Stop the Ride I Want to Get Off

Stop the Ride
I Want to Get Off

An Autobiography

Dave Courtney

First published in Great Britain in 1999 by Virgin Books
Virgin Publishing Ltd
Thames Wharf Studios
Rainville Road
London W6 9HA

A catalogue record for this book is available from the British Library.

ISBN 1 85227 890 0

Typeset by TW Typesetting, Plymouth, Devon

Printed in Great Britain by CPD, Wales

Contents

Stop the Ride I Want to Get Off

Prologue – A Formal Introduction

'My name is Dave Courtney, and despite whatever you've heard of me . . . I'm worse.'

This was my opening address to a jury during one of my trials. And I could have added: 'Whatever you may already think I've done . . . it's true, and more.' But I didn't, of course, because I wanted to get a 'not guilty'. My words were enough to set the scene for my own defence, although my defence team was pretty shocked by what I'd said.

'Dodgy' Dave, Bermondsey Boy, The People's Villain, The *Yellow Pages* of Crime, Heir to the Krays, a right cunt: I've been called many things in my time, not all of them flattering; I've been accused of loads of things, not all of them true. But this is the real story of my life. It is even naughtier than all the newspaper headlines and horror stories written about me by other people. Because of the reputation I've had stuck on me I've also been linked with an awful lot of things that had nothing to do with me. This meant I got given the credit (which was good) but also had to carry the blame (which was bad). Was it worth it? Well, ask me that next time I'm in the dock. Do you think the jury will remember the good or the bad about me? Yeah, exactly.

In fact the things I have been convicted of would fill only a couple of chapters. The rest (and the best) – the things I did do and got away with; the jobs that only the underworld know about; the charges that the police couldn't prove; and many, many other incidents – these form the basis of the book in your hands.

The hardest thing was whittling down forty years of stories

to this. To everyone I haven't mentioned, I'd like to say you are in my thoughts as much as those I have. And if I've opened up any old wounds, I didn't mean to and I apologise, but no one's ever written a true account of his or her life without giving someone the hump. And if I've still upset some people after bending over backwards trying not to, I don't give a fuck.

There's certain people I can't mention cos they're still active, but they know who they are and how important they are to me. If you were on a certain job with me and I've left out your name it's only cos I wanted to protect you. And, in case you're wondering, I've checked with everyone named in the book that it's OK to do so.

I'd also like to say hello to the women I've loved over the years, including the ladies I've been friends with when I shouldn't have.

Now, finally, I've finished with being an active criminal. I've stopped the ride . . . I've got off. But it was a bloody good ride while it lasted and this book you're holding, my friends, is your ticket to it.

1 Giving a Bad Name to Villainy

One time, this guy came at me with an axe in his hand and murder in his eyes. He was proper annoyed, let me tell you. Fortunately, I had a sword in my hand. So I stuck it through him.

Now that's not something you see every day. Or at least, it ain't something *you* see. I've seen it. And I've done it.

Because in some ways you're different from me. Or I'm different from you, shall we say? Unless, of course, you're a gangster or villain or one of the chaps reading this, in which case, How yer doing? But apart from those people, the other readers – people like you, probably – are what we in the criminal world always called 'straights'. It's not meant as an insult, let me add, it just acknowledges that you're 'on the straight and narrow', so to speak. And will probably have no greater run-in with the law than getting a parking ticket. And good luck to you.

But me, I was never like that. I believe, I really *do* believe, that I was born naughty. Born to be a villain, if you like.

If you're young, fit and healthy with your whole life ahead of you, or even a bit older and married with kids and happy, what would make you enter a life where you might risk being beaten, stabbed or shot? What makes you risk being banged up inside, staring at four walls on a twenty stretch? I've had all those things done to me, and done them back. Unless you're one of those unlucky ones who tried it and got burnt on the first go, then you get involved because it's in your blood. It's bred in your bones. You can't make yourself a villain or gangster. Some men try and they always come unstuck; fake, plastic gangsters always melt under heat. And you can always tell by the eyes. Dead giveaway. One naughty man can always spot another naughty man. Look in the eyes, and you can tell the real from the fake. I've seen men beaten to a blancmange because they didn't have that specialness behind the eyes. I've had to do that to some myself, and more.

Which brings up another point: what does it mean to be a villain? Because what I was (or what I still am, according to the Metropolitan Police) is what you, a member of the general public, would call a villain. What the police would call me if you asked them about me is another word altogether. But I don't use foul language. Fuck me, no.

I don't really want to use the words 'villain', 'gangster' or 'underworld', but I will. I don't strongly object to the terms, even though they're not my choice of words, but I realise that they just about sum it up in most people's eyes, so I'll use them anyway (I'm nothing if not obliging). But the truth is this: real villains and gangsters don't consider themselves villains and gangsters, and don't go around 'firm handed' showing they are hard. Not in the least. It's only those who are trying to be one – all the fakers and the on-the-makers – who do that. Please don't think I'm saying that everyone not up there at the top is faking, but at the top there's only room for one.

Real villains call it 'work'. As in, as an armed robber would say, I went out on a bit of work the other day. He wouldn't say, 'I'm just going out into the underworld to meet some other villains to rob a bank, babe. Pie and mash for tea, is it?' To a villain, villainy is work; to a gangster, gangsterism is work. So you might hear of someone who's done a bit of work and got caught. (The bit about 'getting caught' sort of gives the game away a bit, though, I admit. How many ordinary jobs do you get 'caught' at?) You've seen Hollywood films where a Mafia bloke is accused of being a gangster and he says, 'No. I'm just a businessman.' Well, it's like that. It's just that our business – me and my friends and associates – was a dodgy one. An illegal one. I'm not saying it's normal work, by your standards, but it's work nevertheless. And normal to us. Just like wearing a white frock and snogging airport runways is normal to the Pope. Depends what you're used to. If you live a certain life for long enough then out-of-the-ordinary things become ordinary. I wouldn't stick my arm up a cow's arse, but some vets do it every day.

And villains don't use words like 'work' and 'job' cos they're trying to distance themselves from the reality of what they do, either; they're faced with the reality of what they do every time they risk getting banged up for a thirty stretch. They talk about it like that cos it reflects the ordinariness they feel about what they do.

For example, towards the end of my career the Old Bill were raiding my house and smashing the door off its hinges so often that it would've been cheaper to have a revolving door fitted, or an extra set of keys cut. So I did. Then I went down to my local nick, dropped the keys off with the desk sergeant and said, 'There you go, boys, now do me a favour and next time just let yourselves in quietly.' You should've seen their faces. It was wicked. I wish I'd videoed it.

What I want to get across is this: real villains only do their work *on site*. Like builders. You wouldn't catch a brickie slapping a wall up in his living room or a boxer training in the bathroom. Villains are like builders, but they've got more front and show less arse. Villains are not villains in their own front rooms; they're not villains when they take their kids to school; and they're not villains in the bedroom (that's a different kind of naughty). Robbing a bank – well, that's work; printing a couple of million pounds of moody money – that's work; collecting a container full of nicked fags at Dover – it's work; taking some geezer who's been wounded in a gun battle to get stitched up by a dodgy doctor – that's work an' all. Sometimes you'd feel like coming home and saying to the missus, 'Honestly, love, work, work, work! It just never stops.'

It sounds funny, but it's true. When a villain or gangster is in his front room, he's just an everyday geezer (just one who happens to rob banks, etc.). In the same way I imagine very famous people are pretty ordinary at home. I don't expect Madonna dances her way down to the breakfast table every morning, rubbing her crotch at the cleaner. And when you get started on this life, you don't see a card in the local shop window saying, VILLAINS WANTED – RING THIS NUMBER. You just go that way. You're not pushed into it by anyone; you just see the road open up for you and you choose to go down it. It comes natural. It comes natural because that's what you are. If you feel yourself trying to act like a villain then you're in the wrong game. It should come natural. If you're someone trying to be something, you're not it. You don't have to try. You don't have to act. And if you do put on an act, and if you do it with me, I'll see right through you like a fucking X-ray.

Which brings me to someone I know who is a perfect illustration of that. Someone I'd like to tell you about. It happened only last year.

When I first met Guy he seemed pretty imposing to everyone. He was 23 stone, this geezer, a big, pasty-faced fucker with jet-black hair greased back into a pony tail. But as I got closer, I looked in his eyes and saw that he didn't have it. There was just none of that specialness there that you need. In time, even he realised how obvious it was and he started wearing shades to hide it. He worked as a chauffeur for one lovely geezer called Mick Colby. Mick was a chap who didn't take no lip. He's ex-everything is Mick: done the lot, knows all the chaps; a really good fella. So all Guy had to do was stand there trying to look menacing. No one argued with him cos they knew they'd incur the wrath of who he was working for.

The more I ran into Guy the more I knew he was not just a real prat, but nasty with it. A proper bully and thug. He beat up his girl, and she was a real tiny sparrow of a woman too. Made you sick to think of it. He'd always pick on younger, smaller people. If he was working in a club, he'd ask someone for an E, go round the back with the guy and smash him up and take his stuff. Then he'd say, 'The doormen are my mates, what are you gonna do?' Or he'd take a coat off someone for himself. Oh, he was a right cunt, through and through.

Now I didn't mention what I thought of him to the people he was working with because if they hadn't seen it themselves yet they'd just think you were being paranoid or bitchy. It's always better to let people come to their own conclusions about someone. It means more. People generally believe in their own judgement more than in that of others. So, in a case like this, you bide your time. And I did.

Guy got into some financial trouble and I bailed him out. When the time came to pay it back I knew he wouldn't. And I knew he'd have some excuse. They always do. But at the time

I gave him the benefit of the doubt. This was his chance to prove me wrong about what I thought of him. And whatever other talents I may or may not have, I can say this one thing without fear of sounding conceited, because I know it to be true: I am a bloody good judge of character. Very, very rarely do I get that wrong. Often it's been the thing that's saved my life or kept me from doing a lot of bird.

Guy proved me depressingly right.

He'd recently been done for something and the court case was looming and he was a dead cert to get sent down. So I knew what he was doing. He was trying to stall paying me off to keep some funds for himself for when he was inside. I knew this. He knew I knew this, yet he didn't mention it once. If he had, I would've said, 'Fair enough, I understand cos we've all been there. See me when you get out.' That's all he had to do. To trust me to be fair. Instead, he gave me excuse after pathetic excuse. Taking advantage of my leniency, really, though I knew in my heart he wouldn't pay and that I'd just given him enough rope to hang himself.

Like I've said, to the professionals, crime is a business. It's an unusual one, but it still shares similar working practices with more conventional businesses. If you were a top car salesman, for sake of argument, and you didn't go in for the kill on every sale, then the other salesmen below you would see that and want to take over. It's human nature. They want to be top dog and get all the perks. Same difference in my line of work.

And it's not like Guy thought I was the local Cub Scout leader. He knew who I was and what position he was putting me in, so he couldn't even plead ignorance. He was just taking a massive liberty. I gave him more chances, and the more I did nothing about it the more he thought he'd had me over. Big, big mistake. I make it a point never to underestimate anyone. They might just be the one to put a bullet in your back, and why run the risk? Someone once said, Keep your friends close and your enemies closer. I understand that.

One night I was out at Napoleon's casino having dinner with friends of mine: Bernie Lee and his wife Brenda, Frankie Fraser and his Marilyn, four geezers from New Zealand – Andy, Christian, Saska and Zombie – and Jack Adams, a diamond geezer and Ben, his unpopular son. We all had a nice meal and a spin of the wheel.

Driving home with Andy, Christian, Saska and Zombie, taking them back to my pub, The Albion, I suddenly realised we were passing right by Guy's gaff. I hadn't been out chasing him down for the money. The world is too big to search, but too small for me not to run into you, y'know what I mean? I wasn't gonna pull a muscle for someone like Guy. But he had been pretty conspicuous by his absence recently and this was too good a chance to pass up.

I left the four chaps downstairs in the motor and went up to Guy's. Would you believe it – he answers the door all cocky, holding back his dog. A real big hound of a bulldog it was too. (He still lives at home with his mother does Guy, which can be seen as a bit odd for a man in his thirties.)

'Guy,' I said, 'you know why I'm here.'

He went into the old routine. 'Yeah. Er . . . listen, Dave. About that. I haven't got it together yet but –'

I stopped him right there. 'I've heard this all before and I don't want to hear it again. The needle's stuck in the groove on that particular little tune. Let's not make a song and dance about it. Just tell your mother what you said to me yesterday.'

The day before, when I knew what was going to happen, I'd come right to the end of any tether I had left, and I'd asked him a question. I said if he didn't cough up, what should I do tomorrow? He'd said, 'You're well within your rights, Dave, to give me a clump.' Maybe at the time he thought I wouldn't do it if his mum was there. So he was even using his own mother as a shield.

Anyway, he turned to her and told her this and she just nodded, bless her, like she agreed! As soon as the words had left his mouth I was on him. Halfway through giving him a proper good clump I heard this noise and turned to see the bloody dog coming at me. I just saw these snarling, snotty jaws zipping towards me. The bastard was actually in midair, all paws off the carpet, when I punched it as hard as I could right on the nose. Bulldogs are ugly fuckers at the best of times, but I hit this one so hard I nearly made it handsome. It hit the deck, went cross-eyed and staggered off, still growling. Guy, the idiot, just ran into the wall. The dog growled and whimpered.

I turned to finish with Guy and his mother jumped up, shouting, 'Don't hurt him! Don't hurt him!', and then fell to her knees. I thought, What's she up to? I suddenly realised who she meant when she ignored Guy and started cuddling the dog. I thought, Fuck me! Talk about getting your priorities right. I don't know who was most shocked: me, Guy, or the bloody dog. I turned back to Guy and gave him the final, complimentary parting shot. He went over like a tub of lard.

So I'm now stood in the middle of the living room, a 23-stone geezer at my feet and his old lady hand-in-paw with the dog, stroking the dent in its head. You couldn't make it up. I felt like I was on *Candid* bleeding *Camera*. I thought, Fuck me, I've seen it all now. I almost felt sorry for Guy. Mind you, having said that, a good dog *is* hard to find . . .

After showing concern for the dog, Guy's mum soon calmed herself and sat down. She wasn't at all ruffled about Guy being arse over elbow on the Axminster. I said to her, 'What I know about your son, I know you must know. Because he's your son, you know it too. I don't expect you to say you agree with it, but in your heart, I know you know what he's like.'

She just looked at me. She knew. No one, absolutely no one knows you like your mum does. Mums just know. That's why they can still tell you off. Your mum sees you as a little baby and as a boy, when you're too naive to hide your bad points. If you're cheeky, you're a cheeky bastard; if you're lazy then you're a lazy kid. As you grow older she sees you grow more clever at hiding the bits you know people don't like to see. But she's already seen. By the time you get to eighteen, you think you know it all, but she knows your core cos she's watched it grow. It's a bit of a cliché about gangsters loving their mums, but usually the mum is the only one that can still give them a good battering. Well, the way Guy's mum looked at me, she seemed to think he was as big a prat as I did. Some mothers do 'ave 'em.

That one incident destroyed Guy. I don't mean physically, cos the bruises soon heal, but mentally. After that he became transparent to people. He became what he'd always been. That hard front had been well and truly battered down. It was like those Hollywood film sets where the building is just a front held up by a few props. But he'd got away with it for too long.

He'd had a good run out of the act. It was only a matter of time. In fact, I think it had gone on for so long that even he conned himself into thinking it was true. And you know what they say about believing your own press. But when someone treats you in a certain way, with great respect, and you're never tested, it's very, very easy to believe that. The crime world is a fucking hard place and an even harder place to fake it.

One thing that never fails to amaze me is some people's capacity for self-delusion. I can understand trying to con someone else cos you might get a reward, but conning yourself? One of the hardest things in life is to be honest with yourself. Do that, and you're more than halfway there. You won't find yourself doing a 24-carat walk with 9-carat feet.

A few days later, when he'd got out of hospital, he came round to The Albion with, would you believe it, even more excuses. It fell on deaf ears, and he was promptly bashed to bits again. I commandeered his car and rang the man an ambulance.

Everyone heard about what had happened and because they all knew me and knew there had to be a bloody good reason for me doing that – the old bop! bop! bop! – they all turned away from him. Mick sacked him, every other doorman didn't wanna know him, and even his missus gave him the elbow. Then his old pals started saying, 'Yeah, I always thought he was a bit of a prat.' I couldn't even say, 'I told you so.' Time will either prove you right or prove you wrong. I always tried to make sure it proved me right.

The 'real thing' don't act; they *are*. And they don't need to shout because a whisper will do. Guy was a thug and real villains are not thugs. It's distressing really, when you think about it, how some people give a bad name to villainy.

2 Naughty by Nature

The year 1959 was an interesting one. The M1 motorway opened, Russia launched a space rocket with a chimpanzee at the wheel, and Frank Sinatra was in the charts with 'High Hopes'.

And it was even more interesting for my mother because that's when she had me. I was born in King's College Hospital on 17 February. Which makes me an Aquarius, for what that's worth. I don't know anything about all that astrology bollocks to be honest, but I wouldn't mind being a Sagittarius. It's the best star sign for a man to be because the symbol of Sagittarians is half-man half-horse, which means you've got a big dick and a licence to shit in the street. Anyway, one out of two ain't bad. But there you go – you can't have everything.

(One thing I'd just like to say here to all those miserable gits who whinge on about how they have such bad luck that they never win anything. Well think about this: out of 400 million sperm, you were the only one to get to the egg. Just by being conceived you've won the greatest, biggest swimming race on earth. The odds on the National bloody Lottery are only fourteen million to one. Cheer up!)

I was the first born, followed by my brother Patrick and my sister Susan. Maybe if my mum and dad had known then how I was gonna turn out I might have been an only child. I guess they had high hopes of their own about what I might become. Even though I don't regret a minute of the life I've had and wouldn't change a thing.

I know that when people say 'I blame the parents!', it's just so much bollocks. I came from a normal family of very, very good people. I was loved and loved them in return. They did everything for me. The fact that I became what I did was down to me alone. Sometimes you see these discussion programmes on telly with some know-nothing sociologist banging on about criminal elements in society and what made them that way, going on about, Is it nature or nurture? Speaking for myself, I can say that for me it was nature. I really do believe I was born naughty. Then I grew naughty, became a naughty boy, and naughty boys often become naughty men. When that way opened up for me I took to it like my mate Jimmy Five Bellies took to lager. The fact that it came so naturally to me is one of the reasons I'm still around to tell the tale. 'Acting' like a gangster is something you can only get away with in Hollywood. In the real underworld, for want of a better word, only the real thing survives the distance.

In a way I wish I could say I had a deprived childhood; that I never saw any green areas and we never had enough books at school, the classrooms were too full and all that, but in all honesty, I can't. It would be an easier explanation and probably less scary for people to think that. Because, if you do think about it, if what I'm saying is true, then all the reformers and social workers and Lord Longfords in the world will not change a thing about some men. It means there's always going to be baddies because that's just what they are.

I grew up in Camberwell Green, South London. We lived above a butcher's shop on Denmark Hill. As a kid I was as happy as Larry, and I've got a mate called Larry and he is *fucking* happy, let me tell you. That's how happy I was! Dad worked for the Gas Board and did so all his life. He was a really straight-down-the-line, 35-year man. Paid his dues, paid his bills, and provided for his family. He was a scout leader, that's how straight he was. In fact, he made me stay in scouts until I was about fucking 38. Mum was an Akela in the cubs. I was in cubs and scouts for years cos it was cheaper than a babysitter! But Dad was a lovely man, did his bit in the war, worked hard, and was fit and healthy all his life until his later illness. He was strict, but not hard. The real firmness came from my mum.

My mum is an Irish Catholic, originally from Molling Gar, County West Meath. We went back there sometimes when I was a kid and I thought it was the most picturesque but the most boring place on earth. It would've driven me spare to grow up there. I always had too much naughtiness for the country. She was always real pretty, my mum. From good stock. She was one of seventeen brothers and sisters, so you can tell they were practising Catholics; her mother had the full football team plus reserves. Because she'd come from a massive family she knew how to fight. When you're one of seventeen you'd have to, wouldn't you? Fight for bed space, and attention, and everything else probably. So you didn't mess with my mum. And when you got clumped you got *clumped*, mate. And you knew it. But only cos you deserved it.

Mum was a store detective for Woolworth's, which is pretty funny considering the amount of stuff I used to lift from Woolies. She warned me off going up there when she was working and, of course, I never did. I knew what I'd get. Imagine getting nicked by your own mum. And then getting a battering when she got you home.

I was definitely naughty from an early age, and that's why I can say, with knowledge, you are born naughty. And it don't matter what family you're born into either, whether it's a poor one or a plum-in-the-mouth job. If I'd have gone to Eton, I'd have been the naughtiest boy at Eton; if I'd worked on the stock market, I'd have been the naughtiest boy there, like that Nick Leeson. And, if a naughty man becomes a policeman, then he makes a naughty policeman. I've met enough of those to know that's true. I wasn't the only one who could spot it either. While I was still at Adamsrill, my primary school, the headmaster, Mr Gerrard, said about me, 'That boy is going to cause his mother, future wife and the police a lot of trouble.' I just thought, Wow! Fancy having that on your school report.

One Christmas night someone broke into the butcher's shop below our flat and started robbing turkeys. The police ended up coming and chasing the blokes up the street. It started off a bit of a riot with people running round with turkeys under each arm. Nearly everything went. Must have been the only Christmas that the turkeys escaped and the butcher got stuffed. But it led to loads of bother and Mum said we should move. Because my mum and dad had got married on Christmas Day, maybe Mum thought it was extra special and something bad happening like the turkey riot was a bad omen for us there.

From Camberwell Green we moved to 10 Condor Street in Stepney. It was a pre-fab house up on stilts. During the night I'd lie in bed listening to the cats underneath my room scrapping and singing. it sounded like they were right in there with me.

Condor Street was right next to a big, disused hotel. One day I went exploring and found the dumb waiter, climbed in, lowered myself down and got stuck! I was in there for two days. My mum and dad had the police out searching for me. Eventually I was saved by this old tramp who heard me and pulled me up. After two days the first face I saw was this old guy's. He had a long beard and fingerless gloves, like Fagin. And I was Oliver bleedin' Twist. After that I didn't care how much the cats cried as long as I was in my own bed.

Then we moved to Shifford Path, Mayow Road in Forest Hill. I would live here until I left home, and it was here, from this small house, that I made all my best mates and got up to all my early naughtiness. It was Base Camp One for little naughty people.

I wasn't a kid for very long. Or I didn't feel like I was. I was getting up to all sorts of naughtiness beyond my age. I always ended up running with older kids and the fact I acted older than my years meant they didn't mind. And I learnt. I learnt very, very quickly. Without even meaning to, I studied people and assessed them. Tried to work out what made them tick and what made them good at some things and bad at others.

My last school was Forest Hill Boys, the biggest boys' school in the country. Two-and-a-half thousand of the little bastards under one roof. Imagine being a teacher there. Later on, some of the teachers signed up to go to the Falklands just for light relief. The headmaster of Forest Hill later went mental, literally, and had to be carted off to some nuthouse. I'm not claiming any responsibility for that. In fact, I'd like to go 'no comment' at this point!

Everyone remembers one good teacher that had an effect on them, though, don't they? Mine was the drama teacher, John Edwards. He was younger than the rest and got on with the kids easier. I suppose he was our equivalent of a trendy vicar that some churches have. He'd do things like organise a kids' disco at Bell Green Baths. He called the disco The Aquarium, which is funny cos twenty years later I ended up running the security at one of London's top clubs – The Aquarium. I took to drama quite naturally (and I don't mean just causing it) and Mr Edwards saw that in me. He later recommended to my parents that I should go to RADA, but they believed, probably quite rightly, that they'd supported me for long enough and I should go out to work.

When I was about ten going on eleven, me and my mates had two gangs and a little war going on between us. There was my best mate Colin Robinson and his brothers Terry, Peter and Paul, and then Robert Hanson, Tony Smith, Tim Beeches, Raymond Power, Andy Robe, Gary Oldfield, Gary and Geoff Vines, John Barnes, Ian and John Lockrey, Colin Little, the Kings, the Bridges, Godfrey Lewis and Phil Pinock – all too naughty to forget.

One day we were throwing stones at each other on this old bomb site. It was like being in the trenches in World War Two. We were down in one hole and the other lot in another. Really giving it to each other. I found this thin roof slate and stood up and chucked it hard, just as this kid was getting out the other hole. The slate caught him slap-bang on the head – whack! – and knocked him out cold. He keeled over like a chimney. We all stopped for a second, the two gangs, and looked at each other. Then the other lot ran off and we ran over.

The slate was just hanging out this kid's head like an axe blade and, this was the weird thing, even though he was spark out, his eyes were wide open. That really freaked us out. My heart was banging like mad. I thought, Your eyes wouldn't be open like that if you were knocked out. He was obviously dead. Everyone seemed to click on to this at the same second and started shouting, 'Oh, shit! He's dead! He's fucking dead!' One kid started crying. No one was accusing me so I knew in the heat of battle that they couldn't have seen me do it. I immediately went, 'All right! Who threw that?' They all looked at me then. 'Come on! Who threw the slate?' Everyone started denying it or pointing at some other poor bastard. I didn't see why I should get in bother just cos I was a better fucking shot than everyone else. I pointed out how, if we didn't know who'd done it, then we'd all go to prison for the rest of our lives. I said it might be a good idea to push the dead kid in a hole and cover him with leaves and then we'd all get away with it. It was in the middle of autumn so there was loads of leaves around for camouflage. It made perfect sense to me. So we did it. Then every snotty-nosed one of us ran home.

You just deal with stuff as it happens when you're a kid, don't you? When you're scared. Quick as possible to get it out of the way. You don't even think of the future. I used to run away with a few pence in my pocket thinking I was rich, and spend it all on sweets before I'd even got to the train station. Then it'd be, Oh shit – I've gotta go back.

Anyway, later on in the evening the boy's mum came round asking about him. Paul Cook was his name. It was about eight o'clock now and dark, and the street ended up filled with all the mums crying and screaming, saying, 'Where's Paul?' Then the coppers came round and it came out that one of the other kids had told his mum about what I'd done. My first experience of being grassed up!

So I had to go up to the waste ground with my mum and dad and the police. *With my mum and dad!* Can you imagine? They were going absolutely spare. I was shitting myself, thinking we were walking towards a body. But by now I was as much bothered about the hiding my mum was going to dish out to me as I was about killing someone. There was nothing worse, was there, than when your mum said that line: 'Just wait till I get you home, boy!' Like I said, you didn't mess about with my mum.

When we got to the hole, it was empty. It turned out that Paul had come to; he wasn't dead at all. The poor bastard had crawled out from under the leaves and staggered about with a massive headache and a *Tom and Jerry* bump on his head, trying to figure out who he was and where he lived. I thought he could at least have let everyone know he was alive, for Christ's sake. But you know how thoughtless kids can be.

At school I was caned six times a day, every day, for two years. It was so regular they practically wrote it into the curriculum: '9 a.m., morning assembly; 9.30, cane Courtney'. You got a report card with two boxes for each lesson – one tick for proper attendance and one for your work. Or a cross in each box if you did neither. You got a caning for each cross.

By the third lesson I had six crosses and cos I knew, by law, the school wasn't allowed to cane you more than six times a day, the lessons after that were mental cos we all knew they couldn't add any more on. So the last teachers to get the bad lads were absolutely fucked. One time we put a big metal bin over the music teacher's head and battered it like an oil drum. Which I thought was quite inventive and would've probably gone well on the float at the Notting Hill carnival. The musical side of it was lost on him, though. It deafened him up a treat for the next few days.

They ended up putting me and all the naughtiest boys in one big class, '3C2'. It was a proper government education experiment to take all the bad apples and put them in one basket. Which was good in theory, but it ended up being like an early version of prison: we all just learned bad things off each other. In fact, that one class alone was responsible for turning out people who later went on to big-time crime; some of them I still know, as it happens. Funny that.

A good pal of mine at the time was Rob Hanson. He was tall even as a lad and could handle himself, but he was real bright as well. One time when we were all playing up the teacher locked us in the classroom and said we were all on detention. I stood up and said, 'Oh no we fucking ain't!', opened the window and jumped out. Rob followed me. The room was two storeys up and when we landed our feet stung like fuck, but we just ran off. The teacher panicked and unlocked the door before anyone else tried it.

Rob was a good one, and I'm still big mates with him to this day. He tends to leave rooms by the door now, though.

Another time I went to run away from home with Colin Robinson, my mate who had been in on the slate-throwing thing. Col said he was running away so I nicked the neighbours' milk money from under their empties for my travelling money. Next time I saw him he said he wasn't coming after all cos it was his birthday on Saturday and he was getting a camera! I couldn't believe it. He said he'd come with me if I bought him a camera to make up for missing his birthday. And the tight bastard only went and made me buy him one at Tower Bridge railway station! So then we had no bloody money for the train ticket.

We ended up down Walnut Tree Walk by the Imperial War Museum and saw this lorry coming out of a Trusthouse Forté. We jumped on it and stowed away in this compartment bit that was at the back of the container. We didn't know where it was going and we didn't care. Especially when we opened the inside door to the container and saw that it was chock-full of stock. We thought we'd died and gone to pastry and cream cake heaven. For the next couple of hours we stuffed ourselves silly with anything we fancied. By the time we got out we were in Belle Vue, Manchester, near this massive fairground. Eventually we hitched home.

We started doing this regularly: me, Colin, Barry, Les and Mick, Ray Bridges and Danny. Years later, after we'd got to know the lorry drivers, one of them introduced me to a scam. He'd arranged for his lorry to be 'hijacked' by a mate of his and then they'd split the proceeds from selling the stuff. They used me as a witness to corroborate the hijack. And that taught me very early on how important good witnesses are, even if they're making it all up. One of the drivers was a guy called Andy Bergicoff, a big, strong, powerful geezer who was then about twenty, and went on to get involved in larger things. Many years later, around about 1990, he got shot dead in The Tiger's Head pub in Catford, south London. Someone pulled up on a bike, went in and shot him at the bar.

Me and Col would run away from home all the time and go up and down the country. We slept rough in Margate for six weeks once. We'd never buy a train ticket. We'd just wait until someone went into the bog and knock on the door and say we were ticket collectors, and they'd slip their ticket under the door and we'd fuck off with it.

At school once, one of the teachers asked me to wash his car and gave me the keys. I sponged it down, got in and drove it off down the road and crashed it. I wasn't too good a driver then. But I loved cars and, once I got into nicking them, my driving improved. Self-taught, you see.

It got to the stage where I'd walk into class in the morning and my form teacher would say, 'I've already signed you in on the register, Courtney, so you can go now. I don't care what you do, just get out!' I thought, Brilliant. They didn't even dare palm me off washing their cars any more.

2 **Naughty by Nature**

Another money-making scheme I came up with was providing my own school dinner service. I'd get everyone's dinner money off them at school and then take them all back to my house while Mum and Dad were at work. I'd knock out beans on toast for twenty kids. The teachers must have wondered why school was suddenly hit by a farting epidemic. Mum also began to wonder why we were going through a hundred quid's worth of food a week and had nothing to show for it!

I had loads of money. Not just bits of pocket money like the other kids. Me and Colin Robinson, Robert Hanson, Rory Bullen, Paul Bingham, Fat Laurence and Big Ricky pulled lots of stunts. When I realised what a typewriter could do I made up forms for a sponsored swim and got loads of signatures. Then we went back in a couple of days and collected the money. If they'd ever looked carefully at what we'd written down it looked like we'd swam round the fucking world. Twice. Biafra was big at the time; people starving in Biafra. Different causes go in and out of fashion, don't they? So that was another one for the sponsor forms.

During Harvest Festival time at school I'd see all this food coming in and think, Mum could use some of that gear – to make up for me cleaning out the larder when I'd temporarily become school chef. So me and Col made up forms for donations that we'd take round to all the flats. We called back a few days later with a Sainsbury's trolley. By the time we got to the fourth floor it was full, and we still had another twenty floors to go! We ended up with nine trolleys full of the stuff. We were wheeling it all down the street just pissing ourselves. We ended up trying to sell it off to people. Well, that's how Marks & Spencer started off, on a poxy market stall. They'd call it free enterprise these days.

When I was thirteen I broke into a toy warehouse with Colin, Cornish and Bill. Now you think that'd be every kid's dream, wouldn't you? But I was more bothered about how much we could sell the stuff for. We got grassed up by someone and the police came around. I don't know who they'd been talking to but it was funny when they started reeling off the information they'd been given. This copper said, 'There's just three we haven't found yet: David, Colin and someone called Scooby.' What they didn't know was that Scooby-doo was the name of Colin's dog, and they had him down as a suspect. Yeah, Scooby, he was the brains behind the whole operation. At my house they found about 25 Action Men and dozens of Kerplunk! and Mousetrap games. When they saw them all boxed up in the garden shed and asked me to explain, I said that one had been bought for me by my mum, one by my gran, one by my auntie, etc. Even then, caught red-handed, I tried to talk my way out of it.

I was into big boys' toys even then. Like cars. I was nicked for stealing cars. And I got done at fourteen for doing a wages snatch from a building site. I got loads of fines and could have been sent to borstal but always managed to slip out of it somehow. I was older than my years, so if I got caught I'd know how to play the game: I'd always act more like my real age then, so they'd think it was more like a prank and I'd get the benefit of the doubt.

Me and Col got up to loads of things. I had a Lambretta scooter but kept it at Colin's cos I wasn't supposed to have it. I used to take our beagle out for a walk, pick up the Lambretta and let the dog sit on the footplate as I rode around. One day the daft animal only jumped off when we were doing thirty! I still had hold of his lead so he ended up sprinting at the side of me on his back legs. The police were right behind and pulled me over. They must've been thinking, What a lazy-bastard way to walk a dog! I parked the bike, put the dog inside my crombie and made a run for it through Sydenham high street. When I got home with his paws all bleeding, my mum said, 'Just how far have you walked him?'

Colin lived with his nan and could sneak out late when he wanted. It was more difficult for me. I couldn't set an alarm to wake me at two in the morning cos it would wake everyone else. So I got some of that string they wrap beef with and tied it around my toe and hung the string out the window. It worked a treat at waking me up until the night when Colin tugged it too hard. My foot flew off the bed and smashed through the window! I ended up with stitches, a broken toe and a clump off my mum.

When my younger brother Patrick got old enough to be of some use, I'd sneak him out the bedroom window with me to act as look-out. Sometimes, when I went out alone, I'd be gone for three days at a time. (It wasn't until years later when I had my first child that I realised what worry I'd put my parents through, and I immediately went round to see them and apologised for all the hurt I must have caused them.)

I was going right off the rails rapidly. Well, other people must have thought I was going off the rails but I thought I was on the right track. I loved it. I wasn't academically successful at school so now I felt I'd found what I was good at.

Because I was running with adults, I learned adult things. Things like 'seed planting': that's what I called it when I'd put an idea in someone's head, but in a roundabout way, and let them come to their own conclusion about me, but always one that was in my favour. Or I learnt how to change a conversation slightly by dropping little hints that an adult could pick up on. I saw that adults, and particularly ones in authority, liked to think they'd worked things out for themselves. So I flattered them by letting them think they'd done that. And the usual result was I'd get off lightly and walk. It wasn't that I looked older, really. I was no bigger physically than the others, but hanging around with the older ones meant that I had an older attitude and I could always get people to believe that I was older than my years. And confidence in a lie is half the battle.

I learnt an awful lot. And, when I wasn't running with my much older mates, I was dealing with children. So that made me an automatic leader. Even going back to the slate-throwing thing, which was when I was only about ten, I instinctively knew how to take charge and lead. I found that once you've taken on the role as leader, you're treated as such, if you are a deserving one. And you can't go back. You can never go back to following. And people warm to you because, as much as most people don't like to admit it, they do prefer to be led, and not a lot of people want the responsibility of that leadership. But even at this age I fucking thrived on it.

Me and Russell Carter would break into schools and shops, or nick cars. That was always a good earner. This was in the days before car nicking really became a national craze and made everyone get an alarm. Cars were so easy to get into. We'd get old Anglias and Cortina Lotus Mark Is and break them down and sell the bits off – engines and rostyle wheels and stuff like that. I was earning good money. Even though I got caught loads of times, I carried on. It was too easy and the money was too good. I couldn't see myself going to work in a poxy factory.

I got involved with another mate of mine called Frankie B. who did smash-and-grabs. He'd send his sons out to case shops, checking thickness of glass and if they had wire mesh, stuff like that. Then we'd drive around during the day looking for the easy windows. Talk about running with an older crowd – this geezer was 35 years old! He'd nick anything. He'd just get a beer keg, lob it through a window and take what he wanted: tellies or radios. Or he might pass a shop and think, Oh, that's a nice suit, then go back that night and rob it. He'd smash a whole plate-glass window just to get a pair of sunglasses. Proper nutter he was. And he was addicted to it, to getting stuff for free. He admitted to me that he couldn't even bring himself to buy a pack of fags; he'd rather go back at night and do the whole shop just to get his smokes. Mind you, the way this geezer smoked he probably saved himself fifty quid a week. He filled up his whole house with half the local high street. First time I went round there it was like walking into Aladdin's cave. When you saw through the gloom of the smoke from all the fags, it looked like a shop warehouse.

He once nicked an African parrot. A big, blue, fuck-off parrot in a four-foot-high cage. He did the pet shop window and legged it with this thing squawking under a blanket. He put it in the middle of his room. I gave that bird about six months to live before it got cancer from passive smoking. It was the only parrot I heard of that didn't speak; it *coughed*. If you'd gone to it, 'Who's a pretty boy, then?' it would've probably said, 'You are – now give us a fag'. I said to Frankie, 'What you gonna do with that then, the parrot? Hold it to fucking ransom?' He said he just fancied having it. He was like that. If he wanted something, he took it.

All this time, when the other kids were still at school, I was already at college – on the streets. You've heard people call the streets 'the university of life', and it's true. Right from the off I was naturally streetwise and just got better – I got good at being bad. I had an alternative education. My Geography was

the London *A–Z*; my Maths was adding up how much we'd
make from selling knock-off gear and then dividing it between
us; and PE for me was trying to outrun some cunt that'd caught
us up to something. I studied Law through experiencing it and
Biology and sex education through getting birds (the 'home-
work' on that one was blinding). And when you're having the
time of your life, why would you want it to stop? Well, you
wouldn't, would you?

It felt like second nature to me to be like this, but I didn't
really know what would happen next, where I would go with
it. It weren't second nature to my mum and dad, though, to
have a son like me. They were going spare, as you can imagine.
I think I broke my dad's heart, to be honest, because I didn't
turn out how he wanted his first son to be. I got some proper
hidings (Mum always hit harder) but I deserved them.

As a kind of last resort they took advice from my school and
took me along to somewhere called Maudsley Hospital. The
school had told my parents that I was manipulative, on a
constant quest for attention and didn't care what the cost was
as long as I got a laugh. They told me that afterwards, cos at
the time I was up on the roof with another lad I'd persuaded
to go up there with me and moon the playground. Anyway,
Maudsley Hospital was a place for troublesome kids with
behavioural problems like me, supposedly, where they did
psychiatric evaluations. We went up every Thursday for eight
months. The doctor was called Six. Doctor Six.

Sometimes just me, Mum and Dad were in a room with
Doctor Six; at other times we were in a lecture theatre in front
of a hundred medical students watching us and taking notes (I
always wondered if they turned me into some kind of case
study for other future naughties: the Courtney Complaint).
They said I was academically backward but mentally
advanced. One of them summed it up by saying that in an
essay competition I'd come last but in a debate I'd come top.
Talking and thinking was my thing. So the visits to Maudsley
ended up being more painful for my parents and the doctors
than for anyone else. I started to relish the thought of going
and talking about myself and getting into discussions and even
arguments. I was in my element. If they'd followed their own
thinking they would have got me to write about things not talk

about them, but reading and writing weren't exactly my strong points.

They did try to improve that side of things, though. Get this – I ended up having reading lessons from a blind lady. I know, that's what I thought when they first told me. I was like, eh? But she was brilliant. She would read the same book in Braille and teach me as well. Because it happened so late I still remember the first book I read. It was *The Lion, The Witch and The Wardrobe*. Actually, that blind teacher was really nice and I eventually ended up seeing her. She was in her late twenties so, to me, it was like my first real experience of a proper woman rather than a girl. I learnt a lot over those few months. Years later, if anyone asked me if the place had done me any good, I'd say, Yeah – it got me laid. Not exactly what the doctor ordered, but that woman did me more good than the rest of them put together.

Sometimes, during the dinner periods, I'd go over the road to the park opposite. The park would be full of old tramps and winos and they'd all come over and ask me for money for beer. I started to wonder just what they would do for a drink so, for a laugh, I went over the road and bought a cheap six-pack of Skol and some paint-stripper white wine. You wouldn't believe what ended up going on in that park. They would do anything. Within half an hour I had them all competing for the booze: five of them doing one-legged races (backwards); a couple climbing trees to see who could get to the top first; another three or four on the kiddies' swings seeing who could get highest; even two having a punch-up. Oh, it was mental! I started doing it regular. It was too much fun to stop. Tramp Olympics, I called it.

The tree-climbing event was wicked cos half the trees weren't strong enough to support a person. So there'd be this tubby, fifty-year-old tramp bending back down to earth and shouting out to me, 'I've won!' People from nearby offices would walk into the park to have a sandwich and see this smelly, ragged-arsed version of Billy Smart's Circus giving an afternoon matinée. I could have thrown up a marquee and charged admission, come to think of it.

I got so into it one day that I completely forgot about my mate, Gary Vines. He was appearing in Camberwell Green

Court House, right next door to Maudsley, that morning. I was supposed to go in and see him but lost track of time being the winos' ringmaster.

I invited some of my mates down to see all this one day. And this is where I learnt something. Even though it had all started out as a big laugh, watching these winos practically jump through hoops for me had made me think about what you could get people to do for the right incentive. It already got my brain thinking along those lines. No matter how daft the thing was, they were prepared to do it. Now with mates of mine around and with them being a good bit older, as most of my friends were, I started thinking about how I could take it a step further. After laughing about it I realised there were other possibilities. Like getting the guys to go nick stuff out of shops for the reward of a few cans of beer. Or walking into a police station and saying they were driving a certain car at a certain time. That got one of the lads off who had recently got into some car trouble. That kind of thing.

Meanwhile, back in Maudsley, the sessions stopped. They said they were having an adverse effect on me. Even the doctors gave up and suggested to my mum and dad that it might be for the best if I didn't go any more. Charming!

Not long after, something happened that made everything just drop into place – wham! – like that. It was something I'd never forget. It was when I started boxing, first at Honor Oak Boxing Club in Forest Hill, where I was trained by Tom Heckman and Vince, then the Thomas à Becket gym with Gary Davidson and Billy Aird, and finally at Peckham Boys. It was at these clubs that I started to see famous unlicensed boxers like Roy Shaw, Lenny McLean, Jimmy Batten, Teddy Webb and Jimmy Holmes, and also men that would make a big, big impression on me, known faces like Joey Pyle, Harry and Billy Haward, Freddie Foreman, Charlie Richardson, Harry Holland and Charlie Kray. I was already aware of them and had seen them knocking about, but this was the first real look up close. These chaps were the absolute bollocks. This was around the early seventies, only a few years on from when the Krays had been sent down in 1969, and people still talked about them.

Charlie Richardson, Frankie Fraser, Harry Holland, Freddie

Foreman and Joey Pyle were from the same era. Freddie was nicknamed 'The Undertaker' – make of that what you will. Joey was a real classy gent. Both big names with a lot of say. Both from the old-school of villainy. They had stature and style. They'd just stroll into the gym, not swagger (or anything naff like that) because they didn't need to. They would just have so much control and confidence. They exuded that. Sparring would stop and I'd just stand there with my gum-shield half hanging out, thinking, Wow! Get a load of that! They were always dressed really sharp in the best suits and the best jewellery and smoking the best cigars. They were treated like royalty, and to us they were. Fuck me, they just sparkled. These men radiated power and class and to me it was like a real gee-up. I thought, I want that. That's what I want. That's what I was gonna be. I saw the clothes and the cars and the women, the power and all that came with it. And I thought, That ain't come from working no nine to five, mate. That's come from what I'm doing now, but bigger and better.

I'd always loved the romance of crime – always. I absolutely *loved* it. The whole image of gangsters just blew me away: the smartness, the brotherhood, the never running away, the never grassing anyone up. The whole story. The full monty. It all meant something to me. And even this early on I realised that if you went a bit wonky as a boy then you were just called 'naughty', but if you did the same as a man, you were called a villain. That was fine by me. I thought, Well, if that's what I am then that's what I am. Yeah, it made me come over all Popeye: 'I yam whats I yam!'

Seeing these guys come in the gym made me think that if you're gonna be a villain then at least do it with as much style as you can. I think that's important in whatever you do, but even more so if what you do is a bit naughty. If you're doing something that a lot of people think of as bad, then rather than have the world hate you (which would be easy), do it with style and class and make it palatable. You might even win a few over and make some friends. And these men had that in spades – so crisp and classy. I knew they did naughty things, but it had a real air of romance about it as well. In the end, when it comes down to it, everyone loves a good baddie, don't they?

I was a million miles off that stage, but it had given me a

flash into the future of what I wanted. But at this time, me, Colin and our sidekicks weren't so much *The Dirty Dozen* as The Slightly Soiled Six.

Another good scam we got into at this time was nicking wheel clamps. They had only really just come out and were worth good money. We'd buy, say, an old Mini from the auctions for fifty quid and park it up somewhere we knew it would get clamped. Then we'd go back, take off the clamped wheel, put on the spare and throw the clamp in the boot. We'd sell the clamps to a dealer we knew who had car lots all around London. That was a tidy little earner while it lasted and, for the reputation that clampers earned themselves, I don't think a jury in the land would have convicted us.

I did get nicked for the odd thing, though, but I got away with a lot more than not. One thing I did get done for was a burglary me and Col did which went severely pear-shaped.

It was on the cards from the start cos I was the world's worst house burglar. My best crimes were noisy ones. I didn't mind kicking a door in, but tiptoeing around someone's house just did my head in. I just couldn't do it. I'd end up not being able to lift my leg cos it was shaking so much and it'd make me as clumsy as a carthorse. Every time I touched something, it broke. I was useless.

Anyway, Col and me broke into this bloke's house. He was an alky, this geezer, and we found him asleep upstairs. Because, as usual, I'd been clattering around like Stevie Wonder in a china shop, I went on guard duty. Col whispered to me to whack the guy if he showed signs of waking up. He was a big, bearded, hairy guy – a proper bloke – and if he woke up and I gave him a right-hander, he looked like the type to swallow the fist whole and bite the fucker off. On the wall above the bed there was one of them Irish wooden clubs, a shillelagh, so really quietly and carefully I took it down and held it like a bat over him.

Col carried on darting around the room as I stood over the guy, shitting myself. I kept telling Col to hurry up and he was hissing at me to keep an eye on the bloke. All of a sudden the geezer in bed just rolled over. He probably wasn't close to waking up, but that was it; I panicked and started whacking seventeen shades of shit out of him. I just carried on until Col grabbed me and we ran off. And that was that, the end of my early burglary years. Well, I wasn't exactly Raffles – cat burglar extraordinaire, was I? A man's got to know his limitations, as Clint Eastwood once said.

We got nabbed and nicked for that one. And just fined. That bloke must have woken up with one proper big headache, though.

As well as everything else, all the scrapes we got into, me and Colin got in some right scraps as well. With Col living at his nan's with his five brothers, they got away with murder. They all turned out good in the end and got their own businesses, as it happens (and good luck to 'em), but then they were right tearaways.

The first nightclub I ever went to was with Colin and his older brother Terry. It was the Crystal Palace Hotel, or the CPH as we called it. They served Tartan and light and bitter in plastic pint pots. We'd go down there bopping along to 'Love To Love You Baby!' and all those disco tunes. It was fucking wicked, mate. We had the best times. The worst of it was actually getting there. Because of Terry.

I remember the first night. I called round for Col and we planned to go down together along with Terry. I was a skinhead, so I was there with the cropped bonce, crombie and silk scarf and Col was a rocker so he had the long barnet and biker jacket. So, us two were waiting in the hall and I suddenly saw Terry clomping down the stairs – red pants, orange hair, a cape over his shoulders and a big gold spot on his forehead. I thought, Oh *stop* it! It's Ziggy fucking Stardust! I could not believe it. I never knew he was a glam rocker. He was proper well into it. Worst of it was we weren't driving so we had to go up on the bus. It was all right for David Bowie – he didn't have to risk getting his head kicked in on a No. 122. Just picture it: the skinhead, the rocker and the disco chicken. Talk about The Good, The Bad and The Ugly. We were more like the pick 'n' mix gang!

It was outside the CPH that we nicked a bus, one time. I thought, I ain't paying for a cab and I don't want to freeze my nuts off waiting with all the other punters. So we jumped on an empty one that had been left with the engine running and I took the wheel. And then we were away, ringing the bell all the way – ding-a-fucking-ling! Trouble was, I couldn't get it out of first gear, so there we were in a double-decker going 15 mph all the way with the engine screaming, down Crystal Palace Parade and right down Sydenham Hill to Cobb's Corner. You should've seen the faces on the people we passed. One old guy put his hand out and I just went by giving him a V sign and screaming 'Yeee-hah!!' I could just imagine him complaining to the bus company: '. . . and it just drove past me being driven by this rude skinhead, with a bus conductor who looked like a Hell's Angel. And I *swear* that David Bowie bloke was on board!' I tried to stop for the roundabout but I stalled it, so we just jumped out and legged it down Sydenham high street, laughing all the way home. But we had got about three miles in it first. Shame I couldn't get it out of first, though. We could've picked people up, told them the fares had risen to a quid and made a bit of money.

I didn't have much luck with buses, as it happens. Next time a bus did for me was when me and the chaps went up to the CPH again for a night out. Over the road was the travelling funfair so we nipped in there for a laugh before we hit the club. The fairground boys were all toughnuts and always ready for a row at the best of times, even more so when they saw we were with the David Bowie of Peckham.

We all got into a ruck and then ran off to the club, but they followed us and spotted us in the queue. It kicked off again, and one of the fairground blokes stabbed me in the arm. It went right into my elbow joint and stuck there. It was one of those little 50p penknives and this one had a beefeater on the handle. I couldn't pull it out; I was just looking at it thinking, Wow! Fucking hell! It sort of amazed me that I couldn't pull it out.

I ran off down the road, and these cunts only belted right after me, didn't they. Because I was in a brand-new pair of loafers I was sliding all over the place. Then I saw two buses parked up, nose to tail, and went for the little gap between them, but my crombie got caught on the corner. I couldn't move forward or back. They all caught up, and while I was jammed over the bonnet of this bus they all laid into me. And this was when kung fu films were big – *Enter the Dragon* and all that – and every bloke thought he was Bruce Lee and started carrying round rice flails. They just gave me such a hiding and I could do fuck all about it. Oh, they really done me. Yeah, *Enter the Dragon* – Exit Dave Courtney. I had on this really nice Prince of Wales check suit as well and, as well as the knife hole in the arm, it ended up with blood all down the front. I was gutted. Wouldn't have been so bad, but when I was at the fair I didn't even win a goldfish.

Funnily enough, after I left school I went to work on the fairgrounds for six months, travelling around the country with a geezer called Jimmy Botton. We had mental times, and he has stayed a friend ever since. I used to hide inside the ghost train and whack blokes in the cars and throw buckets of water over people! They'd come out the other side, soaked and bruised, thinking, Fuck me – that was a bit much for fifty pence!

I was nearing the end of school now, but I still turned up whenever there was a school trip. We went on one to Abergavenny in Wales and I got up to some naughtiness, as usual, and the teachers got the hump and decided to send me home early. I thought I might as well go back in style so I nicked a car and then decided to go off to the seaside instead. On the way back the Old Bill nicked me for speeding! They told me that the teachers at the hostel had thought I'd gone missing and called out a rescue squad. I thought, Christ, I only go to the seaside and they call out a land, sea and air search party. It's a good job things were a bit different then, otherwise I'd have probably been a regular face on *Crimewatch* by the time I was fifteen.

Another time, me and John Barnes, Morris Tagg and Robbie de Barbour broke the lock on the gates of Mayow Park in lower Sydenham, south London (like we did about once a month) so we could use the paths as a racetrack. I did an Evel Knievel, standing on the saddle of this motorbike, actually standing on it! I went slap-bang into the back of the park warden's car. All the others ran off cos they thought it was a police car. I ran off about two paces, realised I'd broken my leg, and fell down. And ripped my jacket. Then, when I was being loaded into the ambulance I saw I'd lost a loafer. And then one of the ambulancemen found I had an air pistol – a gatt gun – down my pants (I'd forgotten about that), and when

I took it out I shot myself in the foot with a dart. The foot with no shoe. Just one of them fucking days!

And how did my mum and dad react all this time? Listen, they were in *despair*. I do feel genuinely sorry, looking back, at what I must have put them through. It can't have been easy having me for a son. It must have been hard for them to understand why their son was, in their eyes, going ever so wonky. They did try everything, from a good old-fashioned clip round the ear to the softly-softly approach. I mean, I loved them to bits and I didn't want to hurt them, but sometimes you just have to follow your nature wherever it takes you, don't you? And my nature was naturally naughty. Talk about your black sheep of the family. I was fucking ebony, mate.

As a last resort I was sent on an Outward Bound course at Newton Abbot in Devon, one of those Duke of Edinburgh Award-type schemes. I think it was supposed to straighten me out. Which seemed a bit like trying to straighten out a corkscrew with a toffee hammer to me, but I went along with it.

And I *hated* it. We had to go out on the moors and go rambling and fishing and abseiling and potholing and all that country-life crap. I was a city boy through and through. I thought combine harvester was a kind of roll-your-own tobacco. I thought, Well even if I nick a tractor I ain't gonna get very far, am I? What could I do, plough my way back to London?

There was one kid there with me called Eddie Bedford, a big fat roly-poly kid that could scoff for England. This one time we had to go out on the moors and eat what we caught. Most of us got rabbits or tried to get fish out of a stream, that kind of thing. That wasn't enough for Eddie. He tried to kill a pony. We all came back with our catches and Eddie turns up leading this pony, its face all dripping with blood where he'd tried to bash its head in with a rock! That was probably just his starter. I thought, Fuck me, Eddie, start as you mean to go on. What a nutter.

The course teachers were drawn from policemen, firemen and soldiers, and then the rest of us, the kids from the Naughty Brigade, made up the numbers. It was a bit like I imagined it to be in the army. We all lived in a big dormitory. They put you through all these testing things to make a man of you, make you grow up a bit. But I'd already been through the stages. It was supposed to correct me and make me join in with things. That was the big thing, 'joining in'. 'Come along and join in with the others, David!' they'd say. I thought, Oh *please*, leave me alone!

I'd never been one for team games. Not because I was a loner, cos I wasn't, I was really sociable; it was because I hated having to pay the price for someone else's failure. I hated that. You might prepare all month for a football game – train hard, go to bed early, don't shag – and then some prat stubs his toe and your whole team loses one-nil.

That's why I loved boxing. If you get decked in the first you've no one to blame but yourself, and the other bloke that chins you of course. But mostly it's about self-reliance. Being that way taught me not to shirk responsibility. I actually embraced it. Most men love a challenge, or they should do.

What they didn't tell us was that one of the people in the dorm was a spy. He actually slept in the dorm with us and went through all the activities but he was really a policeman. He'd report back on what we were saying behind their backs. When it came to the end and you got your assessment you'd think, Fuck me, how did they know that? That was bang on! But even though I had some black marks they gave me a silver award. Maybe it was just to encourage me the right way, or maybe it was because even though they thought I led people astray, at least I could lead.

I'd found out pretty early on in my life, and by now I knew it was true, that once someone sees you take on responsibility they can't help but warm to you. They just do. And that's really all I wanted. I don't want to make it sound like some poncey plea for understanding, but that is all I really and truly wanted: to have lots of friends. To go everywhere and do everything and have millions of mates and loads of good times. And have a laugh. That was always the most important thing to me. To have a laugh.

I always loved being the jester. I know a lot of kids do that at school to stop themselves getting battered – it's difficult for the bully to smack you if he's laughing – but with me it weren't that. I never had trouble with being bullied. I just always saw the funny side of things first. I remember actually thinking about this at the time and realising what I wanted was something different – to be King and court jester at the same time. That would make you the absolute bollocks. People respect a king because of his power but no one wants to knock around with him cos he's a serious old cunt; and the jester, people like him cos he's funny but won't take anything he says seriously. I wanted both. To make people laugh but also to have credibility so they would listen to me during serious times.

I didn't realise it right at the time, but that was one of the things that came out of the course. I came back from it a little bit different because of that. So if there's one figure who is partly responsible, even if in a small way, for me getting where I am, it's the Queen's old fella, that scheming Duke of Edinburgh. Cheers, Phil.

The things that had an effect on me – leading other kids when I was younger and getting away with murder (not literally – not yet); seeing the Joey Pyles, Freddie Foremans, Wilf Pines and all the others walk in the gym; even things on the Outward Bound course – I took something from them all. But what I learnt wasn't what they wanted me to learn, that I should 'mend my ways' and 'buck up my ideas' and that kinda crap. What it gave me was a stronger realisation of what I was. Every test and obstacle that was put in my way didn't deflect me, they just made me more determined.

There was one other thing, though, that I haven't mentioned yet, which I saw as another signpost towards where I wanted to go. Because the road I was going down was one way.

3 Never Nick a Monkey

It was two things actually. The first was the death of my nan, my dad's mum. Every Sunday the family would visit her, and later on, when she was ill, we went a couple of times a week to look after her. Right from being little I used to love going to my nan's. The house was on Summer Avenue, Denmark Hill. I remember everything there seeming massive. And you know how your grandparents spoil you, cos they only see you at your best and don't have to put up with all the grief that your mum and dad get.

She was the biggest thing in my family; she was the biggest influence. And when she died it really affected me cos I missed her and all that, but in another way as well. Even though she was a real character, I noticed that a few months after her death she wasn't really being talked about that much. I mean, considering the effect she'd had when she was alive. It's a normal thing, I suppose. People just get on with their lives. But it made me think that I wanted to be something. I wanted to be someone who would still be talked about afterwards for a long time. And Nan was special, so that gave me an idea that I'd have to be even more so to get where I wanted to go.

After Nan died I tried really hard to think of things she'd said to me, but I couldn't remember any. And I felt really guilty. How could I not think of everything, or anything? Is this what happens when you die?

And then something she'd said came back to me.

Whenever I'd done something that parents and teachers considered wrong (about every other fifteen minutes it seemed), I'd get the usual finger-wagging lecture or screaming and shouting. Nan was different. She was too smart for that; she knew it went in one ear and out the other. So she'd sit me down and talk to me.

This one time, I'd got in trouble for fighting, hitting another boy. I'd been with an older boy at the time and got carried along with it all. His mum came round to see mine, y'know, the usual routine, and I ended up on the step with Mum gripping my arm and saying, 'Did you hit this boy? Did you?' That kind of bollocks. When my nan heard, she said something different. She said she could see from my face that I'd enjoyed it and it was something that was in me and not gonna go away. She asked me if I'd won the fight. I said I had and she said 'good'. She asked me if he was bigger than me, and when I said he was, she said 'good' again! Then she gave me some advice: 'If you try really hard all the time to be nice to everyone and be seen to be really trying, when you do have a fight people won't think bad of you,' she said. 'If you have less fights you could win them all.'

I thought, Wow! What a thing for a nan to say – she really knows me. She'd seen something that no one else had, cos they were just too ready to believe that I went out looking for trouble. She saw through me. I was only about fourteen at the time yet this lady, more than fifty years older than me and at the end of her life, knew me better than anyone. She was really wise.

At the time she had also tried to bring home to me the truth of those sayings which old people just seem to spout at the drop of a hat: 'All that glitters is not gold', 'Time and tide wait for no man', 'A leopard cannot change its spots', those kind of things. They sound meaningless cos you've heard them a million times before, but she made them true for me. Something like, 'There's nothing to fear but fear itself' was what she said to me. I may not have got the words exact, but I remember the feeling it gave me; that fear sometimes makes you do too much you don't want to. But when you face the fear it disappears (hopefully). I sat down then and wrote out all the sayings that Nan had said to me, and any more I could think of. Then whenever something happened there was usually one of them I could apply to the situation. And it always rang true. They became like my commandments. That was what Nan left for me. Her legacy, I suppose.

The other thing I remember which meant something to me was a school trip we went on to Madame Tussaud's. I was only very young at the time and I didn't even know what Madame Tussaud's was. Then someone said the most amazing thing to me; they said, 'That's the place you go when you die and people don't want to forget you.' I thought, Wow! What an accolade. That sounded like heaven to me.

There was all these figures of kings and queens and politicians, which didn't interest me really, apart from one and that was the model of King Arthur. I was a real window-gazer at school, especially during lessons like History. When the teacher started droning on about something I'd suddenly find the view outside really fascinating, even if it was dead boring. But one thing that did grab me, for some reason, was tales about King Arthur and the Round Table and that sword in the stone. The romance of it all, I think. I thought King Arthur sounded wicked with all his mates, the Knights of the Round Table, and Sir Lancelot his second-in-command. The thing at Madame Tussaud's that really stopped me in my tracks, though, was the section on crime. Most of the models, of royalty and politicians and sportsmen, were things I could never be, but seeing all those famous gangsters and crime figures like Al Capone immortalised there, and people stopping to stare at them, made me think, Yeah, I'd like that. I could do that. Put it this way, I knew I was never going to be Prime Minister or world famous for doing charity work. Florence fucking Nightingale I wasn't. 'The place you go when you die and people don't want to forget you' – that stayed with me a long time.

Finally, at fifteen years old, I left school. I think we were both as glad to see the back of each other. The headmaster's final comments on my end-of-term report were, 'For a boy with such low academic standards he has a high opinion of himself'.

By now I knew what I was cut out for. Seeing those gangsters at the boxing gym had done it. I knew that that's what I'd be like if I had the money. And I knew I wouldn't get it going to work. I did try the 'work' thing, though. I did give it a go. You've got to at least give me that – I gave it a go. Guess what my first job was. Listen to this: it was as a window dresser! Can you believe that? *A window dresser.* But how difficult could it be, I thought, dressing dummies?

It was at Cobb's Corner in Sydenham. A big store. I pretended to be a bit older and cos I'd always acted older it was easy. This geezer interviewed me and when he asked where I'd worked last I decided to embroider the truth a bit. Well, no, actually, that ain't true; I didn't just exaggerate, I downright lied. I could only think of one other big shop, so I said, 'Oh, I used to work at Harrods.' His face lit up then. 'Harrods?' he said. 'Blimey, when can you start?' He took me on then and there.

On the first day he took me round and introduced me to all the different heads of departments: clothing, furnishings, household goods, ornaments etc., all them and more. He'd be saying, 'This is David, the new window dresser. And Dave, this is Mr Jarvis of soft furnishings. He'll give you any prop you want from his department.' I just thought, You silly bastard! You don't know what you're letting yourself in for. If smash-and-grab Frankie could've seen me then he'd have creamed himself. The job lasted until I made a little slip-up: I got caught nicking everything. Honestly, you make *one* mistake!

Some time later I went back into the shop and hid in the furniture department. I climbed into a big wardrobe and the plan was to wait until they locked up. I nearly got sussed when this couple came up to look at the wardrobe and started trying to open the bloody door! I held it from the inside. I think because it was late they didn't bother asking for any help and just left. Finally, I climbed out when everyone had gone home. I was always into gold so I ran straight towards the jewellery department. I felt like I was on a gold rush. The sly bastards had locked it all up though. Big chain shutters from floor to ceiling. So I went on the rampage round all the other departments.

You know what you're like at fifteen. Imagine being let loose round a big store with everything there for the taking. I could have everything I wanted. Oh *listen*, what I didn't have! I put on Farrahs, tonic suits, jackets, then a suit over the top; harringtons, crombies and big overcoats over the lot; stuffed the pockets with sunglasses; Brut, West and Hai-Karate aftershaves; soap-on-a-ropes and creams. I put fishing rods under my arms and air rifles over my shoulders; I got handbags and travel bags and stuffed them until they wouldn't zip, till they nearly ripped, with shoes and statues and even penny chews. I just went mental. I put on a new pair of loafers. I even had a bobble hat on my head, like the cherry on a cake.

Then the fluorescent lights started to flicker and I thought, Hang on! Then they all came on at once. I looked round and saw the police bursting in. I didn't know there was a silent alarm hooked up to the local station. I made a run for it, or, more accurately, I made a wobble for it. I couldn't move. I felt like the fucking Michelin Man with asthma. I must have looked a right sight, hobbling away, dropping the bags and chucking stuff off me left, right and centre. And the new loafers didn't help, sliding me around (bad flashback here of being chased by the fairground boys). So there I was: Fatty Arbuckle on Ice. It wasn't exactly the most difficult catch those coppers ever had to make. I must have weighed 24 stone. I did feel a bit of a tit, actually. At least Mr Jarvis would've been pleased that his soft furnishings hadn't been touched. About the only thing I didn't have on my back was a three-piece suite.

So me and 'work' didn't exactly see eye to eye, you might say. I was less interested in the nine to five than the five to nine I might get sent down for if I was done for anything serious. But a term like that wasn't a serious prospect. Not at the moment anyway.

Then, at sixteen, I left home. I left without having anywhere to go because my leaving was prompted by an argument I had with Mum and Dad. It was entirely my fault, one hundred per cent my fault. But I was 16 going on 38 and thought I knew better. It was for the best though. I needed my own space to do what I wanted. It was the right time to do it.

I don't know it's right to say that it was a relief for my mum and dad, because if your kids are at home you feel like you can still watch out for them, but I was bringing grief to their door whenever the Old Bill called round. The world I was moving in was very different from theirs, that world of scout masters and respectability. They wanted better for me, but they weren't fools, my mum and dad, and they knew I was a bit that way, not a homey nine-to-five type at all. Even at fourteen I had twenty-year-olds calling round to the house asking for me. And I smoked cigars from right early on too. I think that was a result of the early boxing gym days when I saw the big faces come in. I was the only one in my family remotely like this. And one is enough, you know what I mean? So they let me go; they let me go out into the world.

I wasn't exactly sleeping rough, more just dossing down on the floors and settees of my mates. The sympathy wears pretty thin eventually, especially at that age when your friends' mums are getting the hump. I wanted to be on my own and I used all this – the argument, the dossing down – as an excuse to do that. And once you've left home proper you shouldn't ever go back, should you? Not really.

It was good for me that I left cos at home my mum cleaned and tidied up after me, like mums do, fed me and all that. Because with myself I was a lazy little fucker, I really, really was; not lazy with anybody else, but with myself I was. Still am, as it happens. I neglect myself. That's the truth, that is.

So I got a room in 18 Canonbie Road, Forest Hill. Canonbie Road is the steepest hill in London and also one of the highest points in the capital. No. 18 was a big detached house split into bedsits. The place was owned by the old landlady, Ena, and her husband, Butch. They also lived there. And upstairs lived a married lady called Margaret who helped me grow up even quicker (and is still a good friend). The house also backed on to a foreign languages' college, so there was always a fast turnover of foreign students coming and going. It was different from all the other houses in the road; it was a bit like the old Amityville horror house, and right from the start I thought there was something spooky about the whole set-up. I didn't know then just how weird it would get. But I could come and go as I pleased now. I'd always had a lot of freedom, mostly because I'd just done what I wanted, but having a place of my own was something else. So now I had all the time in the world to do my work.

One thing I could never do was break into anywhere that had anyone in it. I'd tried that before (like with the shillelagh guy) and I was just crap at it. All my crimes were against things, not people. I could nick things or kick a door in and go, 'Right! Everyone in!' But doing frauds and scams like putting on a wig and slipping a note to a bank teller saying 'Give me all the money', no, I couldn't do it if my life depended on it. Like cheque-books and carding, standing in line while they checked you out; that's horrible. I'd hate it. You'd never feel in control cos you're just waiting for something to happen.

Recently, over the last few years, they've introduced something they call 'pro-active' policing, which is just a wanky term meaning they get right in there first, at the thick end of it. Well, I was doing that years ago. Pro-active villainy, if you like. Because, in my line of work, I was often out on what you might call 'the night shift', I kept getting pulled by the police. And it was getting to be a pain in the arse. It suddenly occurred to me that the only cars that could drive round London late at night without looking suspicious were black cabs. So I bought one. At sixteen I had my own black cab. Diesel as well, they all are, so you could do a million miles on a couple of gallons. And loads of room in the back for my mates or any gear. I got the diesel cheap from Terry Lawrence, Budgie and Bruzie and his brothers, and Johnny and Maxie Grey down the council yard.

I was making good money. I got up to all sorts of things: running round at night breaking into garden sheds, nicking from building sites; I even nicked a load of garden gnomes and ornaments once. I filled up the boot and the back of the cab with them. I remember pulling up at the lights next to another cab being driven by someone I knew called Lenny Lucas. He looked across and nodded, and then he saw all these painted gnomes on the back seat smiling out at him. It must've looked like the seven fucking dwarves on a night out. I just drove off laughing.

The black cab came in very useful when I went up to Mayow Park one night. I'd taken a shine to the bowling green turf. Beautiful, lush green it was, like expensive carpet. I thought, That's wicked grass, I'll have some of that for the garden at Canonbie Road (come on, you can't blame a bloke for being house-proud). But before I nicked the turf I had to sort out the garden. It was in a real mess, all overgrown with weeds and bushes and rubbish everywhere. There were probably World War Two deserters still hiding out in there.

Now I've always been more light-fingered than green-fingered and, to this day, if I ever got a blister from doing DIY work I'd photograph it, frame it, and call in the local paper to do a feature. It'd make the front page where I live. So, I thought, How the fuck am I going to do this? I'm not slaving over a hot shovel for two weeks, and I can't exactly call the police and say someone's messed up my garden and can they help. Or could I? It gave me an idea. I got a woman friend to make an anonymous call to the Old Bill and say she'd just split up with her husband of 35 years, and that she knew her old man had buried a body in a garden years ago. The address: 18 Canonbie Road.

Next day they came round, banging on the door. Vans of them. For the next few days the back garden was like a circus: tents up with groundsheets and tarpaulins everywhere, coppers in overalls digging for England and sifting for evidence. The neighbours had a fit and our old landlady looked like she was on the verge of a heart attack. I just watched from the window thinking, Go on boys! Dig that fucking garden and lift those weeds. They didn't find anything, of course, and by the time they'd left the garden was clean of all the bushes and rubbish and the earth was all levelled out beautifully. Result! I could hardly believe it had worked out so well. I felt like putting up a little plaque saying LANDSCAPE GARDENING COURTESY OF LONDON METROPOLITAN POLICE. They even paid out £200 in compensation for the inconvenience they'd caused!

So now the Great Bowling Green Turf Robbery was back on. Me and my mates Colin Little, Damian Solly and Pat Fogarty went out the next night and lifted all the squares up and put them in the boot of the black cab. They drove off in their own car and I set off to meet them at the bedsit. It was all going to plan until I was waiting at a crossroads and suddenly the cab's back door opened. I looked round and this little old lady was climbing in and telling me where she wanted to go. I thought, Oh no, fucking hell! But what could I do? She's perched in the back with her handbag on her knees and one of those silly old-person hats like a plant pot. I could hardly kick her out. Christ knows what she was doing wandering around at that time. Senile dementia is a terrible thing, ain't it? Luckily she didn't live a million miles away from me. But it wasn't exactly close either. She was sweet enough, but all the way she was twittering on about this, that and the other. I knew her whole family history in ten minutes.

When I dropped her off, she came to the side window to pay. I said, 'No, it's all right, love. This one's on me. I was going this way anyway.' She was so grateful I felt guilty for cursing when she'd first got in. I told her to mind how she went and said I hoped her grandson got better (don't ask).

By the time I'd got back and done a spot of midnight gardening (whizzing at the time – they were good, them 'blues'), it was three in the morning. I slept in till dinner time and then threw back the curtains to admire my handiwork. I hadn't thought of the fact that grass grows one way, so when I looked down what I saw was like a big chessboard. Now all I needed to do was nick a two-foot-high chess set.

A few days later the old landlady, who lived in one of the downstairs rooms at No. 18, upped sticks and left. Just like that. First I thought she'd just gone off on holiday or something, but it gradually dawned on me that she'd just fled. Everything in her room was just as she'd left it. During the police dig, I'd always thought that she'd looked really really spooked, much more than I expected, even in those circumstances. I started to think that maybe there really was something hidden in the house that she knew about. Anyway, me and the others in the house didn't care. We could now live rent-free. What a touch!

Another good pal of mine was Rory Bullen. One day me and Rory decided we wanted to go off to a kibbutz in Israel. We thought we'd work our way across Europe, following the sun. That was the plan, anyway. We came up with the idea of making money along the way by taking photos of tourists with an animal. But we didn't have an animal. We needed something like a big parrot or a snake. Something exotic.

I roped in another mate, Ricky, to help me out. Ricky was all right, but his brother didn't turn out to be very popular at all. One day he filled my petrol tank with sugar. I saw him immediately after he'd done it and the turn-ups in his Oxford bags were still full of sugar – he was that bright. (I'm still very good friends with his ex, Michelle, and her new man, Paul, but fuck knows what happened to him.) Anyway, Ricky was a good mate and agreed to help me out with the animal kidnapping. The local pet shops just seemed to be full of really sad, dodgy-looking creatures that looked like they'd die before they got to Dover, let alone Israel. So we broke into Crystal Palace Zoo. To get a spider monkey. You could probably pass it off as an animal rights thing these days, say you were 'liberating' the monkey to give it freedom. Well, we were just nicking it.

So one night we dropped off the perimeter wall into the zoo. It was all completely dark and everything seemed to be asleep. It was weird cos everything was really really quiet, and a bit scary – I kept thinking something was gonna jump out of the dark and smash against the bars. You couldn't even tell what was in some of the cages. But you could smell the fuckers and hear them breathing and shuffling around. It didn't seem like such a good idea then as we moved around whispering to each other.

Ricky found the spider monkey cage and I double-checked the sign. Better to be safe than splattered. I didn't fancy tapping awake a silverback fucking mountain gorilla with an attitude. Imagine a gorilla with the hump! I could picture the headlines: LOCAL TEENAGERS IN KING KONG FRENZY HORROR! The cage had two doors, an outer and an inner one. We propped them both open with dustbins and then went in. Ricky was behind me, whispering at me to hurry up – 'Go on, Davey! We ain't got all fucking night!' – y'know, being really brave like you always are when you're only second in line to get your arms ripped off.

It was a cold night, but as soon as I entered the cage I felt this slap from the body heat and the stench. I tiptoed in, and just as I bent down, real careful, to put this sleeping spider monkey in the fisherman's keep-net I had, the monkey sprang up about six feet in the air and screamed like it was being murdered. I was so shocked I yelled. Ricky yelled. Every other fucking monkey woke up and yelled. They all went proper mental.

Well, that did it. That really put the cat among the monkeys. Every other animal in the zoo woke up screaming and roaring and squawking their heads off. It was like they were all going, 'HELP US! HELP US!' I shouted, 'Out! Out!' and we ran for the doors. With the dustbins half-blocking the way it ended up being a fight between us all for who was gonna get out first: me, Ricky or twenty screaming monkeys.

Ricky and me ran off into the park and the monkeys scattered everywhere. We hid behind this big rhododendron bush and then lights started coming on and before we knew it loads and loads of zoo wardens were running about the place. We could hear voices shouting and see headlights from all these jeeps whizzing around. Some blokes ran past the bush carrying rifles. At the time I didn't realise they were dart guns and thought they'd come to shoot us. I thought, Fuck me, they must have been expensive monkeys! What were they anyway, the Queen's Own? It was getting serious. We suddenly felt like Public Enemies One and Two.

We waited until they all seemed preoccupied and then made a dash for it. I *swear* I cleared that zoo wall without even touching it. I did the Fosbury fucking Flop, mate – Olympic style. We hit the ground running and disappeared sharpish. All I could hear behind me was what sounded like a whole jungleful of animals killing and raping each other. God, those monkeys had the hump, and talk about fast. What phenomenal acceleration: from nought to hysterical in two-and-a-half seconds. We should have gone for something a bit more dopey, like Ricky's brother.

So the Israel/kibbutz thing never came off. Me and Rory had a change of plan. We went to Brighton instead.

I never had any luck with animals. The next one was a horse. Me and another big pal of mine, Russell Carter, got this racehorse from Fowl Farm in Biggin Hill. It was an animal rescue centre, but they were going to put this horse down. So we bought it. We got it back to Sydenham Hill and had it living in the cycle sheds by Sydenham Hill Stations estate. Soon we had to move it and decided to keep it, temporarily, in this flat we knew of that squatters had just been evicted from. Trouble was, the flat was on the fourth floor of this block. We didn't want to try and get it up the stairs, so we put it in the lift.

Tower block lifts usually smell of piss, don't they? Where some drunk's done one in the corner. Well, this ended up being the only lift in London with a pile of horse shit in it. Eventually, the police got wind of it. Which wasn't difficult cos the place stank. Me and Russ came round the corner one day and saw them there. God, what a sight it was. Apparently they'd tried to get the horse back in the lift but it weren't having it. It obviously remembered being spooked by the trip up and just freaked out. Then they'd tried to get it to go down the stairs and that didn't work cos horses can't walk down stairs. In the end they tranquillised it, but it fell asleep in the flat and they couldn't get it out to the lift. They came up with another solution, and this is what me and Russ turned up just in time to see: a doped-up horse spark out in a canvas hammock, being lifted off the balcony by a big construction crane that they'd brought in, with policemen and firemen all shouting directions and waving their arms about. Fuck me, it was funny. We just stood down below pissing ourselves. All the residents from the other flats were out on the balcony. I imagined they were thinking, Christ! The DHSS will house anything these days.

Me and Russ had some mental times. We used to go racing down Canvey Island to a place called the Goldmine Club. This was in the seventies, remember, when people were customising their cars with sidepipes and Wolfrace wheels and painting flames down the sides. We had this yellow Cortina Mark II that we'd done up. It looked like a clash between John Travolta's hot-rod in *Grease* and something out of *Wacky Races*.

On this one day when we drove down to Canvey, we ran out of petrol. This other bloke with us called John decided to nick a Triumph Spitfire convertible that was parked nearby so we could drive down in that. He got this sledgehammer out the boot of our car and stood there on the pavement, steadying himself like he was doing one of those 'Test Your Strength' things at the funfair. I was thinking, Wait a minute – flat hammer against soft material . . . this just ain't gonna work, is it? Anyway, this geezer John gave it one almighty swing and hit the roof as hard as he could – whap! – the sledgehammer bounced, shot back as if on elastic and smacked him – whap! again – flat on the forehead. He dropped like a stone, unconscious, and me and Russ just looked at each other for a second and then burst out laughing. I suppose it wasn't funny really – well, not for him anyway – but watching it happen was fucking hilarious. We looked down at him, and I swear this massive square lump, same shape as the hammer head, started growing out of his forehead! All blue and full of blood. It was like a *Tom and Jerry* cartoon come to life. I thought, Well you won't be doing that again, will you? (silly cunt).

Me and Russ got on really well, which is why he gave me a job. He worked as a mechanic at a place called Volks Spares in Sydenham. It wasn't a real job he gave me but, cos we always had a laugh, he liked having me around. So I'd pretend I was a mechanic. I knew absolutely bugger all about cars apart from how to break into them and crash them.

One day, this car drove into the garage. It was a huge American Buick Eight, a 1930s car with big black wings over the wheels, running boards down the side and a massive chrome grill. It was the absolute bollocks this car, and in mint condition. Because I stood there looking like I knew what the fuck I was doing, which I fucking didn't, the geezer got out and came straight over to me. He was a real face in the area called Terry Julian, one of the notorious Julian family. He was more than a bit naughty, y'know, one of the chaps. Anyway, he came over to me.

'Awright, Chief! Brought it down for the sunroof fitting. Russ said he'd do it for me. Is he about?'

Now I know Russ is on holiday for two weeks and this geezer ain't gonna want to wait that long. In the few seconds when my brain was ticking over, deciding what to do, he took out a wedge of notes and threw it on the passenger seat.

'There's a grand there. Should be enough, yeah?'

For some reason, that swayed me. 'Sure,' I said, 'leave it with me.' I thought, How hard can it be? There's more than enough money there to do it and still leave enough for a tidy little earner.

So, like the flash cunt I am, for the next week I just drove around in this American gangster car like King Dick. Because it had a massive V8 engine it was just spunking so much money on petrol. I thought I better get the job done while I still had some of his money left.

This was when the Webasto glass sunroof had just come out and he'd told me this was what he wanted. I priced one up new and thought they were too expensive, so I drove to a scrapyard and got one off a smashed-up Dolomite Sprint. It cost next-to-nothing and would leave me with more profit. I put it on the roof of the Buick and drew round it with chalk. I didn't have any proper tools so I cut the hole with a drill with a cutting bit attached to it. It ended up looking like I'd gone at it with a bloody tin-opener. Worse still, inside the roof were these wooden girders making the framework of the car. Those old cars were built like houses. So now I've got to start cutting the wood and I'm chopping at it with Black & Decker hedge cutters! Stuffing from the headlining was flying everywhere like confetti. A little panic was starting to set in now, but I thought, No, don't worry Davey – it'll look OK when the Webasto goes in.

I put the sunroof over the hole and it dropped straight through on to the front seat. Because I'd drawn around it the hole was too big. Now I was absolutely shitting myself! I thought, You silly, silly cunt – you've just ruined the twenty grand, pride and joy, mint-condition classic car belonging to a local villain.

I always fancied Australia, but I didn't have enough money to emigrate, so I taped an old groundsheet over the hole and parked it outside his house late one night. I managed to avoid him until years and years later when I did eventually run into him again. He just looked at me, and then smiled. 'If I'd caught you at the time,' he said, 'I would've torn you limb from limb. But now it's just a funny story, so let's forget it.' I just thought, Fucking hell! Touch. Cos I knew if I'd been in his position I would've felt as furious as he obviously had at the time – it would take me years to forgive that. Well, you really, *really* would want to get the little cunt that butchered the roof of your twenty-grand car, wouldn't you? I guess if he'd wanted a convertible, he would have asked for one.

So that was my days as a Kwik-Fit fitter down the drain.

The landlady of our house never did come back. The police turning the garden upside down on a body search must have really freaked her out. So we started selling off stuff inside the house. Waste not, want not! But after months of her not being there and paying the bills, the electricity and gas got cut off and I had to move out. And that's when I found the lizard.

When I'd first moved in I'd bought this little beaded lizard but it had escaped in the house and disappeared. I thought it had just run off and probably got eaten by a cat. Now when I was packing up, I moved a box and this dirty great big thing leapt out from a hole in the floorboards. I nearly shat myself. It was about two-and-a-half feet long! Fuck knows what it had been feeding on down there, but it had grown into a right big bastard. It scuttled out the door and that was the last I saw of it.

We all moved out. Now listen to this – this is a strange one: that house stayed empty after we moved out. I mean, 23 years later, right up to the present day, it is still empty and as we left it. The landlady had owned it outright so it was never repossessed or willed to anyone or anything like that. They just boarded it up. I still pass it sometimes and it still gives me the creeps. At night it looks like a proper old-fashioned haunted house.

I got another place in Court Lane, East Dulwich. When I was living here I met Susan. It was at the Crystal Palace Hotel. She was a lovely girl, nice and decent. We hit it off right away and had a real whirlwind romance. After only a few weeks she moved into my flat, and then a few months after that we got married. We moved to Silvester Road.

4 Errol Fucking Flynn!

Then, one Saturday night, my life changed. It was New Year's Eve. It only took a minute to clock over from 1979 into 1980, from one decade to the next, but over the course of that night I left the seventies as just an all-round naughty person and entered the eighties accused of attempted murder.

Me and my younger brother Patrick and all my mates were seeing in the New Year good-style. Susan was there as well – we were still together at this point. And there was Terry Ferry, Roy and Steve Olefonte, Mark Jones, Mark Lambert, Mickey Julian, Roy Hazell, Dave Powell, Andy Bergicoff and Ricky, Mark and Tony Spinks – all of us in The Railway Signal pub in Forest Hill. The place was heaving with people singing and what have you, having a proper London knees-up. We were all pretty merry and I was in the thick of it as usual, geeing everyone along. Patrick decided to go up the road to the local Chinese and get us all a take-away.

When he came back he was in a right state. He staggered in, battered and cut, with blood streaming down his face. I couldn't believe it; he'd only been gone twenty minutes. He told me that there'd been a mix-up at the Chinese and instead of bringing the food as a take-away, they brought it all out on plates. He was only fourteen, remember, still just a kid really. 'They said I had to pay for it, Dave, but I refused. Then all the waiters jumped over the counter and laid into me.' They'd given him a right good hiding. I thought, I'm not having that, a fourteen-year-old boy beaten up by grown men. *And* he's my fucking brother. I'd stand by any mates of mine and they'd do the same for me. Family even more so. It's a matter of honour.

Patrick had got into bits of trouble with me in the past when I used to take him out with me to act as look-out, but nothing like this. I felt protective of him, and this attack on him made me absolutely fucking livid.

So I went up the road to see who's beaten up my brother. I know the head waiter's not gonna challenge me to a duel with chopsticks at dawn. But I'm revved up for it anyway, and I just couldn't let it pass.

It was now five to twelve, and instead of seeing in the New Year I was on my way to give some guys a good seeing-to. The streets were full of pissed-up revellers wobbling about arm-in-arm, singing their heads off, but I was on a mission. And this wasn't just gonna be business, it was personal.

I could see the lights of the Chinese up the road. I walked in, shut the door and faced the load of blokes that turned to me. I could tell that they could see, just by looking at me, that I wasn't there for prawn crackers and noodles. I said, 'All right, who's the tasty bastard who just beat up a fourteen-year-old?'

Because I'm on my own they all started leaping over the counter going, 'It was me! It was me!' like that scene in the Kirk Douglas film where they all jump up saying, 'I'm Spartacus!' I thought, Right, fair enough. In that case I'll have the whole fucking lot of you. One of them went to chop me. I grabbed his hand mid-air, pulled him towards me and butted him into next week. All the others are round me, hitting me, when some of my mates turn up and run in fighting as well. Now, if you've been brought up watching Bruce Lee films you might believe that all those little yellow geezers going 'Ha! Ha!' and chopping at you might hurt you. They don't. A seven-stone man, even if he's hung round your neck, is still a seven-stone man. But one punch from me and, believe me, I'm gonna fucking hurt you.

So they were all jumping round us making these funny kung fu chicken noises and we steamed into them, decking them one by one. Then – get this – this geezer appears holding a sword, something like a big sabre. I couldn't run so I went for him, dodged inside the blade on the backswing, chinned the geezer and took the sword off him. Now it's in *my* hand, and they all jumped back. I thought, Right, now you little bastards. But the bloke I've taken the sword off only jumped up on the counter like he's Hong Kong fucking Phooey. Then he jumped down on me and landed right on the sword point. It went straight through him and I saw it come out his back, smeared with blood. He slipped down off the blade and hit the deck.

Now the whole place was in uproar. The waiters started going mental and grabbing knives off tables in the restaurant. They rushed at us and suddenly I was Errol fucking Flynn, mate! I was slashing and stabbing and the Forest Hill boys slipped into turbo to keep these fuckers at bay. People in the restaurant were going barmy.

I heard the kitchen door bang open and this fat chef ran out screaming and carrying a wok full of steaming oil. I turned and whacked it with the sword, full-belt, and it spilt everywhere. They rushed us again and we did one geezer and then another one who was rushing at me and Terry with two dinner knives in his hands and, again, it went right in deep. There was blood all over the tiles and everyone screaming. Absolute bedlam. Then some more of my pals, who had come up from the pub, rushed in the door behind me and started attacking any waiter that moved. It was now a full-blown riot.

While all this was going on I followed the last guy into the kitchens, and he only went and got this massive chopper! It was sheet steel and must have been three feet long. So shiny, I could see my face in it. We're squaring up to each other, out of view of the others. He advanced and started swinging and I backed down the corridor until we came back out into the restaurant.

What happened next is something I will remember for ever, second for second, cos it was one of the most exhilarating experiences of my life. He's just seen me stab most of his friends, remember – they're all wriggling on the floor in their own blood – and now he was trying to kill me. Literally. His eyes were popping out. I am now in a real battle to the death. With swords. Me with mine and him with the steel chopper. Around us there was all sorts of mayhem in the restaurant. All my mates were getting well stuck in, to say the least.

This geezer started screaming and going down real low, chopping at my legs. I'm thinking, Christ! I'm in a real, proper sword fight. My left hand just naturally went up in the air for balance, and we were at it! The swords were clashing together, people in the street were at the window looking in, the restaurant diners were horrified. And then it happened . . .

He walked into the hot oil the other geezer had dropped, and cos he was only wearing little black slippers, he stopped for a second, and then started hopping about, screaming. I was thinking, Now that just ain't my fault, sunshine! Doc Martens are easily available and you should've got a pair. With him hopping about like a Siamese on a hot tin roof, well that was it; I saw my chance and took it. Ping! I did him. Last but not least the cocky bastard with the chopper got it. He was down and I'd won the coconut.

Now this is the kind of thing that can completely ruin your New Year's Eve. Talk about putting a damper on things. I've gone from doing 'Knees Up Mother Brown' in the pub to swashbuckling the Yellow Peril at the local Chinese. Think about it: it was five to twelve when I set off, so by the time I'm in there, and Big Ben's bonging and everyone else is singing 'Should auld acquaintance be forgot', I'm in the middle of World War Three.

By the time Patrick got out of the pub again and up to the Chinese, we're all just running out. He joined us and we ran back to the pub. Everyone was still singing and dancing. I said we should leave, but they all insisted that we should stay, so we did. Meanwhile, back at the restaurant, the walking wounded only went and called the Old Bill.

This is the major difference between Us – the so-called, for want of a better word, 'villains' – and Them, the 'straight' people (most of the readers of this book, as it happens). We never, ever go to the police. Ever. And if one of us does go to the Old Bill then he isn't one of us any more. He's not even one of you. He's a grass. And in my world that is lower than the lowest. It was OK for those knife-happy gits to go all mental-oriental and attack us when they thought they'd win, but as soon as it went pear-shaped, they called in the police. The cheek of it.

New Year's Eve being what it is, however, with half the world and his missus pissed, and all the trouble that goes with it, the local plod were well stretched. Besides, on New Year's Eve night they probably didn't want to wade into a pub full of geezers, and who can blame them? So instead they sat outside in a car and videoed everyone as we spilled out on to the street. It took them a month to put names to faces, and after they did I was identified along with forty others. Then they whittled it down to the Magnificent Seven with me pegged as Yul fucking Brynner. Or if we'd been the seven dwarves, I suppose I'd have been the one called Stabby.

The Old Bill kicked my door in one morning and, because they were in plain clothes, I thought it was a rival firm trying to have me. So I went at them in the hallway. There's loads of them, but because of the narrowness of the hallway they can only come at me two at a time. It was only after I'd laid three or four of them out and they'd kicked me in the nuts and overpowered me that they suddenly said, 'You're under arrest!' I thought, Bloody charming.

They could've at least said that first and saved a lot of aggro. One of them even kept kicking me in the balls after they cuffed me, the cunt. I said, 'I'd like to see you do that on your own!' (Turned out they were the SPG – Special Patrol Group. See, it's not always nice to be wanted.)

Then, to add insult to injury, the cat jumped out of hiding. Now, I'd just bought this poxy cat for Susan, pure white it was and a right little bastard. I knew what it was like because I had crocodiles at home as well (they were mine) and one time I got one of them out of its tank to freak out the cat. Crocs bark just like dogs and it started barking. Well, the cat jumped in the air, all claws out, landed right on the croc's back and then just ripped it in half. It opened up that little crocodile like a melon! I couldn't believe it. Anyway, so this cat had also taken an instant dislike to me, and I hated it. So while I'm lying there trussed up like a turkey (with some spiteful bastard still trying to turn my balls another colour), it wandered over, real casual, and just attacked my face! It must have thought, This is my big chance! This is where the cocky skinhead gets it! I could *not* fucking believe it. Even the cat turned against me.

Then this copper that's been kicking me in the balls saw its litter tray close to my head. He pulled my head off the floor and banged my face down into it, rubbing my face in it. Then he pulled me out by the ear and said, 'Now say something funny, cunt.'

I looked up, with a juicy little cat turd stuck to my nose, and went, 'I *knew* I should've bought a fucking hamster ...' A couple of the other coppers laughed before they dragged me off the floor and threw me in the van. But at least I had the last word. Well, you've got to make the effort, haven't you?

So on top of the charges against me – attempted murder, carrying an offensive weapon with intent, actual bodily harm, and affray – I've now got resisting arrest and ABH against a police officer. Y'know, for viciously throwing my knackers against his toe-cap. Good job the cat couldn't talk; it'd have probably turned supergrass.

This was the beginning of a big learning curve for me. At this point I'd never been nicked with anyone else. I had always been by myself. I didn't yet realise the significance of distancing yourself from other people who may end up in the dock with you. But 'guilt by association' is something I'd learn about very, very quickly, believe me.

It all goes back to what I said earlier about why I never really liked team sports. I hated having to rely on anyone else. But now, after the sword fight, I'm part of a team, so to speak. All the others are pulled in as well. Now, I might have a fantastic barrister that could get me a 'not guilty', but if the other lads' barristers aren't so good and they get them to plead 'guilty', I have no option but to follow suit (or so I thought at the time).

I got bail. And I stayed on bail for eighteen months. The police deliberately held it over so that my brother Patrick, who was only fourteen at the time, would be old enough to be charged as an adult, not a minor.

So I was out and about for the time being, still doing anything that would turn a quid and give me some excitement – stealing, car nicking, hijacking lorries, robbing department stores. I'd got the old trick of hiding in the stores until after closing time down to a tee.

Then I opened a little drinking den in East Dulwich, between Dog Kennel Hill and Denmark Hill. So every week me and some mates would drive down the coast and cross over to France to get cheap booze. This was years before the big beer and fag runs that everyone does now, so the customs weren't so hot on it. On this one run I took a thousand quid to fill up the Transit with drink. The plan was to buy it, put it in the van and then go have a good time with any money left over before we came home. Trouble was, we had too good a time. When the money ran out we took some of the drink out of the van, got a refund on it and went out again. And then we missed the last ferry back. Not exactly what you'd call a precision run operation. After missing the boat we thought, Fuck it, and ended up staying a week and spending everything. I went home skint. Absolutely potless.

That was the last straw for Susan. She decided to leave me. It was the final one of loads of little things I'd done that had built up to this. We'd married quickly, though; too quickly, really. It had only lasted a year. It was my fault. She was a lovely girl. And if you're reading this, Sue, I'd like to apologise for being a right proper silly bastard when I was married to you. But I'm afraid I'm still the same.

I carried on with loads of money-making schemes. I'd do scams abroad with my pals Rory Bullen and Mickey Julian. We'd go into a jeweller's, me with a moody Rolex already up my sleeve, and ask to see a Rolex from the case. Someone would create a diversion or distraction and I'd take off the fake watch and give it back and walk out with the pukka one. It was easier then, to do things like that. The shops weren't so security conscious with CCTVs everywhere you looked. Ah, the good old days.

Another thing that still worked well for us was hijacking lorries. And this was before they wised up to this one as well, and learnt not to put BELL'S WHISKY on the side of the trailer! Talk about asking for it. The stuff we got was incredible; loads of everything: booze, fags, food, catalogue gear. One time I got a lorry load of the old seventies-style lava lamps. They were wicked. I had over a dozen of them myself going in the front room.

Anything we wanted (and an awful lot of stuff we didn't really want), we nicked. And then we wouldn't just have one of something, we'd have hundreds or thousands. All or nothing. We felt like modern-day Dick Turpins. I suppose you could say it was daylight robbery. But it wasn't. We did it mostly at night.

The best thing that happened, though, was that I met a girl called Tracey only about a month before I got sent down. We met in a pub called the Uplands in East Dulwich. She was very pretty, that was the first thing I noticed of course, but when we got chatting I could tell she was a really happy, genuine person. She just radiated that. Very intelligent as well, and from a nice family. I couldn't help but fall for her. And we really hit it off. I asked her if she wanted to come out with me tomorrow, but she said she was already going swimming with her friend. The next day, I just happened to turn up at the baths, accidentally on purpose, and we got chatting again and we started going out. She moved in with me soon after.

When I've made my mind up about a lady, I've made my mind up. None of that hanging around bollocks, all tentative and scooting round things you want to say. I like a full, bang-on, proper relationship where I can talk to someone. Tracey was a smart lady with her own career in the City, a very straight-down-the-line kind of person. My life at this stage with Tracey wasn't really anything like it would be later on. She wasn't the kind of woman that would have been attracted to a man fully into the kind of lifestyle I later had.

I like a good flirt though, I must admit. I *am* a flirt, always have been. I love women. I know a lot of blokes say that, but they mean it in a different way. I mean I love women's company, talking to them and being around them. I need women as friends more than anything else. I'm not saying I'm whiter than white or that I have been over the years, and I'm not saying that I haven't had the odd shag cos I have, on numerous occasions. But I've always been very very lucky with the women I've lived with.

And Tracey was another example of my good luck on that score. We'd only known each other a bit over a month before the trial and I think most people thought it wouldn't last. But I knew if I got sent down she'd be there for me when I came out. Not cos she overlooked things or anything like that, but just because, at that time, I was nothing more than a slightly naughty geezer. That's how I was when we met and fell in love, and I know it did become difficult for her a lot later on cos the lifestyle I chose would never have been Tracey's choosing.

In the run-up to the trial I prepared to turn up with loads of witnesses to attest to me not being in the pub. Trouble is, there was one thing I wasn't aware of until they showed it to me: the video tape of me coming out of the pub dancing the bleedin' conga, wearing a party hat and tooting one of those party blowers. When the magistrate saw it I don't think he could quite come to terms with it.

'I fail to understand, Mr Courtney,' he said, 'how your mind works; when you can be stabbing five men with a machete one minute, and dancing the hokey cokey and singing "Should auld acquaintance" the next!'

He had me down as a right nutter, I tell you. I felt it was a waste of time even to attempt to go 'not guilty' (or so I thought then). It was to be the first, last and only time I would ever plead guilty. It taught me a valuable lesson and, luckily for me, one that didn't cost me too much.

The 'attempted murder' charge was dropped, but I was done for the others. I only paid for it with a three-year, six-month sentence (and the six months was for resisting an arrest using violent conduct). I'd already seen other blokes learn the same lesson and it cost them fourteen years of their lives. When I got inside I learnt, in the big Criminal College, that I'd made a mistake to plead guilty. And it burnt into me. I never ever forgot that. From then on I decided they could catch me in a bank with a smoking gun in my hand and a bag of money at my feet and a bullet hole in the ceiling and I'd say, 'Who do you believe – me or your lying eyes?'

It was knowledge which would be valuable to me in the years to come.

5 Bird

Prison was exactly what I needed, though I didn't realise it at the time. But not for the reason that advocates of harsher sentences or prison reformers like Lord Longford would want to hear. It didn't make me want to get 'back on the straight and narrow' or 'see the error of my ways' and all that crap, because I still feel to this day that I was right. It just made me realise what price you had to pay and the sacrifices you had to make to go through this intense college course in crime. It was to be a very valuable time for me and one of the best chances of self-education I could have hoped for. It also helped buff the shine on the three golden rules: (1) Never get caught; (2) If you do, always say 'no comment'; and (3) Never, *ever* plead guilty.

I don't know if it was my parents' hope that it would straighten me out, I suppose it was, but I was well past that. The worst thing was that my younger brother Patrick got sent down as well. He got a year at borstal. For what? For being attacked by them bastards. It was ridiculous, but they did him as an accessory. You can imagine how that cheered Mum and Dad up no end. Bad enough me, who they kinda expected it from, but then Patrick. I weren't exactly in their good books for a while.

So the new decade of the eighties began with me in Wormwood Scrubs in Shepherd's Bush. The day I went to prison I got to court really early. I went to the caff for a cup of tea and the guy there said, 'You've got to listen to this – it's just come out,' and he put the jukebox on and Shakin' Stevens came blaring out singing 'This Old House'. Anyway, I went into court then, got my sentence and got taken down. Then Shakin' Stevens became a massive hit and I had to listen to 'This Old fucking House' for about the next twenty weeks it was at No. 1.

When you're in prison, records mean an awful lot to you. They might be awful records, but it don't matter. It's a reminder. Records to men in prison are like those to someone who's just split with their girl- or boyfriend. If you hear the right one it just seems to be speaking to you, and it can crumble you.

The Scrubs was what they call an 'allocation' prison, one where you go temporarily while they work out what category your crime was and where you should be transferred to. They call 'em 'railway stations' because you're just parked up waiting to be sent off somewhere. These prisons they put you in for the first few months of your bird are always overcrowded. They are old prisons with small cells and they put two or three blokes in there (these days it's up to three or four!). They were built in Victorian times when there weren't so many prisoners and people must have been a hell of a lot smaller cos the cells were tiny. You didn't have room even to get a cat in, let alone swing it round.

Even if you were in for something petty you could end up on a more serious charge because if you got put with someone that really got on your tits, you'd feel like killing them. Luckily, my cell mates were all right. They were two geezers called Digger and George. Proper nutcases, but lovely fellas. Digger was in for some charge involving a shootout in the backstreets of Stockwell. My crime seemed petty compared to some. There were some very, very naughty people in there and a large proportion of arseholes.

But you do get some funny times inside. It's one of the few things that makes it bearable. There was this one guy who we had in with us – Jarvis, I think his name was. He used to work on the gameshow *It's A Knockout*. Part of the game was that you could play what they called the 'joker' card and double your points. Anyway, this geezer was having an affair with one of the scoreboard girls who just happened to be married. He ended up killing her husband and trying to pass it off as an accident on a fishing trip. He got ten years for his trouble.

So, one night, about three in the morning, we were lying there; some of the nick was asleep, loads were just half awake but listening, and me and a few others were still up talking. Suddenly, someone went up to his window and went, 'Oi! Jarvis?'

'What?' Jarvis said.

'I was just wondering – how come you got ten years then? Did you get five and play the joker?!'

Well, we all just fell about. Inside the Scrubs there are 500 windows facing another 500, so all you could hear was hundreds of blokes all laughing at the same time.

There was also a big-name band leader from years ago, still known at the time. He was done for drink-driving. And a famous footballer (from Arsenal, I think); he was in there for smuggling Krugerrands. Quite a few footballers, come to think of it. All caught well offside.

And there were three different Johns in different cells down below: Johnny, Big John, and the youngest, John Boy. Come lights out they all started shouting goodnight to each other. It was like the bleedin' Waltons. When it got to 'John Boy', we all jumped up and joined in: 'Goodnight Mary-Ellen! Goodnight Grandma!'

And guess who I saw while I was in there? My old maths teacher! He was in for some cheque-book fraud scam. I used to hate this bastard at school and every time I saw him round the prison I kept thinking of all the beatings he'd given me. One time I put a book down my pants to protect me but he saw the outline of it, took it out and gave me even more whacks for having it there. So what a touch running in to him. He didn't think so, though, cos I made sure he copped it big-time. And I gave him an extra one for being ginger.

Bob Marley died while I was inside and the prison went absolutely mental, all screaming and shouting out the windows. They actually called in reinforcements at one point cos they thought a riot was going to break out. That says something, don't it? Not just about how much his music was loved but also about a certain prison recreation: none of us could let pass quietly the death of King Spliff.

Alfie Hoyle – he was another one of the lads. Over Christmas we were brewing our own beer. The whole landing stank of it. It smelt like a fucking pub. You only had to be stood downwind to get pissed. I was brewing mine in the khazi so if they tried to get the drop on us, I could just hide the pisspot. Anyway, the screws got wind of it, which wasn't too difficult, and we smelt a raid coming so we hid it all in Alfie's cell. When they came up and banged into his cell, the smell just punched them in the face. They found something like fourteen gallons of beer under his bed! From then on we called him Ben Truman, after a beer we used to drink.

It was in the Scrubs that I learnt something that would make me quite a bit of money over the years. I was the association orderly, so I went to get the pool table out for us to play on. It was proper fucked: wobbly, ripped felt, one cushion missing. No one else would go near it, so I had it to myself. I decided to learn to play one-handed and practised non-stop until I was better with one than most players were with two hands. Twenty years of playing like that earned me a healthy amount of dough in pub challenges over the years, mate, let me tell you.

After my time in the Scrubs I was moved to the proper nick, Coldingly Prison in Woking. And Woking's such a one-horse town that even the horse has left. But this is where I was going to do out my time.

When you first go in there you're put in a dormitory with twelve others until a cell comes free. It's OK for a while, it can be quite funny all being together, but then you get your bullies and your snorers and it all starts to wear a bit thin; it starts to do your head in.

One of my best mates in there was Mickey Clarke. He came up with the idea of doing the Ouija board one night and everyone else was up for it. Anything to alleviate the boredom. We waited until it was a full moon, y'know, for maximum spookiness, even though we all thought it was a load of crap. Then on the night, after lights out, we all sat round this table with letters drawn on it and a glass in the middle. Almost as soon as we sat down and put our fingers on it, the glass actually moved! Whether it was people pushing it or not, the bloody glass moved. Well, we all just jumped up and put the lights on. Everyone swore that it wasn't them that had moved it and although no one would admit to it and tried to laugh it off, it really freaked us out. In fact, it really fucked us up for the next few weeks in the dorm. There's all these supposedly hardened criminals not wanting to go to bed with the lights off! It really shit the life out of us that little episode did.

Then I got my single cell. It was a very new nick at the time – an electronic working nick (the only nick you got paid in money). No keys, no screws walking round jangling with keys; just press buttons. And cameras everywhere. You've got a microphone in your cell as well. I thought, Fuck me, what's this – karaoke? The screws talk to you through it and you talk back to them. And there's no bogs in the cells either. They're outside on the end of the landing. You ask to go and they unlock the doors. Cos the landings are all camera-ed out, they can see who's in and out.

I was on the same landing as Chris Lambrianou, brother of Tony Lambrianou, who was well known as the guy responsible for removing the body of Jack 'The Hat' McVitie after he'd been topped by Reggie Kray. I got to be good friends with Chris. He was in for murder. He was a massive, scary-looking geezer. And a born-again Christian, for fuck's sake. Which made him a massive, scary-looking born-again Christian, the scariest-looking bible basher I've ever seen in my life. I bet he made more converts than Christ himself. Imagine this huge bloke looming over you, his eyes saying 'I want to eat your brains' but his mouth saying, 'Have you ever felt the need for God to enter your life?' Research shows that nine out of ten non-believers said, 'Yes, Chris! Please tell me more.'

Another bloke on my landing was this geezer called Big Rocky. Now you've never seen anything like this bloke before in your life. A big black geezer, and I mean black, so black he was almost blue. Six foot three and barrelly with it; not fat, just real big and barrelly. And he had colossal strength. He was a South Londoner from Brixton and the nearest thing to a Yardie I'd ever met at the time.

We got on like a house on fire. We really hit it off. He told me that in summer he used to walk up Rowlton Road with a dirty great machete in his belt. He had this Transit van with a four-foot cube of ice in the back. He'd chop bits off with the machete, pour lemonade on it and sell them as those Slush Puppy things you get from ice-cream men. He thought by doing that it gave him the authority to walk around with this machete in his trousers. He was animal, pure animal. But he was really funny too.

Another one of his convictions was for when he went into a cinema and jumped up on stage in front of the screen, pulled out two .45 automatics and demanded the audience empty their pockets. Imagine that! If you'd been sat there thinking, Wow! I didn't know this film was in 3-D!

Nothing was ever boring with this geezer. For instance, I'll tell you a quick tale about what happened after we both eventually got out of the nick. Rocky's house was knocked down in the re-modernisation of Brixton so he came to me cos I'd always said I'd help him out if he needed it. Get him some work, that kind of thing. So I obliged by giving him this old yellow Mercedes 450 SEL which he thought was the complete bollocks, and the next day he came out with me on a job. I had to go and have a word with this guy in his shop and knew he'd have three or four others with him, so Rocky was my safety net. This shop was on a main street in full view, so I didn't want us to attract any more attention than necessary. I told this to Rocky and he turned up wearing his version of incognito smartness. I saw him from about half a mile away, strolling up the street towards me: bright white trainers with green stripes, a three-piece suit that would've looked OK if he'd been four stone lighter, no shirt or socks, a buttoned-up waistcoat, a large brown leather hat containing all his locks, and more gold chains round his neck and wrist than the local Ratner's had in their window. I wanted smart and sensible, and I ended up with Huggy Bear. I didn't have the heart to say anything cos he was so proud of the effort he'd made. 'Yo, Davey!' he said when he reached me. 'Me look like a bloodclat solicitor!' I told him he didn't look fuck all like my solicitor.

When we went into the shop, which was a car accessory place, the geezer looked round when the bell went ping, took one look at Rocky behind me and made a dash for it from behind the counter. Rocky picked up this car battery with one hand and threw it about fifteen feet. It whacked the guy right on the head and he dropped like a dead weight. I'd never seen anything like it in my life (actually, that's not true; I had seen something like it. When Rocky used to do the shot put in prison he'd throw the shot right *through* the chain-link fence). So then, when I'm bent down talking to the guy, Rocky came up behind me, put his long arms over my shoulders and picked this geezer up by the flesh of his face. So now we were nose to nose, and he looked like a bloodhound. Like I say, the guy had phenomenal strength. Dress sense? Not so good.

So Rocky was OK by me. Prison is where I learnt that I wasn't prejudiced. Outside I'd come from a certain kind of place and gone into a certain kind of lifestyle where blacks and whites didn't really mix. I found out, when I was inside, that I wasn't like some of my mates or people I worked with; I took people as I found them, and if they were straight with me then I was the same with them. I'm not saying I deserved a medal for that or anything, but that's just when it really came home to me.

So getting on with the other blokes certainly makes life easier when you're banged up together 24 hours a day. It can, on the other hand, be a complete fucking nightmare if you get paired up with someone you clash with. If you're in a cell 23 hours a day with just one hour for exercise, you can imagine. Me, for example, I snore like a Volkswagen, like a proper Volkswagen Beetle. Now, if the other geezer can't sleep because of it, that means next day he's tired, and then it happens again the next night and before long he's ready to stab you in the eye with a toothbrush. Or you might move in with someone with a really bad hygiene problem. It doesn't even have to be a big thing like that. Sometimes the tiniest things, over a long time, can become a big proper problem if you let them. One guy I was in with, it was the way he ate crisps. That's how daft it can be. He'd suck the bits off the ends of his fingers and just the sound of it drove me absolutely fucking mental. Luckily for him he weren't in long and he left before I snapped (his fingers). Some weren't so lucky. I did have some nightmare ones where I'd only be in the cell with them for ten minutes and hadn't even unpacked my kit before I'd be in the block for chinning them.

If you got a good 'un, though, it would be brilliant. You'd strike up friendships in prison like you'd never had anywhere else in the world. This might sound weird, and don't take this the wrong way, but it's almost like a relationship. You end up knowing the geezer better than you do your own missus. I know only people who've been inside will really understand that, but I'll try to explain it for the rest of you.

Think about it: you spend 23 hours a day, seven days a week, every week of the year for maybe two years with this bloke. You get to know what makes him laugh, what makes him cry, when he farts, when he wanks, when the kids' birthdays are and what holidays he's been on. You know when he's down and when he's upset and what cheers him up. You see him going through every single solitary emotion and how he handles it. Which is something your family or missus don't even see cos on the outside you hide different bits from different people, don't you? But there ain't no hiding in a poxy little cell. It can go one way or the other: annoyance can turn to hate and friendship almost turns to love. And when you see a man live with stress, pain, rage, fear, nerves, everything, all of it, and help him go through it, and he helps you, you can't help but strike up a strong bond of friendship with someone that you know everything about. And when it's time for them to go, if they're due to go first, you can actually feel tearful, to be honest. Truthfully, it's gutting. You're losing your best mate. You know you'll never ever know someone like you know your cellmate. And you know the next bloke in is gonna take another year to get to know that well. And when you've felt the concerns and fears, you genuinely feel for other men in there cos you know the pains they feel or are going to feel. And that never leaves you. Even when you're out, if you hear of someone getting a stretch you still feel a knot tying in your stomach.

For me, going from running round on the outside, having the time of my life with my mates and generally living life to the full, to being banged up was fucking not nice. Not nice at all. I'm not saying my little bit was any harder than anyone else's, but to have your liberty taken away for the first time is very very nasty. But it is also enlightening, and made me realise for the first time the truth behind that old saying, that in times of hardship you find out who your true friends are (as Nan used to say). So getting banged up was like being dragged out of a party in full swing and then thrown into a dentist's waiting room, just sat there listening to the drill and knowing you're next.

One of the big things that made it easier for me inside was having an excellent relationship outside with my missus, Tracey, who'd moved in with me three weeks before I got sent down. She was the perfect missus for a prisoner. I knew she'd wait for me, and she wrote to me every day – every single day. She was honest, loyal and supportive at a time when I really needed it, and for that I'll love her always.

Knowing that, at the time, gives you strength. It really does. When you get back on the outside and see old mates, they say one of three things: they didn't know what to write; they'd left it so long they felt they couldn't start; or they just never seemed to have the time. That really hits you. Because inside you've got nothing but time. Too fucking much of it. It's easy to forgive, but you don't forget.

There's a saying that goes 'The missus does the bird as well as the man', and I'm here to tell you that that's true, it's absolutely bang on. In some ways, for the woman it's harder because it's like being in an open prison for them. It's not often spoken about or acknowledged either, which is wrong. There's so much the woman has to deal with: silly jealousies; guilt over going for a night out (even though they're not up to anything); guilt over not being able to do anything about her fella inside; not knowing whether to say something's gone wrong at home or keep it to herself and, if she does that, risking it might be mistaken by the man for hiding something else, like he might think she's met someone; pretending not to be bored by the same old prison stories; being in a dilemma about what to wear – should she wear something sexy to please him, or dress down? Little things turn into big things. It can be like tiptoeing through a minefield for the woman.

And, on top of that, she has to hold her end up by being brave. There's nothing worse than the wife coming in crying about how bad it is out there because that just makes you feel useless. No one sees all these things the woman has to live with – how she'll go to bed with one of his shirts so she can still smell him and feel near to him, or how she might be late for work in the mornings and risk getting the sack because she's sat waiting for the postman to arrive with a letter. Or worrying if when he gets out he's gonna start again, and is he ever gonna stop? Or how, when he's inside, no one looks after her with a couple of quid. People do say 'if you need anything just ask', but then they leave it at that, knowing she's not the type to ask or is just too proud.

Prison is also the worst place to have an argument with your missus cos then she leaves and the man has 24 hours a day to do nothing but play it around his mind. Often he'll put two and two together and come up with something well wide of four. Then she'll get it in the neck the next visit. They have to put up with all that.

Tracey was perfect, though. Took it on the chin. Didn't whine about financial needs, and showed she knew I was hurting and all that. And she grasped, early on, the importance of letters. You can learn more about someone from a letter than from talking on the phone. It brings out another side of people. I can't stress that enough, really. I saw blokes fall in love with their wives all over again because of the letters they sent them.

The same kinda thing happened with me and Tracey. She fell in love with me in prison. I hadn't known her that long, remember, before I got banged up. So we'd met, and she'd touched me and been with me physically for a few weeks but then spent over a year getting to know me through letters and visits (there were no phones in prison at that time, let alone your own colour TV). I suppose, in a way, it was like an old-fashioned courtship.

As long as you can shut the door behind you, you can fight the world and win. Keep your wife happy first and you can fuck the lot of them. And that's bang on. But if you have fucked about and stuff like that, then she's usually gonna find out while you're inside. I don't know why, but when you're inside, you always get some bastard outside waiting to tell your wife if you've been screwing around. And when you're inside you are in the wrong place to try to explain to her just how unimportant those things were. I've seen hard men inside fall to bits when they've got a Dear John letter.

Another thing is when guys come out and instead of seeing the missus first they go off down the pub with all their mates. That's a big mistake. Most men don't know that. They try and keep their mates happy. And the woman can see how pleased he is to be out and with his mates, and she knows she has to hold her tongue, even though she's thinking he should give her a week of his time first. She doesn't want to start moaning, although it's mostly her who carried on visiting him, not his mates. The man forgives his friends for that, but his missus finds it harder. Women can see something in men that men can't see in other men. And time inside has stood still for him, living in a prison regime, but it has been months and months of hardship for her. He hasn't had to worry about going back to the house alone every night. So keeping your relationship with your lady happy and strong means you can fight the world and win – you can fuck the lot of them. A good woman is the key to a man's strength.

If you're safe as houses indoors and the wife stays with you then you can fuck the system. I've seen it and I've done it. That's why I could take the piss out of it. And the screws know that too. That's why it's common policy among some of the officers (not all of them) to try and hurt you at home. If they can fuck up your home life, they will, cos they know you won't be able to handle your time. It's a very common occurrence, if a prisoner is writing to his wife *and* a girlfriend, for the screws to swap the letters over and put them in the wrong envelopes while all the mail is being vetted in the sorting office. Sometimes, they'd even go to the lengths of holding one letter for days, just waiting for the other one, say to the girlfriend, to come through. How fucking snide is that? And they wonder why riots kick off.

Talking of riots. About nine months into my sentence we all heard of the outcome of a trial that had been going on. This prisoner had been kicked to death in his cell down at Brixton and the screws stood accused. When news came through that the screws had been acquitted of kicking the guy to death, parts of Coldingly just blew up. Loads of things got smashed to fuck, people were barricaded in their cells. Like us, for instance: me, Rocky, Dave Hazeltine, Alfie Hoyle, Mickey Clarke, Paul and John Harty, all squashed in a cell. We put the bed over the door and holed up all night with baccy, booze, a bit of puff, a radio, a pack of cards and Monopoly (the 'Get Out Of Jail Free' card always went down well). It went on for one night and got so bad that the prison guv'nor even interrupted his golf, or whatever the fuck important thing he was doing, to come all the way back up to the nick. They smashed the glass in the cell doors and doused us with water extinguishers. Eventually the guv'nor came down to address us all.

Like I said , one of the guys with us was John Harty. Johnny was the absolute bollocks, a proper man's man. He was a very promising professional boxer with Frank Maloney. And one of the funniest men I've ever met.

So the guv'nor walked up and he went, 'Most of you are going home in a few months, but John Harty over there, he's got another eight years. He doesn't care what punishment he gets, and carry on like this and you'll get it with him.' He paused, and we just looked at him like the dozy cunt we thought he was. He carried on regardless. 'Just think about that. Because if you continue to do what you're doing, you're going to cause a catastrophe.'

Quick as a flash, Johnny stepped forward. 'Excuse me, guv, but you don't know what a catastrophe is – we've run out of fucking *tea bags* in here!'

I thought, Oh yes! Bosh! We just killed ourselves laughing.

Johnny was another one of those guys who looked like he could suck your eyes out for breakfast but just happened to be really funny. He was also one of those guys who, as hard as he was, was destroyed by his wife leaving him while he was inside. Later he was murdered in Parkhurst. Stabbed to death in the kitchens.

Of course one of the things which ain't funny about doing bird is the fact that you can't get laid. Some of the blokes on longer stretches turn gay, but not many. I couldn't see it happening to me, but I don't condemn it. I can see how it happens. It's not my cup of tea, but stranger things happen at sea, as they say.

So I was all set to be a nun for however long I was in there until Mickey Clarke told me about hospital visits. He said that if you went on the sick they'd take you to a prison hospital and when you got a bedside visit it would be in your cell. The screw would just sit outside so you'd get some time with your missus.

At this time we were doing some outside work at Reading train station. Soldiers were brought up from Bisley to escort and guard us. It was winter, and really, really cold, and our job was to clear snow off the tracks and clean them, similar to an old-fashioned chain gang type thing, like you see in films. So the plan was this: Mickey was to whack me on the head with a shovel. I'd say I slipped and hit my head on the track, then thank you, goodnight, and hello hospital bed and a bit of natural healing from the missus (I had a visit due next day). That was the theory anyway.

Come the day, we were all working away on the tracks, freezing our bollocks off. Because I knew what was gonna happen, every time Mickey came near me I started cringing, just waiting for the clump. I squashed my head so far down in my shoulders, if it wasn't for my big nose I think it would've sunk right in. But it's really, really hard, when you know something is coming, not to react. Every time he passed I tensed right up. To anyone watching it probably looked like I was suffering from severe constipation. This went on for ages, and I was dying. I thought, For Christ's sake just do it! When it finally came, it felt like the silly bastard had taken a ten-yard run-up cos when he hit me full belt – whap! – right on the back of the head, I went semi-unconscious. And you can imagine the clang a shovel makes on a head.

My eyes nearly fell out. That's what I remember most. My eyes seemed to ping right out on springs, like those joke-shop glasses. I fell forward, so numb that I couldn't move my hands out, and landed face down – smack! I'm laid there in the snow, half-dead, thinking, Oh cheers, Mick! (Afterwards he told me that when they'd picked me up I'd left this body-shape in the snow, cartoon-style. And also, the reason it had been so hard, he said, was because he'd tried to do it quick, to catch me unawares, and in doing it quickly . . .) Anyway, I mumbled something about slipping and banging my head on a rail and they carted me off in an ambulance with suspected concussion.

I spent the evening in the hospital, knowing that next day Tracey was due to arrive for a visit. In the morning I took a mouthful of tea and Weetabix and made sure I spewed it up in full view of the doctor to make him think I was still suffering from ill effects. When Tracey arrived they told her I was in hospital, but the silly bastards didn't even say what it was for and that I was OK. Now she knows I'm not the sicky type – barely had a day off work in my life (and that's not just cos

I've never worked!) – so by the time she gets in to see me she's crying her eyes out, thinking I'm at death's door or something. On top of that, because it's really snowing, she's wrapped up like Tutankhamun on a skiing trip: wellies, three pairs of tights, jeans, jumpers, scarf and balaclava. The works. It was like pass the bleedin' parcel just trying to get her undressed. And we haven't exactly got all the time in the world. All the time this is going on, another con keeps popping his head round the door to say daft things like, 'You OK for biscuits in there?' just to make the screw think everything's all right. What a palaver. Worth it, though. Well, it always is, innit?

But the funniest thing I ever saw in there was this (oh, listen to this, just *listen* to this!). There was this old guy inside for nicking money from someone's account. George was his name. He was an old bloke, a really sweet old gent as it happens; 65, upper class, paid his TV licence and all that, never been in trouble his whole life. But he'd gone and embezzled loads of money. Two to three million, as it happens. He was really rich anyway, but I guess he just wanted more. He was puzzled how we all got stuff like fags and toothpaste and silly little luxury items that you can't get inside. He couldn't see how we got all this gear on £2.50 prison pay. One day he asked me. I told him it was through selling 'puff', but he just looked dumb, so I had to explain.

'Puff. Y'know? Cannabis . . . for a bit of a smoke. Get your lady wife to bring a hundred quids' worth in.'

'I see,' he said in this proper posh voice he had. 'And would you sell it for me?'

' 'Course I would, George.'

I filled him in on the score, how she'd have to bring it inside in a Durex so he could put it up his arse.

Next thing, we're in the dorm on visiting day and George has prepared himself: got no underpants on, undone the crotch seams on his trousers and baby-oiled his arsehole so when she slips it to him in the Durex he can slip it inside himself. (Just a point here, by the way. You would not believe some of the containers that people bring in, expecting you to shove up your arse – triangular-shaped and wrapped in sharp tin foil. If the person is a masochist, no doubt they'll tell you! So, if you've got someone to visit, try to make the package soft and turd-shaped. Preferably the skinny ones. Thank you.)

Anyway, so we're all sat there taking visitors. I'm talking to Tracey, but I've got one eye on George and his old lady. Now George's missus was something else. She'd come in with the mauve rinse and everything just immaculate, but she had this permanently pained look. Like she didn't know how she was gonna explain this to the neighbours. She was probably a nice lady, but she just had that look about her – like she had a yard of ice cubes up her arse. I just hoped that George had the same talent with his backside.

Anyway, he started to look as pained as his missus, did old George. He caught my eye and tried to smile but he looked right uncomfortable. We found out why when visiting ended and we all got back to the dorm.

George dropped his pants and there was this thick black oil leaking out his arse! Me and the lads all stepped back as one, in formation. It looked like something out of *Tales from the Crypt*.

'George?' I said. 'What the fuck is *that*? You look like you're shitting treacle.'

'It's opium, David. My wife said it was the best.'

Oh, fuck me sideways, I thought.

Now, get *this* – this is what had happened. It turned out that the old dear, bless her, had gone to their home and asked their driver to get a hundred quids' worth of best puff, and he'd gone and got the best, which is opium oil. No wonder George had looked so bloody pained. Full of this oil the Durex had wobbled like a jelly. He'd managed to slip it slyly between his legs but only got it halfway in his arse before he put his finger through it. It was just pouring out of him and down his legs – pure black oil.

So, this is what we did. We knew this oil was pure opium, really tasty stuff, and we thought, Waste not, want not, as my old nan would've said. We skinned up loads of joints and started wiping them down his legs to soak it all up. We were rolling and wiping them and passing them back as fast as we could. If anyone had walked in at that point, this is the sight that would have greeted them: a grey-haired, 65-year-old, upper-class geezer called George bent over a table with one foot on a chair, while a bunch of cons crowded around his wrinkly old arse rolling joints in what looked like his diarrhoea. We could hardly do it for laughing. For ages afterwards, just the thought of it would set us off. Someone would start laughing for no apparent reason and you'd think, Yeah – George and his missus! Half Bonnie & Clyde, half Darby & Joan. You lose your dignity in prison, no doubt about that. Well, George did anyway.

The funny times aside, doing bird also taught me an awful lot. Or, more accurately, I made sure I learnt. Not everyone does. Some geezers just lie in bed and wank all day. Prison teaches you to get your priorities right. You learn how you handle yourself in different situations; how other people handle themselves; the right and wrong things to do; what violent people do to hide their weaknesses. You're actually living with some horrible, lying people and when you're away with them you learn how to see through people, straight to their bad points. When you come out you know what bad really looks like. I came out knowing how to spot them. Then when I met someone untrustworthy it was so clear, it was like I could see a visible line down them made of all the lies. Because, by then, you know what it looks like. And once you learn that, it's something that gets better every day. I couldn't do that before I went inside.

As well as the bad 'uns I met the good 'uns too. Real characters and proper class people. Men like Rocky, Paul, Tony White, Johnny Hart, Mickey Clarke, John Short, Phil Moredew, Frankie Fraser and Joey Pyle, all good chaps. Joey was one of the men I'd first seen all those years ago coming into the gym. He was one of the old school and a top gent. And now I got a chance to meet him and learn from him. (To this day, I still do.)

Being locked up for the first time at a fairly impressionable age (I was only just twenty when I got the sentence), I was open to learning. I learnt what was a good baddie and a bad baddie, a liked baddie and a disliked one. And I had the sense to learn from the good people like Joey. But, unlike some of the other younger blokes inside, I was never so much in awe of the older ones that I just listened to all the fantastic things they'd done. For one thing, if they were banged up inside then everything they'd done obviously hadn't been perfect.

Mostly, when I met men inside and studied them, what I

really wanted to learn was not what they'd done right but the one thing they'd done wrong. I thought, If I can gather all those 'wrongs' together then they'll give me a better chance of being right – they'll give me an answer. If I'd met you inside at that time, that's what I'd have wanted to learn from you: the one thing you done wrong. And being in prison I was surrounded by nothing but men who'd done at least one thing wrong. What a brilliant place to learn. Talk about a college of knowledge. It was like being at Open University, but with bars and big gates (not *that* fucking 'open', then). I didn't waste the time at all. If I did something out of turn or said something I shouldn't have, I never did it again. I sponged everything up.

Whatever world you move in, you find it's a small one. If you're a DJ, say, then you get to know lots of other DJs, make friends and then work opportunities open up for you. That's what it was like for me. My world was the so-called 'underworld'. When I knew this to be my choice of profession I decided early on to make the right friends and do right by them. I thought it was simple and blindingly obvious to do this. It's just a matter of long-term thinking. I knew the importance of the future. You make the wrong moves in any profession and it has only one effect on your future: it means you ain't got one, mate. So I looked on this as my apprenticeship.

Towards the end of my stretch they sent me up to Brams Hill, which was like a college for the hierarchy of the police force. Sir Paul Condon used to stay there. It was a cushier little number that everyone is given at the end. Because I had only a quarter of my sentence left they gave me an outside job. We used to do gardening jobs, mow the meadows and look after the deer, stuff like that. They'd drive us up there in an old army lorry. I used to get mates of mine to drive up there as well and hide loads of booze and puff in the fields for me. I'd tie bits of string from my waist, all different lengths, and hang these bottles down under my clothes. I was bringing so much beer back I was clinking when I walked. I sounded like a fucking cow bell.

I served eighteen months of the three and a half and made friends inside that I knew in future would help me and be good allies to have. I looked at it as a sort of audition. I conducted myself in such a way that they could see for themselves what kind of person I was, and that that person was the kind they'd want to associate with on the outside.

Being in prison made me realise exactly what kind of person I was. It wasn't so much like a homecoming, more like being reunited with long-lost relatives that you didn't even know you had. It made me realise what I was, or, should I say, what I was gonna be. Looking at the guys around me I saw rights and wrongs; I saw that there was a morality even in crime; and I saw something that I think I'd always known, deep down, from when I first saw guys like Freddie Foreman, Joey, Harry Haward and Alex Steen walk into the boxing gym when I was a lad: that it was possible to be a villain in a dignified manner. And that was right up my street.

I didn't even realise at the time how much I was learning in there, but I was. If they'd asked me on any day if I wanted to go home I would have said yes, of course. But the time I'd done was so very valuable to my learning. It made me realise I wanted more than I knew I could get from normal work, all the nice things of life that I saw my dad slave all his life for and still never get. That wasn't going to be me. And there was only one way I was gonna get those things. I'd seen what the punishment was if you got caught and knew I could handle that, so now I was gonna go bang at it.

So I came out smiling into the light of Woking after eighteen months inside. I now had the knowledge so it was easier to get on. One of the pieces of advice given to me by the older, wiser guys like Joey Pyle was, believe it or not, get a job. And they meant a proper one, not a bank job. In this game, as soon as you knock the nine to five on the head then people notice you. Especially if you've still got money. Where's it coming from? What's he doing? It attracts the wrong kind of attention. The day you sack your normal job is the day you are regarded by the police as a professional criminal. However little you're dabbling and however unimportant you think you may be compared to the big boys, it don't matter. The police imagination runs riot and they end up crediting you with a lot more than you are actually doing, and then they give you the attention they think you deserve. So from that day on you are, to them, a professional criminal. To avoid this you had to have, and keep, an ordinary job.

So I became a dustman.

6 A Flash Bastard, but a Nice Flash Bastard

No matter how long you do inside, walking out the gates is always a bit of an anti-climax cos you just build up so much in your imagination about what its gonna be like to walk out the door. And if you've done twenty years or two years you want to get out just as much, and you build it up so much in your head that nothing could possibly match up to it.

Don't get me wrong, it's brilliant to be out, course it is – it's really really good – but, everything seems different: the roads seem a bit wider than you remember, the buses are a bit redder than before and everything seems noisier and more manic. You also notice what's moved on because it all comes at you at once rather than gradually: a new bus shelter's been built or a local shop's closed down and reopened as something else; the nextdoor neighbour's changed his car – silly things like that. Well, first of all they seem silly, then a little bit scary as well. I suddenly realised that everything had gone on as normal without me. I'm not saying that I expected the world to stop or nothing, just because I'd got banged up, but the reality of it really struck me. You think, Fuck me, everything would just go on and, apart from my family and friends, it wouldn't make a blind bit of difference to anyone. And I'd only done eighteen months.

Try to imagine what it must be like coming out after twenty years! Same time as I was released this other geezer was let out. He'd been inside since the early sixties. When he went in it was all sixpences and shillings, and Elvis Presley and The Beatles in the charts. Now when he comes out there's hole-in-the-wall cash machines, Michael Jackson, *Star Wars* at the pictures, and Elvis and John Lennon are both dead. Get your head round *that*. Some guys were in so long even Rod Stewart had changed his hairstyle by the time they got out. And fuck me, that is a long time.

I remember, when I was in Coldingly, talking to one guy who got a long stretch many years ago for an armed robbery. The whole thing went a bit wonky and someone ended up getting shot. When he got sent down it was all drainpipe trousers and short back and sides. By the time he got out it was slap-bang in the middle of punk rock. There was still amazement in his voice even when he was telling it to me: 'I couldn't believe it, Dave. There was these geezers walking round with blue hair! In big spikes! And wearing dresses and make-up and earrings, some of them. Proper blokes as well, not birds. I couldn't fucking believe it.' He thought blue-haired Martians had landed. That's how it can fuck your head up when you're taken away from the world. You feel like a fish out of water.

So when I came out it was more like a case of 'stop the world I wanna get back on'. It didn't make me want to stop what I was doing, just made me determined to do it better so I didn't get nicked.

I've always made it look like it's no big thing going to prison, then when I'm inside I made everyone think I was having a good time, but, naturally, like everyone else, I wanted to make a big show of coming out: stretch limo waiting for me, champagne for the screws to show no hard feelings, that kind of thing. I suppose I was always a bit flash, but always tried to be nice with it. In fact, I had a business card made up saying just that: DAVE COURTNEY – A FLASH BASTARD BUT A NICE FLASH BASTARD. So I came out to a waiting limo and Tracey stood at its open door, all smiles.

There was something that I felt I approached differently to most people: I never trusted anyone else other than me to tell my story to a judge. With such high stakes I wouldn't trust anyone else with my liberty. Right from the time I'd been sitting in court with the others I'd looked around and thought, Hello! I can shine here! So I did. I kept cool enough to crack some jokes in court and even make the jury laugh. And that's always the best time to do it, during difficulties. Anyone can be cool, calm and collected as fuck when things are going well, but to keep cool when all around you are losing theirs, as they say, is more difficult. That was always my forté.

Prison only has a stigma about it when you're a young man. That's when people pointing the finger and saying 'He's been inside' affects you most. When you're older it means absolutely fuck all. To the older guys it doesn't have that stigma cos it's so inbred it's part of the job, almost like going down the social club for a pint.

After I came out, I didn't realise I had changed until I started talking to everyone else, and I felt I now had this little edge. And whatever changes it had made to me were well received by my friends. I'd found out, by being in prison, that this – being a villain – is what I was all about. And I intended to be a fucking good one. I knew that it came naturally to me; I understood the law, I could read people and work out situations; I knew the whys and wherefores and didn't mind having a tear-up – and a lot of that was what I learnt inside. I now knew, *really* knew, that I was cut out for it.

When I'd gone into prison I'd been living in a proper man's flat: the bed was held up with dirty books, mirror on the ceiling, dartboard on the wall at the foot of the bed, a baseball bat on the wall and two crocodiles living in the front room. A real, normal, proper man's gaff. I also had three cookers. Two of them were to sell, but I never mentioned it, funnily enough, so that must have looked pretty strange to Tracey. I could've said I was training to become a top chef (like she would have believed me). By the time I came out Tracey's family, in particular her step-dad Barry, had thrown away every stick of furniture (which, by the way, I'd nicked from outside shops) and redecorated it into this beautiful little flat. It was a really nice surprise. That made it an even better homecoming.

Also, when I came out I had loads of new contacts and it was easier to get on. That's when I took the advice to get a proper job and became a dustman. It was in Dog Kennel Hill, Southwark. It was a wicked job to have cos after I'd done my round I was finished by, say, half ten in the morning and then I had the rest of the day. Although it was a proper job, it was my way round getting a *proper* proper job, if you know what

I mean; something with a real strict clocking on and off kind of carry on. That wouldn't have done at all. After I finished my rounds I had all day to go out meeting people, finding work and doing jobs. But my kind of jobs.

On the dust I worked with a great bunch of blokes: Terry, Steve, Johnny Lawrence, Budgie, Frankie Brock, Ray Bridges, Bill, Kenny, Danny the Nutcase, Peter Reeves and Keith Eves. Even doing that job, which sounds boring, we had a good laugh.

One thing that weren't so funny was when a bin fell on me. It had been really snowing and I slipped and this big bin I was holding fell and squashed me. What should be the first car round the corner, but a police car. They called an ambulance. The damage the bin did meant I went on the sick. The odd thing was that the coppers said they witnessed it all, which they never! I think they just wanted to come out of it as heroes. Honestly, you can't trust anyone!

It was about this time that I made what turned out to be my last attempt to do something legit. Tracey's sister, Jan, was married to a guy called Leslie who was a fireman. I thought that job might give me all the things I wanted: excitement and surges of adrenalin. Those things were right up my street, and certain legal jobs like being a fireman could have fulfilled that need. And you'd also get all the brotherhood thing with it too, y'know, like your little team. So Leslie got me an interview.

Driving there in my black cab I got stopped by the Old Bill, so that weren't a good start. The day didn't end too well either cos the test was four hours long and I failed it. Academic things had never really been my strong point, especially maths, and the test seemed to be mostly that. And then I had to go to court for getting pulled by the police. By this time I'd got enough unpaid parking tickets and speeding fines to sink a battleship. Which gave me an idea. I had a mate in the Navy so I borrowed his uniform, the full fancy dress kit they used for parades. And that's how I turned up in court. I told the magistrate that one of my five brothers had used the cab and I didn't know which one it was so I was willing to take the blame.

'It was while I was in the Falklands . . . I'm sorry, I didn't mean to say that,' I said, playing it humble. 'Let's just say it happened while I was away.'

Not fucking guilty. Fines and tickets wiped out. *Yes!*

So then I started on my kind of work, the stuff that would later earn me the nickname, 'The *Yellow Pages* of Crime'. You remember the old *Yellow Pages* advert? 'Let your fingers do the walking' it said. Well, a lot of light fingers were doing a lot of walking – walking off with nicked tellies, dodgy cars, and moody this, that and the others. My end of it was introducing people to the right people to do the right job, and taking a cut out of it. Like a sort of alternative employment agency, if you like. Or an early version of the AA, y'know? Even if I didn't do something myself, I always knew a man who did. It didn't even seem like what I was doing was illegal. Someone might ask me about knock-off tellies, for example, and I'd whizz through the old mental pages to 'TVs (knock-off)' and it would say 'see Johnny' or whoever. And in that situation, your brain gets trained into making money. I acquired, early on, a horrible habit, whenever I was introduced to someone, of saying, 'Hello – and what do you do?' So I knew where I could slot them into the *Yellow Pages* in my mind. I still do that today. And I remember them all.

I had lots of things on the go by now. I even started DJing (anything to entertain and get a reaction) at The Railway Signal and another pub called The Albion, owned by Brian Kean. I played golden oldies, that was my thing: all the old rock 'n' roll and Motown stuff. One time I got booked to play a place called Dr Jim's on Croydon high street, owned by Jim Wylie. So I went in there with my two boxes of records and walked slap-bang into a blues party! The place was full of black guys dancing to heavy dub reggae. I thought, Hang on one fucking minute! Talk about feeling like you've stepped out the lift on the wrong floor. I was playing the last set of the night so there was no way I couldn't go on. I got up and banged 'em out: Elvis, Roy Orbison, Jerry Lee Lewis, Otis Redding, Sandie Shaw, Dusty Springfield, the lot. There were a load of puzzled faces, I can tell you. Have you ever seen a dreadlocked Rasta trying to dance to 'Great Balls of Fire'? Fucking funny, mate. I made a few converts, though. They left at the end of the night singing, 'Yeah, man – always somethin' there to remind me!'

As well as all the wheeling and dealing I was also doing a bit of doorwork, a bit of debt collecting, and I'd gone back to boxing. I'd never really left it, always went to the gym to keep sharp, but now I went into it professionally. In professional boxing you realise pretty quickly if you've got what it takes. I knew I was never gonna be world champion, and it's not my style to do anything unless I can do it well.

One of the best things to come out of it was meeting someone who went on to become a great pal of mine. It was when I was on the card at a boxing show held at a college. The changing rooms were communal, and that's rare in boxing. Hardly ever happens. So the geezer that I'm gonna be fighting is in there, and I'm giving him dirty looks. He was a big, handsome-looking bloke and I thought, You ain't gonna look like that by the end of the night, mate. Anyway, he only comes over and speaks to me. And he had one of the poshest voices I'd ever heard. He made Prince Charles sound like a retarded navvy.

'Hi there,' he said. 'I'm Jonathan. I believe we will be boxing next. I'd just like to say may the best man win, and whatever the outcome I'd like to buy you a drink afterwards.'

I thought, Fuck me! Is this guy for real? 'Look,' I said, 'you ain't even gonna want to look at me afterwards cos I'm going to rip you to pieces, mate.' Cocky little bastard, I thought.

What I didn't know was that Jonathan (or Posh John as I later came to call him) was a rugby player, a Sussex county cricketer and a proper trained boxer. First round, I came out like a bear with a wasp up its arse, growling and swinging. Jonathan, boxing by the book, danced around, picking me off with his jab – ping, ping, ping! He made me look a right cunt. Second round, I used all the tricks I'd learnt: the thumb in the eye, the head, the knee. That kind of thing. That's 'by the book' where I come from; me and John had just read different books, that's all. By the third round we were both wary of each other. It was scored a draw.

And afterwards he did buy me a drink. I learnt that he was the only son of a multimillionaire, his dad was a baron and he'd grown up on this huge estate in Hastings. You'd think we would've had absolutely fuck all in common but we got on really well straight away. That was because what I immediately saw in John, despite the poshness, was naughtiness. He was just naturally naughty. He was the perfect example of what I said before, that naughty men are born not made. We had that in common. We got on like a petrol factory on fire. We went on to have loads of escapades, which I'll tell you about later, and in time he became one of my closest friends.

So after five professional bouts I went into the unlicensed game. Not out-and-out street brawls, but illegal boxing matches. We called them 'straightners' – much smaller gloves and the rules were more lax. You might get two guys fighting who were different weights or ages. One might be a football hooligan who wants more fights than he gets every Saturday at the match or a tasty pub brawler that wants to do the same and get paid for it, and the other might be an ex-professional boxer who's too old to get licensed.

I won my fair share, but I would never embarrass myself by saying I was good at it. I was a fucking good tryer, but when you saw men like Roy Shaw, Lenny McLean, Columbo, Stevie Earlwood, Harry Starbuck, Jimmy Batten and Fred the Head, you knew you were never gonna be the best. I realised that I only had two or three good rounds in me. I didn't understand what it was to back off or pace myself. I'd go absolutely berserk in the first round looking for a knockout. By the middle of the third I'd used so much energy you could've knocked me down with a well-aimed fart. When it got to that point I decided that I'd rather be disqualified than knocked out in front of everybody. I always had enough left in me for a kick or a bite or to grab the geezer by the scrag and stick the nut on him. Not so much the Queensberry Rules as the Mike Tyson Technique. Out of seventeen unlicensed bouts I was disqualified in five. Not bad going.

I wasn't even doing it for a living, to be honest. I was doing it so I could stand up somewhere and have five hundred people chant my name. It was a platform for that. That feeling, when you're carried out of the ring on people's shoulders after a win, is amazing. And however good a brickie or plasterer or dustman you are, no one gives you a round of applause at clocking-off time. I never walked down the street with a bin on my back to find all the neighbours out shouting, 'Da*vee*! Da*vee*!' I guess it goes back to the 'entertaining' thing and the acknowledgement that I wanted. Boxing was just like being on stage for me.

I didn't always get roses at the final curtain, though. One time I boxed at a show in Woodford. I was fighting a guy called Patsy Gutteridge. Lenny McLean was due on after me. Now there was a man who was a fighting machine. The three guys in my corner were Amon Ash, Harry Holland and Santos. On paper, I should have beaten this Patsy geezer. He was fifty something and I was supposed to be in my prime. But he was so hard this bloke that when he hit me in the side he bent me like a banana. I doubled over with no air left in me. I knew the next punch would knock me out so I quickly went to nut him and get disqualified. But when I threw the nut I split my own head open. The cunt even had a rock-hard head! I saw Patsy outside in the car park afterwards and had a few words, but everything was OK. But because of the nature of these events, where every fighter brings loads of mates to support him, my mates and Patsy's didn't see eye to eye. They all ended up having this massive row in the car park with me and Patsy trying to calm it down!

Lots of the fights were in Grey's Inn, but I had fights all over the place: Crystal Palace, the Queen's Hotel, football grounds and even one at Luton car plant. A couple of them were raided by the Old Bill, but I was never questioned or arrested. One of the weirdest ones I had, and probably the most embarrassing, was at Lewisham Town Hall. I was still inside the dressing room and and all set to go when the other guy's cornermen came round and said their man couldn't fight cos he had a boil, or something, under his arm. Fair enough, I said, and then retired to the bar with my mates. A couple of hours later, near the end of the night, this geezer's cornermen only came running up and said they'd lanced the boil and we would be fighting next! Now, I'm sat there with four pints and ten hotdogs in me, but I can't refuse cos all my mates started cheering and shouting, 'Go on, Davey!'

I climbed in the ring not feeling too good about this. I'm at a disadvantage to begin with. When the bell went and I moved out I sounded like a bucket of water in the back of a car. For the first round I kept my distance (not my usual style) and hoped that things might settle a bit. After the bell for the second things went from bad to worse. He ran out and whacked me right in the guts. And I threw up right in his face.

Four pints of warm beer, two packs of peanuts and hundreds of hotdog bits (and where the carrot bits came from, fuck only knows) came up and hit him slap-bang in the mush – *smack!* It was unbelievable, like a thick rope of sick flying out my mouth. I felt like that bird in *The Exorcist*. I think everyone half-expected my head to twist right round and my eyes to glow red. I wanted to turn to the crowd and go, 'And for my next trick . . .' but I was still bent double in pain. My opponent shouted out and tried to wipe the puke off himself, but cos he was wearing gloves he couldn't do it. He went mad, running blind round the ring looking for a towel. And I was disqualified, which I thought was a bit rich. As far as I know there's nothing in the book ruling out puking in the face of your opponent. I think it should have stood as a TKO.

Another funny one was when I went down to Crystal Palace stadium with my mates Eric and Sue. There was a massive athletics track event going on. Just as we got in I saw that the 1500 metres was coming up to the last lap, with Olympic champion, Daley Thompson, leading. Never one to miss an opportunity, I dropped my pants so I was in my shorts and T-shirt. Then I jumped the barrier, ran out on to the track just as Daley was taking the bend, overtook him (cos he was shagged) and won the race – *And Courtney breasts the tape to win by ten yards. What an achievement for a young man just out of the Scrubs!* I ran off back into the crowd. A bit later, when I was in the stand, some of the other athletes recognised me and had a go at me, trying to make a citizen's arrest or something daft like that. They were absolutely fuming about what I'd done. Everyone else thought it was fucking funny! Anyway, I had a go back at them, obviously, and got nicked for GBH! I got probation for that one. But I had beat Daley Thompson; they couldn't take that away from me.

It was the end of the year, though, which gave me the best result of my life. Tracey had got pregnant as soon as I got out of Coldingly. No shock there really, we'd had a lot of making up to do, and on 18 December 1982 she gave birth to my boy. She was 48 hours in labour! We'd had weekend breaks that didn't last that long. Men don't know no pain like that, do they? Well, only the ones that've had to shit a bowling ball. A mate of mine, Stevie Street, sat with me at the hospital.

We called our boy Beau. Tracey came home with him on Christmas Day and that was the best present that I've ever been given. Nothing could top that. That's better than any boxing prize or Christmas present or flash motor all rolled into one. A man's first son is something really really special, and Beau is.

I started to get on when I was employed by John Boy doing security work, working the doors of pubs and clubs and shows. John Boy was the Mr Big of doormen at the time. I worked with Lenny McLean and the Firm at places like Camden Palace with Basil, Ray and Steve; Browns with Alex and friends; Dingles; Stringfellows with Dave, Alex, Mark and the Simms brothers; The Fridge and just about any other club you could mention. My fellow doormen were all tasty fellas like Ned Rawlings, Mickey Jackson, T.J. Santos, Steve Bogart, Big Warren, Norman, Funny Glenn and American Football Tony.

I was training at the Thomas à Becket gym when Gary Davidson asked me to do the security at a professional boxing show at Lewisham Town Hall. Two coachloads of rival supporters started some trouble and I sorted it out well enough without going OTT. I used a little diplomacy rather than just outright force and this way of handling it made an impression.

Most of my work was in the south and east of London when what I really wanted to do was move up to the West End and the big clubs and proper nightlife. I did do a couple of nights up there but I couldn't take my own firm – it was all sewn up there already, business-wise. That would change, though, a bit later on as I gathered more men around me and my own firm of doormen started to grow

But I had finally found something at which I excelled. I'd been through all different kinds of villainy, if you like, trying this and that and finding what I was good and not so good at. I liked boxing but wasn't good enough to get as far as I would've wanted to. I needed to find what I liked and what suited me. Security and protection work was that. It suited me right down to the ground. I found what I was good at was working for and looking after the kind of men who in my game needed protection. The feeling of belonging, being part of a team; the smartness of it, all dinner-suited up with the chaps around; the circles you moved in and the people you met:

everything about it was made for me. I was cut out for it big time.

I also started getting into debt collecting. This would be the thing that would always be my bread and butter, and later made my name known. I went on loads of jobs and quite a few with Lenny McLean. Now, Lenny looking like Lenny was sometimes enough in itself, but he was a fearsome fighter as well. I saw him perform in unlicensed bouts. He'd come into the ring, tense himself so the veins stood out on his neck and then roar at the top of his voice. You could see his opponent thinking, Fuck me, isn't there somewhere else I should be right now?! Working on the doors with him and doing debt collecting together, I got to know him well. Because most of the geezers on the Firm were real giants of men – guys like Lenny, Dave, Theo, Benny and John Boy – Lenny gave me a bit of advice. He said that cos I wasn't big enough to scare by size I should go about things differently. Put more importance on what I said to someone and the way it was said, to get the result I wanted. 'And remember,' he said, 'people will talk about what you've done afterwards so give them something to talk about.' That stood me in good stead for years after.

One time me and Lenny had to go to see this bloke at a restaurant in Hounslow. Him and his partner had split and he still owed the guy fifteen thousand pounds. When we walked in the place was full. Lenny stood in the doorway, filling it, and all the diners turned, looking really alarmed. The owner was stood at the back of the room, shitting himself. Calm as you like, and in that deep voice of his, Lenny said to the customers, 'Don't worry, none of you are gonna get hurt. We've only come to kill him!' – and pointed at the owner.

The geezer started shouting, 'Call the police! Call the police!'

Lenny said, 'You can call the fucking SAS, mate, but you're paying the money!'

The owner turned and ran and Lenny picked up this massive tropical fishtank and threw it. It went right through the swing-doors of the kitchen and smashed open. The water hit the ovens and all this steam poured back out into the restaurant. It looked like smoke, though, and everyone started screaming cos they thought the place was on fire. I do believe the guy paid up not long after. Funny that.

Another time we had to go on a job in Essex to see this car salesman who owed money. We got to the car lot and I approached the office to have a word with the guy first. No point in steaming straight in and Lenny throwing cars about if the bloke's open to reason, is there? Before I even got to the office, two blokes came out and approached me, and another one, who I wasn't even aware of, started coming up behind me. He was holding a wiper blade down by his side. Whether he was gonna use it as a weapon, I don't know, but Lenny, who'd been stood in the background, saw the sun glint off it and thought it was a knife. He ran up behind the first two blokes, grabbed their heads from the back (one in each big hand) and just carried on running! I stepped out the way and he rammed them both into the side of a car. One went headfirst into the quarter-light and the other hit the door pillar – double smack!. You couldn't help but wince. Lenny turned back to me: 'Well, that evens it up a bit!' The owner had been watching from the office doorway. He disappeared back inside and we caught him rummaging in a drawer. He gave us a set of keys for a car worth a good bit more than the debt.

I remember my very first debt collecting job. I was stood there on this doorstep with my bollocks in my hand cos I hadn't done it before and I didn't know what to expect. Who should open the door but Mick McManus, the wrestler! Mick was one of the most famous wrestlers in the country and I'd grown up watching him on *World of Sport* on Saturday mornings. I thought, Oh thank you God, thanks a fucking bunch. Mick McManus just looked at me and went, 'Yeah? What the fuck do you want?' I just said I'd got the wrong house and walked off. But what a one to get on your very first job. It's the only time I ever wished I was Big Daddy.

After debting with Lenny I got a job working on a boat. No, not as a bleedin' sailor; it was on a ship called *Tattershall Castle* which was moored up on the Thames by Victoria Embankment. It had been turned into a nightclub. I did the security there. Working by the river at night it was absolutely freezing. The wind comes up the Thames really cold. We'd be wearing tights, long johns, tracksuit bottoms, two or three T-shirts, a dinner suit and a crombie on top. You looked like a bodybuilder even if you weren't. And if you pulled a bird, when you stripped you took off four stone. She'd be thinking, Hang on! I thought he were a massive bloke.

Ned Rawlings had just come out the Navy and he came to work with me. Ned was this six-and-a-half foot pro boxer – very handy, and exactly the kind of bloke to have on your side. Ian Waddley worked there too, a real force to be reckoned with in the doorman world. Jonathan (Posh John) also worked alongside me there some nights as well. Like I say, because he was a successful businessman in his own right he didn't do this for the money. He did it for the buzz and cos when me and him got together we always had a ball.

Tasty geezers were needed on the *Tattershall* cos it was absolutely mental. We'd only have three doormen and on some Saturdays when the London teams were at home there'd be all the visiting football fans from Leeds, Liverpool, Manchester and Newcastle flooding in. All of a sudden London had seventy-five-thousand, lairy, drunk northerners out on the town. The guv'nor at *Tattershall* then decided he didn't like football fans any more and we were supposed to keep them out. All three of us. So it kicked off big-style. Real, proper fucking fights, let me tell you: gangplank gone, people thrown in the Thames, the lot. We only needed a set of swords each and it would've been like *The Scarlet Buccaneer*.

One night I was on control duty upstairs and I heard 'Dave! Dave!' coming from down below, so I ran downstairs and Ned and Funny Glenn had got this massive Irish bloke against a wall. He was so enormous that they were just hanging off his arms and legs! There was no way they were gonna push him over. I just slipped on my duster and bam! clumped him one. He was out of it then, really dazed. I got him under each arm and started to walk him up the gangplank. On my own. All of a sudden he came round and grabbed my neck. His hands were massive, like a big vice choking me. So now I've got this lairy, hairy-arsed, twenty-stone Paddy growling like a grizzly and trying to screw my head off. It was freezing that night, as usual, and cos I'm wrapped up like a mummy I can barely move. I managed to drag him to the edge, though, and this is where it all went a bit pear-shaped.

I was wearing something around my neck at the time that I really treasured. Some time before, someone had nicked a forty-five-grand tiara and I'd helped them sell it on. It'd been split for the jewels and melted down. Afterwards I'd still had some of the diamonds and gold. I had the gold made up into a huge dice with the diamonds for dots. It was the absolute nuts. I wore it around my neck on a big, thick gold chain.

Anyway, me and Paddy were tussling and I was whacking him but, because I was wearing four stone of clothes, I was running out of steam. I had him up against the rail and I thought, Because he's so much taller than me, and his bum's higher, if I push him over he'll go. And he did. But as he started to fall he grabbed the dice. I instinctively pulled back, and the chain popped. He dropped over the side, into the water, holding my diamond dice in his hand.

I couldn't believe it. I was absolutely fuming and started going, 'You *cunt!*' All over the top deck of the ship were these tables with big umbrellas. When they're lying down folded they're like spears. So I picked loads up and started chucking them down on him. But they were all opening up in mid-air and blowing down! It ended up with about twenty big brollies floating in the Thames with this big Paddy in the middle going mental. They had to get the fire brigade to lift him out. Then they pulled me in and nicked me, but nothing came of it. He got a visit and dropped the charges. So my gold and diamond dice is still down there. Fuck raising the *Titanic* – I want that dice back.

All the other clubs finished at two, but *Tattershall Castle* went on till three, so when all the other clubs shut all the doormen came down to mine. By the end of the night we'd have about thirty doormen there. I had this 1960s Mark II Jaguar and one night one of the other doormen asked me if I'd lent it to someone. I said, 'No.' He went, 'Well I've just seen someone getting into it!' We all ran outside and the bloke who'd just broken into it saw us all tearing over and tried to get out to run. But he couldn't cos the driver's door was a bit dodgy; it had dropped, like old car doors do sometimes, and you had to lift it to open it. But he didn't know that so he just pushed the button down. Now he was shitting himself cos there were about thirty suited-up monsters surrounding the car screaming at him to get out. He was shouting at me through the window, going, 'I'm sorry! I'm sorry!' I thought, You fucking will be.

There was a mate of mine called Rocky there with me that night, and when the geezer started to get out of the car, Rocky said, 'Leave him – he's mine.' Then Rocky started dancing around doing all these kung fu moves and making all those stupid chicken noises. Like he's Bruce Lee or something. The other bloke just stood there, crapping his pants. Rocky took this massive run-up, leapt in the air and shot forward with both feet out; the other geezer took one step to the left and Rocky went flying past – screaming – and disappeared into a bush! Well, we were all just bent over pissing ourselves and the guy took his chance and ran off. Rocky's head popped back out of the bush, twigs in his ears and looking like, 'What happened?!' *Fuck* me. So much for the Neighbourhood Watch!

Another time this geezer pulled up at *Tattershall* in a bubble car, a proper bubble car. They're mad-looking little things. We were all looking at it, but instead of taking it as a compliment, the geezer who'd driven up in it got all cocky. Anyway, later on some trouble broke out in the club and this guy and his mates were involved and he just ran off. So we got his bubble car, me and a few other doormen, lifted it straight up and threw it in the Thames. It bobbed on the surface and floated off. We watched it for ages until it finally threw in the towel and sank. I never knew the car got its name from the fact that when they sink they make loads of bubbles on the way down.

There was another car-trick we used to pull. We'd pick up a car by the back and put the rear wheels on two stools, and then do the same with the front. Then you just wait for the geezer to come out and find his car two feet up in the air. He'd stand around gob-smacked, not knowing what to do until we appeared like Good Samaritans and lifted the car back down. We did it to Ned Rawlings's car once. He just got in the car, cool as you like, and drove it right off the stools! I thought that was real class. I'd always tried to do things with a bit of style myself. That was important to me. It makes people remember what you do. No one had ever seen anyone do what Ned did that day and everyone who saw it still talks about it. Like I am now.

I decided to turn up for work on the *Tattershall* in as stylish a manner as possible. I had this speedboat of mine that I'd done up myself. So I'd get dressed for work in the dinner suit and tie and then put these waterproof overalls on top so I didn't get soaked in the boat. Then I set off up the Thames. Just before I reached the *Tattershall* I took off the overalls, cruised up alongside in my suit and threw the rope to someone on the river wall. It looked just like James fucking Bond turning up for work.

Ned Rawlings was the guy that burnt my face one time. Accidentally. Me, Ned, Terry Turbo and Adam drove up to see someone that was supposedly gonna blow my legs off. There was a gun under my seat and I was driving. Just as we got there the guy came out, and clocked us, but instead of running away he ran in front of the car, putting his hand inside his jacket. Ned reached for the gun first and fired across me and out my window. He missed the geezer, but the flame from the gun barrel singed my lips to fuck! The geezer did a very good impression of Linford Christie and fucked off up the road sharpish (I couldn't have caught him if I'd been in a Ferrari). We made an appointment for Ned at the optician's not long after. That burn from the barrel did hurt. For weeks after, as well. I looked like someone who'd been giving a blow-job to a Formula One-car's tailpipe.

Talking of racing cars. Around this time we all started going down to Brighton for the day, me and about twenty other pals, mostly doormen. One day we decided to have a race back up to London – like in that film *The Gumball Rally*, or *Smokey and the Bandit*, that kind of thing. We were all at an age when we were into fast cars and tear-arsing around, and every geezer likes to think he's a good driver, don't he? So we had a bet. Everyone put thirty quid in so there was six hundred quid or more in the pot. We raced back to London, running red lights. I only came third because I was in my own car, a Triumph Stag V8, and I didn't really want to wreck it.

It became a regular thing, though, and next time I was prepared. I knew that if I got a rental car and paid extra for their insurance, I could completely fuck the car and not have to pay for it or even lose anything off my own policy. Touch! Sierra Cosworths had just come out, so I got one of them. Black with big fuck-off alloys: a real monster.

On the day there was Ray Bridges, Amon and John Ash,

Santos, Tony Rawlins, Jimmy the Greek, Mickey Jackson, Lloyd, Marky Mark, Rick, Jonathan (Posh John), Adam, Mick Warrel, Imran Khan, Jamie and Bobby Frankham, Paddy and Mel, Seymour, Big Joe from Gravesend, Stevie Two Pints and Danny Dolittle. (I'd first met Danny in a holding cell beneath the Old Bailey and cos he had a stomach complaint I gave him my trifle. Which turned out to be a very good move cos he ain't stopped giving me things back ever since.) Most of the fellas had also wised up to the fact that using your own car wasn't the thing to do. So they had fast old bangers or, mostly, nicked cars. Half of them had screwdrivers hanging out of the steering columns.

We drove down to Brighton in the morning, had a bevvy and got ready to set off about two in the afternoon. Sixty-five miles from Brighton to Trafalgar Square. We assembled in this car park and counted down to blast off. The races were always started by a stunning young lady called Karen, who I became close to and still see today.

But straight away it was a case of 'Ground control, Houston – we've got a problem!' because the exit of the car park was single file and we all bottle-necked. Eventually, we all flew off like bats out of hell. It was just mad. Completely mental. We all took out-and-out diabolical liberties on the road: speeding, running red lights, going up on pavements, nudging other cars out the way.

I was near the front, screwing the arse off the Cosworth, when I saw Posh John ahead at a red light stuck behind a van. Danny was tearing up behind me in a Jag. The lights were two-lane, so I pulled alongside John, bumper to bumper with this Sunday driver out in his Morris Minor in front of me, and then floored it and pushed the Morris over the lights and went round him. Danny followed me through the gap but I accelerated away. Loads of us got pulled by the police, but as they stopped one, another five of us would fly past. They even started setting up road-blocks to stop us. I smashed fuck out of the Cosworth, but I did win the race. By the time I took the car back to the rental place, totally battered and with the doors practically hanging off, it looked like Coco the Clown's circus car. When I pulled up outside, the guy in the office looked like he'd just shat himself. I handed over the keys.

'Sorry, mate,' I said. 'Had a bit of a prang when I swerved to avoid a dog. Y'know, one of these days, being an animal lover is gonna be the fucking death of me!'

The car rental insurance thing gave me another idea. Listen to this one, you might be able to use it yourself one day. A mate of mine, Ray, had blown the engine on his motor. You can't claim for that on the insurance, so now his car was worth fuck all. I said that for a bung I could make sure he got a pay-out. He said fair enough. The plan was simple: I rent a car, pay for the rental company's insurance (about twenty quid extra), and smash head-on into Ray's. I then accept responsibility, they write his car off, he gets a lump sum from his insurers and Robert's your mother's brother. Yeah, I know, it sounds too good to be true, don't it? But it works, believe me. I even arranged for one of my friends, Bizmark, to be out on the pavement as a witness. I came up with the idea of videoing it as well.

So, on the night, Ray's car is parked up outside his gaff in Peckham and he's sat next to me in the rental with a video camera up to his eye. Now, actually doing it, actually bringing yourself to deliberately crash at over 40 mph, is *fucking* difficult. It goes against all your natural instincts of self-preservation. So as we were approaching, and the engine was screaming through the gears, we both braced ourselves and went *urrggghh!* tensing up for the smash. We hit his car head-on – wham!! – but cos the seat belts give a bit before they catch, the car went Bang! and Ray shot forward. The video camera he was holding hit the windscreen, and the eyepiece smashed right into his socket. I sat there with Johnny next to me moaning in agony, steam and water pouring out of the bonnet.

Ray was left with the biggest, blackest, black eye I've ever seen in my life. It was like something off *Tom and Jerry*. What a shiner that was. Massive. It took about a month to disappear. It looked like a big purple fanny. He got paid out, though. And I've still, to this day, got that video tape. The end of it is a minute-long shot of Ray's feet after he dropped the camera. You can hear him moaning on the soundtrack and me going, 'Fuck me! You all right, mate?!'

That was another case of my animal-loving instincts making me 'swerve to avoid a dog', as I put it on the claim form. That weren't the last time I did that little scam either. I often wondered if any of the car rental blokes met up at some insurance industry 'do' and swapped stories. 'Christ! Did that happen to you as well? Hang on . . . the customer wasn't a big skinhead by any chance?'

One night me and a few of the lads on the *Tattershall* decided to break into this leisure centre. It had a gym, swimming pool and a room with loads of arcade machines. We were after the money in the machines. That might sound small-time, but if you hit them at the right time we're talking twenty, maybe thirty grand's worth of coins in those machines.

Me, Lenny and Big Chris got in there all right, but there must've been silent alarms and the Old Bill were swarming over the place in minutes. We split up and ran, but I ended up in the locker rooms with no way out. There was nothing I could do but hide in a locker. Now I ain't saying it was a squeeze, but I felt like I'd been fucking buried alive. Only time I was ever jealous of an anorexic. I could hear the coppers roaming about outside. I waited until I was sure everyone had gone and went to get out, but the door wouldn't budge. I'd only gone and locked myself in! What a bastard. I didn't even have enough room to get a decent kick in. I pushed the door till it was bent out above and below the lock, but the cunt of a lock wouldn't give. I was trapped in there for seven hours with some cunt's smelly trainers and gym gear. I ended up gasping for air like a landed fish. What a way to go – death by jockstrap. I started rocking the locker backwards and forwards till it fell over. What a fucking noise that made. Sounded like a washing machine falling down a lift shaft. Anyway, eventually I managed to break the door open and finally got out just as it was coming light.

It weren't all fun and games, though. One night on the *Tattershall Castle* all these butcher boys from Smithfield market came on a stag do. One of them got a bit lairy and started causing trouble and got thrown out. The rest followed him. I weren't working that particular night but I got told about what happened.

A few days later I was working the door with Posh John, Nick and a couple of others when twenty of these butcher boys came steaming back on to the ship screaming blue murder.

They didn't know we were different doormen from the other night and I don't think they gave a fuck. All of them were tooled up and they just went mental.

Now, that night *Tattershall* had been hired by this crowd of theatre goers. They'd gone to a show and come back here for a party. So, cos all the blokes were in dinner suits, the butcher boys thought they'd walked into a doormen's convention and started laying into them. The bar and dancefloor just turned into this massive battlefield. Everyone fighting, the women screaming. Me and John ended up in the middle of it all, stood back to back to protect each other from getting clumped from behind, whacking and nutting as many of these fuckers as we could. The fact that these other poor cunts in dinner suits were mistaken for doormen was a bonus for us cos it meant that the Smithfield lads were running everywhere.

Just as I gave this one guy the old Courtney Crumbler and he hit the deck, I heard a cry and saw that Nick was down on the dancefloor. A knife had been stuck *right through* his hand. He was pinned to the floor by it and these cunts were kicking him round in a circle! I grabbed a fire extinguisher and went fucking berserk. I smashed two of them and then grabbed the extinguisher by the hose and started whirling it round to back them off. John ran over and hit this one geezer so hard he took off. Then things got really bad.

It must have gone on for ten minutes or more, like a big saloon fight in a cowboy film. It went on for so long that the river police got there before the ordinary police. They pulled alongside in their boat and started climbing in through the windows like pirates!

The fire extinguisher I'd been using was dented to fuck. I rounded off the evening by setting it off and covering everyone in foam; then did a bow, caught a few bouquets and that was the final curtain.

During this time I'd done a few bank jobs. The hours are good, plenty of time off (especially if you get nicked) and the wages are fucking phenomenal. A lot of people I was associating with were at it so it just didn't seem a hard or unusual thing for me to get into. I liked the way these people lived, I liked the lifestyle and I didn't know anything else that could fund it. Once you've tasted that life you can't go back.

We did a few banks, a few wages vans, a ferry and a disco boat. We'd go in four-handed, usually, me and three other doormen pals. In, out, away. No one hurt. One time we ended up with two hundred and fifty grand to split between the four of us, and the driver. He was in on it. In fact, most big-money jobs are inside jobs. Most of them, not all. The driver had said to us, 'I'm driving, it's me you've got to say "Give me the money!" to. It's me that's got to lie on the floor and not look at you when you tell me. Just do that and I'll do it.' So we did, and he did.

And the worst thing to do is actually do it, and do it well. Because then it seems too easy. Once you've done it successfully it's hard *not* to do it. For instance, I could work on the door of a club for twelve hours, have five fights and get a hundred quid. Or, get a thousand quid for a debt collection that might take half an hour. Once you've done that it's hard to go back to the door.

The kind of bird you get for an armed robbery, though, is enormous. But the number of people that are involved and that know you're doing one, that spooked me. Again, it's the old team sport thing: I might do a perfect job but Harry over there, he screws up and we get nicked. And what a fucking job to get wrong. You're then looking at big-time bird. So I got out of that game pretty sharpish. Not out of fear, but out of good sense. I weighed up the risks and probabilities. Like I say, the wages were good, I just didn't fancy the extended holiday you get for screwing up. All the money in the world is no good to you if you're banged up. For me there were better ways of making money.

Afterwards, and since then, I did much more in the way of putting people together that wanted to do work. I ended up doing more of that than the actual deed itself. Part of my *Yellow Pages* service. At the same time, you can't give advice to people about something unless you've actually done it yourself. That's my philosophy: don't theorise unless you've done the practical. Whenever I come up with an idea for a scam or dodge, I always test-drive it myself. Bit like those American test pilots trying to break the sound barrier and all that. What was that film about them called? *The Right Stuff*, I think. Well, I had the right stuff for finding out how to do the

The Wrong Stuff. With people coming to me for advice, as they seemed to do more and more as time went on, I couldn't afford to let them down with dodgy advice based on me just imagining something.

But the excitement from doing a successful job is amazing. Does it give you a buzz? Oh, *stop* it! You get a fucking hard-on, mate. Well, *I* did anyway. The best time for my missus to get hold of me was after I'd just had a good row with someone or I'd just walked in with a bagful of cash. Fuck the oysters.

So, after my brief time in that game I decided to concentrate more on the other things that started to kick off big-time for me: debt collecting and door and security work. And I was meeting all the right people.

And a few of the wrong ones.

7 One Wedding and a Shooting

I came out of the King Tut pub in Peckham about half eleven one Friday night. I had a beige cashmere crombie on. There was a little yellow Escort Mexico with a black vinyl roof parked by the kerb. A geezer got out, youngish bloke, and walked towards me. He said, 'Dave? Dave Courtney?'

I said, 'Yeah,' and moved towards him.

As we got nearer I could see that he was frightened and I thought, What the fuck is he frightened for? I wasn't gonna do anything to him – I didn't even know him – and just as I realised it was because he was gonna do something to me, it was too late. He'd been sat out there for Christ knows how long, building up to this. His hand came out of his pocket holding a 9mm Luger.

Everything went into that strange kind of slow-motion which happens at times like this. I thought, Fuck me, I'm gonna get shot – and in Peckham! So much for the romance of crime.

It happened quick, but I remember everything. His hand went up high and then started coming down to get a bead on me. I started dodging. The gun levelled at my head and I thought, Not the head! Then he aimed lower and I thought, I'm gonna get it in the gut! Then lower still until he seemed to be aiming at my balls, and I thought, No! Not the fucking nuts! I thought, Jump, Dave, jump, and I tried to leap over the bonnet of a parked car. Just as he shot me.

What does a bullet feel like? Forget about all those things in films. A bullet is round, not sharp; it don't cut the skin, it just hits and bends it in as much as possible until the sheer force breaks it through. It feels like a big fucking hammer, and that's the God's honest truth. I know cos I've been hit by both.

I was in mid-air when the bullet hit me in the shin. I went arse over crombie. The force of the bullet shot my leg up high in the air and bashed my head on the ground. When I came round there was an ambulance beside me. It went *DEE-DOH!!* with the siren, just once, as if they were trying to wake me with it! I nearly had a fucking heart attack as well. My mouth was bleeding and my face hurt from hitting the ground. I could feel this dull pain in my leg and knew then that I'd be OK. I was supposed to be boxing soon and started worrying whether I could make that. You think of silly things at the time.

They had me laid up in hospital for a few days. Dressed the wound and stitched me up. Worst thing was that they posted a copper in the room in case someone had another go at me. This plod was there 24 hours a day at the foot of the bed like a fluffy toy. I couldn't even have a wank, that was the worst of it. And I was too old to play tents and have a sly one.

My mates came round to visit. Someone rang Tracey and told her. She asked where I'd been shot and he said Peckham, the div. She went, 'No . . . where in the body?!' When she knew it was the leg she automatically knew I'd be OK. She didn't visit as much as she could cos it pissed her off that all my mates stood around the bed talking about it.

That might sound blasé, but let me explain something: being in the kind of work I was in, it was par for the course that at some point I'd get shot at, or shot. I wasn't working as a registered child minder so there was a certain amount of expectation of it happening and acceptance when it did. I mean, I was still a working dustman during the day, remember, and me and Tracey had a perfectly normal home life. People on the outside looking in might think, Oh, the poor woman, but it weren't like that at all. I kept my doorwork and stuff like that very much separate. It didn't intrude on our lives at home. But also that's what I mean about the life you live, or the life I was living – throws up things that ain't really unusual to that lifestyle. You accept that and deal with it. A zookeeper is occasionally gonna get a mad chimp throwing monkey shit at him, but if you went there on a visit you wouldn't like it. That's not exactly on a par with getting shot, I grant you, but same difference, as they say. So people in that walk of life took it all in their stride. Which is more than I could do with a bullet hole in my leg.

At this point in my life I hadn't seen my mum and dad for a couple of years because, after bringing trouble to their door when I was younger, I felt it best to keep some distance later on. And we kind of drifted on like that, like you sometimes do. So, by the time they would've heard about the shooting it was all over and done with.

I told the Old Bill I didn't know who was responsible, and I didn't. Not the geezer that had put one in me anyway. Most parts of the country have gangs of long-term unemployed blokes with fuck all to do and even less money to do it with. It ain't that difficult to offer someone a few hundred quid and turn them into a shooter. They go, Here's the gun, here's the address, here's the car; drive there, shoot him, throw the gun in the Thames, leave the car where it is, and never tell another soul. And there's no possible way in the world you can get caught for murder if there's no connection between the hitman and the victim and no one talks. So I didn't know who the shooter was. But I *did* know who'd ordered it.

It had come from me sticking up for someone who was in the wrong, but I stuck up for him anyway because he was a mate. I put my weight behind him even though I knew that. I let friendship cloud my judgement. Bad move. Lesson learnt. It taught me always to make sure I was in the right, always to have a good reason for my actions. Debt collecting, for example: always make sure the guy genuinely owes the money so then you're just collecting, not robbing. I was still relatively young, and I'm glad I learnt that lesson then and that it cost me no more than a few nights in hospital and the charming, witty company of one of our local constabulary.

But, like I say, I did know who had ordered it. And that geezer mysteriously vanished not long after. He came down with a case of permanent missing-person syndrome. Funny that. Fucking hilarious, you might say.

And then I got married. 1984: what a year.

On the day of the wedding, in the church there was a vicar in the dog collar and cross. And a backless suit showing off his knickers, fish net stockings and suspenders.

That was me actually. The real vicar was dressed more normally and was probably wondering why he'd agreed to do the vows at a fancy dress wedding. Which it was. That was my idea. It was so funny when you walked into the church. The only wedding that had Batman, Frankenstein's monster and Humpty Dumpty sat on the front pew. There were loads more: the Three Musketeers, cowboys and Indians, Sir Lancelot. Some clever bastard even came as a gangster, Al Capone style. Beau was in a little miniature dinner suit and bow tie I'd had made for him. There were hundreds of people there.

Tracey wore a normal wedding dress. She didn't know about the fancy-dress thing until she walked in the church and got a load of me in my get-up, looking like I'd just come from Perverts Anonymous. With Dracula stood one side of me and my best man – get this! – on the other side dressed as an Egyptian mummy. You could say that Tracey was ever so slightly surprised. Well, it's supposed to be bad form to upstage the bride, ain't it? But how can you avoid it when your wedding is a cross between *The Rocky Horror Show* and Madame Tussaud's? Tracey later said that knowing me she should have expected we wouldn't have a run-of-the-mill affair.

When it came to the part when the vicar asked, 'Does anyone present know of any lawful impediment to this marriage?', Batman looked at Humpty, Humpty looked at Frankenstein's monster, and everyone looked at me, stood there in stockings and suspenders. I think the general feeling about answering any question over 'lawful impediment' was 'No comment!'

Instead of the usual white Rolls for leaving the church, I went for something a bit . . . how can I put it? Different, shall we say. It was one of those 'Big Foot' American jeeps with the massive chrome wheels. You should've seen Tracey's face when she came out and saw it. She laughed about it, though. It weren't the most romantic way for a bride to leave church, I admit, but it wasn't boring. Because the jeep was about twelve feet high we had to give her a fireman's lift to get her in. Quite handy that her brother-in-law *was* a fireman, as it happens.

The reception was something else. It was down Lordship

Lane at the Catholic Club. Bit embarrassing for the geezer dressed as the Pope, but there you go. Between him stood at the bar giving out blessings with a pint in his hand, and me walking round in a dog collar and backless outfit giving my arse an airing, you could say we raised a few eyebrows. Bet they didn't drop for a fortnight.

Our party was upstairs at the club and another wedding reception was being held downstairs. Two geezers from that one came up and gatecrashed ours. They were pissed and started making an awful nuisance of themselves. I politely asked them to leave and got absolutely no respect back – I think the suspenders and garter belt undermined my authority a bit – so I gave them a little clump and sent them packing. One of them got a kick up the arse from the Pope for good measure.

Good job I weren't a practising Catholic, though. I'd have been in confession for fifteen years. And you should have seen the wedding photos – it was like 'Spot the Normal Person'.

Wow. Shot and married in the same year. I don't know which one scarred me most (joke, Tracey).

8 Queen's and the Short-arse of the Law

My name got put up for this job that came up doing security at a club called Queen's – the Queen Mother Reservoir Yachting Club. It was in a place called Colnbrook, near Heathrow airport. All the pilots and stewardesses and businessmen from all over the world went to Queen's. It was also just up the road from one of the biggest gypsy camps in England. I'm tellin' you, this place was massive. Must have been two thousand vans, and God knows how many gypsies ('pikeys' or travellers, as we call them) in each one. It was like a proper city.

It was a big job to take on, doing the security at Queen's, and a tough one. The gypsies used to come up the club and have it, big time. Whatever you say about pikeys they do love a good fight. They're brought up on it: parents belt the kids, kids belt each other, littlest kid belts the dog, the dog belts the cat and the cat turns into a right handy little bleeder. You'll find some of the world's most nervous mice on a gypsy campsite.

Every Friday and Saturday night there would be loads of fights. It had got so bad that local doormen couldn't work there cos the pikeys would find out where they lived, call round ten-handed and give them a kicking at home. There was another little stunt the pikey lads used to pull. Because the club was next to the reservoir, up on a hill, the road to it went round and round until it got to the top. The gypsies would wait for a car to come down and then get a couple of boats (there were loads of them parked up) and push one in front of you and one behind. Then when you were trapped they'd converge on the car and batter the doormen in it.

So the club decided to bring in an outside firm from London. And that's where I came in. I jumped at the chance. I went down there knowing no one knew who I was. There was a little bit of the old cavalry-coming-to-the-rescue thing about it as well. We'd drive down the M4 like *The Dirty Dozen* on an away-day with *The Magnificent Seven* – yee*ha*!

When I took on the job I told the guv'nor of Queen's who'd brought me in, a guy called Vinoo, exactly how I was going to play it. I decided I was gonna take on twice as many doormen as a normal club should have and pay really good wages. If you're going to do something then do it right, right? A couple of really handy fellas called Clint Dyer and Airport Dave worked on the door with me.

The weekends there were wild. Oh *stop* it! It was abso-fucking-lutely mental. The thing about the gypsies is, because they scrap so much, if they lose it don't matter. In their eyes that's something that's bound to happen cos they fight so often. So they'll just come back next week and have another crack. One thing they don't do, which earns them a lot of respect, is they won't grass anyone up to the police. If they came out of a row worse off, like I say, they'd just wait until next week and come and have another pop.

They weren't difficult to spot either. When most of the geezers coming in were international businessmen and airline pilots, and all the women were either stewardesses or local birds done up to the nines (like my friend Jo), it weren't exactly hard to spot a wild-eyed pikey clumping up to the door. Who do you fly for, mate, Romany Airlines? That'll be the one with outside bogs and hanging baskets from the wings, then? They do know how to spend their money on themselves, though. But even if one approached the door wearing a thousand-pound suit, silk shirt and enough gold to sink Pavarotti, I'd just look down and see these muddy boots. Dead giveaway, every time.

My respect for them grew when I realised they really were a law unto themselves and there's no one with better, more natural, fighting ability. Much later on, ironic after the current troubles, I favoured them as allies when I needed help. People like the Franklins, the Lees, the Smiths, Gary Eastwood, Joey Moore, and the Grants.

Sometimes it was like a Wild West outpost. One night this

van drove up towards the door and just carried on coming. And coming. We leapt out the way and it smashed right into the doors and wedged there. I thought, I've heard of gate-crashing but that's just taking the piss. Then they set the telegraph poles on fire so we couldn't phone out. That was a sight and a half, these big columns of flames going up like massive fireworks. And they regularly blew the windows in with shotgun blasts. I saw the local glazier so often I had him on my Christmas card list. If any of the airline captains had a near miss with another plane at 40,000 feet, they'd just say, 'Ah, that's nothing. I go to Queen's on a Saturday night!'

I had a right tasty team of lads working with me: Don Kelly, who was one of the best fighters I've ever seen; Big James, a bodybuilder; and Jeff, who turned out to be a grass and got me nicked. Part of our job was also to protect the trout they had there, and the yachts. The fish I weren't interested in. If I'd had big plans to move into catering, maybe. But it was the boats that got me. Christ, you've never seen anything like it. It was a millionaires' playground down there so there were thousands of these really expensive yachts.

Now the good thing about yachts is – and remember this if you ever get a chance at one – they don't have any ID plates like a car, so they're not traceable. They don't have alarms. And they're really difficult to secure. And I was surrounded by them. Touch! Guess what . . . yeah, you're ahead of me now, aren't you? I went into the export–import wholesale yachting business. In other words, exporting boats from deepest West London and importing them to East Dulwich. We'd just hook one up to a car and drive off with it. I mean, they were so easy to nick it would have been criminal not to. I would never have forgiven myself. We'd tow them back up to London and swap them for cars. I had some mental cars: Bentleys, Jags, Triumph Stags. I used to get fun cars as well just cos they were funny. An ice cream van, for instance. Me and the boys would drive round in it with the Popeye music on. Kids would run up and then see this big hairy-arsed doorman lean out like Lurch off *The Addams Family* and go 'Yeesss?!' and they'd run off crying.

The best one, though, was a hearse. A big, black Austin Princess coffin lugger with a chrome grill. That was wicked.

You could take the flat-bed out which the coffin would rest on and make the back into bench seats. We'd drive back up from Colnbrook in it after Queen's shut at two o'clock. By half two in the morning we were flying through the middle of central London. Picture *that*: ten sixteen-stone, flat-nosed, joint-smoking monsters squeezed into a hearse doing 90 mph up Tottenham Court Road. And because we were all blacked-up in dinner suits we just looked like the world's maddest, most unpunctual, undertakers. You could see from the faces of people we passed in the streets that they were thinking, Fuck me, they must be late! The best ones were the people that had obviously just come out of a club and were stoned or completely off their heads. They'd see us blast past with Don stood up through the sunroof yelling his nut off and me with my arse out the passenger window, and you knew, you just *knew* they were thinking, I am never *ever* taking drugs again! I eventually sold the hearse to some good friends of mine from a very famous biking house in Woking who helped me out a number of times.

Mental things just seem to happen sometimes. This bloke I knew used to break into dentists' to nick the Novocaine. One time he came round my house with a bag full of gold teeth he'd got from one of them. Seven and a half pounds it weighed! Anyway, I bought them. I took the bag to a jeweller's to have the gold melted down and made into chains and rings. The cunt only waited till I'd gone and called the police. He thought I'd been going around knocking people's teeth out until I'd saved up this huge bagful.

The police raided Queen's looking for me. Now, at Queen's, we had a camera behind the desk so that if any stars came in we could take their picture. But no stars ever came in Queen's. So whenever someone got knocked out in a fight we'd take a photo of them spark-out on the deck. We pinned all the pictures on this board at the front desk, so only staff could see it. You didn't want customers seeing them cos they looked like illustrations from Hannibal Lecter's Home Cookbook. It was a real ugly montage of mashed faces. I didn't even think of it at the time, but when the Old Bill came in they took one look at all these photos, put two and two together and thought the teeth had come from all these people in the pictures. Even when I was trying to explain it I could see, in their eyes, it just looked too good not to be true. I felt a bit unlucky over that one. I mean, what are the chances of that happening? And I got nicked for it.

But listen to this! This was the best one. One night I was looking round and I clocked a yacht parked up there. I thought, I've never seen this fucker before! It was unbelievably impressive. A real peach. It was really really streamlined and all aluminium, and so big that its trailer had twelve wheels. I'm having some of *that*, I thought. So I hooked it up and took it. The mast was still up and, hardly being Captain Birds Eye myself, I didn't know how to get it down. I drove back to London hoping I'd go under a bridge low enough to snap it off.

Next day, Sunday morning, and I'm sat at home having breakfast watching telly. This news report came on about the theft of the vessel belonging to the British Olympic yachting team. They said something like, 'Due to production and development costs, experts put its value in excess of twenty-eight million pounds.' Then they showed a photo of it and I had a coughing fit on a mouthful of cornflakes and pebble-dashed the front room. I looked out my front window and saw the same yacht that was on the telly, outside my house, with loads of local kids playing pirates on it. Turned out that rather than test it at sea where it could be photographed, the Olympic team had been doing secret speed trials at Queen's. And there's me thinking I might get something like an E-type Jag for it. I got dressed, hooked it up, drove it off and dumped it. We do crap enough at the Olympics already, don't we, without me getting the blame for us missing out on another bronze.

Working at Queen's I got the respect from people I was working with. I earned respect down there and learnt an awful lot about fighting. Rows broke out so often that it helped you polish up your act. It was another big chance to shine, and I loved that. We had some right proper fights there and saw some terrible violence. I've seen some awful things in my time, but one of the worst things I ever saw happened there.

Outside the door at Queen's, to the left of the entrance, there was a security light on the wall. It was the prime position to stand there cos with it shining down on you – suited up, arms crossed – all the security lads knew if they were under it it made them look the absolute bollocks. You looked like you'd just been beamed straight down from Planet Doorman.

This one night a big black fella who worked the door, called Lloyd (Big Lloyd, actually), was stood there. I was stood just in front of him, to the side. Something whizzed out of the dark of the car park; I felt it, actually *felt* it fly by me, humming like a wasp. I turned as Big Lloyd cried out. Whatever it was had hit him on the side of the face and broke his jaw clean off at the hinges. It was only held on by skin and he was actually holding it in his hands to stop it swinging. His tongue was flopping out about a foot long, like a roll of carpet and his teeth were everywhere – all out on the floor like broken mints. Fucking disgusting it was. Proper repulsive. Like an X-rated cartoon.

Lloyd was taken inside to wait for the ambulance. Looking around outside I found a massive wheel nut, like off a Transit van or something. No one could throw anything that hard, and there had been no sound, so it must have been fired from one of those hunting catapults. You know, the aluminium ones with industrial strength elastic. They're like silent guns. That powerful.

When you work the door, throwing troublemakers out, you always get threats made. Half a dozen a night. Most of them come to nothing, but the odd few do. They might even wait until a week later before they come back to have a go at you. There's no way you can remember everyone, but that one person can easily remember you and know where you're gonna be. We didn't even know who it was that had fired the bolt. Someone with a grudge after an argument, obviously.

Every time me and the boys returned to London after the weekend down there, we always had the best stories to tell. We'd meet up with other doormen who mostly worked in West End clubs and they'd tell us about breaking up a few fights or chucking out some lairy punters. We'd be like, oh . . . right . . . well, we had a van rammed in the doors, telephone poles set on fire, the windows blown in with a sawn-off, ten fights with gangs of marauding gypsies, two cars turned over and someone slapped in the mush with a trout. And then rounded off the evening by nicking a twenty-eight-million-quid boat. Pretty average really, but next week we're expecting real trouble.

I didn't know it at the time, but real trouble was on the cards a little later at Queen's, concerning some drug dealer. Before that happened, though, I was having a pretty good time. And always finding something to laugh about or, as was always my aim, doing something to make other people laugh.

Let me tell you about this one. I've named this chapter after this incident cos I liked the title I made up for it so much. Well, it's my book, I'm 40½ and I'll do what I like. But listen, this was one of my funniest little things.

When working at Queen's we'd get this stripogram geezer coming to do shows there. He was one of them Chippendale types with long hair, shaved chest, cobblestone stomach and an ever-ready supply of baby lotion, that kinda thing. He was a nice enough fella and I got on well with him. Joe was his name. Me and him had this running joke. After he arrived at the club and was walking around, if I saw him before he saw me I'd run and kick him up the arse, and if he saw me first he'd do the same. Silly, I know, but if you want something mature, go buy an old fucking cheese!

Anyway, one of his stripping outfits was a policeman's uniform. Always popular with the ladies, that one. He'd rip it off on stage and end up in his G-string. Like they do. One night, I was upstairs looking out and I saw Joe walking across the car park in his copper's uniform. I was already planning where I'd wait for him in the club to jump out and kick him when he suddenly stopped and started inspecting car number plates. It was then that I realised it was actually one of the local police out there. I thought, Christ, good job I didn't run out and kick him in the car park. Then I thought, Yeah! What if I *did*?

There was about half a dozen of the chaps standing with me by now, looking out. I thought, Right! I'll have you. I turned to the others, real calm. 'Er ... I fancy kicking him up the arse.' They all looked at me like, yeah, don't we all? 'No,' I said, 'I'm *really* gonna go and kick that geezer up the arse.' And, having said that, I ran downstairs with some of them coming after me cos they thought I'd gone mental.

Outside, I waited a moment until his back was to me and then sprinted over towards him. I knew I'd only got one chance, and if he turned and gave me a look at his face, it couldn't work. As I got closer I noticed he was a bit of a short-arse as well, for a copper. I was loping up behind him thinking, It's outrageous – no standards in the police these days; no wonder no one mentions the long arm of the law any more. By the time I got to him I was going flat-out and I gave him such a *massive* kick up the jacksie that he lifted, rolled over the bonnet of this car and disappeared from view. Oh, it was amazing. He flew. I felt like phoning NASA to claim launching the first policeman into deep space. I looked back at the club and every window upstairs was full of faces, either laughing or completely gob-smacked.

Now, I know that even if I can't talk my way out of this and I get done for it, all it will say on the charge sheet is 'Accused kicked officer in behind', which looks like nothing, doesn't it? It sounds like something out of the playground. And I know he can't add another bit on to it, saying, 'But he kicked me really, really hard!' because that just looks even more pathetic! So I ran round the car, and just as he's getting up, looking in agony and trying to put his helmet back on, I put my hands up and went straight for the Oscar (Best Lead Actor). 'Oh, fuck me, mate! I am sorry, officer. You're not gonna believe this but . . .' And then I went into the full story about the stripping policeman and our little running joke, and why don't you come back to the club, I said, if you don't believe me; honest, it's true guv – the boys will tell you.

So I led him back to the club and all the chaps came down and started backing me up. I've got to give them credit, they all slipped into it automatically. In fact, talk about a right bunch of Robert De Niros, it was like they all got in a contest for the Best Supporting Actor. One went, 'Davey, what *have* you done! That ain't Joe!' and all that kind of crap. Never mind that Joe is a good foot taller than this copper and has long blond hair. He weren't to know that.

What with him still being half in shock from navigating the bonnet of an Escort, combined with a dozen big, flat-nosed geezers stood round him offering tea and sympathy, I think he was completely overwhelmed. 'OK, OK, I believe you,' he said. And then he mumbled something daft like, 'Make sure it doesn't happen again.' I thought, No need, mate! Once is enough. I can live off this one for years. He walked away trying to stay composed, but he was practically mincing. He looked like a gay John Wayne.

The best thing, though, was that we had it all on video. The security cameras look out over the car park, obviously. So we all ran upstairs laughing like idiots and played it back straight away. It was such a pleasure to watch. The camera was at a high-up angle so it got the bits I didn't see when I did it, like him landing on the other side of the car, right on his head. Each time we played it back, we just collapsed. We kept rewinding it and every time I toed him up the arse we all winced and everyone went, '*Fuck*ing hell!'

I kept the tape. That was my reward. Well, if you scored the winning goal at Wembley you'd want the match ball, wouldn't you? And I've still got it. Maybe I should send a copy off to one of those telly programmes, *Police, Camera, Action!* Can't see them using it somehow, though, can you? (And if you're that policeman and you're now reading this, I don't expect you to admit it happened to you, but when you go to sleep at night you can do so knowing you have one of the most famous arses in the London underworld.)

And don't you just hate it when someone shows off? Especially over something crap. I was in The Greyhound pub in Dulwich with some pals when this bloke walked in with one of the first mobile phones. Now when mobiles first came out they were like a breeze-block with a handle and a receiver stuck on! Not very mobile at all, really. Anyway, this geezer sat down and plonked this big thing on the floor. Then he starts taking calls on it and talking really loudly so everyone's looking. It was probably just his mum calling to say, OK, I've rung you twice like you said, now what?

Stuck on top of this box the phone was in was its actual number, pressed out in that blue ticker-tape stuff you do yourself. I leaned over and had a look then walked off to the bar, called Tracey and gave her the number. Two minutes later his phone goes off. He's making tutting noises by now, like it's a drag being so fucking popular and up on technology. Anyway, he answered. Then I heard him say, 'Dave? No, love, I think you've got the wrong number.'

Which is when Tracey answered, 'No, I don't think so. He's the chap sat directly behind you in the leather jacket.'

He turned, looking puzzled, and asked me if I was Dave. I said yeah, and quickly took the phone off him and launched into my own really loud bit of chat. 'Hello, babe. Yeah, you? I'll be home about half past I think, or thereabouts. OK. Love you too. See you soon.' And then I handed the receiver back to him. 'Cheers, mate.'

He asked who it was. I told him it was my missus. He looked like he'd just staggered out of a home for the permanently bewildered.

'But . . . how did she get my number?'

'Oh, my lady could find me *anywhere*, mate. Absolutely anywhere. Never underestimate the power of a woman.' And then I turned back to drinking with the lads.

That fucked his little head up good and proper for a few hours. He's thinking, Hang on – I've just paid £800 for this thing, it's bang up to the minute, and yet this geezer behind me, his missus just called *him* on it! But the first mobiles were so unmobile that you'd have to be a bit of a prat to lug one around. And baiting too-straight people is always good fun.

There was this pier down in Hastings where Posh John lived and whenever me and him walked along it the fishermen would get all huffy and start tutting about it (another lot that do the fucking 'tutting'!). You know what fishermen are like if they think you're disturbing the fish. So we thought we'd give the fish and the fishermen something to really be disturbed about, something to really tut about. Like a Mark II Cortina going off the end of the pier. That should do it.

We bought it for eighty quid at auction. Took the doors off and took the windscreen out. It was automatic. And purple. The pier had all these old nobbly bits down each side (but enough about the fishermen) but it was open-ended where the boats pulled up. We drove through town in this purple Cortina with no doors and windscreen looking like the advance search party from a clown invasion. Then we pulled off the street, down a ramp, hit the back of the pier and I floored the pedal. All the fishermen jumped and we blasted past at about 70 mph, whooping and blaring the horn. The car really juddered on the boards; I couldn't even say 'fuck' without it sounding like I was laughing. It had been scary before thinking about it but zooming towards the end now it got worse. Seat belt or no seat belt, that had been the question. 'Bust head' or 'get trapped and drown'? And you never appreciate a windscreen until you ain't got one. We flew off – *Arrrgghh!! FFUUUCK!!*

We got a little glimpse of sky and then a big fucking look at the water. The Cortina nose-dived. Massive *BOOM!* when we hit, and all this black water smashed into the car. We both swam free, but we had to do it underwater and push away from the car. Watery grave time for that old shed. We thought it'd be like in the films, straight out off the end like a plane. No one told us they put sandbags in the boots of those stunt cars to balance them out.

We climbed up the ladder on one of the pier legs and then rolled out over the boards and got up slowly. Both of us stood there in the sun, dripping wet, clothes plastered flat, both with one shoe missing, stood in a puddle each. And with a dozen fishermen just stood looking back at us.

Jonathan's cut-glass voice saved the day and made the moment: 'Errm . . . they've actually *moved* the car park then?'

9 Raving Lunacy

Something that had first started when I worked on *Tattershall Castle* and then through at Queen's continued to grow, and that was my doorman and security work. I'd learnt things about that little world in the best way possible – by doing it myself – and from the best there were – men like Amon Ash, Lenny McLean, Roy Shaw and Harry Haward. I already had my own boys working in places in South London and further down south in Hastings (a club called Saturdays) and Margate (The Golden Horseshoe). The West End clubs were already sewn up, contract-wise, but I had a foot in the door there as well cos that's where I worked personally.

I never got into any conflicts or aggro over door contracts because I'd seen too many others make that mistake too many times. Years later, when the rave scene really took off and there was massive money to be made, that kind of aggro got really bad. At this time, though, I did what I always did and took the long-term view. I just went about being nice to people. I've always made a point of that and it's always paid off. Five minutes of your time to talk to a geezer that no one else bothers with can pay big dividends even if it's years later when he's come on a bit. Actually, it wasn't as coldly calculating as that might make it sound. I do genuinely like talking to people and making people laugh and, fortunately, people tend to warm to you because of that. That's just common sense to me.

Some firms advertise by saying 'No job too big'; my policy, in security work and debt collecting, was no job too small. I took them all and did them as best as could be done. I applied that way of thinking to people as well. I always took time for the little guys. It's all very well an MP impressing other MPs in the House of Commons with his speeches, but unless he's got the backing of the voters, the masses, then he ain't got no future.

Because I was always very, very professional about what I did and made sure I never let people down, my little firm of doormen just grew and grew. I never had to go out looking for contracts or trying to get them from other firms because people saw how I operated and eventually came to me. Which is a big compliment. Like I always say, it's nice to be wanted – except by Scotland Yard. So whenever any of the other firms needed any extra hands to help out, they called me. I was more than willing to oblige.

How it happened was like this. There were major firms like Amon Ash's 'Titan', Lenny's 'Firm', one called 'Panther', Lance, Elliot and Lenny and Manny Clarke's boys, and, of course, Carlton and Big Phil's boys. And if they needed extra blokes at short notice, or when a big event demanded it, like when the football season kicked off, they would call me and I'd send some of my boys out to make up the numbers. For instance, when the Milk Race, the bike race, went through London, all these spectators lined the streets to watch. Thousands of them got on *Tattershall Castle* and the ship began to sink below its water line! We had to pile on and get people off quick.

And I had some of the biggest, best, tastiest fellas about, mate, I can tell you. Proper ones. All good, handy lads. So I ended up being in the position of getting on with all the other firms. They might not always get on with each other, but they all got on with me and I got on with them. And as their firms grew and grew and got more work and did bigger jobs, then so did mine cos I needed to expand to fill the need.

We worked *Tattershall Castle*, Dexters (with Joe and Gary), the Vibe Rooms (with Alan, Adam, Simon and Adrian), the Hippodrome, Equinox, Maxims, Heaven, Limelight, the Astoria (with Brian), Stringfellows (with Shaun and the boys), the Gass Club, the Park in Kensington and EC1 in Farringdon – oh listen, everywhere. Every fucking where. From it all starting, within a year or so I had a hundred and then nearly two hundred doormen working for me. It just went mental and really blossomed big-time. I ended up actually having more men working for me than the other firms had because I supplied blokes to all of them.

And what was this time of my life like? Well, let me see: I was doing a job I loved with all my pals and loads of other people I liked; I was making big money and staying out all nights surrounded by birds, booze and best mates; driving in flash cars from one club to another after I finished work; hanging out with pop stars and Hollywood celebs – and all of it in the best city in the world. Yeah, I was *that* close to suicide.

No, *stop* it! I was having the time of my fucking life.

I worked the door at the Limelight in Shaftesbury Avenue. The Limelight was an old church converted into a club, and at this time, late eighties, it was definitely *the* place to be. The VIP lounge there was the most exclusive in London. Everyone wanted to be in there and every star from Boy George to Sylvester Stallone did end up in there. Friday and Saturday nights were mental: queues of punters around the block, crowds of onlookers and tourists in the street just watching and star-spotting, limousines pulling up and stars getting out, paparazzi buzzing round. The Limelight was just opposite the Palace theatre at the crossroads of Shaftesbury and Charing Cross, and at the end of the night's show all the theatre goers would spill out. They'd stand there in their suits and with the missus on the arm, looking over at us, and, all dinner-suited up with bow ties as we were, we looked smarter than them! And working at the Limelight I probably saw more drama in a year than that theatre had done in its whole lifetime.

One night when I was working I heard all this commotion outside in the street. I came out to the door to see what was going on and the whole street was cordoned off by the police and fire brigade. Loads of people were stood round looking into the sky. Up on top of one of the buildings next to the Palace, and slap-bang opposite us, was this geezer on the edge of the roof threatening to jump off. You could see his little trouser legs flapping in the wind. They were all trying to coax him down but he weren't having it. Well, this went on for fucking ages and all the time no one could get into the Limelight because of the cordon in the street. We're all getting more pissed off waiting, and so are the punters who can't get in. Over an hour later and they're all still talking to him; a guy's on top of the fire engine ladder saying, 'Listen to me! Listen.' So, as a joke more than anything, I just shouted up, 'Oh, why don't you just fucking *jump*!! Get it over with!' And he did. I swear to God, he did. He jumped. Six storeys drop it was, too. *SMACK!!* on to the tarmac. I couldn't believe it. In case you're wondering, the fall didn't kill him. But the fucking landing did! Right on to the road. Urggh.

I just backed into the club quietly.

Another time I had a ruck with the guys from the band Sigue Sigue Sputnik. Remember them? No, no one else does either. They tried to look punk but ended up looking more like a bunch of transvestites on an away-day. I had to throw one of their mates out and the singer and one of the band ended up having a go at me. So I had a go back. I ended up with mascara and lipstick all over my duster!

All the English New Romantic bands and pop stars came in the Limelight: Spandau Ballet, Duran Duran, all that crowd and everyone round them, and all the American groups when they were touring here. Any Hollywood star that was in the country came down. One came down the club one night and really pissed me off. As he came in he took his car keys and just threw them into my chest and walked in. Like I was some kind of car park attendant. I thought, You bad-mannered, cheeky, cheeky cunt! So I nicked his car, obviously. It was this amazing, massive, six-wheeled Range Rover with blacked-out windows. I jumped in it and went round picking up some mates from other clubs. We'd never seen a six-wheeled Jeep before. We drove around for nearly an hour, drank the mini-bar dry, called everyone we knew on the carphone, did wheel-spins at traffic lights, the lot. I thought he'd be in the club for a couple of hours so when I got back I thought no one would be the wiser. Trouble is, the prat had only gone in for twenty minutes and decided to leave. He'd been stood at the door going berserk. I told him some crap about driving past the doors of the club looking out for him but I must have kept missing him. Then I tossed him the keys. I liked the thought that when he got his carphone bill it'd have itemised calls that sounded like the sign on Del Boy and Rodney's old van: New York, Paris and Peckham!

London has its own ethnic communities and they all have their own firms and organisation. The Chinese, the Turks, the Asians, etc. The Limelight being so close to Chinatown, I got to know a lot of the Triad members that came in. They have a hard reputation. I got to see some of that ruthlessness up close and to witness their coldness first hand. It was after some trouble we'd had in the club with this Chinese guy who was dealing drugs. If he ripped someone off then he just said he was a Triad to scare them off. He wasn't a Triad member, though, and word got back to them that they were getting the blame for his behaviour. Loss of face is a big, big thing among those people. You don't fuck with that.

Late one night this Triad guy came into the club to see me. I didn't know him by name but I knew what he was and who he represented. He said he had something to show me outside. We left and went down into this underground car park nearby. I had no idea what it was really about, I just thought he was gonna show me some knock-off gear that he thought I could shift. That sometimes happened.

We walked down the ramp into the car park and it was almost empty; just a few cars dotted about. There was a Transit van parked up and two other Chinese guys got out when they saw us approaching. They opened the doors at the back and moved away. Inside was the drug dealer geezer who'd been causing all the hassle. He was laid across the floor of the van with thick white tape binding his ankles and wrists together. His hands were behind him and there was a wooden pole like a broom handle across his back with his elbows hooked around it. White tape was wrapped around the bottom half of his face, covering his mouth. He started straining to look up and his eyes were wide open.

Before I had a chance even to really think about anything, quick as a flash and without batting an eye, the first Chinese guy, who was now stood next to me, pulled out a 9mm automatic and pumped three bullets into this fucker's chest – bam! bam! bam! – quick as that. He just sagged back on to the floor. The other two blokes slammed the doors shut. Not a word was said. The guy who'd shot him didn't even look at me. Not one bead of sweat came down his face. Not one. They all just got into the van without a word to each other and drove off.

I was just left standing there in the middle of this deserted car park at two in the morning having witnessed *that*. Something I wish I'd never had to see. But it did leave me with a very, very healthy respect for what those people were capable of. Doing that, to them, was no more than swatting a fly. And it was for nothing really, just for respect. And to show their loyalty and honour by shooting the geezer in front of me. That is cold behaviour though, ain't it? Absolutely fucking steel cold.

The doorman security thing had really kicked off for me. I had all the benefits of it: hundreds of blokes working for me and all the perks that came with doing the door on all London's major venues, but with none of the aggro. Because my boys were used by the other firms I never had my name down for a licence, so even though I was known to the police, they didn't know the extent of my business.

It was when I was working at Queen's that I'd met this eighteen-year-old kid called Wolfie. He was a real lovely, active, happy, raving geezer. The bollocks. My kind of guy cos he was always up for a laugh and real happy-go-lucky. Raving had just started, and Wolfie was right into it. He gave me my first trip. That was when I was at Queen's and it really fucking blew me away. I'd never had anything like it in my life. I remember looking at the carpet and seeing the colours move. I felt like my brain had been put in upside down. I decided I'd treat us both to champagne.

When I walked across the dancefloor, even though no fucker was anywhere near me I was going, 'Excuse me! 'Scuse me!' and taking big steps to avoid these people I thought were really close. I didn't know at the time, but Wolfie was watching and laughing his nuts off. When I got to the kitchen I bent down to this case of champagne and all the foil tops started sparkling really madly at me like little silver eyes or something. Just then, the guv'nor Vinoo appeared and said, 'I hope you're gonna pay for those.' I thought for a second, cos I knew I'd been caught, and said, 'Well . . . I am now!'

Then, during the Limelight time, I had my first experience of a real rave. I was working the door of the club Heaven in Charing Cross. It was a gay club and they had a Saturday night thing called 'Spectrum'. It was at the height of Acid-House raves and the first time I'd seen full-blown ravers in all their glory. The club was just rammed with these kids going absolutely mental – all these half-naked sweaty bodies dancing non-stop, waving their arms in the air, blowing whistles, shouting out and dancing on stairs and tables and anything they could get up on. Some of them had white gloves on or swimming goggles. The music was banging out and everyone started shouting 'Acceeid!!' I was walking through it all in my dinner suit and bow-tie thinking, *What* the fuck?! A whole boatload of Ecstasy had obviously been consumed in there, but that was all new to me. At the start I was shitting myself, to be honest. I looked around and thought, Just look at that geezer's eyes! And that one. And his. I thought I was in some kind of annual outing from Rampton High Security Mental Hospital. And all these geezers being loved-up to fuck on Es, they were coming over and trying to hug me. I clumped a couple, I must admit. What a berk. But I felt really out of my depth.

Anyway, after hours and hours of this I started to realise they were all harmless. Much more so than normal clubbers. They were too much into having a good time even to think about anything else. At first I hadn't wanted anything to do with them and just thought, What the fuck are they on? Then I found out exactly what they were on.

I started to calculate how many were here, how much they'd paid to get in and how eager they were for more, and saw what they were paying for a can of pop or even a bottle of water to cool down with. I thought, I'll have some of that. This is a right little earner. I saw the future of clubbing, Lord, and I said Halle-fucking-lujah! Praise be to Acid.

That night was a real eye-opener and the start of my days as a club promoter. I called Wolfie straight away and made plans to open my own place. I got this venue on John Ruskin Street off the Walworth Road in South London, just down from Elephant & Castle. The mainline train track ran over there and I bought one of the viaduct arches to turn into the venue. So we called the club The Arches. I put Wolfie in charge.

We did minimum preparations; no fuss or gimmicks, just this bare railway arch with a stage and DJ console knocked up out of scaffolding. We painted all the walls black. We nicked some Portaloo toilets from a building site up the road. Just hooked them up and drove off, ripping all the pipes out. We drove for about a mile with all this shit and fluorescent green chemical stuff pouring out the back. In fact, we had to drive around till it all ran out otherwise they'd have been able to follow the trail right to our doorstep. We put them in a corner of the arch and dug a big hole beneath them. (Later on, when it rained heavily one night, the hole backed up and spilled everything out. People were too off their heads to care they were dancing in shit!)

The Arches became the first, the very first, all-night rave in London. When every other club shut at three o'clock, mine was still banging at six, or seven, or eight in the morning. I'd leave the Limelight at two in the morning and go straight over to The Arches. By the time I walked in, with about a dozen other doormen, everybody was already well on one and raving away. I wish you'd been there – and a good few of you of a certain age that were in London at that time will have been – but for the rest of you I'll try and describe it.

Lunacy. That's what it was. Absolutely brilliant lunacy. The best kind of madness. Hundreds of people poured into the club from everywhere. Word got round really quick about this place down John Ruskin Street. We didn't advertise. Didn't need to. The Arches became like this little legendary thing among clubbers. Other promoters came, DJs came along asking to play, the streets outside were jammed with cars. In fact, on the first night we dropped a bit of a bollock. The cars spread out so far they even covered East Street on the other side of Walworth Road. This is where the market was, so come Sunday morning all the barrow boys turned up and couldn't get on. They went completely mental. Never get between a market trader and his pitch, that's my advice. So from then on, as well as working on the door and inside, I had some of my boys out in the street directing traffic. And all around the railway arches there were these flats. I knew they wouldn't like the noise, so every Saturday night we'd knock on doors and give all the residents a bottle of champagne. Some of the older ones didn't even drink and ended up with cases and cases of champagne stacked in the room.

The Arches was an illegal rave, by the way – did I mention that? Or did you just naturally assume? Well, you were right to. It was about as illegal as they got. But we didn't give a fucking monkey's. It was probably the best place in London to be and, like Wolfie's namesake in *Citizen Smith* used to say, 'Power to the people!'

First time the police paid us a visit was really funny. In front of the door were these thick iron gates that we closed and locked with a massive chain and padlock. So when the Old Bill arrived we just opened the door but left the gates locked and spoke to them through the bars. I said, 'Yes? can I help you?' And they told us to break it up and turf everyone out, and we just went, 'Err, no. I don't think so,' and closed the doors! They were left outside going, 'You *cunts*!' cos they knew they'd never break in.

Ecstasy really changed lives, though. For the better. I do believe that. Football thugs turned into love-a-dove ravers. Even hardened doormen got into it. I remember, one time, walking through the club thinking, This is just the best! It was jam-packed as usual with dancing nutters; sweat running down the walls and music banging out. No one had seen anything like it before, even the hard-core ravers. We had dustbins all around the club packed with ice and filled with free apples and ice-pops, and a girl in a *Playboy* bunny outfit walking round with an ice cream tray around her neck full of ready-rolled joints. They were a quid each! People just couldn't believe it. It's a shame the name had already been taken cos this place really was Heaven.

At one point I looked around and then I turned to one of my boys and asked where one of the other lads was, a guy called Norman. He looked around and then pointed up and said, 'Oh, he's there.' And there was Norman on top of a speaker, this sixteen-stone doorman geezer with his jacket off, shirt undone, dancing away off his head and giving it loads – brilliant! That just summed it up. I thought, Wow! Stormin' Norman.

We had DJs playing there that went on to become big names on the club scene. Fabio and Grooverider and Danny Rampling. They all played for us at £25 each. It would cost you more than that just to *think* of booking them these days. The DJs we booked included Randle, Ramsey and Fenn, Dean Lambert, Dominic (who later ran 'Spreadlove' at the Gass with

Andy Swallow and Johnny; that place became almost a
religious cult), Norris d'Windross (DJ of the year), Stevie Jay
(of Stringfellows fame), Creed (now Britain's most famous
rapper with chart successes), Junior, Danielle Montana,
Brendan Block, Mickey Finn, Steve Perry, Carl 'Tough
Enough' Brown, DJ Flighty, Steve Wright (now Kiss FM), and
Rob Andrews (who'd played at my wedding). Practically
everyone bar Tony fucking Blackburn. They all loved it down
at The Arches; all the Shoom people.

Looking back, it was something special. We hit right on the
crest of the wave of raving going off really big. Right time,
right place. And everyone with the right attitude. What really
did for us, though, was when we started advertising. I had
flyers made up and handed out everywhere. The police then
just thought we were taking the piss. Pretty soon we had
undercover Old Bill in there. Not like we couldn't tell who they
were: the dodgy, scared-looking ones in the corner.

Wolfie approached a couple of them once. 'Rumour has it,'
he said, 'that you two are of the flat-footed persuasion.'

Eighteen months after The Arches opened, it all ended with
as big a bang as it had started. If you dig out a copy of the
Independent dated Tuesday, 22 August 1989, you'll find a full
page devoted to the raid. The headline was THE PARTY'S OVER AT
AN ACID HOUSE UNDER THE ARCHES. In the article there's even photos
of the Territorial Support Group being briefed before the raid,
and photos of the raid itself. That just shows how much the
police wanted us, that they had gone to the trouble of having
photographs taken showing them preparing for it, and then
inviting press photographers so they could be there on the
night to get pictures of all us 'Acid-House ravers'. One of the
pictures even has a caption that says, 'Officers are told that
with these type of people anything is possible'.

On the Saturday night/Sunday morning of the raid, this is
what happened. A convoy of 150 plod descended on us, believe
it or not. The Territorial Support Group were in bulletproof
body armour, flameproof overalls and steel helmets with visors
and little radio microphones. Just a little bit fucking
overdressed for the occasion, you might say. But then we were
all evil Acid-House ravers, weren't we? They'd come prepared
for our little 'locked gates' trick as well with an hydraulic ram,

an angle grinder, a thermic lance (whatever the fuck that is), sledgehammers and probably James Bond in reserve for all I know.

The paper says that the police 'went straight to the known dealers and put the handcuffs on', which is not what happened. When they started bursting in, anyone inside that had anything just dropped it on the floor. By the time the Old Bill had got in and switched on these massive arc lights which blinded everyone, there was no way of telling who had had what on them. So the police just picked something off the floor and then grabbed someone and said, 'That's yours – I saw you drop it.' At the first signs of the raid, the few who were dealers had even thrown their night's takings away. On the floor behind the bar there were big, rolled wads of money. I wonder what the Old Bill did with all that? Just a thought. In fact, about the only thing the newspaper did get right was when it said, '. . . and the toilets were a disgrace'!

They arrested 26 people and cuffed them with plastic disposable handcuffs. Wolfie got pulled in as the organiser. One of the photos shows him being arrested or, as it says, 'Officers accost some of the teenagers'. The police thought of Wolfie as one of my 'lieutenants', as they called him, but he stuck to his story of being the organiser. Eight of the ones arrested were charged; all of them but one got sent down. The trial was a real farce. One of the officers changed his story halfway through because another had already said what really happened and it didn't go in the police's favour. So the other officer came in and said the first one was mistaken! During the trial, which lasted six weeks, I wasn't allowed to be named so they just referred to me as 'Mr X'! And Wolfie was called 'one of Mr X's trusted lieutenants', which is just about guaranteed to turn any jury against you. We knew then that the jury would come back with 'guilty', but we thought the sentences would be for about a year or eighteen months. The judge was Hugh Morgan, or Huge Organ as everyone nicknamed him. He lived up to that name when he handed down two-, three- and four-year terms. And Wolfie got *five* years! Get that! Five fucking years – for nothing. That broke my heart, it really did – broke my heart. Because Wolfie was just something else.

The authorities were scared by the whole rave thing, though.

To them it was like a new version of what rock 'n' roll was in the fifties – kids being led astray by 'Devil's music'. But it weren't nothing like that. Everyone was just having a fucking good time. Because the police had invested so much in the raid that morning it had to be seen to work. They were out to set an example, and so were the courts and Huge Organ. Wolfie only got a few months' parole as well and served nearly four years. That was more criminal than anything we were doing. Anyway, Wolfie's out and about now and we're still great pals.

Even though The Arches stopped after eighteen months, during that time I'd made inroads into the clubbing scene that would stand me in good stead in years to come. I ran more club nights afterwards and I made friends that went on to much bigger things. Hector went on to do Ministry of Sound, for example, which is now the biggest club in London and the best club in the world (I later did the security there with Nod and Zed and the boys).

It was at the Ministry that I met a geezer who went on to be one of my biggest pals, Brendan McGirr. Turned out he was one of the few who could be as silly as me on a night out, which I instantly warm to in a person, obviously. So we got on like a petrol-soaked kitten on fire, did me and Bren. As it happens, I'm now really glad he's on my side cos with his twisted little genius of a brain I wouldn't want him as an enemy. (And I'm glad he finally turned away from the priest-hood because the celibacy would've killed him.)

That's one of the best things about clubbing, though, ain't it? The people you bump into on one night that go on to become best mates for years afterwards. And after being involved in that lifestyle I didn't look back. Because I never ran around hiding in shadows and cos I was always a bit in love with the whole entertaining thing and putting my face about, it started coming up trumps for me. People would see me out in clubs having as good a time as them, not stood in a corner doing the 'I'm bad' bit. And because I was really having it, then people approached me. Sometimes it was just to say hello and sometimes it was to ask for work, or offer it to me.

Around this time something funny happened which came from me being out and about on the club scene. It showed one of the downsides of being so visible and everyone thinking you're a mate. Like I say, I was running an awful lot of doormen on the London club scene at the time. Most of the clubs had my doormen. It was a proper little firm. Not a firm in the sense that it had a 'family' name that we were known by, like all the others – the Brindles, the Arifs, the Arnolds, the Nashes, the Krays, the Richardsons and Lambrianous – but more because of the size of it and the number of things that my boys were involved in. I'm sure we got on well with all those people. Some, of course, I see a lot more regularly than others, but I consider them all my friends.

Anyway, I remember this meeting that was called between some of the big-known firms and faces from up north (including Tommy from the Midlands) and one or two of the big boys from London. They all attended with their own very seriously naughty-looking men, and they *were* serious-looking as well. It was called to try and sort out an escalating problem over a missing million pounds. So far three deaths were the result of the argument.

The reason I was at the meet was I was a good friend to all parties there. Adam and Birmingham John accompanied me. And, keeping it nice and classy like us Londoners try to do, we had the meeting in a conference room at the Dorchester, and I'm sat there with all these proper tasty faces from all the big firms. I'm just looking round at the people sat around this big table and thinking, Wow. I was just chuffed to be there. The cars these geezers had parked outside were impressive enough alone.

If you'd tried to impress people like this they would have seen right through you. When people do deliberately go out of their way to try and impress someone they usually fall flat; they do the wrong thing at the wrong time or in the wrong way. It comes across worse than if you hadn't bothered. I'm a firm believer in it's better to just get on and do what you do and, if you do it right, people who appreciate that will recognise it and you have a friend and ally.

Anyway, we're all sat there when suddenly, right in the middle of the discussion, I heard someone calling out, 'Dave? Dave! Davey!' I turned round and through the glass doors I saw this geezer waving at me. I didn't know who the fuck he was. He sauntered in and he was wearing a hooded T-shirt, a belly bag, tracksuit bottoms, Ray-Ban sunglasses and odd Kicker boots. All the chaps at the table, who were all suited-up to the nines, turned and looked at him like he'd just personally pissed in all their soups. He bounded towards me going, 'Davey-boy! Da*vee*!' I knew what it was. He was obviously some guy that I'd said hello to weeks ago at some club and he'd gone away suddenly thinking we're best mates. I didn't know him from Adam (sorry Adam) but he'd obviously remembered me!

Everyone was looking at me now. I thought, I do *not* believe this. It was like someone had set it up to try and make me look a proper cunt. I knew I couldn't deny I'd ever met him and risk getting into pantomime territory – no I don't, yes you do, no I don't, he's behind you! – and I couldn't give him a warm welcome cos he looked like the type to just plonk himself down in a seat next to me. I knew then what I had to do. Now, this ain't the most politically correct solution, I admit, but I was in a bit of a fucking spot. Just as he reached me I rested my cigar in the ashtray, stood up – real calm – and chinned him with one quick punch, bop! He went down on the carpet, spark out. I turned to the waiter who was hovering nearby. 'Deal with that for me, mate, would you? Thanks.' Then I sat down, picked up my cigar and turned to the others as if to say, 'Carry on, chaps'. Out of the corner of my eye I could just see these two mismatched Kickers trailing on the carpet as the waiter dragged him to the door. I didn't say a word more about it, but I could tell they were all looking at me thinking, What the fuck was that all about? But nicely handled, Dave, anyway.

Now I know that whenever I went out in clubs after that little episode, I must have, at some point, walked into a club where this geezer was. Stands to reason, it's the law of averages. And he will have seen me, thought I had some grudge against him and left the club! Or if he was with some mates of his that saw me first and they went, 'Look, it's that Dave Courtney – he's all right!', he must've said, 'No he ain't – he thumped me one time just for fucking saying hello to him!' So, if you are reading this, Mr Odd Kickers, at this point I'd first off like to apologise to you for the clump, and secondly I'd like to thank you. Because that little bit of action that day helped crack it for me with those guys who were there and saw it. So, cheers. And next time you see me out, come up and introduce yourself. I'll make it up to you, honest.

Then I started doing some work with an ex-CID officer, Steve, and two gypsy brothers, Gary and Peter, at a place called Junction 13 (owned by Bryan Adams) just off the M25. It was a cowboy-type country and western style gaff. A sort of disco/burger bar place with twangy music. The punters were all check shirts and moustaches. And that was just the women.

One of the blokes I employed to work at Junction 13 for me was Northern Billy. Billy's a frightening sight in daylight, let alone on a dark night: a six-foot-four, eighteen-stone, scarred ex-boxer. And he's from Manchester, so the accent works a treat.

Anyway, the owner of the club decided to go on a trip to America and, knowing that, his son Terry arranged to have a party at the house while his dad was away. At the last minute, though, his old man decided not to go away and came down to the club instead. So now he's in the bar with me when I get called to the phone.

It was Terry on the other end and he was in a right state. The party'd been gatecrashed by loads of people and they were refusing to leave and going mad smashing stuff up. The boy had called me to go and sort it out. He panicked even more when I told him that his dad wasn't even in America, he was in the bar with me. I told him that I'd get up there and then made some excuse to his old man for having to leave.

It was a pretty big house, and when I saw the state of it (the gatecrashers had broken up the garden furniture to make a bonfire!) I knew it was past the talking-and-being-reasonable stage. There was a lot of them as well, so I had to do it like a proper nutcase, a real scare-tactics job. I burst in with a chain and club and went mental. That was enough for most of them, but some were so pissed-up they decided to have a go and I had to clump a few. Then they all started to leave.

One of the gatecrashers backed his car out the driveway and hit mine. I told him he had to pay for it, which I thought was fair enough, and he gave me some money to cover the repair. I don't know if any of them called the police, but none of them knew who I was anyway and I didn't hear any more about it. I thought it would stay that way.

Now one day a pal of mine called Lou, who now runs The Aquarium nightclub with Timmy, Heidi, Tony and Paul, said he wanted to take me to a meeting to see one of the Lambrianou twins. He asked me to please bring some of the boys with me. I assumed he needed some assistance and some villainy was gonna take place, so I took along Northern Billy, Scouse Jamie, Mad Jack and Algerian Joe. When we got there we walked in and it was only a born-again Christians group! It was run by Chris Lambrianou, Tony's brother, and the guy I told you about that I first met when I was in Coldingly: the scariest-looking Christian you'll ever see. If the Romans had thrown Chris to the lions I fucking know which one my money would've been on.

So, we all walked in, me and the boys. We're all crombied-up and in black shirts and suits – the lot. Full gangster rigmarole. We looked like the local mafia come to rob the collection plate and extract protection money from the organist. Chris came up and hugged me and thanked us for coming. 'I'm glad you're going to become one of us,' he said. I thought, Eh?!

What Lou hadn't told us, the little monkey, was that this group had asked their members to bring along people they knew who were the most unlikely to become converts. They said if they could just convert one of that kind, then it was worth ten of the others. It had a kind of logic to it, I admit, but looking around at us lot I thought they might have bitten off more than they could chew. I mean, what's the odds on someone called Mad Jack or Algerian Joe suddenly finding religion? Yeah, I know, that's what I thought – stick with the lottery.

Anyway, we sat there and listened to it all. Billy was funny. He could not believe he was in the middle of this. At one point one of the speakers said, 'Tell me your sins! Tell me all your sins!' Billy just said, 'How long you got?'

That year, 1987, ended on a high when Tracey gave birth to our daughter, Levi. We could have called her Jean, but then the best jeans are Levi's, aren't they? And she was the best.

10 Lights, Camera, Action!

Then something happened where I was supposed to go to prison. Or I mean it looked like I would and everyone seemed to think I would.

It was due to this geezer at Queen's who sold cocaine. To be quite honest, if you haven't got certain drugs in certain clubs then you haven't got a club. People might not like to hear that, but it's true. (If I told you I'd never had a line or an E now and again, I'd be a liar. And if I said I'd never had any puff or whizz to stay awake, then I'd be the biggest liar in the world.)

The drug of choice for the punters at Queen's was, mainly, coke. They were the kind who could afford it: they were older people not bits of kids; and all the airline pilots and stewards (as if they didn't get high enough on a regular basis). The guv'nor, Vinoo, didn't know anything about it, but the doormen, being on the frontline, always know what's going on inside.

Now, if someone ain't causing any bother and is being very discreet then it has been known for doormen to turn a blind eye. Especially me. And sometimes one person being allowed to deal inside made it less trouble than if there was two or three. There's no price wars or battles over whose turf it is. The geezer selling charlie normally did it pretty low-key. He'd sit over in a corner with his gorilla close by and have a couple of blokes over at the bar to do the running for him in a pleasant manner. Everyone knows it goes on, so the best you can do is try and keep a lid on it and any grief it might cause.

Anyway, one night this dealer was well out of it. I think there was too much getting high on his own supply. He was dancing out on the floor when he suddenly pulled a gram of coke out and started cutting it in half and putting half in a fiver. Now that was just taking the piss. It was well out of order and made it impossible for me not to say something. I approached him and calmly told him to be more discreet. Coked off his box though, as he was, he weren't exactly bothered about getting a nomination for the World's Most Reasonable Man competition. He immediately took offence and started screaming and shouting at me. While I'm trying to get him out before it escalates into an even bigger scene, the two helpers of his come running over along with his gorilla. I let him come on and then took one step and chinned the big cunt straight off, knocked him out. Then, trying to get the others out, a big punch-up broke out. So all the other doormen jumped in to help and we threw them outside.

That weren't enough for them. The big guy had come round by now and they all came back to the door and had another go. I was fucking outraged. First they'd been in the wrong and now they were really trying to give it to us. I weren't having a running battle going on all night so me and the other doormen, Clint Dyer and another Dave, laid into them with baseball bats and gave them a proper *proper* good hiding. They staggered off to their car, and just as they drove off they fired a few shots out the window at us. What I didn't know then was, because of the state they were in, further down the road they crashed their car into a wall. Then the Old Bill ended up on the scene and the dealer fingered us for giving them a battering. By the time the police came back up to nick us the club was shut and we'd all gone off back to London. They decided to come back next week to get us. But we didn't know all this at the time.

In the meantime, during the week the dealer started ringing up the club saying that they were coming back to get us and we were gonna die, they were going to shoot us, and all those kinda threats. Now if I know some fucker's going to come up and shoot me then I'm gonna make sure I shoot them. That's the bottom line. I'm not going to stand there like a fucking fairground duck waiting to be dropped.

So come next Friday I had a shotgun in the car.

Before Friday came round one of the doormen that worked for me, this geezer called Jeff, rang in sick. Which was the first time in two years of working with him that he'd ever done that. So that all seemed a bit iffy. I still didn't know that the police had been up before and were due to come back, but Jeff did cos he played rugby with the fuckers. He also knew they were gonna raid us cos he was the one that told them I was planning on having a gun there. It was all part of his plan to get the head doorman's job from me. So he suddenly gets ill. I pulled in another bloke, Kelly, as a replacement. He was the brother of James Abola, a pro boxer and one of the tallest heavyweights there ever was.

So that Friday I'm stood on the door as normal when suddenly these two blokes by the cig machine turned round and jumped me. I thought, Fuck me, I know they only give you sixteen in a pack, but don't take it out on me! Then half the queue, which were also undercover police, launched in. It was like a big signal for everything to kick off. The back doors of a van in the car park burst open and loads of Armed Response uniform boys jumped out. Squad cars came tearing round the corner with the full light show going, and even a fucking helicopter that had been hovering above made an appearance. Talk about 'Lights, camera, action!' Only thing missing was Eamonn Andrews jumping out with a big red book saying, 'Dave Courtney - *this* is *your* life!'

They started searching the club for the baseball bats but they couldn't find anything. So they went for my car, which was right by the door, and found the sawn-off on the passenger seat. *Fuck.* They lined up a right shopping list of charges against me: grievous bodily harm (section 18 GBH), malicious wounding, carrying an offensive weapon with intent, attempted murder (all of them for the baseball bat thing), and possession of a firearm. I went 'not guilty' to all of them. The fight as well. Even though my other doorman, that prat Kelly, had turned Queen's Evidence against me.

I got banged up on remand in Reading for six months, then I got bail. When I came out I got a call from this guy who said he was from the BBC! I said I didn't even know you were looking for a new presenter for *Blue Peter*. He went, 'No, Mr Courtney, we want to make a documentary on you.' What with me being so naturally shy and retiring, I had to think about it for, ooh, maybe a thousandth of a second before I said, 'I'll be ready in ten minutes.' The geezer from the BBC, Marc Munden, tells me they're making a series of documentaries called *From Wimps to Warriors* and they want me to be in it. I said, 'Look! Are you trying to make me look like a wimp?' Now, because I'm not laughing when I'm talking to him, he takes everything I say deadly serious. He starts saying, 'No no, we want to feature you as more along the warrior lines, and doing the debt collecting.' I said fine.

Over the years I've found that because of my shaven-headed look, if I keep a straight face I can get away with saying the most stupid things and people aren't sure whether I'm serious or not. They daren't laugh in case it wasn't meant to be a joke and I might get offended. And I find all that really funny so I have a giggle with it sometimes. I'll drop an example in here before I forget. You'll like this one.

Years later I had a Rolls-Royce, a big beautiful white roller – Silver Wraith II. Wicked or what? The Silver Wraith is the really big one as well. When you sat in the back, if it was a clear day you could see the driver. Anyway, one time after me and some of the chaps had just come out of a club and we were driving home, I saw these two guys on the pavement and pulled alongside them and wound the window down.

' 'Scuse me, mate,' I said, 'am I going the right way?'

He walked up to the car looking baffled. 'Err, I don't know – where are you trying to go?'

I said, 'That's *nothing* at all to do with you! Just give me a straight answer: am I going the right way?'

He went, 'Errm . . . yeah!' And I said thanks and drove off. Now I don't think I could get away with that if I looked like Julian Clary. They are silly little jokes, I know, but let's just say I'm trying to keep in touch with my inner child.

Anyway, so the BBC are now following me around filming me and my friends and family. Tracey, Big Neil and David, Marky Mark, Norman, Warren, Anne, Joanne, Steve Bogart, Wolfie, good old Ray and my old pal Robert Hanson were all caught on camera. Loads more as well; a cast of fucking thousands, mate. If we'd had the right costumes we could've done a remake of *Ben Hur*.

They were going to call the programme *Bermondsey Boy*. I ain't even from Bermondsey, but some of the stuff took place there and they liked the sound of it. They filmed me doing my debt collecting in the weeks running up to the trial for the thing at Queen's. The film crew knew they were on to a good thing cos I was odds-on favourite to get sent down. Against me I had GBH, attempted murder, possession of a shotgun, three geezers I beat up picking me out the ID, another doorman grassing me up – the works. So the crew were creaming themselves. They genuinely believed I'd go down cos it looked like I was. They even thought I had a proper touch getting bail! Not only do they get film of me at work but it all fits in with their idea for the film: seeing whether or not prison changes a man for the better. The director told me that they had actually got permission from the Home Office to film me inside, and then they'd film me when I came out to see my reaction.

Although I didn't share it, I could understand their certainty about the outcome of the trial. Not only were there witnesses against me, including police testimony about finding the shooter, but also Kelly, my doorman, had given Queen's Evidence (I didn't even know he was gay!). Because he was studying at college to be a youth worker or something, the police had told him this was going to screw all that up, but they'd let him off if he grassed up Dave Courtney. So he just went *blurgh* and spilled his guts. What kind of example is that for the youth of today? I ask you.

So I went around doing my usual business, but now I had a film crew in tow. They stuck with me everywhere and got all the naughty things first: debt collecting, repossessions, rent-a-clump, evicting squatters, having fights with bodybuilders, etc. The full monty. They encouraged me to be worse as well to make me look better, by comparison, when I came out. That's something you don't know till you do telly; behind the scenes they really egg you on to go OTT. They filmed me doing loads of debt collections; having fights with loads of big old lumps who all lived together; rucking with Hell's Angels look-alikes, all sorts of rows. The worst one, though, was when I called round to this geezer's house to get £200 back that he owed the bookies. What happens but a 75-year-old man opens the door. And I'm stood there with a knuckleduster in my hand in case it's a big muscley cunt that goes for me.

I went, 'I'm looking for a Mr Robinson who owes money to the betting office – is that you?' He said, yeah, and I thought,

Oh great, now I'm fucked. I can't say that I'll let him off cos the cameras are there. I can't threaten him cos he's an old man. I'd rather he'd said, 'No it's not me, it's my six-foot-four, karate-expert son, shall I get him?' (To make it worse he only ended up being the dad of one of my friends!) Anyway, the old geezer's daughter only pops her head out and then starts emptying the phone box for money. They got £160 together. It was a real awful, awful situation.

We left, and as soon as I got round the corner (with the cameras still on me), I went, 'Aaww, *fuck*! What was I supposed to do? What *was* I supposed to do?' Some of the crew were laughing cos they knew how bad it had looked. They were well chuffed.

The next Sunday morning I was doing my regular thing, which is taking my little boy Beau to Dulwich Park. I had this green Austin Champ Jeep that we went in and Beau loved that. Mark Munden, the director, and the BBC crew are all with me at the time, sticking to me like limpets. Anyway, I got this call from a mate of mine, Mark. He had a job for me. I knew already he'd been getting grief from some lumps down at a gym in Peckham that he used. Now, when he'd gone for a night out with his missus to the Laserdrome club, one of these gym guys was working on the door and started giving Mark more grief. Just cos the guy's a big muscly cunt with all his mates around, he feels safe to take a liberty with Mark, and in front of his missus. So Mark was calling me to ask if I'd clump the geezer for him. He was at a place called the Matrix gym in Peckham high street. So, there we are, bombing down to Peckham in an army jeep with a film crew in the back hanging on for dear life. They fucking loved it!

When I got to the gym the crew couldn't follow me in cos they're not allowed to film me doing anything illegal (allegedly). But Beau did come in with me. No risk to him, no risk at all. The girl on the desk said that the fella wasn't available cos he was on a sunbed. I said that'll do me fine. I walked past, pushed through the louvre swing-doors of the room and saw him lying there, toasting himself with those stupid little goggles on. I banged the lid of the bed down on him and then whacked him, hard, four or five times. The perspex behind his head shattered.

I waited until he came round enough to hear me. 'Listen, you ever take a liberty again with a mate of mine, and never mind the sunbed tan, I'll fucking spit-roast you!' I left him looking a lot paler than he'd started out. (Funny thing is, years later he went on to be on telly quite regularly, presenting a popular TV show.) And if that little incident sounds familiar to you it's because they later used it in the film *Lock, Stock and Two Smoking Barrels*, with Vinnie Jones playing me.

Then they filmed me on a night out. And I mean a real, proper, man's night out: me and twenty other doormen on the town at a Chinese restaurant called Gracelands. It had a Chinese Elvis impersonator who sang things like 'Heartblake Hotew'! I had all the firm around me drinking champagne; the whole matey gang thing.

I had no visible means of income at the time cos I'd given up the dustcarts a while back, and the Criminal Gains Tax had just come in. That meant they could empty bank accounts. Fucking criminal, if you ask me. Emptying banks – that was our job! So I invested all my money in rare cars. This was at the height of the classic car boom. I bought an E-type Jag convertible for twenty-two grand and it was worth twenty-six grand within a year. I also had a Cadillac Coupe de Ville, a Thunderbird and Corvette Stingray, a Riley Pathfinder, an Austin Champ Rolls Royce Jeep, numerous Mercedes, a couple of bubble cars and some Harley Davidsons. You could safely say I had no reason to catch a bus for a while, put it that way.

They practically lived with me, the BBC! It was like Invasion of the Life Stealers. They filmed me getting dressed, having breakfast before I went out on the job. I daren't even have a wank. They even got me in the bath, and that was, without doubt, the most embarrassing thing that's ever happened to me. Not cos I was naked (I couldn't give a monkey's about that) but because of the way they did it. The director asked me to dip under the bath water and then come back up slowly so they could get this shot from above with my face emerging. Fair enough. What I didn't know is that they got my whole body in and there, floating in the bubbles, was my dick, shrunk up like a chestnut cos they'd kept me in water for 35 fucking minutes! When the programme came out you wouldn't believe the amount of piss-taking I suffered from my mates, saying, 'Ain't you got a little dick?!' British Broadcasting *Cunts*.

I got my own back, though, big-style.

Around this time I was also working the door of an exciting little pub called 'Lilliputs' run by one of my old boxing trainers, a lovely fella called Billy Aird. Yeah, exciting was one word for working there. Someone once shot at me from a car when I was on the door. They missed and I jumped in my car to chase them. Trouble is, at the time I was driving one of the many heaps of shit from Ronnie Cheeseman, a car dealer in Peckham. This particular car was two-tone – rust and mould – and did about nought to sixty in a fortnight. So the cunts got away. Shame that, cos it would've been the only drive-by shooting that turned into stock car racing.

Just before the trial they filmed me saying ta-ra to all my mates, selling some of the cars to get some money in, getting rid of the door-security contracts, and all that kind of thing. Winding up the empire, if you like. Then there was me kissing Tracey goodbye and saying goodbye to Beau and giving him my boxing gloves. It was worthy of Walt fucking Disney. I was nearly in tears myself when I watched it afterwards. But that's cos I was laughing.

Before we went to court the film crew asked what my defence was. I said 'I'm going to go "not guilty" until I get to court, and then when I'm on trial, say, "Yeah, I did it *but . . .*" ' The crew looked at each other and then at me, as if to say, You're going to prison then, Dave. (I didn't tell them what that innocent sounding '*but*' was gonna lead to.) 'You're a villain,' they said to me, 'and you're going to get done. But we wish you the best of luck.' I thought, Yeah . . . right. Well, to be honest, in a way I think they meant it cos I'd got to know them quite well and I think they were surprised I wasn't this raving monster that people sometimes think you are when they've read a few headlines about you. Especially when the headlines are SWORDFIGHT BLOODBATH AT CHINESE RESTAURANT! But, in another way, they couldn't afford for me not to get sent down. The whole film rested on it.

I left them outside on the steps of the court. They couldn't come in and they knew they wouldn't be filming me walking back out, but they could get some footage of me being taken away in a police van on my way to the Scrubs, or wherever I got sent.

I went to the bog before I entered the court and, inside, I saw this barrister's wig by the sink. He must have been in one of the cubicles. I nicked it and walked out. It turned out to be the wig of the guy prosecuting me, so my case was delayed for nearly an hour while they found him a spare!

So, eventually, I walked into court (with the wig still in my pocket) to see all my mates in the public gallery along with loads of press from the papers (cos word got around about the BBC filming), all the police involved, the barristers, the jury and the judge. OK, rewind and recap: I'm facing GBH, attempted murder and firearm possession backed up by a positive ID, police evidence and a grass's statement after Kelly's turned Queuey on me. If this was a soap opera, at this point it would end with 'and tune in next week to see Courtney's fate.' But this ain't no soap and I know I'm looking at a five to ten stretch before the next commercial break.

My excuse for me having the gun was going to be this: after word got round about the trouble from the coke dealers and them taking pot shots at us, some gypsy came up next week and offered to sell me the gun. I said that I didn't want it, but one of the doormen inside might. But cos I didn't want him taking it inside I said he could leave it in my car. After he'd gone in, that's when the police pounced. That's what I'd always planned on saying and that's what I said. I even produced twenty witnesses from the queue outside to say they saw the pikey put the sawn-off on the passenger seat. Even the police had to admit that when they'd searched my house they'd found no other guns or any cartridges.

Then I got what I'd been waiting for. My chance to address the jury. Directly. Fuck the prosecuting council; even though he's the one asking me the questions, I turned and spoke to them. I remember it almost word for word.

'As a doorman I feel as if I am policing the nightclub. Putting me in a dinner suit just singles me out as the figure of authority, as a policeman's uniform does with him. Now, if a policeman tries to arrest you, you can go quietly. If you resist, then he'll use force. If you start kicking up enough fuss he'll pull out his little bit of wood and bop you with it. If it gets bad enough and seems to be life threatening, they'll even bring in guns. That's what the police do. And it ain't too far away from what I do.'

I stopped there and looked at them. They were all looking right back at me. I didn't turn round but I could hear complete silence behind me from everyone in the court.

'Yes, I did it, *but* . . . that night I was in the nightclub and saw drug dealers taking an out-and-out liberty and I asked them to leave. I don't condone what they do, but I knew it was going on. I told them not to insult me by doing it so openly cos I've got to be seen to be doing my job. They refused, freaked out and started using some force, so did I. If they'd stopped hitting me then I'd have stopped hitting them. Then they got worse, ended up with a good hiding and ran off with their tails between their legs. And took a good few fucking shots at us on the way. I left thinking I've done a good job and then next week I'm being arrested!

'If I'd pleaded guilty I automatically go to prison, the bad guys get off, and you don't even get the chance to hear me telling you this. So I'm going "Not guilty" and giving you something to think about when you go back in there to deliberate. *If* you go 'guilty' then the bad guys get off *and* get a couple of grand in compensation. That's all I have to say.'

I knew when they went back into that little room that I had them on my side. I knew they were thinking, Well, if we say 'guilty' to the GBH the others get off with it, and even though he's said he's done it, even admitted to the gun in the car, they *did* shoot at him the week before, so . . . All that was going round in their heads. If I'd gone 'guilty' to it, like everyone thought I should, I would never have got that chance. And if you can appeal to a jury's common sense then you're halfway there, even if it means they go against some technicality of law. Cos they like to feel they've got some power and influence – which they fucking have when they can send you down for ten years! But if you trust them to do the right thing then they can't help but acknowledge that and like you for it. I cannot overestimate how much difference it makes to get the jury to know you, rather than the image they have of you. The number of 'not guiltys' I've had because of that, or because I've made a jury laugh. We'll get to a few of those later.

They came back in, and as the judge read out each charge the jury foreman answered, 'Not guilty.' It was only for the possession of a firearm that I got 'guilty' for. I knew that would happen anyway. It was in my car and so, technically, in my possession. My prints weren't on it though, and I got a suspended sentence. Which pissed off the Old Bill ever so slightly, I can tell you. And talking about pissed off . . .

I walked outside to the BBC film crew who were still on the steps. 'Not guilty, boys,' I said. 'I'm a free man!'

It was a race between which one of their jaws hit the floor first. They just looked at me.

I said, 'What? Don't tell me you're not happy for me?'

They all said congratulations but none of them were doing cartwheels. I thought, Have I just put a right hole in your boat, mateys? I knew their version of what they wanted the documentary to be was fucked up good and proper.

Oh dear, how sad. Never mind.

When *Bermondsey Boy* was shown, though, it had big repercussions for everyone involved in it, not all of them good. It made me high profile and really visible, which had its up and its down sides. The downside was that it made me so visible that some of the gatecrashers I'd thrown out of that party (when I'd been working at Junction 13) saw me on the telly and recognised me. They rang the fucking police and said, 'I know who it was now – it was that big skinhead that was on TV last night.' I thought, Thank you God, thanks a lot! Talk about trial by television.

I immediately got pulled in and charged. I was now looking at seven charges of GBH (one for each gatecrasher that had been clumped) and one count of robbery for taking the money off the geezer that had bashed my car! So now I know what to do when the car insurance company takes more money off me when I make a claim: I'll charge them with robbery. I was told I had to go back in a week's time for an ID parade. I did that, but the ID parade wasn't conclusive and the police got it into their heads that I'd intimidated the witnesses. Well, I ask you.

When the Old Bill came back round to my house to re-arrest me they found me at the top of the stairs on crutches. Remember that accident I'd had years ago when I was a dustman? Well, that injury often recurred, especially at times like this. Must have been all the stress and worry, I guess. One of the curses of being sensitive, I find. They got an Army ambulance from the TA barracks on Camberwell New Road, nicked me and took me to Brixton prison. I went straight on to the hospital wing and did the whole of my six months on remand there. Lenny McLean was also in on remand.

And who should also be in the hospital with me but John 'Mad Dog' Mangan. We had some mutual friends, like Big Reg Parker who owns Sharpes Gym, and Billy Dalou. John was one of the old school from the Kray days. Like another 'mad' one, Frankie Fraser, John was physically small but carried a big reputation. He was famous for once having been shot nine times and living to tell the tale. Every time he took a drink I expected him to leak like a sieve. He was in the hospital wing with some heart problem. Not surprising, really, as he was now in his sixties and still doing armed robberies. His getaway transport was a Shop Hopper.

Once, when he was in court, after the judge had sentenced him, John stood up and said, 'I don't fucking care! I've done more porridge than the three bears!' That is a class line. He really played up to the 'Mad Dog' thing and conned all the screws into thinking he was properly mental. He'd do daft things like break out into song, full voice, in the middle of the night and carry on for hours. Sometimes I got woke up at three in the morning by one of his mental renditions: 'Ayye deeed it . . . mmmmyy waaayyy!!' He sounded like Frank Sinatra with piles.

The coppers on my case were also going mental cos I was in the hospital wing, which is quite cushy, and getting visitors all day. I was even getting shagged. I worked the old hospital visit routine that I'd used in Coldingly. Let's put it down as physiotherapy.

Anyway, before the trial I went up for bail. The night before that I was screaming in agony and crying out for painkillers. I'm no doctor, but it must have been the stress again, bringing it all back on. The next day I couldn't even sit up and they had to lay me flat on the floor of the meat wagon and cuff me to the seat. On the way to the court I looked up at one of the coppers sat over me. I couldn't resist it.

'Typical NHS,' I said. 'I knew I should have gone fucking private!'

The police opposed my application for bail on the grounds that I was a danger to the witnesses. My barrister jumped at that one. He said, 'Let me get this correct. You want to refuse Mr Courtney bail on the grounds he may intimidate witnesses and yet he was arrested on crutches, spent his remand on the hospital wing and is too unwell to get up the steps into the dock to defend himself. And has been up seven consecutive nights *in hospital* and in agony! I for one, your honour, am unable to see any threat at all.' The judge agreed, and gave me bail.

I hobbled out of court and found the police waiting on the steps outside. I suddenly felt much better then, as it happens. Could it have been the lifting of that awful burden of further incarceration? Fuck knows, but God ain't the only one who moves in mysterious ways because I smiled at the coppers, picked up my crutches under each arm, ran down the steps two at a time, jumped in a waiting car and drove off. I'm not rude though – I *did* wave.

By the time the actual case came to court, 47 witnesses turned up to say I was somewhere else at the time of the alleged crime. Fuck me – lucky or what?

And that was only one of the downsides. Also, because *Bermondsey Boy* was one of the most hard-hitting documentaries of its type that had been shown, it caused loads of controversy and complaints. The producer was sacked. Peter Watson at the BBC got in hot water over it. And I weren't too happy about the finished result.

After I'd got the 'not guilty' it had screwed up the original point of the film, so instead they concentrated on all the worst things and really played that up. The way they cut it, it looked like I woke up first thing, grabbed a knuckleduster and then went out seven days a week clumping people. But out of all the fights with big lumps and bikers and what-have-you, guess which was the only debt-collecting job they featured? Yeah, the one with the old geezer who owed the betting office £200. It had been designed to show me in the worst possible way, and everyone began looking at Dave Courtney in a bad light. I could see how it looked to people: me driving around in flash motors with all the rent-a-clumps. Even how they showed me describing a fight I had with a fella made me look racist, when everyone who knows me knows I'm not. I've always had black mates, and later married a black woman (my Jennifer) but, at the time when this film was made, racism was ferocious. I'm not saying it still ain't around, I know it is, but back then it seemed worse and people were real open about it – no shame about it – and real nasty.

And me out with all the firm on the nights out didn't go down too well either. On top of all that was the fact that when I'd come out of the court and the film crew asked me if I'd done it, because I know I can't be tried twice for it, and also because I'm buzzing after the result, I said, 'Course I did it!' (People knew that anyway – I'd already admitted it in court.)

The press also republished the story about the Chinese waiter stabbings, and all that went national and I became a bit of a celebrity. If you've earned something falsely then people can begrudge you having the glory of it, but if you've earned it proper then there's no reason why you shouldn't get off on it. And I did.

Funnily enough, despite all the controversy over it, *Bermondsey Boy* was put forward as the British entry for Best Documentary at the Cannes Film Festival. And it won! Marc Munden later told me that he wouldn't have made the film as it turned out but, after I'd got off the charges, he just had to put something together from what he'd already filmed. While he was in Cannes he also met an American woman who later became his wife, so it turned into another case of good coming from bad.

Whether I wanted it or not, my future was picked out then in those terms, and by how people saw me. I could hear my little nan on my shoulder with one of her old sayings, about how you're judged by the company you keep. Bang-on that one, Nan. Suddenly I had five hundred new 'mates' that were all lunatics. Loads of right nutters saw *Bermondsey Boy* and thought, 'He's all right, I wanna be Dave's mate,' but anyone half respectable didn't want to know me. I'd got known as a violent debt collector who loved having a row and didn't give a fuck.

Although every man likes to put out that he's leader material, most of them aren't. Most men need guidance. I know that. And because I came out of the programme as leader material I suddenly had a ready-made army of people ready to do . . . whatever. It made me a very well-known debt collector. I just got offered so much work that I would've been a fool not to take it cos it was gonna make me rich. It led to me going all over the world doing debt collecting: America, France, Sicily, Malta, Portugal, Belgium, Spain and even Australia.

But, I never *did* get that offer of a job as *Blue Peter* presenter. Funny that . . .

11 Let Me Tell You How Fear Works

Fear works like this: it plays on two things, what you know and what you imagine. For instance, if you've ever had your nose broken you'll know if it were less or more painful than you'd imagined. So, two things: (1) if it weren't as bad as you'd thought it would be, then some of the fear of that happening again has gone and you're stronger for it; or (2) if it was absolute fucking agony then you'll be frightened of it happening again and that'll make you weaker. If, on the other hand, it's never happened to you then all you can do is imagine it. And more often than not people imagine things to be worse than they are. So you can use that. If you want to frighten someone then it's best if it's over the unknown. Because what people don't know, frightens them.

I learnt that the threat of violence is a lot worse than violence itself. That's worth more than kicking in doors and going apeshit cos once you've done that you've got nowhere to go. If you're clumping someone and screaming, 'I'm gonna kill you! I'm gonna kill you!' and then you don't . . . what do you do then? Halfway through the beating the punches don't hurt any more and the guy knows you ain't gonna kill him. He's thinking, Well, he keeps telling me he's gonna kill me but it ain't happened yet. And that's when he decides not to pay you. Then you've left no room to go any further other than topping the bloke. So I did it the other way, through talking and seed-planting. Fear tactics. And that carried on working on him after I'd left.

And as well as using their own mind against them you can use other people's. Every man's weakness is his woman. A man will suffer a lot of stuff himself but will be able to stand very little being endured by his missus. Fact. It's human nature. Like I said before, I've seen the hardest hardnuts crack in prison because of a woman.

The trick was this: visit the geezer at home when his missus is there. Don't say anything to her apart from being really respectful and apologise for having to come into her home like this. Then do your bit explaining the situation to the guy. No raised voices, no shouting and screaming, just a calm explanation of what he owes, when he should repay it and what will happen to him if he don't. The other point to make is that now I've been employed to recover the stolen money (cos that's what a debt is, at the end of the day) then what that means is that half of it is now owed to me. Half of the debt owed is mine, and if the money isn't paid back I'll make sure he has a hard time enjoying it. Then you leave, stroking the dog on the way out and quietly closing the door behind you. 'I'll see myself out' was a good last line, leaving him in the room with his missus.

What happens then, before you've even reached the car, is that she goes absolutely mental at him. Telling him to pay back the money he owes and saying he had stolen it after all and what if the kids had been home, and how can he put them all through this, etc., etc. That's worth more than beating a guy up. If you're lucky she'll go on at him for the next ten hours solid and you'll have the money in the morning. If you can get the missus on your side, that's the key.

Now that might sound like a naughty one, using the woman, but you know yourself she's never gonna get hurt. It's an avenue that even the police use. They know that if they raid a house and find something, a gun for instance, the geezer's gonna go 'no comment' and so will his missus. So they nick them both. The kids get popped into care and it's a real fight to get them back. So the police keep both the bloke and his missus, just waiting till the bloke holds his hands up and says, 'OK, it's mine, guv.' It's a proper strategic tactic used by the police. They even stake out the place until they're sure that no one but the man and his wife and the kids are home and nobody else. Cos if you've got a friend there, or a relative, they can legally take charge of the children and that's one worry gone. So the Old Bill swerve that one by nabbing you when they're sure the kids will be taken. Believe me, it's true. You might not want to believe that of the good old British bobby, but they've learnt how to do that and they've seen it work. I've seen it. I've watched men who are as strong inside as me about going 'not guilty' hold their hands up to a charge. You could threaten to kill that geezer and he wouldn't say nothing, but they get to him through the wife.

They've used it on me. Twice. One time was a few years later, after Tracey, when I was with my missus Jennifer. Someone tipped the police off to a weapons' stash in a flat below me. They said they were told it was mine but it weren't. Whether they were told that or they just realised they could use it against me cos it was nearby, I don't know. Either way they kicked my door in as well to nick me. I weren't home, as it happens (they got that bit wrong), but Jenny was and they nicked her. Jenny didn't say nothing. She is the best, mate, believe me; the best missus any man in this walk of life could have. If they ever took her in they got as little back from her as they would from me. I've been lucky on that score. Tracey was a strong one too.

Anyway, when I heard about it I knew I had to find the guy who owned the stuff from the flat before the police found me. I didn't find him, but he got word about what had happened and, give him his due, he didn't do a runner, he came in and owned up to it.

The lack of shouting when you're telling someone what you're gonna do is always more scary, and that's something you learn off your wife. If she's screaming and shouting, 'Piss off! Don't come back!' then you can deal with it. But it's when she says, very quietly, that she's had enough and she don't want you there any more – that's worse. You know that's the last straw.

I'll tell you something now, if you haven't discovered it already: women have so much more fucking sense than men, they really do. They just don't seem to have the same hang-ups and baggage and dodgy pride and all that mental crap about doing the right thing.

So what you're doing when you say those things to people, when you plant that little seed in their mind, is you're actually getting them to beat themselves up for you – mentally. And they're helping you by doing it. You scare them and then they carry on scaring themselves. They're thinking, He said he'd do this and he said he'd do that and he said he'd get away with it and he looks like he would and, fuck me, it would really fucking hurt and what if it hurts even more and what if he kills me, and when does the fucking bank open?! Or thoughts to that effect. If the right thing is said in the right way then you can recover a million-pound debt without lifting a finger. Without even raising your voice.

Now that might all seem an awful bit naughty, but is it any naughtier than nicking, say, £100,000? Because if you hadn't done that then you wouldn't be in that position. (I got jobs from five hundred pounds to four million, from Peckham to Australia.) Let me put it this way. If, for example, your accountant or business partner rips you off for a hundred grand and then declares himself bankrupt and gets away with it, or even gets caught and serves a bit of time inside, what are you going to do? One day your bank account says £100,000, the next day it just says £0. You might have worked forty years for that or you might have made it in a year. Same difference: you want it back. How could you get it back if all the legal options have failed? You could come to me. I would get it back. You might not like how I do it, and by this stage you wouldn't even care, but I would get it. After *Bermondsey Boy* I got more job offers than a two-bob tart doing a two-for-one special promotion.

I took half of the debt owed, but my rules were this: before you come to me, go through every possible avenue you can to get your money back – police, solicitor's letters, lawyer's threats, court actions, citizens' advice, the United Nations, the Samaritans, letters to your MP, going to your big brother, wishing, praying, and *Jim'll Fix It*; then, when you're fucked and completely finished, I will go and do it for you, for half. And half of something is better than all of fuck all. As my maths teacher used to say.

If people have tried to get your money back for you already and it ain't worked, none of it, then I know what tactics *not* to use. That made it easier. When it got to that stage, again, there were two ways of looking at it: (1) it's a hard job if it's got this far; (2) I now know what not to do, so that narrows it down.

A lot of guys might be more vicious and ruthless on a job and it ain't worked, so I know that road isn't there for me to go down. And that's when I started doing it the psychological way. And that became my way of doing my work.

The other major rule I had was this: make sure that I was in the right. I knew that what I was doing afterwards – the visit to the geezer that owed – was legally wrong, but I made sure I was morally right. It wasn't robbery, it was debt collecting. It was the bloke that owed who had robbed. Even if I got nicked afterwards, I had that justification. So I vetted what I did.

And being the one to take on these kind of jobs got me known for it. Sometimes it'd be a job that other geezers in the trade had tried to do. Sometimes it would just be some ordinary bloke that had seen everyone else and believed me when I'd said I was the last resort. Either way, by taking on the toughest jobs you lined yourself up for the most acclaim. Which, along with the money, I thought was just reward.

Like in any business, there's levels. When I first started doing it I might be collecting for the bookies or for unpaid furniture, stuff like that. Or TVs and cars with the odd bigger money job coming my way. Then it grew to bigger and bigger jobs.

I was cracking it off as a debt collector and doing really well. I was employing tons of doormen, and because they were only working Friday and Saturday nights then they had the rest of the week to do fuck all. So they worked for and with me on the debt collecting.

Like everything else I'd done it just seemed to evolve. I'd always had an idea of how I wanted things to go, but I'd never really chased it or pushed it. I just had this feeling that things would come when the time was right, and they always did.

I was never short of partners whenever I went on a debting job. Dave Legeno, or 'Lone Wolf' as I called him from his American wrestling days, was one of the best.

One time me and Dave had to go down to Margate to see this geezer. Now this was a strange one. This bloke had first got in touch with me with an idea for bringing cars from abroad into Ireland, not paying tax and then flogging them. He was something in the motor trade and he made it sound like a proper little good plan. He used to come up to see me to discuss it.

So I set up a big meet between him and some guys I knew would come in on it with me. I brought these people down from their places and put them up in hotels. We waited. And nothing happened. And then more nothing happened. It turns out that Mr Big Idea had just been lying all along. He was a bit of a gangster freak and he'd just lied his bollocks off to get to meet me. He'd read about me and wanted to say hello, so he did it through some invented business. Which I might have taken as some kind of backhanded compliment if me and this other geezer hadn't just thrown two and a half grand at the whole thing. That's how much we were down, what with travel, top hotels and entertaining for all the blokes I'd brought into this.

The original guy just fucked off. He changed his phone numbers so I couldn't get hold of him that way. So me and Dave saddled up and rode down to that old outpost and one-horse town, Margate. So much for acting like Butch and Sundance, though, because the geezer weren't even in! But his missus was, as it happens. I apologised to her. Said I didn't really want to bring my troubles to her door and explained how her husband's little ego trip had cost me and my partner two-and-a-half thousand pounds.

'Please explain it to him,' I said, 'because if I see him before he's paid it I'm gonna hurt him.'

I didn't think his lady saying that little speech to him would have quite the same effect as I would have got, somehow. It didn't, and he didn't pay.

Round Two. We went back. She opened the door on the chain. I heard him shout from inside, 'Hang on, I'm coming!' I thought, That's a lie if ever there was one. I charged the door, smashed it off its hinges and ended up flying down the passage on top of it like a surfboard. I shouted, 'I'm in!' He came running out one of the bedrooms, and jumped straight through an upstairs window! He dropped into the garden, rolled in all the glass, got up and fucked off! I thought, Wow – what a compliment that was, for him to risk doing *that*.

His missus was scared now. I calmed her down. 'You know me,' I said, 'I've spoken to you before, you've got my home phone number, here's fifty quid for the door and I apologise for that. I'm not gonna run up streets to catch your old man but I will get him and he will pay me what he owes. You know that, he knows that.'

When he got back his missus probably gave him a bigger battering than I would have. He paid.

Two of the guys that often did the jobs with me were Jim and Big John from Birmingham. Now John is a lovely fella, and I'm not just saying that, he's a genuinely nice bloke, *but* – you just knew there was gonna be a 'but', didn't you? – you would definitely not want to get in a row with him. He's a big, big lad and very tasty with it. He's actually a successful businessman in his own right, a millionaire believe it or not, so he didn't do this with me for the money. He just loved the buzz. Bit like my mate Jonathan Evans in that respect: the naughtiness was born in them. And if that's what you're like then no matter what happens to you along the way, that's what you are. And Jim was a big, loveable, cuddly bunny rabbit, ha ha ha.

A funny one was when we went up to Scotland to recover this debt from a guy who'd ripped someone off. He was a professional conman. He must've been a good one cos just as we got to his house he was walking down the drive to get into a new Porsche! Now that gets you zero sympathy to begin with. He owed money and he was driving around in *that*. It was a really sunny day and he looked up when he noticed something block out the sun. He turned round to see the total eclipse of John. He just froze, with the car door open. I spoke directly to the guy.

'I hate working with him,' I said, pointing to John, 'cos he stops the sun glinting off my knuckleduster.' He looked down at the duster and then jumped in the car and slammed the door. Luckily the window was already open and John just reached in and pulled this guy out through the hole. He was a big geezer, but John is just so strong that when he pulled him out, the window frame *bent*. John let go and stood back.

Now the geezer's stuck there, half in, half hanging out, jammed like a square peg in a round hole. His arms were pinned to his sides but he started shouting and trying to fight, the dozy bastard! Fuck me. We stood there laughing at this fat geezer paddling away with his arms inside the car. Then I stepped up to him, real casual, as if we stick people in car doors all the time.

'Right, listen . . .' I said. I could see John out the corner of my eye trying not to laugh any more cos this was the serious bit.

Now we all know why people rip other people off – for the money, of course – but you might wonder why they do it to blokes who are connected enough to know guys like me. The client that'd hired me knew how to contact me (or someone in the same trade) and the conman knew that. So why do it? It's simple really: they always think they're the special one who'll get away with it. Always. Everyone secretly likes to think they're different from all the mugs. Even the blokes who scam really ordinary geezers – nine-to-five, bloke-next-door types – even then they don't realise how accessible guys like me are. I've been hired by sixty-year-old cardigan-wearers who've never had so much as a parking ticket their whole lives, and they've managed to get hold of me.

This geezer was a bit different, though. He wasn't a one-off scam merchant, he did it for a living. So that called for my little Repeat Offender speech. With a bit of the Terminator thrown in for good measure. He'd stopped struggling by now, and was just stuck there looking up at me. I do love a captive audience.

'Listen, I don't blame you for doing your little scam, but this time you've been caught and I've been brought in. I don't care if you've done this twenty times before and got away with it or if you'll do it twenty times again and get away with it, but this time you haven't. *This* is the one that you knew would happen eventually, the one where you've got caught. Accept it. And pay.' John stepped forward for dramatic effect and put the geezer in the shade again. 'It's nothing personal,' I continued. 'I do this professionally, and if you pay you won't see me again. But if you don't then you can run, you can try to hide, you can shoot at me, you can call the police or the Seventh fucking Cavalry, but I will come after you, and I will get you.'

We left. We left him like he was, actually. So as well as a bent Porsche he probably ended up with a really bad case of sunburn. He also paid.

On the drive back I told John about something I'd been

With Mum and Dad

With Colin Robinson

Cap'n Dave, with John, Jenny and Danny

At The Albion, My pub

With Warwick outside my old flat

John Boy

With Patrick (Patsy) Gutteridge

With Posh John (Evans)

Drew, Jennifer, me and Jenson at my villa in Marbella

Jenny and ex-Mr Universe Selwyn Cotterell performing at the launch of the record, 'Who is he?' at the Hippodrome

Looking cool with Courtney

Beau, Chelsea, Levi;
I love 'em lots

Afloat in St Katharine's Dock

My stocking was full that year

Ian Tucker, me, Jenny, Eric the Viking

Hector, me, Don

Seymour (lifelong friend), me, Wolfie

(Back row) Floyd Brown, Maurice Smith, Johnnie Ash R.I.P., Eamon Ash, Ned Rawlings, Robert Lopez, Mick Robinson, Nigel Foster, Barry Littlejohn. (Front) me, Rocky, Posh John

Roy, Kevin, Steve, Sean, John, Dean, me, Paul, Chrissie the Greek

Big Mark, Warwick, Terry, me, Alan, our host

Jeff, James, me outside Queen's

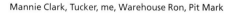

Mannie Clark, Tucker, me, Warehouse Ron, Pit Mark

Outside my Crazy Mondays club: me, Boris, Jenny and Julia with a posse of top DJs

At Ronnie Kray's funeral:
(Left to right) Me, Frankie Fraser, Reggie Kray, Lance Clarke *(behind)*, Ian Davies

At the opening of mine and Joey Pyle's gym. Charlie Richardson, Joey Pyle Snr, Bill Murray, Roy Shaw, Rod, Joey Pyle Jnr, me, Rick English, Freddie Foreman, unknown, Tony Lambrianou, Lloyd. The painting behind Roy Shaw is by Charles Bronson.

Joey Pyle, Roy Shaw, Frankie Fraser, me, my brother

Lenny McLean

Freddie Foreman, Dave, Beau, Christian, me, Marcus, Tucker, Frank, Chris Hammer, Mad Pete, Tony Lambrianou

Johnny Fleming, Al Benson, Marcus, unknown, Howard, Matt, me, Terry Turbo, Big Albert Chapman (Elbow Rooms), Dirty Adam, Been-There-Seen-It-Done-It Bernie, unknown, Freddie Foreman, Joey Richardson, Frankie Fraser, Welsh Bernie, Joey Pyle

Big John, me, Francis, Felix and Steve McFadden (both from *EastEnders*),
Terry Turbo (my partner in One Nation)

Me with Nigel Benn

Arrested by *The Bill*

Happy 40th birthday: Steve McFadden,
Mrs Joey Pyle, Bill Murray, Barbara Windsor, me

tempted to say to the guy, one of my favourite lines from a film. It's in that gangster film from the sixties, *Get Carter*, when this fat geezer squares up to Michael Caine. He says to the fat bloke, 'Don't even think about it! You're a big man but you're out of shape, and I do this for a living.' Oh yes! What a wicked line that is. But our fat geezer had been old enough to know that film and I thought it might undermine my argument a little bit. Anyway, he weren't the only one out of shape. So was his fucking car.

John was the one who did one of the best moves I've ever seen. We were on another job and this idiot tried to have a pop at him – a mistake that ranks right up there with the asbestos wok and the chocolate fireguard. John whacked him in the belly so hard that the geezer jackknifed, bent double, still standing but with his head between his knees. John just put his arms around him and picked him up like that. Like a folded deckchair. Then he went, 'Where d'ya want this putting, Dave?' That's John, a black belt in origami. Have a go at him and he'll fold you to death. John was also the one who introduced me to the dodgy doctor in the Midlands that would stitch up bullet holes and stab wounds with no questions asked. If you go to hospital with them injuries they have to call the police.

Doing the debt collecting big-time, like I was now, you do so many jobs that anything you can think of will happen eventually. I mean, they weren't always perfect jobs. There were good, bad, funny, mental, and just downright laughable ones. This one time me and Marcus from Margate (now there's another massive geezer) travelled four hundred miles to find someone. That was up in Scotland as well. Right up. We couldn't go by plane cos of something we were taking with us. Something that might set off a metal detector or show up on the X-ray as ever so slightly gun-shaped. I wrote the address down on a Rizla so I could just swallow it in case we got pulled and searched by the Old Bill. So we got there after a four-hundred-mile, five-and-a-half-hour journey and Marcus pulls out the map. And I pulled out the address. Only I didn't. Because I couldn't find it. In fact, I had lost it.

At this point Marcus, whose muscles even have muscles, tensed up and nearly bent the steering wheel in two. First off, we'd come a lot further than he thought we would because I'd just said Scotland, y'know, that bit just above England, and it hadn't sounded ridiculously far. Three quarters of the way there, though, we realised it was the *top* bit of that bit above England. The real Haggis-munching, sheep-shagging, skirt-wearing, ginger-beard depths of Scotland. And then I'd lost the address. We couldn't get in touch with the bloke in London to check, and Marcus really had to be back in Margate the next day, so we turned around and came back. Before we set off Marcus got out, bent a lamp-post in two and tied it in a knot. His little, harmless way of getting rid of pent-up aggression, bless.

That's another thing, come to think of it: the way that people think because they're a few hundred miles away they can't possibly be found. Or that you'd even bother trying. It's cos some people only come down to London once in a blue moon; it makes them think it's a real long haul. But I travelled all over doing jobs, so five hundred miles was nothing. It did feel longer when you lost the address, though. Ask Marcus.

This thing about blokes thinking they're safe if they are a few miles away cropped up in another job. This particular one had everything: the good, the bad and the ugly; laughs, cock-ups and rose cutters. This guy lived in Brighton and thought that London was a million miles away, but Londoners think that Brighton is round the corner. Anyway, he was a proper nasty little piece of work, this geezer. Proper horrid little junkie. And he owed big money to this guy that owed money to me. He'd borrowed it and then just smoked it all away on fucking crack.

I rang him and I told him it as I saw it: that the guy who owed money to me couldn't pay it because he hadn't been paid by him, this Brighton guy. Now it's a little bit naughty to jump the queue but, in this case, I was going to knock the middle man and go straight to the source. And the reason he wasn't paying the guy who owed me was cos this middle man was a bit of a prat and couldn't do anything about not being paid. And he knew that.

'So before all that happens,' I said, 'you pay the money, cos I've taken the debt and it's me you owe it to. I'm not gonna beat up the prick in the middle for you, like you want me to, just so you can think the debt is wiped out. I'm not falling for that silly little trick.'

He didn't pay. I rang him again. No joy. Then I couldn't get him on the phone. One of my boys went down there for me and found him, rang me on the mobile and handed it to this guy. I said it weren't too far for me to visit his silly little seaside town. He said, 'You ain't coming down here.' I told him that if he carried on trying to humiliate me I would cut his fingers off. 'Oh well,' he went, 'you've got to do what you've got to do.' Oh dear oh dear, I thought. That's just ever so slightly the wrong thing to say. Then to top it all, him and his little gang beat up the fella that had gone down for me.

I'll tell you something now: it ain't good news that travels fast, it's the bad. Good news travels last. Ask Trevor McDonald. *News at Ten* wouldn't have even got to the first bong if it had to rely on good news. And I knew he was proper bragging about having me over on this one. 'You ain't coming down here,' he'd said. So I went down there. Me, Lone Wolf Dave, John, a geezer called H and loads more. Two carloads of us all tooled up. I walked up to the door of the club this guy went to. Now I know, more than anyone, what it's like working the door and I don't like taking trouble to another doorman. So I gave them a choice. I said I'd appreciate it if they'd go in and get him for me but if that was a no-no then I was going in myself. And if they even *looked* like I was gonna get any grief I'd smash them and the place to pieces.

He took one look at us and said, 'Go straight on through.'

The club was jam-packed, absolutely rammed with ravers going mental to this ear-bleeding dance music. So we're all squeezing through this human wall of people, and I'm going, ''Scuse me, mind the bat please, mind the baseball bat, thanks.' There was no way we'd find him, so I decided to make an announcement. I tapped on the glass of the DJ's booth, but he just motioned for me to wait. I tapped again. He ignored me. So I gave the glass one almighty big tap with the bat – *SMASH!* That got me in. I whacked the decks and there was that awful ripping noise when a needle flies across a record. That killed the music stone dead. Silence. Total silence. Five hundred people went from dancing to some rave tune to just standing in dry ice and looking up at this geezer in the booth with a bat resting on his shoulder. I bent down to the microphone.

'I'm looking for Gary Travis.' Everyone looked at each other. 'Is he in the building?' Not a fucking sound. 'Don't tell me no one knows.' Nothing. 'Don't make me put on my Bay City Rollers album.' A kid walked forward and handed me up a piece of paper. I said, 'Thanks, grass,' and we left as quietly as we'd come in.

It was an address up the road. I bounced off the door five times. The cunt had a double-locked firedoor so he must've been used to pissing people off. By the time we got in and ran upstairs I was fucked cos I'd been having an argument with that front door for the last ten minutes. To top it all off, he wasn't there!

Back in London I called a proper meeting. I'd heard now that he was saying some things – that I'd found his missus at his flat and slapped her around, that he was waiting for me and he'd take me on, blah blah blah. Just being as snide and lairy as came natural to him. I found out that he was gonna be at a rave on the pier next week and because he definitely now knew I was on the warpath he would be prepared. So we went down with five carloads this time. Big John, Dave, H, Andy Finlater, Warwick, Northern Billy, Big Mark, Mad Jack and many more too numerous and naughty to mention.

On the way down, I thought, This is a proper little army this is. Fuck Brighton! I want to invade Poland. Straight through France and on, boys!

After I'd made that little threat to him before, I'd started thinking, Well, what if I did lop his finger off? (1) he can't stand up in court and say it cos he thinks of himself as a big gangster and he can't be seen to grass; (2) no one else will care because they know what he's like: he's been terrorising the local community and everyone knows he's got it coming. I knew if he just got a hiding that he'd heal and he'd still owe me the money and still mouth off and lie about me. Like I've said, if you act like a gangster then at some point you'll get called on it and when that call comes you better have something more to fall back on than old Jimmy Cagney dialogue.

Anyway, we found him and after some resistance we won

him over to our point of view. Big John standing on his chest and pinning him to the floor helped. And it just came right off. I'd barely even applied any pressure and – pop – his little finger hit the deck (those rose cutters, though, they are sharp). So that was one little piggy that wouldn't be running all the way home.

And he paid, oddly enough.

I was getting loads and loads of work because I'm not a hidden-away type of character, I'm approachable. And cos I was in the nightclub world, and not walking around growling like a grizzly, I just seemed to end up knowing every fucker! I knew all the firms. I'm not saying I knew every criminal in Britain, but I knew all the key players in the cities. And people like those controlling the football gangs.

Loads of things started to happen. The doorman thing had gone bang! – massive. The debt collecting went berserk (I thought of applying for a Duke of Edinburgh Award). And all these things just naturally led on to other things. Just by being there and doing things properly, things seemed to take off.

I was providing security for just about anything you could think of: concerts, music festivals, nightclubs, outdoor raves, indoor tennis, unlicensed boxing, diamond couriers, sex orgies, fetish parties, street parties, illegal card games with a couple of hundred grand on the table, underworld meetings, bodyguarding film and rock stars, protecting racehorses, patrolling turkey farms at Christmas (don't ask), controlling street parades and New Year's Eve celebrations. I even provided gay-friendly doormen for those kind of clubs and things like the Gay Pride march. It was easy to spot my boys on that day; they were the ones in the turquoise suits asking each other, 'Does my knuckleduster look big in this?'

Because I'd always been out and about so much, meeting people, chatting away, saying 'How d'ya do; *what* do you do?', I got to know an awful lot of people. This had gone on for years, so I'd built up a massive database, for want of a better phrase, of loads of different people who did loads of different things. Mostly friends, friends of friends, colleagues, associates, that kind of thing. It weren't really intentional, but I always did love meeting people. I found that most people have something to offer, something they're good at.

That's where I got the reputation for being the alternative *Yellow Pages*. And if I let my little fingers do the walking, I'd find you doormen, doorwomen, debt collectors, protectors, dodgy tellies, iffy cars, whiffy stereos, moody money, bootleg videos, fake passports, new IDs, fresh birth certificates, snide licences, hideouts, alibis, witnesses, weapons, legal advice, illegal advice, lawyers, loans, loan collection, bent coppers, prostitutes, male escorts, porn films, bank robbers, safe breakers, getaway drivers, cat burglars, dog breeders, light haulage, heavyweight boxers, boxing promoters, DJs, rave dancers, lap dancers, club owners, pub singers, record producers, sculptors, terracotta makers, writers, bikers, mopeds, go-peds, dopeheads, yachts, car lots, bankrupt stock, 'quack' doctors, private nurses, Daimler hearses, gamblers, bookies, bent jockeys, straight bananas and counterfeit luncheon vouchers. I was gonna buy Del Boy's little yellow Reliant Robin van, but there wouldn't've been room to paint that little lot on the side! And articulated lorries are so expensive.

The straight bananas I might've needed some extra time on, but the luncheon vouchers? Oh, just listen to this. My mate had a printer's and he'd print up anything but money. Moody money's a good one to do if you can stand the risk of the amount of bird you'd get for it if you were nicked, but my mate just did things like petrol coupons, cinema vouchers, book tokens, concert tickets, luncheon vouchers and Green Shield stamps. In a roundabout way it was like printing money cos you used these tickets and vouchers to get stuff for free.

Now these things were fakes, but then again they weren't, because he printed them in *exactly* the same way, with the same inks and the same papers as the originals. So I know they're moody, but they're dead real. Anyway, he printed thousands and thousands of Green Shield stamps. I mean, pallet loads. Rows and rows of them. The only hassle now was getting enough books to stick them in. So he just printed his own books.

We went through the catalogue choosing all the stuff we wanted: TVs, stereos, leather three-piece suites, fitted kitchens. Anything we took a fancy to. Some of the stuff for ourselves and some stuff to sell on. I spent ages tearing out the stamps and sticking them in books and, like a silly bastard, I did it by licking them. Couple of hours later my tongue swelled up and stuck to the roof of my mouth, actually fucking stuck there. I had to be rushed to hospital to have my stomach pumped! I'd swallowed something like a quarter of a pint of glue.

So I bought a sponge.

And the luncheon vouchers! He made hundreds of thousands of them. He bought a seventeen grand Mercedes and then sold it to me for thirteen grand. And all with moody luncheon vouchers. You can get luncheon vouchers worth up to £75 each. He'd do twenty-two grand's worth and then sell them to big companies for ten grand. A Mercedes out of luncheon vouchers – get a load of that!

With the tickets he made we went to Wimbledon tennis, football at Wembley and Pink Floyd in concert. Loads of things, cos this was in the days before they started putting holograms and all that crap on the tickets. The geezer made an absolute packet out of it. He now owns hotels. The best thing about it was that when he first started the printer's, the government gave him a grant to set up the business. And then he decided to do that with it. Talk about private fucking enterprise!

Another time a geezer came round my house with ninety-thousand pounds, all the notes coloured half mauve with security dye, and said, 'What can I do with that, Dave?'

I said, 'Buy something off Stevie Wonder.'

He'd been on some job, and when they'd sprung the case, this silver metal attaché case, the security device had gone *boof!* and dyed all the money. He was only a minor player in the job and they'd told him to incinerate it, but he brought it to me. I invited him in.

I got a roll of Sellotape and a pair of scissors, two intravenous drips of black coffee, and we stayed up all night long carefully cutting the notes in half. Then we pushed them together and Sellotaped them. Each half had different numbers, of course, but without spotting that they looked exactly the same. If the notes had all been the same value, all twenties or all fifties, we would've got forty-five grand, but the denominations were all different. Still, by morning we'd made fourteen grand from absolutely fuck all, really.

I had another dyeing experience. How about this one! Another geezer I knew got into ringing horses, same way they do with cars. He opened his own company – about a hundred quid to register the name – and set up as a horse trader. He bought this mega-expensive stud horse, and then declared himself bankrupt so he had to sell the horse for 150 grand. Then he got some old nag that's the same age and build as the stud, and me and him started working on it. And because when you buy a racehorse or a stud horse you get papers with it listing its distinguishing marks (bit like a log book with a car), we knew exactly what to do. Mark a white spot on its tail, make a little nick with a Stanley knife where it's supposed to have a scar on the tendon, and tattoo its ID number inside the ear. Only one problem left: this horse was brown, and the stud was black.

We got these big, thick, black rubber gauntlets, like vets wear. They were a bit like fisherman's waders, but for your hands. We started dyeing the horse black. Every bit of it. We dyed its gums, inside its ears, up its nostrils, the red bits in its eyes, its eyelids, its tail and mane, its body – everything. The bit under the saddle is always shaved short, the hairs are like little pins. So we did that as well. Anyway, we're dyeing this bloody horse for over three hours and getting a real sweat on. When we'd done I took the gloves off and my arms were jet fucking black! What I didn't realise was that those little pins of hair on the saddle bit had pricked through my gloves when I was rubbing the dye in. I couldn't believe it. I scrubbed it and scrubbed it with brillo pads till I bled, but the skin didn't even go pink. Then I scraped it off my fingernails and that just looked worse. It looked awful. Big black hands with white nails. For nearly a month I was walking round like Al fucking Jolson.

The horse ended up being sold in Saudi Arabia, with copies of its papers, for 150 grand. The real stud horse was still over here waiting to be sold to someone else. So some silly Arab's got a gypsy carthorse that originally cost three hundred pounds and it ain't even black. Try finding people to do those kind of things in the ordinary *Yellow Pages*!

12 Getting Away With Murder

I didn't really box that much any more, but I'd have the occasional one now and again. It weren't for money or anything, it was just for the thrill and the entertaining bit – being the centre of attention and all that.

I had this fight one afternoon at an unlicensed event held in a disused warehouse on Old Street. It's the same place where the Aquarium nightclub is now, but then it was just an unused building. As usual, it was a real no-frills affair. Dark and dingy with sawdust on the floor. No hotdog stand, just a trough. On the day there were hundreds of people there. All blokes. A boxing match, especially an unlicensed one, isn't really a place for ladies. It's a proper man's thing. At any one of these events you'd find enough testosterone to power another moon shot. Fuck me, look! The first boxer on the moon, and NASA had nothing to do with it. Three hundred blokes just started shouting, and it fired him up there!

There were so many there, about three or four hundred, that they were hanging off scaffolding and standing on chairs and boxes to see. And when you walk out into this big crowd it's amazing: everyone roaring, the place mostly dark apart from the lights over the ring; and you get nearer and nearer the ring, walking through the crowd, hearing people shout your name. It's fucking electric, the atmosphere. The good thing about it is that all your pals are there to lift you out when you win; the bad thing about it is all your pals are there to see you carried out if you lose. Walking out into the crowd is exciting enough to give you a hard-on, but the thought of losing in front of your mates can drag it out of you a bit.

Now, a lot of people confuse unlicensed boxing with the bare-knuckle, back-alley stuff. It ain't. Joey Pyle was the promoter of this event and, with Roy Shaw, was mostly responsible for unlicensed boxing really taking off in London. He had applied to the British Board of Boxing to go legit, but because of who he was they knocked him back. So he thought, Fuck it, and set up his own anyway. Like you would.

So the unlicensed game started off as an alternative to the licensed one, but because of the characters it attracted it soon went a bit more off-beam. You'd get blokes from all walks wanting to fight, all sorts (and I don't mean Bertie fucking Bassett): football hooligans, hardcases, headcases, nutters, headbutters, over-the-hill boxers, never-even-been-up-the-hill boxers, ex-pros, current pros out to make a few quid, and applause-junkies like yours truly.

Lenny McLean was the most famous one. He weren't the best when it came to technique, but he was ferocious, and that tended to wipe out any technicians. He was a good showman too. I once saw him lean out the ring and grab his opponent by the hair before he'd even got in the ring! That was a sight – Lenny trying to pull a twenty-stone geezer through the ropes by his barnet. By the time the opponent did get in he was mentally destroyed. And half bald. So the unlicensed game became known for Lenny's fights when really a lot of the men were actually just good boxers and fighters. But people always sniff out the blood, don't they? Human nature, I guess, like slowing down to have a good nosey when you pass a big car smash. Other superstars of the game were Fred the Head, Harry Starbuck and, of course, Roy Shaw. Roy was, and still is, a legend.

A lot of pro boxers used to come down from Scotland as well. They'd change their names from Angus McHaggis, or whatever, to something really believable, like John Smith. They were good fighters, but cos you need to be really high up the ladder to make any money in licensed boxing, they could actually make much more doing the unlicensed.

And the rules are more . . . bendable, shall we say, than in the licensed game. You'd get guys of different weights fighting each other or blokes with ten or even twenty years between them. You knew when your opponent had his great-great-grandson as one of his cornermen that you were on a winner. When you touched gloves at the start, the ref would say, 'I want a good clean fight, no low blows or use of zimmer frames!' Well, maybe I'm colouring it up just a little. As my nan used to say, If I've told you once I've told you a *million* times – don't exaggerate!

Anyway, so there I am, in the ring with about thirty of my mates cheering me on. Let's see now, in no particular order of naughtiness, there was Ricky English, Wolfie, Stormin' Norman, Big Ricky, Don, Scotty, 'Hippodrome' Robert, Welsh Bernie, Big Memmy and Jamie Daniels and the rest of the Glasgow crew, Northern Billy, Fat Laurence, Funny Glenn, 'Warehouse' Ron, Tucker, Big Birmingham John, Irish Jim, Steve Raife, Marcus, Louie, Brendan, Fergus and Pat, Danny Dolittle, Ted, Warwick, Robert Hanson, Mick Warrel, Andy Finlater, Colin Robinson and Colin Little, who were two of my old naughty school pals, Ronnie Bridges, who I also went to school with, and, last but not least, Tinky Winky before he went on to bigger and better things in the *Teletubbies*. Listen, the things I could tell you about Tinky (or the Big Wink, as he was known to us). Oh, and (I nearly forgot) Mickey 'Five Holes'! Guess what? Yeah, apart from the ones God first gave him, Mickey had another five holes. Someone shot him that many times while he was in bed. At the time I said to him, 'Mickey, just get a decent fucking alarm clock! Lot less painful, boysie.' My cornermen were Amon Ash, the guy I first started the doorwork with, and Santos.

That happened you see; you brought all your mates along. Because these events weren't advertised it was all through word-of-mouth or mates and pals. In fact, if the police had ever really busted one of these things they would've collared half of London's underworld. And the crowds alone were ferocious enough, so you can imagine what the guys doing the security for the night were like. The word 'gruesome' springs straight to mind. And because there were about five or six bouts on per event, and each of the dozen or so boxers brought thirty or forty mates each, there'd usually end up being more scraps outside the ring than in it. You could've stood with your back to the ring all night and still seen some bloody good rows.

My opponent for the night was Buster 'the Rhino', would

you believe, a big northerner from Scunthorpe. Turns out he was a seaside red coat and he'd brought half of the Butlin's holiday camp down to cheer him on. I took one look at this ugly fucker and thought, If this turns into a knobbly knees contest, I'm completely fucked.

I soon found out why old Buster was called the Rhino. There's me thinking it was cos he had a big nose. Wrong. It was because of the way he charged out and headbutted you. It's a rare occasion when another fighter beats me to the butt, mate, but it was the first fucking thing he did! I thought, God help the poor fuckers at his holiday camp. Hi-de-fucking-hi, indeed!

The bell went, and I returned to my corner. Amon and Santos gave me some advice based on their in-depth boxing expertise. 'Butt the cunt first!' Amon said. Santos nodded. 'Yeah, butt the cunt first.'

As soon as I heard the bell ding for the second I came out like a bullet. Buster had the same idea, though, and we banged together like two stags clashing horns – *wham!!* Because my head was lower down, his forehead smacked right on to my crown. He went down on one knee and the ref started counting. Buster jumped up at the count of 'one', though, far too early. He was still dazed. I laid right into him.

I knocked him around the ring. I could've knocked him out, but I wanted to prolong it and show off. I've never been one of those fighters good enough to do the old 'Ali shuffle' routine, but even I started giving it a bit. It was like a violent version of *Come Dancing*. I only just stopped short of doing a pirouette. Well, you've got to have some restraint. Good job there's no rules against being a cocky bastard, otherwise I'd have been disqualified from half my fights.

Afterwards, I went into The Foresters pub with all my mates. The guv'nors of The Foresters were Dave Thorpe and Tommy Mulholland. They'd sort of sponsor me for some of my fights and I'd have the name of their DIY shop, Decorating Masters, all over my kit. They suggested I even put it on the soles of my boots for when I ended up on the canvas. Cheeky cunts.

I was really buzzing in the pub and buying everyone drinks and champagne and generally having a laugh celebrating. Loads of pals were coming up to congratulate me, slapping me on the back and rubbing my head, that kind of thing. I wasn't showing off in a bad way, I was just getting off on something that I'd achieved. I had won the fight, after all.

Anyway, there was someone else in the place watching all this and taking an instant dislike to me because of it. I'd known this geezer for ten years. Not 'known' him as in we were friends, but knew of him and occasionally ran into him. And in that ten years I don't remember seeing him smile once, let alone laugh.

It wasn't the best kept secret what this guy was. He was a professional hitman, a shootist who lived out in Tenerife. He was a really, really naughty geezer. He was usually only in this country when he'd been brought over to do a job. 'Most everyone in the pub knew that, and he just sat there lapping it up. Then I bounded in with everyone after the fight and he got the right fucking hump at me being the centre of attention. I was stealing his little bit of thunder. Or that's how he obviously saw it. Me? I was just having a good time.

I saw him looking over at me but I didn't want to get into anything, not now when everyone was buzzing, on a high and having a good time. I went out of my way to avoid even making eye contact with him.

I walked away from the bar at one point and went to use the phone. This geezer only followed me over and started putting money in the jukebox right next to the telephone. Now it was obvious something was brewing. I hadn't even finished dialling yet. But I kept it really polite.

I said, 'Do you mind not putting that on for a second while I make a quick call?'

He just looked at me and then carried on pressing the buttons, just to be a pain in the arse, and walked off. Music started blaring out, some Status Quo crap as well, which is offensive enough as it is, never mind the bad manners. I couldn't hear a thing now, so I pulled out the jukebox plug.

I thought he might have something to say about it, but I wasn't expecting what happened: he ran over and went absolutely fucking apeshit, as if he'd just caught me in bed with his wife *and* his bird both at the same time. He started raving at me, 'I'm gonna fucking do you! I don't care who you think you are, I'm gonna kill you. I'll fucking kill you!'

Now, in my walk of life you get that said to you quite a few times, especially when you're working the doors, usually when you have to throw out some pissed-up aggro merchant. Most times it comes to nothing, though I had been shot at outside clubs before. But, when the time comes when someone says it to you and they really mean it, you *know*. You just know they do actually mean it.

People in the pub were trying to calm things down, but I looked at him and I knew what he was doing. By ranting and raving at me and saying those things in public he was doing something that I sometimes do to myself, which is, putting himself in a position where he could not back down. If you make a rod for your own back and tell enough people you're gonna do something, then you have to do it. I know that, so I can see it. Sometimes I can be a big softy (no, really) and let things go that I shouldn't, so I make a point of telling people what I'm going to do and that makes me stick to doing it. And he'd just done that. Even as he'd first started kicking off, I'd been wincing inside thinking, Please don't say what I think you're gonna say. But he did.

Anyway, he was led away from me, but kept looking back and saying I was a dead man. I looked at him and thought, You have just deliberately painted yourself into a corner, mate – you have given yourself a task you know you can't back down from.

Talk about putting a fucking damper on the evening! I tried to make light of it so as not to spoil everyone having a good time, but it weren't no surprise to me when I got home later that night and started getting phone calls from people saying that this guy had been asking about me, trying to find out where I lived, etc.

The next night I was double-aware of everything. Every noise outside the house or any car that pulled up outside. I moved Tracey and the kids to another house where they'd be safe. Then I started getting calls from people I knew who owned pubs and clubs. They'd all heard about this guy and what was going on and asked me not to visit their places in case he tried to shoot me there. They didn't want the risk of being shut down. I thought, Fuck me, this has gone too far. And all over nothing, really.

Now I know this guy would usually pull ten to fifteen grand for a job, but he's gonna do me for free. There's no backer behind him, it's just something very, very personal to him. And obviously being the kind of man you've got to be to do that job, he ain't gonna think twice about it. There's only three things that can happen in a situation like this: (1) hope he don't do it (which I know he will), or if he does do it hope he misses (which I know he won't); (2) run away – which was completely, *totally* right out of the question; and (3) do him first. I ain't gonna hope against hope he has a change of heart cos I know he won't. And I'm not going to wait around until he tries to shoot me just to give me a reason to shoot back. I wouldn't have got the chance anyway. I certainly ain't gonna run away, never in a million years, and I'm not going to live in fear of something happening to me or my family. I now knew it was only a matter of time before he got to me. So all I'm left with is what anyone in their right mind would consider an act of self-defence.

On the chosen night, I visited a certain nightclub. I knew I'd be filmed on the security cameras going in. After a while I left by the fire exit, drove round to this guy's, shot him before he shot me, and went back to the club. At the end of the night I left by the front entrance.

Eight the next morning the police came round and arrested me. It was common knowledge what the guy had been saying. The police have one of the biggest grapevines in the world, next to the underworld's. There was no evidence against me. It was all down to whether I grassed myself up or not. Well, that was a big 'not' in my book. And because I said 'no comment' to everything, they charged me.

I did some time on remand. I didn't tell them what proof I had. When I went to court I just produced the video from the club which showed the date and time and me entering and leaving, and the witnesses that saw me in there.

Not guilty.

When I came out there were loads of reporters there waiting for me. After the Chinese waiter thing, the *Bermondsey Boy* documentary, the fact that I was known to visit the Krays and all the nightclub things that had happened like the big raid on The Arches, I was quite high profile and fair game for the press. The reporters all crowded 'round and asked me if I did it. I couldn't resist.

'Yeah, 'course I done it,' I said.

I knew, by law, you couldn't be charged twice for something you've been acquitted for. I thought, You want something to write about then I'll *give* you something to write about. Me just being cocky again, I guess.

That little admittance was a bit of a bombshell, to say the least. Talk about 'Hold the front page!' They had a fucking field day with that one. I was even more high profile now. They already had me down as a Kray-twin associate, controller of one of London's biggest security firms with hundreds of doormen, and now as a self-confessed killer. You could say that my application to become a registered childminder was in serious jeopardy. It publicly set the standard for me being seen as a right cocky bastard, or a flash cunt, or, as Freddie Foreman said, a cheeky monkey – whichever of those you want to use. 'Cheeky monkey' was a bit of a fucking under-statement, though. (That was the last thing you would've expected a chap like Freddie Foreman to call you.)

The police requested the pleasure of my company down at the station after that little thing on the court steps. I went along willingly. I'd nothing to hide. They just couldn't get their head around why I'd said it.

'What did you get out of it?' the interviewing officer said to me. 'I can't see what you'd get out of that.'

Again, I couldn't resist the wind-up. I said, 'Well, you must be blind cos I thought it was fucking excellent!'

That didn't go down well. During that talk at the station it was made quite plain to me in no uncertain terms, and by a senior police officer, that from now on they would be on my case for as long as it took for them to bang me up. So now I knew I'd have to be double alert for the Old Bill, as well as any fucker that wanted to shoot me. Sometimes it just never rains but an elephant pisses on you.

Anyway, what had been done just had to be done. That seems an awful thing to admit to: killing a man. But from the very beginning of my career, when things started to get really serious, I made a conscious decision. I decided that I would never do anything that I couldn't justify. Right from debt collecting for unpaid Tupperware to topping someone. Because as well as having to live with your family and friends and what they think of you, you also have to live with yourself. People on the outside of it all just don't know the score and probably never will. They only know what you read in the papers. And often the papers don't let the truth get in the way of a good story. But the people in my business knew the score with this guy. Even the police did; they ain't stupid. They knew what had been said and who he was and what he was capable of.

I know, because I know me, that if I had to shoot someone there would be a fucking good reason for it. And I'd be risking a fifteen stretch for it, but I would do that. I would risk that and even live with the fifteen if I got it because I know that if it had got to that stage then there must be no other option: my life or my family's lives were in danger. And all because of some geezer's jealousy in a pub one night. But, as they say, there's nothing so queer as folk. Apart from gay elephants.

So, that really put the cat among the canaries, the old 'of course I did it' routine. That well and truly shot my name into the headlines. Typical – not one word about my many good deeds for charity. Like all the work I'd been doing with unmarried mothers, for instance.

I didn't let it get me down, though. If at first you don't succeed – so much for skydiving . . .

Around this time I got into the acting game and started getting quite a bit of work as an extra through Lesley, the agent at Central Casting. I'd already done TV work, but then I moved on to films. The pay was better, and the grub, but the hours lousy. It's all waiting around, that's what film sets are. Hours of waiting for a few minutes' doing. Plenty of lights, plenty of cameras, but not much fucking action.

I was in *Chicago Joe and the Showgirl*. Emily Lloyd and Kiefer Sutherland starred in that. I didn't know, until I was talking to Emily Lloyd on the set one day, that her old man is the one who plays Trigger in *Only Fools and Horses*. *Bullseye!*, that was an old-style British comedy with two old-style stars: Roger Moore and Michael Caine. As big a star as he was, Michael Caine didn't run off to his dressing room after filming like some of them do. He hung around and chatted to everyone. Nice geezer. The director was Michael Winner. Now he's different, for want of a better word.

I was also an extra on the set of *Hamlet*. That weren't too pleasant. Stood around under the lights in a suit of armour, sweating your bollocks off while Mel Gibson fucks his lines up. Well, he weren't fucking his lines up, to be fair, but they were just coming out a bit too Australian. And call me old-fashioned, but that don't really suit William Shakespeare. Anyway, this went on and on and I thought, I'm gonna faint here and look a right proper cunt. He fluffed the next line as well. I flipped the visor back on my helmet.

'For fuck's sake, Mel,' I said, 'get it right this time, I'm close to fainting!' I thought he'd take it as a joke.

'Get him *off* the set!!' he shouted.

I was escorted away, but I shouted back, 'No need to get so mad, Max!'

Silly. Anyway, I nicked the outfit on the way out. I decided to keep it on. Bit of a bastard getting into a taxi in a full suit of armour, though. Best thing was, this blindin' cabbie didn't even bat an eye. 'Where to, mate?' he went. 'Tower of London?'

But the best ones were the big battle scenes. The casting agent would call me cos she knew I'd bring loads of the boys down to make up the numbers. I'd take fifty or sixty doormen down to Pinewood studios. We'd take off our dinner suits and put on these metal ones. This one time we went down to be soldiers in *Henry V* and do scenes in the Battle of Agincourt. Kenneth Branagh, this film starred, so at least the accent wasn't the wrong side of the world. Me and loads of the lads went down, still buzzing from working the door the night before and having proper fights. And then the film people gave us swords and said, 'Go fight!' We were like, 'Yes! We will not be defeated!' even though we were supposed to be on the losing side. They put all these special concealed arrows on you. Each one is set on a timer. When the timer goes off the arrow pops out so quick it looks like you've been shot.

Brian Blessed, who was acting in the film, was also directing this bit. Well, you know what he's like, don't you? A big, bearded geezer with a voice like a whale farting through a megaphone. A real theatrical fella. So we're all running through the smoke and flames and Brian Blessed's being pushed around on this camera on railway tracks through the grass, and music's blasting out of these big speakers. Suddenly, my arrow went *ping!* and popped out. I thought, Fuck that, I'm not being dead, and snapped it off. There's smoke everywhere and you really think you're fighting. Or was that just me and the boys? We laid a fair few out, though. We were really giving it some. Fuck me, it was fun.

Until the music cut off. Everyone stopped, and this massive voice boomed out, 'YOOU BOY!!' Everyone seemed to look at me. Brian Blessed shouted again, 'YESS! YOU!' I thought, He cannot mean me! 'This is the year *four*teen *fif*teen!' he said. 'And they didn't wear *fucking* Rolex watches!!'

Yeah, it *was* me. Cunt. I'd decided not to take the Rolex off earlier cos I didn't fancy leaving it in the changing area. So I'm stood there with all the lights shining on me and Brian fucking Blessed being wheeled towards me on this little camera train. I thought, I might as well just stab him straight through the heart now!

Robin Hood – Prince of Thieves, that was another one. Or 'Grown Men in Tights', as we called it. Kevin Costner was in this one. Another accent that was only a few thousand miles off the mark. I took about thirty mates with me to this one. We all stripped down to our pants and queued up for uniforms. The girl handing them out looks up at the next in line and says, 'Saxon,' and he gets his kit. Then the next guy, she gives a quick look – 'Saxon.' Next – 'Saxon.' 'Saxon, Saxon, Saxon.' Then I step up. 'Peasant.'

I said, 'You what? I ain't being a fucking peasant.'

'You're not tall enough for a Saxon.'

'Get me a bloody box, then,' I said. 'I am *not* being a peasant.'

Anyway, she made me be a peasant. I didn't wanna be a Saxon anyway, really. Bastards.

Then I was in *The Krays* film. Had to happen really, didn't it? Not that I believe in typecasting, of course. I did like to test myself now and again and play someone who *couldn't* shoot. But fuck me if in this I didn't end up playing John 'Mad Dog' Mangan! I'd actually run into the old geezer in the prison hospital a while back during the Junction 13 thing.

Batman was a good one. I played a policeman as well. I was stood next to Jack Nicholson on that gantry when he gets thrown down into a vat and turns into the Joker. Jack Nicholson was another big star who was normal and down to earth, just chatted and had a laugh. Not that they shouldn't be like that, but a lot of them act like it's beneath them.

I think the only thing beneath Jack was this little dancer he picked up one night when me, him and a mate of mine all went out drinking. That was a proper good night out. We knocked back plenty of bubbly and tore the ends off a fair few cigars that night. Then he went off to his hotel, grinning and laughing. What a fucking excellent geezer. And one of the few who was actually taller than you expected.

One guy who was smaller than you might expect, because his reputation was so big, was Frankie Fraser. I'd met Frankie lots of times over the years when our paths crossed. Frankie was known for having spent over forty years in prison. It was different times then. Doing a lot of bird was seen as proof you were hard, which everyone knew about Frankie anyway. He was a legendary character and more of a figurehead now, but through knowing him, and the older premier division chaps like Joey Pyle and Freddie Foreman, it came about that I visited Reggie Kray and got to know him very well.

Reg and Ronnie Kray had been inside for the best part of twenty years with no sign of getting released. They'd been given life sentences with a recommendation of a minimum thirty years. But life very, very rarely means life and thirty-year terms aren't often served either. It was a fucking outrage they'd been in so long and would likely be in even longer. I know what you might say, that they were both done for murders and all that, but we've all read about people who've done the same and been let out after ten or fifteen years, even child murderers released back out on to the streets only to do it again. And people who've killed what you might call 'civilians' as well. The twins had done in a couple of villains, which ain't denigrating those men's lives, but they knew the risks of the kind of life they led. In a few years' time Reg and Ron would be sixty years old – what kind of threat they were supposed to be I just don't know. It just goes to show how notoriety and infamy can go against you. Everybody knows they were only kept in because they were 'The Krays'.

I did benefit-show boxing matches for Reggie and Ronnie as part of the campaign for their release. It was something I continued to do for years, and I considered it a privilege to be part of that.

I first went to visit Reg when some problem arose outside and it was gonna lead to someone getting hurt. It'd started with a fight and then a few reprisals and could've quickly got out of hand. Reggie heard about it and knew one of the blokes involved. He didn't want him to get hurt. He'd also heard a bit about me and must have thought I was someone he could talk to. Which I took as a great compliment cos Reg and Ron were really the figureheads of that old-style villainy where honour and class had meant something.

We had a really good meeting, and Reg said he hoped I might be able to smooth over the aggro that had been brewing. I think when you've been around a bit and seen as much as he had, you realise what's worth fighting for and what's not. And I suppose when you've been inside for so long you've got all the time in the world to think about how things should be.

Anyway, the bother did end up getting sorted out without any more casualties.

The next thing that happened to me, funnily enough, was one of those situations, those little troubles that escalate into pretty fucking big ones. But it was one of those that couldn't be smoothed over no matter how you looked at it.

13 Once Bitten

Funny how friendships can turn. One minute you're on good terms with a bloke, the next he's bitten your nose off. Don't you just hate it when that happens?

It came about through doormen trouble, really, among other things, but that was it mostly. When you have fifty to sixty working for you, and you've personally vetted them, then you know them and you can go round the clubs and see them. But when it starts to grow, as it had, and you've got three hundred people working for you, then half of them you don't know. At its height it grew to five, six hundred, and this is what led to them being called 'the biggest body of muscle' in London. Every time my name was in the papers they dredged that little phrase up. It made it sound like there was a colossal, sixty-foot hardnut stomping around the streets and crushing cars with his feet.

The way it had grown was like this: it had gone from first me, then me and my mates, then me and loads of my mates, and then others until it was mates of mates. But if there were four on the door I could at least say that two of them were known personally to me; the others I didn't know but they knew the standard I expected. Because if there's a fight down the club and the doormen beat up two blokes, the two geezers don't go away and say Steve, Charlie, Fred and Harry beat us up, they say Courtney's boys did it. So you get the credit *and* the blame for a lot of things that are fuck all to do with you. Because you're the one in charge. And being in that position brings everything down on you. If one of your men gets shot, for instance, he can't do anything about it cos he's got a big hole in him so everyone says, 'What you gonna do about it, Dave?' I'm thinking, Wait a minute – I wasn't even there! At least fill me in on exactly what did happen so I can decide. Do we lie down? Do we cause a ripple?

So decisions came down to me that weren't really in my plans. I'd always wanted to earn a few quid, get on, meet people, have a laugh, enjoy what I was doing and where it was taking me and get the perks. But I didn't foresee the full extent of the problems it brings.

Don't get me wrong, I ain't having a moan, cos I could have got out any time I wanted. Most people con themselves that they don't have any choices in life – do this, work here, marry her, buy this, get tied up with loads of crap you don't want. But you're a lot more free than you think. The only thing you have to do, the only thing you have absolutely *got* to do, is die. Everything else is window dressing.

There were times when other security firms came in to try to undercut me, but I weren't gonna get into the old doorman-wars syndrome. I might have lost a contract but as long as I could place my boys who'd lost their jobs on another door somewhere else and keep them in work, that was my only concern. And I knew that the money the venue was saving by employing a cheaper firm wouldn't seem like a good saving. In the long run they always came back to me. Quality isn't always the cheapest bet, but it's the best one.

Sometimes doormen left other firms to come and work for me and someone would get the hump and say I was nicking them, but it weren't like that. I never sought them out, they came to me. Because I looked after my blokes. If they did get in trouble I'd get them the best barristers; if they went to prison I looked after their families. So they felt a sort of allegiance to me to be good and behave and do things proper. And they felt that way for the right reason – cos I looked out for them – and not for the wrong reason, like because they were afraid of me. In work, having someone afraid of you is the worst way to get the best out of anyone.

I looked at my outfit as more like a bunch of freemasons than hardnuts. If one of my doormen was a plasterer during the day, I'd get him work from people I knew who needed plastering done. Or if he was a car salesman I'd buy my cars from him. It made everyone feel there was some unity.

I think that way of doing it just came about so naturally because that's where I'd started out, on the door, and I'd just loved it and loved hanging around with the fellas, and everything that went with it. And they could see that in me. They knew I was one of them and I'd never dream of acting like I wasn't.

Whenever I got a new door contract I'd always work the first few nights myself with my fellas. Sometimes we'd turn up and the manager left it till that night to tell the other doormen they were sacked. Because he hadn't dared do it before. We would turn up not knowing this and the manager would use us as back-up. So through no fault of mine that led to some fights.

Apart from the new contracts I didn't really do the doors as much as I used to. There was the odd time when some club would ring me up and say the police had just taken all their doormen away, so you have to go do your bit. But when you're running so many men there is a hierarchy, there has to be, that's how you run things. And that's the basis that people are done on when they're nicked; as a lieutenant, a sergeant or the colonel.

I'd known this geezer Alan for some time. We were actually good mates. Then things started to go wrong. First of all, his brother started going out with an old girlfriend of mine and, for some reason, this caused friction. Not from me, I didn't care, but it did from the other side. There was an element of the doormen contract thing in all this as well, but that ended up getting a little more personal. It just got out of hand and he took any excuse to hate my guts. Any excuse. There was a million other little things involved, each one not too niggly on its own, but they all amounted to too much. Difficult to pinpoint which exact straw was responsible, but the camel was definitely in intensive care.

I went to see him in a pub one night. I went over to have a chat and told him to knock it on the head. He wasn't in the mood to be reasonable and started accusing me of this, that and the other. I left with nothing happening. Afterwards I heard he was saying that the reason he didn't do me was because I was carrying a gun, which is a lie. Everyone knows that my chosen weapon is the knuckleduster. In time I became known for it. I swear by them. They've helped me even the odds against much bigger guys than I would have beaten ordinarily. Some people carry knives and guns. I'm a firm believer in only carrying the tool that you're prepared to do the time for. And I know myself from experience, on the occasion when it's been necessary for me to carry a shooter, what they do to you psychologically. The feeling of power it gives you is immense. You burn with it. You feel untouchable because you nearly are. In that situation it's too easy for something that would've been just a fist fight to get well out of hand. When that red mist comes down, people just lose it. That's why in America, people end up shooting each other over an argument about a garden hedge or whose dog shat on whose lawn.

Anyway, the next time I saw him, we bumped into each other in a nightclub up the West End. We made eye contact on the way in. If we hadn't have done that I would've swerved the confrontation because I was with my missus and he was with his. But when I got in he started kicking off, throwing ashtrays on the floor at me and then taking his coat off to prepare for a row.

I walked over and said, 'What's the problem?'

He started squaring up to me, and said, 'If my missus wasn't here I'd kick the shit out of you!'

She was clinging to his arm for dear life, nothing more than eight stone, including her handbag.

I said, 'Look, Alan. You're eighteen stone. If you want to take a swing at me your missus ain't going to stop you, same as my missus ain't gonna be able to stop me. The reason you're not throwing a punch is cos you know I'll throw one right fucking back.'

Out of respect for the doormen working the club I didn't want to end up rolling around fighting on their floor. I told Alan to arrange a place where we could fight without his wife being able to restrain him.

'And,' I added, 'bring a few of your pals because I don't want you saying later that I jumped you from behind with a load of my mates.'

Next Saturday night I got a phone call from him saying that he'd arranged a venue for the next day. It was in this large beer garden behind The Royal Court pub at the back of the Old Kent Road. He worked down the Old Kent Road as a doorman at The Frog and Nightgown and he had a lot of doormen working for him as well. Because of this dispute between us, a lot of his doormen were fighting with mine. It was escalating. I thought, I can mend it once and for all with this geezer and solve the little war that's brewing.

On the Sunday morning I woke up to a beautiful, sunny day. You were probably reading the Sunday papers over cornflakes and trying to shut out the noise the kids were making or staggering in from a club with a thick head. Lucky bleeder. Me? I was preparing for a fight to the death. That might sound a bit heavy on the drama, but I knew it was true.

I knew it because I knew him and what he was like. And he knew me. We both knew how far we'd go. It had got to the point where I might have to kill somebody in front of nearly two hundred witnesses. Or he might do me. If I ended up spark out I knew he'd carry on giving me a kicking. Against a much bigger bloke I needed all the edge I could get, and the two brass lumps in my pocket would do it. The knuckledusters would help as well.

Now if you're ever going to get involved in anything which is a bit scary, what you don't want is time to *get* scared. Y'know, time to think about it. Well, I had all fucking day to do nothing else. If a fight kicks off right next to you, you might have to defend yourself, but because of the speed of it you could be up against my mate Nigel Benn and you wouldn't give a fuck cos you ain't had time to. If you did have time you'd realise that Nigel Benn would hammer you like a tent peg.

Now I'm not gonna tell you about the time me and Nigel were running together on a beach in Tenerife while he was training for a title fight and half a dozen Brits decided to take the piss out of us. They started throwing sand and other stupid stuff. To cut a long story short, I ended up standing side by side with Nigel Benn and having it big-time with a contingent of 18–30s. If I said I wasn't trying my best to show off in front of Nigel I'd be lying, and from what I could see he weren't doing too badly himself. If he keeps it up he could be quite good at it. Not only is he one of my closest friends, but he's also the best boxer I've ever had the privilege to lay eyes on, and one of the best DJs as well. Oops, I weren't gonna tell you about it, was I? Sorry, Nige (and hello to Caroline and the kids).

But like I say, what I'd learnt and used during debt collecting was that what you *imagine* is usually worse. In this case, that didn't actually turn out to be true. This had to be the exception to the fucking rule, didn't it?

So all my pals started coming round. Carloads of them, until there's sixty or seventy geezers in my house. It ended up with them shoulder to shoulder in the hall, in the living room, on the stairs, even outside in the bloody garden. I had to put a few up on the roof. Tracey was flying round making sandwiches and bringing tea and biscuits. She said, 'There seems to be an awful lot coming round today, Dave . . .'

Now, my policy with my missus is this: if there's a need to worry, babe, then I'll say worry; if there isn't, then I won't. Simple as that. It ain't an easy life being a woman in this particular walk of life. This was my way of protecting her from the pressures of living with me. I wouldn't tell her anyway, as it happened, even if there was something to worry about. Ignorance isn't always bliss, but you know what they say about a little knowledge. Tracey knew I was going to have a row with somebody, but as far as she was concerned I was just going for a relatively harmless afternoon punch-up. Albeit with nearly seventy other blokes! A lot of the lads were tooled-up, and five or six had shooters. It might turn into a bit more than a spectator sport. I mean, the fight's just me and the other geezer, but if he ends up jumping up and down on my head and veins are popping out, then my boys will jump in to try to save me. And if it's the other way round, then his boys will do the same.

Eventually we set off. Tracey stood at the gate, not realising the severity of the occasion, calling after me, 'Bring back some milk, love, if you don't forget.' And I'm waving back, smiling, and giving her the thumbs up, thinking, What the *fuck* am I doing?

One thing that cracked me up, though, was my old mate, Marky Mark. Some of the boys were tooled-up and Marky, who was sat next to me, went for the lump in his jacket, and what did he pull out but a fucking camera! I said, 'Nice to see you've come prepared. But if you expect me to say "cheese" in the middle of the fight, you can fuck off.'

There must have been over a dozen motors leaving my house that day. All bumper to bumper like a president's procession.

Sun bouncing off the bonnets and seventy of London's naughtiest crammed inside. I'm at the head of the line in that Daimler Princess hearse of mine with everyone in the back on the bench seats.

It was strange, though, this massive procession of ours. It even felt like that to me and I was part of it, so fuck knows what it looked like to anyone that saw us pass. And with there being a hearse at the head of it I imagined they thought, Poor bugger, but *fuck me* he was popular! It probably looked like the annual seaside outing of the local Mafia. We didn't even stop for red lights, just drove on through. Onwards and forwards! Felt a bit bad when we flattened the nun, though. But she was on a zebra crossing, silly cow; it was like camouflage.

Living as I did in Peckham, it was close to a half-hour drive to The Royal Court, which gave me even more time to think about it. Half of me was going *argggbh!* and growling to psyche myself up, and the other half was saying, 'You're a proper silly cunt for getting into this.'

When we pulled up there was a big crowd outside. On the way in we were stopped on the door to be searched. I was outraged. I said, 'You're fucking joking, aren't you? You're just privileged to be here to watch this, don't start telling me what I can and can't do!'

The geezer looked at me and said, 'Sorry. But he's out the back waiting for you and he's clean.'

Well, what could I say? I handed over the dusters, and that's my edge gone. We walked through the bar and by now the adrenalin's pumping through me. The lads were all around me as we walked through. When we came out the back into the beer garden they split open and I came out from the middle. That's when I saw Alan.

He was standing on the stones in the centre of this circle of about 150 spectators. He was wearing a boxer's bollock-guard, tracksuit bottoms, a sports vest, oil all over his upper body *and* he'd only gone and shaved his head! I thought, Talk about being well fucking prepared. He looked drugged up as well, stood there growling like a grizzly bear with piles. At this point, I must admit, in all honesty, I suddenly felt a burning desire to return some library books which were long overdue.

Things were most definitely *not* going according to plan. He was all pumped up and looking like an even uglier version of Arnold Schwarzenegger with a red-hot poker up his arse, and there was me, the posey bastard that I am, dressed like I'm going to a nightclub. Sharp threads, jewellery, aftershave – the lot! Well, you've got to have some standards, haven't you? I mean, come on, tracksuit bottoms and a vest? I ask you. I wouldn't be seen fucking *dead*.

It kicked off and we went at each other. And this is a weird thing – throughout the whole fight there was quiet. Not loads of shouting and cheering-on like you'd think. Just silent, like you'd think it'd be at an execution. Which made every whack, clump, kick and butt seem even worse because you got the full-on sound effect. And it ain't that comic-book noise you hear in the films neither, it's the real thing.

He rushed me and I side-stepped and gave him a big crack in the face. He swung back and clipped me, and I stuck a left in his gut and caught him across the eye with a right as I moved away. He was a big geezer, so I knew if he grabbed me I was fucked; it'd turn into a rolling-on-the-floor wrestling match. Which, with his weight, I didn't want. But cos I was smaller than him I was quicker. We started trading punches, boxing the stomach, and a few clumps in the mouth. I caught him a kick on the knee and he buckled a bit and I got in some proper whacks to the head.

I was winning, and getting proper cocky about it too, and this was infuriating him. Everyone was still silent. All the crowd just became a blur, but we were fighting in this weird quiet. This made him worse cos there was nothing for him to feed off. He lunged at me and grabbed for my arms. There was a real crack when I butted him away, but he came straight back, grabbed me by both shoulders and ran towards me! Now I had these fucking leather-soled shoes on and I just started backpedalling and slipping until we both fell over. With me underneath.

With him on top of me it was like being under the full weight of a Mini with the wheels off. I knew all the pushing and struggling in the world wasn't gonna get this cunt off me. So we ended up locked, with him holding my hands. We couldn't throw punches, either of us, so we resorted to butting each other. And to cap it all, he had the breath of a bear as well, and I was getting the full blast.

So we'd now locked horns on the ground, both burning up energy in the struggle and practically sagging against each other with tiredness. Then he said something which puzzled me enough to stay in my head for years. He looked up over my head, then back down at me. Quietly, he said, 'Sorry, Dave,' and clamped his jaws around my nose and bit down hard. His teeth pierced into the bone and blood began pouring into me, filling my mouth. The pain was just in-fucking-credible. So much that it wipes out all your thoughts. It was real, white-light pain. Like an electric shock, but one that I had to have for *thirty* seconds.

It entered my mind to say, 'No more! No more!' I did genuinely think that, but something in me just wouldn't let me do it. The natural reaction was to pull my face away, and when I did, his teeth snapped over the bone and cut right through the flesh. It sounded like ripping paper. I actually heard his teeth clack shut and saw these snotty strings of skin between them! The end of my nose was now behind his teeth, on his tongue. He turned and spat it out, and I saw the blood spray after it. I was thinking, *That's my fucking nose, that is!*

The sheer agony made me lash out. I ripped a hand free and punched him with everything I had left. One of my fingers punctured his eye and sank in the socket, popping the eyeball out. Blood spurted out all over me. He screamed and flew back like he was on elastic. His hand went to my face to push himself off me and I bit a chunk out of that as well.

He was standing now – well, staggering – and holding his eye on his cheek. I could see the tendons it was hanging on and all this white and green snot with it. When I stood up I saw one of the weirdest things of my life: I saw double. And I mean no fuzziness, no blurry bits, just a perfect, exact, crystal-clear double image of the geezer. I thought, Wow! This is fucking amazing – two ugly bastards. I thought, Trust him to bring a mate. He could've told me he had a twin, the slippery bastard! So now I didn't know which one to go for. When I lifted my leg to move forward it was trembling, and I wasn't sure if it would take my weight. My eyes were streaming from the pain of the nose going, but I moved forwards. I spread my arms out so I could get whichever one of him was real, and we bashed together again.

We threw a few more punches and started rolling about and he bit me again, taking a lump out of my ear. I thought, This is definitely the last time I fight a man before dinner. I was almost expecting knives and forks to be thrown into the circle. We already looked like we were covered in ketchup.

By now we'd both run out of steam, and breath, and everything else. I couldn't have blown the cobwebs off a nun's crotch if my life depended on it. Everyone dived in and started pulling us apart, and I heard a shout of 'Old Bill!' And that was it. Game over.

As I was walking around I could see the shock in people's faces, just real horror. They'd come to see some fisticuffs, so to speak, and ended up witnessing a cannibals' tea party.

The fight had lasted about six minutes, which might not sound a lot, but when you're going at it all-out it's a long fucking time, believe me.

My lads led me away, and his did the same. Steve Bogart picked my nose off the stones and wrapped it in a hankie. First time anyone else but me has picked my nose, come to think of it. All the chaps were with me, of course. And here, at the risk of sounding like someone giving an acceptance speech at the Oscars, I must name-check those who deserve thanks: Ricky English, Lenny Lucas, Robert Hanson, Norman, Neil, Warren, Brendan and, of course, Steve, who had my nose in his top pocket.

Before I knew it, we were in a car and off to hospital. Some pain is so bad that it numbs you to it, kind of cancels itself out. But I was still getting these stabs of pain that made my eyes float. We set off for King's College Hospital. (I later heard that Alan was taken to Queen Mary's to have his eye pushed back in.)

Steve was driving us, and he was pretty upset, actually. Because it was his car and I was getting blood all over his lovely, grey velour upholstery. Steve said, 'I wouldn't look in any mirrors if I was you, Dave.' I flipped the passenger sunvisor down and saw the gaping hole where my nose used to be. The wound was so deep the blood was black. It was one of those strange situations where, even though you're involved, you almost feel like you're on the outside looking in cos things are just too weird to believe sometimes.

At King's they sent for a dentist to stitch me back together. Apparently, dentists are called in to do some of the most delicate, intricate stitching. I wondered if he'd recognise the teeth marks and realise what had happened. As Steve stood there unwrapping my nose from this little bundle in his pocket, it did remind me of when I used to go to kids' parties and, on the way out, remember, you'd get a bit of cake in a napkin. I don't know if it was the pain making me light-headed.

The doc stitched my nose back on, but the nostril just kept caving in. They decided to put some corrugated material underneath and lay the flap of skin over it and stitch it, and then do the same underneath; more skin and more stitching. There was no blood in it, no flexibility or life. But I thought, Well, there are worse places to get bitten and lose all feeling. Can't say I ever had an orgasm while blowing my nose, to be honest. So I ended up laid up in bed for three days receiving the usual bedside visits, grapes, Lucozade, death threats, etc.

I was given the message that a threat had been rung in from the other side. Straight away some of my boys came round and mounted a 24-hour vigil. They were carrying shooters in case they had to defend me. And I love 'em for that; that they would do that and risk everything that goes with it, just to help me.

At this time, I was starring in the BBC programme *The Paradise Club*, playing the minder of old Dirty Den himself, Leslie Grantham. The series was going well and I was getting recognised and what-have-you, so when news of the fight broke, I had the press and police all over me. The story was tabloid heaven: ex-*EastEnders* star, ex-con, the BBC and cannibalism all rolled together in one bloody story! It made the front page of the *Sun*: TV TOUGH GUY IN PUB BRAWL: NOSE IS SLICED BY BITE! Subtle as ever. They used 'before' and 'after' photos of me as well: 'before' looking my usual gorgeous self, and 'after' with a face-full of bandages looking like a wounded rhino. Some said they couldn't tell one from the other. Cheeky monkeys. They even brought up the Chinese swordfight story from ten years previous, again. Christ, I thought, you make *one* mistake . . .

The Old Bill came round to make a few enquiries. They

knew me by now, so they must have known what I was going to say. Maybe, after the publicity, they just wanted a good nosey. Which was more than *I* could give them. Anyway, we went through the usual Q and A. When they asked me who had done it, I said I'd been bitten by a dog.

The younger copper said, 'If you want us to protect you, you're going to have to do better than that. Who was it?'

Now, I've just been through one of the hardest fights of my life, had my nose bitten off, my ear nibbled, bitten off another man's finger, popped his eye out, and I've now got to suffer Dixon of Dock Green at my bedside. Pointless him even asking, anyway. No one grasses no one else up ever. Ever. Not if you're a proper one. Whether it's someone who's cheated at Scrabble or just tried to fucking top you. No exceptions, no excuses. I stuck with the dog story, but they weren't having it and were still offering me protection.

I looked up off the pillow. 'I think it's highly unlikely the dog will find this ward, officer, don't you? It wasn't fucking Lassie!' That put an end to it.

Eventually, things were sorted out between me and Alan. The outcome of the fight was rated as a draw. I'd usually have doubts about that kind of verdict but, to be honest, it was as close as you could get. So the result was 'even', and we got three stars in the *Good Food Guide*.

In the end, though, I did get those doormen contracts.

The one who'd brought the camera, Marky Mark, worked for *Auto Trader*, going around taking snaps of cars for the adverts. The film in the camera was already half full of Sierras and Fiestas, so he just finished it off on the fight. Then he took it to the chemist's to be developed as normal. I wouldn't have minded being a fly on the wall when that little roll of film came out the machine. It went from photos of cars to two blokes making a meal of each other. They must've thought, Fuck me! They *did* disagree about the price of that Escort!

Best of all, though, was when I was still in the hospital and Tracey came to visit me. On the way out she was pounced on by some journalists looking for a quote. And did she give them one. She's just left me with my nose only just stitched back on, a chunk out my ear and my face bandaged like a mummy.

'How is your husband, Mrs Courtney?' one of them asked.

'Well,' Tracey said, 'he just looks his normal self.'

That was such a good little joke she made that, even though it was one of them situations where it genuinely hurt to laugh, when I heard what Tracey had said it was worth the pain.

But Tracey, like any mother, knows all about pain cos a few months later she was in labour for the third time. I was there, like I'd been at all my kids' births, doing my bit, holding the mop and bucket and mucking about as usual.

I said to one of the nurses, 'I do hope this one's human – I couldn't live with another alien!' That went down well.

And we had another beautiful girl. Well, not so beautiful when she first appeared, but then all babies look like Winston Churchill chewing a wasp, don't they? She was gonna be another classy addition to the Courtney clan, so we named her after a classy area of London. Battersea.

Stop it! Only joking, you silly sausages! We called her Chelsea, of course.

Battersea was her middle name.

14 Fighting Talk

OK, while you're listening, I might as well make myself useful and give you the benefit of my experience. So, if you're gonna have a row, here's some tips.

There's two kinds of trouble: the unexpected and the kind you know is going to happen and can plan for. The first one is the most usual. Now, in this case, the best policy is to try and smooth things over, if possible. A bit of humour can work wonders and it's always better to make a friend than an enemy. In my life enough trouble came my way without me going out looking for it on top. That's just silly, to do that, and the law of averages says the more fights you have, the chance of you coming a cropper increases.

Personally, I'd never swerve one if it meant losing face or respect. That ain't worth it, or it wasn't to me, anyway. You might be different, and that's all right. If someone's giving you verbal grief and you really don't give a toss what they think, fine. You can walk away thinking to yourself, Well, that prat obviously mistook me for someone who gives a flying fuck what he thinks.

Regret is a bad thing, though. You see what most people don't know is that the fear of clumping someone (and getting a clump back) is much worse than the actual reality. And the ones who know that work off that fear. I used that policy myself in the debt collecting. A physical bruise, though, heals much quicker than a mental one.

Be nice. It's easy. Don't be all lairy and risk offending someone for no good reason. Especially if you can't back it up. Some bodybuilders, not all of them by any means but some of them, go down the gym cos they're small inside and they think the bigger they look the safer they are. And those ones get ripped apart. Which is another golden rule: don't let your mouth write cheques that your talent can't cash. You'll just end up getting a bigger hammering than Jesus's hands.

If a row does look like it's inevitable, then smile. That's right – smile. Worst thing you can do is start growling cos then the other bloke's defences go up. What I always did was this: I'd smile at the geezer and motion to him that I wanted to have a quiet word in his ear; usually he'd relax a little and turn his head to hear what I had to say (believe me, the number of times . . .). Then he's presenting his jaw to you on a plate, and *wham!* Then, once it starts, all bets are off. Maximum violence as quick as possible. (The Marquess of Queensberry can go fuck himself cos in a street fight he'd have got his arms ripped off.) What you don't want is to be rolling around on the floor for hours. Most blokes have only got a few minutes' good rowing in them before they start puffing.

The second kind of trouble is the one you know is gonna happen and you can prepare for it. That's a real touch, actually, to be in that position, cos you can make sure certain things are on your side. First, make sure you've got back-up cos it's pretty certain the other bloke will turn up with his mates. It don't mean everyone immediately jumps in, but if you're getting your head jumped up and down on then that's when you need your mates. His will do the same.

Knuckledusters? I swear by them. Chances are if someone's picked on you it's only because he thinks he can handle you. That's just logical, ain't it? To pick on some monster who looks like he can hammer you is just plain mental. So, better to be safe than sorry. Imagine that the other bloke's got an edge and even it up, or give yourself an advantage.

Guns and knives are out, in my book, unless I was gonna get shot or stabbed myself. Then it's just levelling things out. And only carry the tool you're prepared to do the time for. Just having a weapon on you will get you bird, and actually using it means you might as well join a fucking good book club for the amount of reading time you're gonna get inside.

You'd never believe the importance that clothing can have in a fight. No, straight up, I mean it. The number of tasty cunts

I've seen come a cropper because they were wearing a real tie and not a clip-on. If that knot is grabbed and tightened, don't matter how big and hard you are you're going to suffocate, mate. You can't fight anyone if you're fighting for breath. Or, another tip: if you do grab a tie (or some hair) then immediately straighten your arm and lock it. The strongest man will not be able to unbend himself from that. A locked arm is fucking strong. All he'd be able to do is bite your leg. Which I wouldn't want doing to me, but in that position I'd do it myself. You vegetarians out there will just have to come up with a plan of your own. And, if you do bite a hole out, stick your finger in. I *know*, it sounds awful, but it's not as bad as being laid up in traction thinking, Oh, I do now wish I'd been as nasty to him as he was to me. And I've already told you how leather-soled shoes cost me my nose. Sometimes, even now, I think, Fuck! I wish I'd worn my Docs!

Tempting though it is to turn up for a fight looking like a flash cunt (now who could I be talking about there?) it's not always worth it. I've lost count of the number of really wicked and expensive suits and jackets that have ended up looking like Robinson Crusoe's cast-offs. I used to have one particular jacket that I wore if I knew it was likely there would be some aggro. It was really soft black suede with tassles down the arms and back. I know it might sound a bit risky having tassles that someone could grab, but when you get to a certain level you can get away with some things. Not recommended for a beginner, though. Don't try that one at home, folks. The advantage of that little piece of clobber was that it made me feel really good, and it looked the bollocks. I called it my battle jacket.

And talking about moves that you shouldn't ever try yourself, the best, classiest fighting manoeuvre I have ever, *ever* seen in my life was by a mate of mine called Kevin. When Kevin came out of his stint in the Foreign Legion he came back to England. He was kicking around not knowing what the fuck to do, really. After doing what he'd done he couldn't just go do some ordinary job and have some prat of a foreman tell him what to do. So he came to see me and asked if I had anything he could do. I got him work on door and security work.

Now Kevin was the best fighter I've ever seen. No, actually, he weren't just a fighter, he was a trained killing machine. I've seen them all – nutters, hardmen, boxers, judo experts, the lot. Kevin had all those bits and a little bit more.

One night we were out in Turnmills nightclub waiting to meet someone. Then in walked the biggest man I have yet seen to date. He must have been seven-foot tall, 28 stone and with a 34 inch waist. A massive black guy. His head alone must have weighed four stone and his jaw was huge, like a bag of cement. I thought, Fuck *me*! It was just abnormal. He was like a freak. And he had a T-shirt on! Kevin turned to me at the bar and said he thought that must be the biggest man he'd ever seen in his life. I agreed with him.

'Listen,' he said, 'if you can have it with him and win, you've got to be a good fighter, ain'tcha? Cos he's got to be one tasty bastard!'

Without thinking anything of it, I agreed with him again. No argument from me on that one. The geezer was like a spray-painted iceberg. Next thing, I look round and Kevin's walking up to the guy! The big geezer's sat there lapping up all the attention and he thinks Kev's another one coming up to give him a compliment. Which he ever so slightly wasn't. Kevin bent down to the guy's ear.

'You have got to be,' he said, 'the biggest, dog-ugly cunt I've ever seen in my life.' And then he walked back and told me.

I was like, no – that's not my way *at all*. Like I say, enough rows come your way without looking for them. But that was Kevin. He did it for the challenge. Not even to show off, because I knew that if that club had been empty apart from him and the other bloke, he would've done exactly the same thing.

See, what it was, Kevin hadn't had many challenges lately, after doing what he'd done for a living. He'd gone from abseiling down embassy walls and swinging in windows with a machine gun, that kinda shit, to working on the door in London. You imagine replacing one with the other.

The big bloke came up to me and told me to tell my friend to watch what he said. Then they ended up having a little fracas. And the bigger you are, the more of you there is to go at. The bigness don't always count. And Kevin didn't throw anything that wasn't designed to really hurt, disable or kill you, depending on how he saw fit. He knew all that nose-into-the-brain stuff that you think only works in films.

So Kevin went for him and he just *ripped* this big geezer to pieces. He fucking destroyed him. Anyway, the black geezer was helped upstairs and we started getting ready to leave. Kevin went outside the club, but, while I was still inside, the ugly big geezer followed Kevin out and went for him again! This time with a bit of scaffolding pole. And Kev done him again, completely battered him. The big guy was a head doorman and one of his boys ran up and stabbed Kevin in the back and ran off. Lee was his name.

We went looking for him, and Kev came with us. He weren't bothered about his wounds and he refused to go to hospital. He just wanted to catch the geezer. Anyway, this Lee had fucked off and we went back to my place. Kevin insisted on having a bath and smartening himself up cos he didn't want the nurses to see him in a mess! Fuck me, the bath water was just totally red. He was bathing in claret. It was proper pumping out of him. When we finally got him to the hospital he was in intensive for a while, and in hospital for a week.

It weren't until something like four years later that me and Northern Billy caught up with that Lee geezer when we found him working at the Gas Club. We kicked absolute fuck out of him. And then again down at The Frog and Nightgown for good measure.

Anyway, getting back to the best move I ever, *ever* saw, which was one of Kevin's (no, that last story wasn't it!). It was when these two geezers went for him. He bopped the first one in the belly and doubled him over, clamped his head in his arm, gave a little fancy backheel and knocked him out, dropped him (without even looking at him), took one step forward and met the other guy with a right hook that knocked *him* out. All in about ten seconds: bang – bend – backheel – drop – step and *smack*! Oh, it was so fucking stylish I nearly came on the spot, I swear to God. It was that little backheel, like Maradona doing a cheeky pass, which was the absolute bollocks. And it knocked the geezer out. He'd barely even hit the floor before Kevin had decked the other.

Kevin didn't work *for* people, he worked *with* them. He had that army thing: Us and Them. And I just warmed to that in him. That whole 'brotherhood' thing is right up my street.

At the end of the day the most important things in a row, as in life, are a big heart and strength of mind. And I don't care what they tell you, the meek will *not* inherit the earth until the strong fucking tell them they can!

And if you get in a row with somebody, it's not always about strength. Sometimes you have to play it clever.

Something happened only less than a week after I'd had my nose stitched back. I'd come out of hospital and I was at home with Tracey and the kids. In the middle of my breakfast one morning there was a bang on the door. I opened it to find this guy stood there. He was a scouse geezer and straight away he started shouting at me.

'So you're supposed to be the hardest thing in London, are ya? I've just drove 250 miles to fight you, you cunt! Come on – me against you, north against south!'

So I'm stood there on the doorstep, still in my dressing gown and holding a fork with a saveloy on the end of it, looking at this divvy scouse git going mental at me in my front garden. Not exactly the best way to start the day. He'd obviously seen the front-page photo of me when the *Sun* had done a story about the fight and about me being in *The Paradise Club*. I still had a massive bandage over my nose, all taped to my face. I knew I couldn't have a man-to-man with him cos just one touch on my nose and I'd fall down in agony. It was only a few days since I'd had the fucker stitched back on, remember! And now this idiot was asking me out for a fight. Some mates of his were waiting in a car out in the street. I couldn't risk getting even a finger laid on my nose, so I needed an edge.

I said, 'Hold it a minute. Don't fall into the trap that everyone else has. I only play gangsters in *The Paradise Club* and *Minder* so everyone thinks I'm a real one. That's how I ended up this way! I ain't even a fighter.'

He started to calm down a bit, but I was still wary. He weren't completely convinced. I'm still stood there like a lemon in my fucking dressing gown, big bandage on my face and holding this sausage on a fork and trying to convince him I'm normal. I talked to him some more and invited him into the house for a drink. He dropped his guard and started to come in.

I said, 'I don't want you to have driven 250 miles for

nothing, but it's all a myth. You know what kind of crap they put in papers.'

Then, as he walked in, I hit him with the fork. I'll never forget this image, it's stuck in my head (bit like the fork was in his): I hit him really hard in the forehead with the fork and, as it hit him, the saveloy pushed up the handle as the fork went in. The fork bent but the handle was still sticking out at a right angle – with this silly sausage hanging on it! He staggered against the wall and I smashed the fuck out of him. I couldn't afford for him to get in even one punch cos if he got the nose I was fucked. So I bashed the living daylights out of him, really gave him a good hiding, and dragged him outside and threw him in the road. A couple of people jumped out of the car, but they just stood there.

That must have been a sight and a half: this fucker laid out in the road with a fork in his head and, cos my dressing gown had come open by now, me stood there in my underpants with a bandaged face looking like some mental Egyptian mummy. Before I went back in, I turned to the blokes stood by the car: 'You can keep the fork. *And* the egg whisk I stuck up his arse!'

You see what I mean about what happens when you get well-known for something. You get both the good and the bad, the acclaim and the blame. I got to meet the good chaps but it also meant I was sought out by a lot of nutters and divs. I mean, imagine travelling 250 miles to pick a fight with someone you've never even met!

But when it comes to having a row, always best to get things over and done with as quickly as possible with minimum fuss and mess. None of this rolling around on the floor lark.

I was out in a West End club one night with Ian, Junior, Jack, Jamie, Big Joe and Little Joe, Bob with the café, Jason, Floyd, Lee, Gary Barron, Ricky, Margate Pete, Dave Hawkins, Shaun, Dean, Kevin, and Biggins – a proper little army. I weren't working the place, just on a night out, but my boys did security there. Anyway, I went to the toilet and when I came out a really massive brawl had broken out – forty or fifty people giving it loads. There was nothing anyone could do and it was just getting worse and worse.

I was on the edge of it looking down, raised up on these steps that led into the club. I thought, I'll do a flash, cocky one here. I went into my inside jacket pocket and then fired two shots into the ceiling. Everyone screamed and stopped dead (well, not *dead* – that would've been a fucking unlucky ricochet!). Bits of plaster fell down from the roof, there's the smell of gunsmoke, the music's stopped and the whole club's looking at me.

'Right! Everybody who wants to fight, go outside and have fun. Cos we just want to dance!'

Unusual, but effective, you might say. I do like my little sayings cos I know they are gonna be talked about afterwards.

Another difficult one happened in another club, the Limelight in the West End. My mate Dean Lambert was DJing. I was working that night with Jay, Dave, Wish, Cecil and Robbie from Propaganda. About forty American football players came in. They'd been doing some kind of exhibition game over here. Now these geezers are top-of-the-range fridge-freezer size. And that's without the padding. Necks like tree trunks and heads like flattened bullets. Suddenly, just like that, they all started fighting in the VIP room. All of them. I stood back and watched. I knew that this was one situation where my input would have absolutely no effect whatsoever. Then, as suddenly as it had started, it stopped. Like someone had blown a whistle!

They all began leaving, and as the last few got to the door I stepped forward and went, 'Yeah! Get out, the lot of you, and don't fucking come back!'

The manager was stood outside and he heard this and thought I'd taken them all on and thrown them out! So that was a nice little touch cos he went round telling everyone that Dave Courtney had thrown out the whole of the New York Giants!

Lots of times when you throw someone out of a club they say to you, 'I'll be back!' Mostly nothing happens, so you get used to it. But sometimes you look at someone's face and think, Hang on – this little fucker means it. This guy I threw out once was one of them.

He'd caused some trouble and I'd dealt with it. It's not that I'd called for assistance or asked any of the others for help, but when something like that happens doormen just automatically help each other out. He didn't get a kicking or a hiding, he just got carried out. Which I think was worse, because his friends didn't help him and the embarrassment of it all was too much.

He came back half an hour later and asked for me. I went out into the foyer and he pulled a gun on me. A big silver automatic. His face was all twitchy and veins were banging out of his neck. He started shouting: 'Now what you fucking gonna do? Now what you *fucking* gonna do, you and all your mates?!' I could see from his eyes he weren't trying to do it all casual; he was fucked up in the head. He was pointing the gun at me all the time and everyone was stood around watching, not knowing what to do.

Before I said a word, I turned my back on him. 'Go on then,' I said. 'You get famous for shooting Dave Courtney in the back, you coward. You get known for that!' And I started walking away.

He started screaming, 'Turn round, you cunt! Turn round!' but he just couldn't shoot me in the back. As pissed off as he was, and even more so after I'd said that, he just couldn't do it. Which is what I'd been banking on. He knew he'd go down as a famous coward because I'd already made a point of saying that. I can't say that I didn't get a little twinge between my shoulder blades as I was walking away, though.

It was all caught on the cameras in the foyer, and one of the doormen took the tape out and passed it around for people to watch. So that became a bit of a talking point. The police nicked the geezer, but I refused to press charges. They came round to the club for the tape, but we put another one in the machine. *Close Encounters of the Third Kind*, I think it was.

Me and Tracey separated. It weren't that we fell out of love or grew apart, really, but we just wanted very different things. She was always a good, hard-working lady: worked in an office in the the City. She did like a night out, but not the raving and nightclubbing like me. I mean, I wanted all that and everything that came with it in London, seeing everyone and going out, the whole lifestyle. I'd been turned by the lights of London, I suppose.

Tracey wanted to move and live in Kent. Which is natural for most people, that's what they aspire to – the quieter life. I weren't that normal – or what was normal for me, shall we say, was something else. I liked it a bit louder with the volume up. Living in a cottage weren't for me cos I hungered for something else. After a month in Kent I'd have been out in the garden biting off flower heads.

Everything that I had I didn't really want to knock on the head, but she didn't want the worry any more of me coming home with half a nose. Tracey used to say that when she first met me I was just a cocky dustman! Which was true. I'd gone from a donkey jacket behind the door to a bulletproof vest. So me and Tracey's relationship became a casualty of my lifestyle, really.

What I was now I hadn't been when we'd met. Well, no, that ain't strictly true, really; I was still the same, but what I did had changed. That had been difficult for Tracey, I know. But the change had happened so gradually over the years; it didn't suddenly go from that to this. It's like when you bump into someone and they ain't seen your kids for a while and through their eyes you realise how much your kids have grown. I think Tracey had waited, thinking that my lifestyle might start going back to more like how it was before, but that weren't gonna happen. We both knew that.

We could have sat at home until we ended up hating each other, but we're both too clever to have let that happen. We just had to go our own ways. Tracey had given me a lot of great years and three beautiful kids – Beau, Levi and Chelsea. Those are things that no amount of money can buy you; they're just the best gifts. Tracey had been a proper good mum and devoted herself to the children.

We remained good friends afterwards, and still are to this day. I loved her from when we first met, and always will.

15 Jennifer

So then I went back to my bachelor pad days and got a flat in Forest Hill. I moved in with a friend of mine called Warwick who I'd known for years. We'd first met in Hastings with Posh John. Warwick was and is a lovely geezer, one of the most genuine and nicest people I know and someone that I'll always wish all the luck in the world to. One time when we were out for a day with the families, Beau, who was still only a little boy, fell down into the water at Surrey Docks. I weren't nearby but Warwick, without hesitation, jumped in fully clothed and pulled him out.

The flat turned into a bit of an open house and we had an array of people living with us, on and off: Mr Finlater, Fast Car Ricky, Mad Jack, Big Marky, John Saint, Billy, Hippie the Fly Tipper, and two guys called Willy and Wayne. They were the best car thieves I've ever met. Inseparable, they were. They had a Fiesta with WHERE THERE'S A WILL THERE'S A WAYNE painted across it. I thought that was the bollocks. With all these blokes in the house they did used to bring home some right old dogs and slappers. One time this bird came in and I'm not saying she was a pig but I was talking to her brother Perky and he said she'd bounced more balls off her forehead than Kenny Dalglish.

Anyway, it all got a bit silly so we all chipped in and got another gaff for communal use. Warwick moved out to his own place and I started sharing with an old friend of mine called Dave Legeno. I'd first met him when he was doing doorwork at a club called Paradise in Islington. That was the first official all-night rave place. My club, The Arches, had been the first very-much-unofficial one.

Dave was a book in himself. A few years ago he'd been arrested for a couple of revenge attacks against some blokes that had stabbed a mate of his. He got charged with GBH and ABH (and loads of other letters of the alphabet) but he jumped bail and flew off to America. He bought a Harley and did the full-blown cowboy bit, riding round the West, working the door in bars, with a different babe in every one. He had loads of adventures, mate. He ended up busting the jaw of an FBI agent, like you do, and going on the run. They had him down as being 'Armed and Dangerous', which he fucking was, and fifty of them staked out his house. But he escaped that one! He also did a smuggling run from Mexico with loads of puff. When he met the connection he found they'd actually loaded the car with heroin without telling him. So he bashed up the geezer (too right as well), took the money and fucked off back to England. Washington tried to extradite him but couldn't do it. Dave even went back to the States six months later on a false passport, the cheeky git. Get *that*! That's a proper little film on its own.

By the time we were flat-sharing he'd got into the American wrestling lark that had just kicked off big over here. A right tasty outfit called the Peacock Gym had just sprung up which also did boxing promotions and ended up being the best all-round boxing gym in Britain. It was run by the Bower's and Co. Another fucking lovely bunch of geezers, but you wouldn't want them as an enemy.

Dave's stage name was Lone Wolf and he had these mental American Indian outfits. Oh, listen, he was something else. And cos he'd been in the States so much he'd picked up the accent. He came across as being a genuine Indian raised by fucking wolves! He'd appear last on the bill with all these lights on him and music blaring out and everyone chanting, 'Lone Wolf! Lone Wolf!' Some of the other wrestlers were top as well – guys like Ricky 'Too Sexy' Hards, Mick 'The Priest' Warrel and Big Ron 'Mayhem'. The Bower's built the whole show around Dave and another fucking big nutter called Mr T who was an absolute replica of the original Mr T. The only difference was that one was real and one was an actor.

So sometimes I'd get home at night and find this six-foot-four wrestler in a loin cloth sat cross-legged in the living room, strumming his guitar with a fifteen-foot Burmese python wrapped round him. Y'know, just your everyday story of two ordinary blokes sharing a gaff.

Fang, that fucking snake was called. It had to be fed live animals, so Dave would give it rabbits. I'd sit there watching this huge cunt of a snake turn a fluffy white bunny into a bump in its throat. That put me *right* off my bangers and mash. As if one wasn't enough, he got another one as well, an eight-footer he called Spike. Fang was such a greedy cunt he even ate the other snake. Dave caught it when there was only six inches of Spike's tail sticking out of the other one's mouth. He grabbed it and pulled it right back out. And fuck me if it didn't live! I'd gone from married life with Tracey to living in my own Tarzan film. I half expected Cheetah to come knocking on the door asking if I wanted to come out to play.

I ran a new club now called Futures. The club was owned by Harry Haward. Futures ran from six on Monday morning until two in the afternoon. You might think there'd be no call for a club at that time, but there was. The hardened ravers would go to some club on Saturday night, like Ministry of Sound, then go just round the corner from the Ministry to Arches (not mine; one run by Terry Ranjams and Heidi) all day Sunday, then to the Gas Club Sunday night, and finally down to Futures on Monday morning. It was the last resort, literally. All the mass of weekend clubbers and everyday workers had gone home by then, which left all the nightclub people finished until next weekend. So they all came down to mine – doormen, DJs, club dancers, bar staff, waitresses, club owners, villains, celebrities, hard-core ravers, sex-show workers, prostitutes; everyone, just everyone. All the night-people. It was just crammed full of the most naughty, *naughty* people in London. It was a haven of naughtiness, put it that way.

I had no doormen working there. I weren't gonna pay some-one to look after my own club. Anyway, as you might imagine, or maybe not, there was very rarely trouble. And when the Gas Club shut everyone came down this little place of mine. The most colourful characters London has to offer were down in that little club Monday morning. Jam-packed with lovely ladies as well. It was really mad.

The police came round and said, 'We don't know what

you're doing in there but it's really nice for us to know you're all under one roof!' I thought that was a wicked line, and it just about summed the place up. We started sending flyers to the police station. The copper told me that he wasn't making any deals but, as long as they didn't get called out to the club, then they wouldn't come. They were just letting us know that we weren't pulling the wool over their eyes. Another Old Bill told me they'd had three separate police units following three different people around the country and they all ended up at my gaff on a Monday morning! A copper said to me, 'No guessing game needed about the kind of clientele *you* have, Mr Courtney!' That was another good line.

I did another do at the Fitness Centre on Southwark Bridge. With me was Stormin' Norman, Steve Bogart, Big Warren, Funny Glenn, Nutty Neil and Jim. The usual suspects, in other words. One night I hired an act to come and play – five black women, all sisters: Helen, Sam, Corinne, Julia and Jennifer Pinto. Julia and Jennifer were identical twins. Jennifer was the singer and rapper and watching her on stage just blew me away. I thought she was the sexiest, classiest thing I'd seen. I guess you could say it was love at first sight. It was like a bolt from the blue for me.

I went up to her after she'd come off stage. I thought, No point in messing around here; I've never been backward at getting to the point. 'I don't know if you've got someone else at the moment,' I said, 'but I want you. I've got to have you – not as a shag, I don't mean it that way, but as my woman.' I think she was a bit taken aback, to be honest. But I think she liked the directness of it. We went and talked. And talked and talked. And then later, shagged and shagged. We got on blindin' right from the word go.

She was in her early twenties, nearly ten years younger than me. She was smart, strong, sexy, classy, all those things you'd look for. In fact, I knew I'd found what I was looking for without even realising I'd been looking, if you know what I mean. I knew Jen couldn't be anything but good for me. Jenny was with someone else at the time and had two babies, Drew and Jenson. She weren't happy with the guy, but was scared to leave. I said, 'If I could make him go away, would you not want him there?' She said she'd love him to leave, so later I had a quiet word with the geezer and he left.

Jenny didn't know nothing about me, really, so she didn't have loads of preconceived ideas that might put her off or even attract her to me for the wrong reasons. We could just get to know each other as we really were. And that's always a big, big weight off, ain't it? When you can meet someone like that and trust them immediately. None of that game-playing bollocks.

Much as I hated to leave Lone Wolf Dave, and Fang and Spike, we moved in together straight away. And in case you're wondering, I didn't fight for custody of the snakes. Dave was the wrestler, and I didn't fancy tussling with two huge rabbit munchers either, thank you very much.

I quickly filled Jen in on what I was and what I did. She accepted it, like I knew she would, cos I could see what kind of woman she was. Like Tracey, she was a good girl and strong with it. Tracey had waited for me when I was in prison and that had meant an awful lot to me. I knew Jen would be the same type if she had to. That makes a bond with you. A real bond.

I told Jennifer everything because I knew I could trust her implicitly. She said to me that she was Plasticine and trusted me to mould her into whatever I wanted her to be. That might sound odd, and later when the papers started interviewing us they always quoted her saying that. As if it meant she was weak or something, but it weren't that at all. She said she saw qualities in me she liked. 'I feel like I know you, and your faults,' she said. 'Make me into what you want me to be so I'm always going to be here.'

Jenny brought the life out of me and took ten years off me. I was honest with her cos that's what I wanted back, so if I asked her something she could criticise and it wouldn't be for no other reason than that she cared. And she helped me grow the way I wanted to be – to turn the razzmatazz, the media, the nightclub thing, the gangsterism, the infamy, all of that, into something else. She was my mirror image. I got all the pats on the back, but she was my spine.

Is this all getting a bit slushy? I don't mean it to be (Dave Courtney, the Mills & Boon years!). Actually, I don't fucking care cos I'm just being honest. I've never been one who thinks that being a man means never saying what you feel to the people you love. That's just bollocks. I tell my kids I love them, I've always told the women I love that I love them. Everything else, as they say, is just window dressing. And my first job *was* as a window dresser, remember? So I know just how much bollocks that is!

It did raise a few eyebrows in certain circles, though, me living with a young black lady and her two kids. A lot of the people in my circles were not, how you might say, the most liberal-minded. In an awful lot of people's eyes it was un-believable what I done. There was some disapproval at the beginning.

I never felt I had to explain my choice of missus to anybody, and if anyone ever did need it explaining I'd ask them to come stay with us for the weekend. If at the end of that they couldn't see why I loved her, then I couldn't tell them. They all loved her to bits. And ten years down the line, still at my side, she is the first lady of London. In a way, we made it sort of hip, for want of a better word, to be like we were in my world. Even if some of the other blokes had wanted to do what I'd done but hadn't, for various reasons, then I think they looked at us and thought, Yeah – that's how it should be.

After visiting Reggie one day I got the idea of Jennifer and her twin Julia doing something about the Krays. It was too good not to do – one pair of twins singing about another. And from that came our little rap duo, the Courtney Twins: Jenny Bean and Sugar Baby. How sweet does that sound? We wrote a song with Master P called 'They Took The Rap' about the injustice of Reg and Ron still being banged up. I took Jen and Julia to meet Reg and see what he thought. He loved the idea and liked the words so we recorded it. And when it was released we didn't exactly have to go knocking on doors for publicity. Two rude black girls managed by a villain and rapping about the Krays – the press just went mad for it.

We posed for a publicity shot with me all black-suited up and wearing shades, and the girls either side of me in hot pants and with knuckledusters hanging round their necks. It was taken in front of The Blind Beggar pub where Ron shot George Cornell. It was a wicked photo, and they used it everywhere.

Jenny and Julia performed the song at a protest rally for the twins held in Hyde Park and, get this, they were even lined up to play at the opening of the EuroDisney place in Paris! But Disney got wind of just how naughty the Courtney Twins' stage show was and dropped us. Fucking charming. It's OK for Donald Duck to walk around with no pants on though, ain't it?

Later on, Jen did another rap track, this time about me getting not guilty for the shooting thing. It was called 'Who Is He?' It had gunshot sound effects, which was a bit naughty (nothing new there then), and me saying 'Not guilty!' over the music. It was wicked. We did a 'Dub Minder Mix' and a 'Dodgy Dave Mix'. Bryan Adams and his son, Terry, recorded and produced it at Hatch Farm studios, Chertsey. It sold 18,000 copies and all the DJs in the clubs played it willingly. Normally five to ten thousand copies would get you in the Top Ten, but because the hierarchy of the music business saw Dave Courtney as the manager, they wouldn't put it on *Top of the Pops*.

We had a launch party at the Hippodrome in front of three thousand people. Jenny was carried out on stage on the shoulders of Big Noel and Mr Universe, Selwyn Cotterell, with loads of other bodybuilders all around them.

Who needs the Yanks? We were giving them proper gangster rap!

16 Payments Due

People are usually surprised when I say I think we have the best police in the world, but I mean it. They go out on the streets with nothing more than a wooden stick and a pointy hat, not tooled up to the back teeth like the American coppers. Mind you, they're not that good cos they've never really had me, but there you go – can't win 'em all, boys, can you?

And one they definitely didn't win was when I was driving down to Reading with six shotguns in the boot. I was going to get them sawn off professionally by this fella I knew with a cutting machine (I've never been that keen on DIY myself). So, there's me and my mate, Ian Tucker, tootling along on the motorway when this motorcycle policeman comes alongside and motions me to pull over. Now I know it's not for speeding because I've been keeping an eye on that. Well, you would do with half a dozen shooters in the back, wouldn't you? Be plain daft not to. So I know it's either because he's had a really boring day or just cos he don't like the look of us. There must've been something about two lumps in a Jag that got him wondering. Honestly, ain't discrimination a terrible thing?

In the half minute it takes me to pull on to the hard shoulder loads of things start whizzing through my brain. I know I'm now looking at a ten stretch just for having them on me. That's a mandatory sentence for firearm possession – no 'ifs', 'buts' or 'maybes'. What a bastard. I've walked free from really tough ones in the past, ones that 'most everybody else thought I'd get a guilty for, and now I'm gonna get fucked for this!

I pulled over and stopped and the copper parked up in front of me. What went through my head was this: if he takes his helmet off and clocks me, I'm done. Because I'm on the motorway I can't run and I can't drive off; there would be no point anyway cos he would've already ID-ed me. So then it's a fifty-fifty chance whether he'll ask to look in the boot. Probably more like seventy-thirty actually, cos he's pulled us on general suspicion anyway. And that ain't good odds in my book.

By now he was off the bike and putting it on the stand. I knew I'd only got a few seconds. I realised then what the only way out was, and acted on it. That's always been a strong point of mine – decisiveness. Coming to a decision and then acting on it. Loads of people can do the first, but not the second. What's the point? If you do that you just end up full of 'what ifs'.

I got out of the car and approached him. He was already walking away from his bike towards me and I already had my fingers through a duster in my right hand, held down by my side to hide it. I made sure I was all smiles.

'Sorry, was I going too fast?' I said, and he started to lift his helmet off. I knew he couldn't have seen me properly with the helmet still on and the visor down, not clearly enough for it to stand up as a positive ID. So just as the helmet lifted, his chin was exposed and presented to me on a plate. *BOOF!* I whacked him smack on the button. I fucking *lifted* him. He was out before he hit the deck. I think you could safely say it wasn't exactly what he expected.

Where he'd fallen was right in front of my car. His bike was in the way as well. I thought, Charming! The bastard's blocked me in! Those BMW bikes are big, heavy things as well, and with its wheel locked at an angle it started to turn away from me. So I just pushed it over.

I jumped back in the Jag and drove off, pretty chuffed, to be honest, at how things had turned out. I realised that that had probably been one of the hardest shots of my life. The room for error was almost non-existent. I couldn't have afforded it to turn into a roadside brawl if I hadn't caught him square with the first pop. The Old Bill wouldn't have been so chuffed about it all when he came round, though. I thought, I bet that's one that will go unreported back at the nick. I didn't hear anything else about it. I do love it when a plan comes together.

The bloke with me, Ian Tucker, had become a good friend of mine after we'd met doing a debt-collecting job. It was right in the middle of a spot of real action-packed stuff – guns being pulled, people getting hurt – and in situations like that where you've got to grab your bollocks in your hand, you immediately see what a man is made of. I got to see Tucker at his best, saw straight away what he was about, and it led to an instant friendship.

We'd both been employed to do the same guy, and it was when we were both doing some investigation about the bloke that we learnt about each other. So because of the urgency of the job we had a meet and decided to hook up together.

This geezer owed six million pounds. The biggest single debt I'd ever been employed to recover. Now you've got to frighten someone an awful lot to get them to pay that kind of money back. An awful lot. Because I know in the same situation . . . me, personally, you'd have to shoot me dead to get that back. And that wouldn't get you it back. So it was a fucking hard one.

It came about when this bloke, John, who had his own company, bought a six-million-pound health farm in Surrey. The taxman got in touch with him and asked him where the money had come from. This solicitor, who ended up being in on the scam, told John he could get him out of it. He said he knew a multi-millionaire businessman and if John paid him a hundred grand he could sign the health farm over to this other geezer and he'd say that he'd financed it. The health farm would still be John's, he was told, but just not in name.

This John is such a nice fella, a really lovely guy, that he didn't think any bad would come of it, so not only did he sign fifty-one per cent over but he paid the guy the hundred grand for the pleasure! Of course, the first time John tried to set foot back in the place the geezer went, 'Get off my property!' Get *that*! John tried every single legal way to get it back, but he couldn't. Legally he was fucked. Imagine that – six million quid nicked from right under your nose.

So, that's where me and Tucker were brought in. We targeted the solicitor and the businessman. First I went up to see the solicitor to have a word. Big house, Porsche in the drive, the usual. He was in this study of his, a big oak-panelled room. I asked him to please stay sitting down and just listen.

'I don't want you to speak. This is for me, so I know I've said it and I know you've heard it. I know you're probably not going to act on what I'm gonna say but I have to at least give you that chance. I would like you to give the money back or sign the property back over before I get further involved in this or you will end up not being able to spend it or enjoy it, I promise. But if I don't get it back from you, I'll make sure your life is so bad that you'd rather give it back. I feel I have to warn you because I know what I'm capable of. I don't want any comment from you, I just want you to know.'

The businessman's house we visited at night. Another big place that was. We had to make sure we got the right bedroom. He was asleep with his missus so I tapped him awake. Now, waking up and seeing a big skinhead and all six-foot-four of a geezer who looks like Tucker stood at the foot of your bed at two in the morning is enough to make anyone wish they had an en suite bathroom. Or plastic sheets. His missus rolled over as well and nearly jumped out of her skin. I told her to calm down and turn back over because this wasn't for her. But then when I'm talking, even though I'm talking to him, I know it's being heard.

'I haven't come here to hurt you,' I said to him, 'just to give you a proper, genuine chance. Just give back what you stole. Cos you did steal it and you know you did. Don't even insult me by arguing about that. You're not losing something that's yours, just giving back something that ain't. I'm not gonna touch you.' I gave him a little backhander in the face. 'That's how easy you are to get to.' I slapped him again. 'But next time it won't be a backhander. I'll be in and out of here, your wife will be still asleep and you, my friend, will be dead.'

Neither of them did anything about it, which ain't too surprising considering the amount involved. Like I say, in that position you'd have to chop off my arms and beat me with the soggy ends to get me to even think about it. The more money owed, the more drastic the tactics have to be to get reimbursed. And when someone doesn't pay you have to act quickly because fear goes away.

The next time we visited the solicitor, my mate Big M was with me. We waited for the guy to pull out of his drive and into this lane in front of his place with some little traffic lights at the top of it. When he stopped for red we pulled up behind in a black BMW 5 series and got out. Big M opened the passenger door and jumped in. Big M is one scary-looking geezer an' all. The geezer turned to his left and gave a little yelp. I reached through the window, took the keys out of the ignition, he turned to his right to look, and I gave him a little backhander. 'That,' I said, 'is just the tip of a pretty *fuck*ing big iceberg! I'll bury you under the rest of it.'

The Porsche had this fancy chrome gearstick. Big M put his hand on it and leant forward. I don't know where more veins were popping from – Big M's arm or the solicitor's head. There was this awful creaking noise and Big M bent the gearstick in two. It was like something out of *The Incredible Hulk*.

We drove off, and because it was a long straight road I could keep the Porsche in my rear-view mirror for ages. He just stayed inside it, sitting there with the lights changing from red to green and back. The other geezer also got another visit. And John got his business back.

Meeting Tucker led to me and him going on a real spree of little adventures. Oh, there was millions of them. We planned the jobs well beforehand but never discussed them in the car on the way there. We'd just put on an old sixties pop and Motown tape and sing our way there. We'd sing along to stuff like 'I Heard It Through The Grapevine', but making up our own words – '*Ohhh, I guess you're wondrin' how I knew, 'bout your plans not to pay what's due!*'

We collected anything from money to cars to speedboats even. On that last one we went down to Margate to see about a speedboat which hadn't been paid for. Before we even saw the guy we clocked the boat, so we got in and started it. These blokes heard us and came out shouting. We drove off and they jumped in another boat and chased us. So we blasted out of Margate harbour with this other speedboat giving chase. It was a real James Bond moment. They were both fucking fast boats. We were hitting waves and flying up, water soaking us. Then I thought, Wait a minute! We're not *nicking* this boat, so why are we running? I spun us round and started heading back towards the other boat. They panicked and turned and we ended up chasing them! I let them outrun us, and then took the speedboat back to its owner.

We used to have this phrase that we used when we got into a situation where a row was brewing. To tip each other off when the moment had come to go for the knuckledusters, we'd say, 'Let's go for gold!' We were at a wood yard one time, seeing this guy about money he owed. He walked out to meet us looking a bit wary. Just as I thought Tucker's gonna do the 'going for gold' bit, he started talking to the guy about wood! Big discussion about ply and all that crap. Then Tucker said what he's actually after is banister rail. The bloke went, 'Sure, mate, got some of that.' Tucker weighed it up in his hands like some kind of banister rail connoisseur. And then whacked the guy on the legs with it. He fell over, naturally.

'Right,' Tucker said, 'what we're actually here for is this.'

Which reminds me of the time someone broke into my car and nicked some stuff of mine, including a solid-gold knuckleduster. I was fucking fuming. The press did a story about it and I took the opportunity to offer a five-grand reward for the duster. Anyway, I was at home with Tucker when this geezer turned up at my door with my duster for the reward. I said thanks and asked him where he got it. 'From the glove compartment,' he said. I couldn't fucking believe it – it was the actual geezer who'd nicked it! And now he expected the reward. Fucking *cheek* or what?! I slipped the duster on, admired it a second, and then whacked him out cold. I did give him a grand, though, cos I didn't want him to say he'd been stitched on the reward. But I weren't giving him fucking five (except that bunch of fives when I clumped him, you might say).

Another time me and Tuck burst into this guy's house and found him in the bath. Now that's got to be the worst place to be, outside of being caught on the crapper. Well, you can imagine how vulnerable you'd feel in the bath. So we're stood over him and he's sat there with his knees to his chest. It weren't really a 'going for gold moment' cos he's not exactly in a position to threaten, but we did it anyway for effect. I said, 'Look, mate, there's two of us standing here, both wearing knuckledusters, and from here all the help I can see you've got is a soap on a rope.' He paid.

Tucker shared my thing of enjoying having a little dig at the Old Bill. He also had my natural aversion to queuing in traffic.

One little episode combined both when we got stuck at the back end of this mile-long queue of cars. We knew at the front of it there'd be the usual thing, just a few traffic cones around a road digger leaning on a spade. So Tucker pulled out, flew down the wrong side of the road at about 70 mph and dived into the front of the queue. Who should be sat at the head of it but two coppers in a Panda car. Tucker slammed on the brakes, skidded us to a stop and reversed right back up to the police car. I thought, What the fuck is he doing now? One of the coppers jumped out and ran up to us.

'Thank God you're here!' Tucker said. 'I was just looking for some of your lot. There's a really big fight going on back there and someone's bleeding from the stomach.'

The copper said 'Fuck it!' backed up a bit and spun round. They drove off, and so did we. Different directions. That was a wicked little one.

Tucker has got a bit of a thing about speeding. I made the mistake of going pillion on this racing bike of his. We were blasting around on it when we passed Brands Hatch race track. There was a meet on and the side gates were open to let this truck out. Tucker suddenly leant the bike over, shot us through the gates, past all these screaming stewards and straight out on to the track! We were blasting round overtaking all these 150 mph Formula Two cars with me going '*Arrggghhh* – you cuunnt!'

I don't mind going fast in cars. I do a bit of that myself. But only in the early hours of the morning when the streets are quiet – your honour. The Old Bill pulled us up one time . . . no, actually it was about 57 times, but this one time they did it was about three in the morning. The copper was one of those who have the snidey routine down pat.

'Bit of a James Hunt are we, sir?' he said.

I said, 'I do hope that's not rhyming slang, officer.'

He asked me if I was aware that I was doing in excess of 100 mph while straddling the white lines. I explained that I was only doing what it said I should do on my licence. I got it out to show him.

'There. See? "Tear down the dotted line".'

Hundred-pound fine and six points. I thank you.

One they didn't thank me for was when they pulled me over

again one night and found eight knuckledusters in the car. I explained that I'd already registered them as stage props for Jennifer's show. Which is true – I had. Part of the image of the show was her wearing dusters around her neck and even having one shaved in her hair. They took me in and took the car apart searching it. They found nothing and eventually believed me about the dusters (but only after I'd proved it with some registration form I had). When I came to pick the dusters up from the desk, though, there were two missing! A gold one and a gold and diamond one. I'd been robbed in a cop shop! I caused a right stink over it. Eventually, another officer came downstairs to deal with it. Then they took me out to the car to have another look and, surprise surprise, what turned up under the front seat? The two dusters. And this from a car they'd supposedly searched with a fine-tooth comb half an hour earlier. Funny that.

I had another run-in with a stripper about this time. Remember the one with the geezer at Queen's and kicking the copper up the arse? Well, this was another proper little silly one. This guy I knew was a really straight businessman in his fifties. He was another one who was just a really nice guy but, like a lot of nice guys, he got taken advantage of by not-so-nice guys.

His wife had gone to some Chippendales-type strip show. She ended up being one of those that goes on stage, gets blind-folded and has a banana put in her mouth. You know the kind of thing. Everyone knows what to expect and it's all good fun on the night. Anyway, one of the strippers left the act and went solo.

A few months later the old guy sees posters up everywhere advertising this stripper's new show. On the poster is a big photo of his wife sucking this banana stuck out of the stripper's crotch! Now he knows his old lady's been to the show and he ain't bothered about that, but half of London seeing the photo is another matter. Not an easy one to explain to the grandkids when you're taking them to see their grandma and they spot a poster of her the street, is it? 'Guess what I saw Nan doing, Mummy?'

So he rings the stripper and asks him if he wouldn't mind changing the picture. Right off the bat the guy is really nasty to him, saying that he's spent two-and-a-half grand getting the posters done and another five hundred having them put up. The old guy says he understands and offers to pay all that just to have them changed. The stripper says he's got a big summer season coming up going all round the country and he don't care about this geezer and his wife, and then tells him to fuck off.

The old bloke rang me (he sounded proper distressed) and said he'd rather pay me the two and a half to make sure the posters were changed. I said fair enough.

So we got this woman to ring up and book the stripper for a hen night do at her home. She asked him to do it in a copper's outfit (that was my little touch). She lived in a block of flats and, on the night, me and Tucker waited outside in the car park. We saw the bloke pull up and get out in all the clobber, full-on policeman's uniform. We got to the lift first, held the doors for him and stepped back. He walked in and saw me and Tucker looking at him. Now, whether he thought Tucker and me both looked a little on the naughty side, I couldn't say, but he stopped and smirked like he thought we were worried cos he was Old Bill.

'It's OK, guys,' he said. 'I'm not *real*!'

Me and Tucker looked at each other. I said, 'Oh, that's strange, cos *we* are,' and *smack!* I whacked him spark-out. The pointy hat flew off and all his long hair fell out. He collapsed, and as I caught him the whole uniform just ripped right off in my hands! Then I realised that they're only held together with Velcro so they can whip them off in the act. I thought, What a good idea!

We tore the complete outfit off him. He started to come round and I explained the situation over the posters. He was still groggy, though, and we just left him there on the floor. As we walked away I heard the bell ping and the doors close as someone from the flats called the lift up. What a sight they'd have seen when the doors opened: this sun-tanned Tarzan lookalike flaked out in the lift wearing nothing but a leopard-skin G-string. I just hope it didn't give some old dear on her way to bingo a heart attack.

Bingo! Now that's another one! That reminds me. Listen to this. The tabloids got into this big sales war and started offering a million-pound prize with these bingo cards they gave away. This was before the National Lottery, so a million quid was big news. And because people were sending in thousands of these cards the people sorting out the winners could've easily nicked one.

I was called in to do the security for the *Sun*'s bingo. What they did was hire the Connaught Rooms in London and have maximum security. Each counter got a box with twenty envelopes to open and each one was watched while they checked. Now, how they got these sorters was to advertise the jobs at £75 a day, seven days a week if you wanted it, cash in hand. Well, they just weren't ready for the number of people that came for these fifty jobs. Three thousand people turned up at the place. I was only gonna do it with me and two other doormen, but they rang me up really early in the morning and said I'd better bring some more. So I went down there at seven thirty with Tucker and a little army and saw these thousands of people waiting outside. No cars could get up the road. It was mayhem. There was no real queuing order. It was all a bit mental, with people arguing about who was there first.

There was this one bloke, a big African geezer, who was really giving it some; a real mouth almighty. He'd elected himself as the big voice-piece and was shouting and screaming the odds. He was just getting more lairy by the minute and egging everyone else on. I had a few more boys with me than first planned but we would've still got swamped if they'd rushed us. Anyway, this geezer's taken it on himself to do the Che Guevara bit and he's really giving it some. I knew that to get any respect here and nip all this in the bud before it turned nasty, this fella had to get a clump.

The Connaught Rooms have these grand, marble steps. The crowd was at the bottom and this fucker was halfway up with a few other bravehearts behind him waiting for the revolution to start. I thought, I know – I'll do a proper casual little move here: bop him in the belly to bend him over, then whack him with the knee; that'll look the absolute bollocks. A black dinner suit on marble steps looks wicked anyway.

Now what happened next was a bit of a surprise and a bit of a not-a-surprise. I know that different countries and continents of the world breed different types of fighters. A lot of orientals are into the old martial arts and use their feet more, for instance; a lot of your African geezers, on the other hand, look on their teeth as a major weapon in their armoury. And they're right, because they are. If you get bit hard it don't just hurt on the bitten part, it hurts all over your body. I knew that from experience, of course, cos I'd already had the amateur nose job done on me. The sensation is a powerful fucking thing. It goes right round your body like an electric shock. Like a cattle prod, I imagine, although that's one of the few things I haven't suffered, as it happens. So if you're going to fight someone who looks like a biter, make sure your first shot takes his teeth out. Better to lose a knuckle than get eaten.

So, I walked down the steps and everyone was looking, and he started walking up towards me. The guy had three stone on me and was about two foot taller. Even when he was three steps away we were at the same height. I whacked him in the belly – he bent over; I brought my knee up and went *bang!* – he sank his teeth in and went *chomp!* I was hopping around on one foot with this cunt hanging on to my leg like a pit bull! So much for the casual move. I couldn't get him off. His teeth were right in tight. The lads all ran over and beat him off and dragged him away. Next thing I knew the police came up and nicked me. I couldn't exactly deny it because there were three thousand witnesses. Even I couldn't swing that one in court. So I was nicked.

Then his brain started swelling and he was taken to hospital. The police put off charging me cos they didn't know whether it was gonna be attempted murder or murder. I thought, Fuck – I've just given myself a fifteen stretch over some silly fight. They took me to the hospital as well to have a tetanus jab and, cos he's only been over from Africa for a few months, there was talk about AIDS as well. They were frightening the life out of me.

AIDS was the big news at this point. Not that it ain't now, but then was when all the information films were on TV and everyone was paranoid. Strange, though, that whole escalation over the years: first it was VD, and a visit to the clinic; then herpes, which was with you for life; and then AIDS, which would kill you. What next? You stick you're dick in and just explode?

Anyway, when they searched him they found a big Gurkha machete in his jacket that he'd just never got the chance to use. It turned out that he was wanted for loads of things, in this country and back in Africa. He'd been thrown out of the police force back there! Too much biting in the line of duty, probably. They found loads of dodgy gear back at his house as well. He was just a bad cunt anyway, so they dropped the charges.

And all that over fucking bingo! *Thirty-three . . . teeth in the knee!*

Nude bingo. How about that? No, I'm not offering it as an idea, I'm telling you. I've done it! Well, not played it, but I organised it. Nude bingo, with male and female strippers and comedians as entertainment. We had a comedian called Al Benson and an absolute genius called Don Crosbie. You could sit down stark bollock (or fanny) naked and play bingo. *Two fat laydeees . . . there they are – on the front row!* It was just a really naughty afternoon. You might wonder if there would be any takers for it, but there were hundreds, mate, absolutely hundreds. Tucker done it with me and the other doormen I had working were Marcus, Marc Ives, Eric the Viking, Jimmy McGee, Peter Hivton and Mick (and I brought Ian Edmondson with me as a mascot). Even Mr Green from Maidstone was let out for the day to come to the party.

See what I mean about doing security on anything and everything? No job too small, no job too big. I even did Madonna. So to speak. That's what you call a proper star. And she's a lovely lady too. We got on well. I was backstage at one of the gigs with Jen, and Madonna said to me, 'You're a nice guy, but not my type; I do like your lady, though.' I thought, wicked! I'd actually pay to see that.

Talking of going down under, me and Tucker went debt collecting in Australia. This guy had cheated his partner out of over a hundred grand and fucked off to the other side of the world. And he thought he was safe. Silly sausage.

We found him. He'd bought a beach-front bar with the money. He was there behind the bar in a Hawaiian shirt and making an arse of himself with the young birds, mixing cocktails like a bald Tom Cruise with a pie-eating problem. I caught his eye and he looked back like, 'Yeah? I'll be with you in a couple of hours, mate.' I kept staring at him and he started to look a bit wary. When he came across he just thought we were getting pissed off about not being served.

He said, 'What can I get you two gents?'

'I'll have a pina colada,' I said, 'and one hundred and twenty thousand pounds please.'

He sort of bleached a bit in the face. Quite a lot, actually. Purely by coincidence Freddie Foreman and Tony White walked into the same bar and ordered a drink. I'm not quite sure if this helped or not. But what a touch, I thought (ha ha).

I said, 'Look, if the cocktail's a problem, forget it. But the other thing – no forgetting. You've been *found*, mate. And if I can find you here, I know I don't even have to threaten you.'

But I did anyway. Well, practice makes perfect. I explained that it was neither here nor there to me whether he paid or not. If I didn't get my cut out of the money he gave back I'd get the same amount for taking him out to sea to play with the sharks.

He paid.

The funniest one, though, the cheekiest thing that me and Tucker did, was a lot closer to home. It was at the South East Regional Crime Squad's annual Christmas party in Bexley Heath. A mate of mine was employed to do the catering for it and he got me a couple of tickets. I thought, This is just too fucking good to miss.

So, on the night, who turns up at the door but me and Tucker. We'd deliberately got done up in our finest gangster regalia: all black-suited up, black shirts, crombies and every gold ring, bracelet and chain we had. The only thing missing was a couple of violin cases under our arms. The geezer on the door tearing tickets nearly had a heart attack. We gave our real names and he checked if we were on the list. He couldn't do anything but let us through. Practically every copper from the area was there, right up to the most high-ranking. The fellas all stood together talking shop and all their missuses chatting away. Me and Tucker walked in like a double dose of the Black Death and the whole place just went, *What the fuck*?

We walked around swigging wine, eating cheesy nibbles and saying hello to officers we recognised. We'd see one of them across the room and shout, 'Oi! Mr Jarvis. It's me! Remember that GBH thing I got off with?' They just couldn't believe it. You could see them thinking, You cheeky, cheeky cunts.

We stayed about twenty minutes just to rub them up the wrong way, had a couple of dances with their wives, shook a few hands with the chaps and, to top it all, I only dropped the jackpot on the fruit machine! Then we fucked off and went down the club to tell everyone about it. The Old Bill didn't find it half as funny as we did. What ever did happen to the laughing policeman?

Most of the time I could get a laugh out of most things. That's always what I aimed for. Life's too serious anyway if you let it be. But the next thing I got involved in was a challenge for even me to find something funny in it. It weren't funny at all, as it happens.

17 Going Dutch with Dougie

I was offered a job with a bloke I knew called Dougie. I never, ever really liked him and he always looked on me as a bit of a threat, I think. But the job seemed simple enough and I would come out with twenty grand for a couple of days' work. Which ain't bad in anyone's books, is it?

The deal was this: some guys in England were due to be delivered two containers' worth of Benson and Hedges to avoid paying the duty. Now these had already been through customs so they were full packs, wrapped and ready for the shelves and, in the quantities they were talking, worth a lot of money. And this was before every man and his mother were smuggling stuff on the booze and fag run like they are now. The other people involved, the suppliers, were from Holland.

The geezers at our end who had organised it weren't really gangsters, they were more like businessmen, pen-pushers on the make. They might have felt like gangsters to each other, but not to a real one.

Anyway, Dougie spoke Dutch, so that's why I figured they'd given him the job as the money courier. He had little else going for him as far as I could see. Apart from anything else he was a dirty fucker: lank, greasy hair, and he didn't wash or clean his teeth so he had bad breath and BO that could bubble paint. One time, a few years ago, in a drunken rage he'd shot someone dead, so they say. The other guy was unarmed, but it was enough to get Dougie his naughty little reputation from that one crappy piece of action. He'd been running round on the gas from that incident for years. He scared a lot of people. To them he was that English bloke who speaks Dutch and had shot a bloke, and it sounded like something heavy to them.

Me and Dougie were to take near on half a million in cash to the Dutch guys. Like I say, I was on twenty and Dougie got a little more. The deal was that when the containers cleared customs at Dover, their driver got out and ours got in. After checking the gear was all there, he'd phone me and Dougie at the other end and we'd hand over the cash. Pretty simple. What could go wrong? Well, if at that time I'd made a list of what could go wrong, by the end of the whole episode I could have ticked them all. All apart from one – the one that would have said, 'I get killed'.

Right from the off I started to have a bad feeling about the whole thing. It was arranged that I have my money up front, but when I turned up he didn't have it. So we started the day with an argument. He started nicking money out for expenses and stuff, and I could see he had no money at all. I had to get paid, so how the fuck could I refuse? But I was there now, the people I was doing this for were proper so, in for a penny, in for twenty grand.

Like I say, it smelt bad from the beginning. About as bad as Dougie, come to think of it.

Now half a million quid in sterling takes up a lot of space. You've probably only seen it on telly with some Lottery winner holding up a briefcase full of what they've won. You can't exactly pocket it, and I didn't want to be lugging around a big bag of cash. So I changed it into Swiss francs and in francs you can get really big denominations. Say, the equivalent of £500 notes. So it was all nice and compact. I put it in all the pockets of the jacket I was wearing.

Even though it was summer I had this big cardigan on underneath in case it got cold at night. Dougie wore this cheap-looking, sixties-style shiny suit, well past its sell-by date, that he thought was the height of class. It didn't even look like it was supposed to be that shiny, more like it had just been badly ironed. I thought, Fuck me, I've got 500 grand on me and I'm going on a mission with King Mod.

After crossing on the ferry we drove off into Belgium in this red BMW 323i convertible of mine with me at the wheel. It was beautiful weather so we had the top down. Not really a good move cos it put Dougie on full public display. He wound the seat back till he was practically horizontal and lay there like he was on a beach sunbed, with a fat joint in his mouth as big as a cruise missile. When he'd first rolled it I didn't know whether he was going to smoke it or launch it at fucking Iran.

I dealt with some business I had to sort out with this geezer in Belgium and we drove on to Amsterdam to stop the night. We booked in a hotel and I left Dougie there while I went to visit some old mates of mine. They were Outcasts, a biker group which was at war with the Hell's Angels. They often get mistaken for the same thing by people who don't know cos they look the same – all the biker gear and colours and riding round on choppers and all that – but they're a group on their own. They've had big wars out there with the Angels for years. Killing each other left, right and centre. In one gun battle a bazooka was used. That's how heavy they can get. I didn't often get out there to see them, so I met up with them for a few bevvies and we shot round town on the Harleys.

The general public opinion over here is that bikers are dirty, scruffy bastards always at war. But over there they are looked on in a different way. Bike gangs are really big in Holland. Really organised. They're very big and very naughty with it. They're a law unto themselves and run loads of things. They're like outlaws from the old West with bikes instead of horses.

I told them what I was doing over here and when I said where I was going, they said to be careful because that area was a bit naughty, a bit skew-whiff on account of the drug wars. People were grassing each other up, ripping each other off, setting each other up and topping each other. A lot of shit going on. Not somewhere that your local travel agent would recommend, in other words.

One of the Outcasts, Phil, a good mate of mine, asked me if I was tooled up. I wasn't. Initially, I hadn't really thought it would be necessary. Only as we'd driven up and I realised that Dougie was gonna be an even bigger liability than I first thought, did I start to consider it. Phil gave me a .38 snubnose revolver, like American cops use. A tidy little fucker that's small enough to conceal but carries a fairly big round. I weighed it up in my hand and immediately felt a bit better.

I've never carried guns, as a rule, unless it was really

necessary. Only carry the weapon you're prepared to do the time for is my philosophy, as I've said, and I never wanted to get banged up for simply carrying something. Some have different views. I understand the attraction, though. There's no doubt that when you're carrying a gun you feel much more confident, believe me. And that's why they're often carried by exactly the kind of people you wouldn't want within ten feet of you – twitchy little insecure fuckers with no self-confidence who know they're weak at heart, or guys that go into mental rages over nothing. Phil was smart enough to make sure it was a revolver too. They don't let you down. Little tip for you here: never, *ever* use an automatic. They look like the bollocks, all neat and shiny, but they can jam. Why use something that *could* go wrong? Never understood it. Because there's never ever a time when you pull a gun when you can afford for it to go wrong. I've known a few people who had automatics jam on them and they were fucked in a big way, mate. And they also leave spent shells behind when they're popped out by the mechanism. They then become evidence. If they're found.

So I felt a little better. The .38 was already carrying six in the drum, but I asked anyway if they had any spares. Phil just looked at me.

'If you can't get the fucker with six,' he said, 'you're in the wrong business.'

For which I had to give him ten out of ten for observation. He was abso-fucking-lutely right.

Next day, me and Dougie got set to go off to the meet. For breakfast, I had the closest thing I could find to an English fry-up and Dougie had a wake-up joint, the first of many, and the Dutch equivalent of Weetabix, a big lump of weed. Weetafix. He was in seventh heaven cos over there it's legal. The smoking cafés have menus with every kind of hash, weed and resin you could want. I'd normally indulge myself, but I wanted to keep my wits about me. I knew by now that I'd have to be aware enough for the pair of us. Dougie was already half-gone and we still had an hour's drive ahead. He had a hippy heart, that was his trouble, and how many hippies have you heard of making good villains? (No, actually, I have met a few in my time – the exceptions.)

Over breakfast I tried to get more details out of him about

the job cos he'd been a bit too vague for my liking and I wanted all the ins and outs of the operation because I didn't want to be relying on him when we got there. But he was too strung out to make sense and I tired of trying. It was hard work. He was just saying to me, 'Don't worry, man.' I'm thinking, Don't fucking 'man' me, you silly bastard. But he was a bit older than me and he'd offered me the job so in effect I was working for him. In that situation you can feel you have to agree and go along with them whether you agree or not. Which was another lesson learnt: agree with an idiot and you're only one step away from turning into one yourself. He was playing boys' games in a man's world and his casual attitude just made me doubly aware of the possibilities.

The alarm bells were really ringing now. This geezer Dougie was not exactly what you'd call 'together'. Several marbles short of a full bag. I could see now he was a piss-head and total junkie. Druggy Dougie. Anyway, I had the cardy tied round my waist and the .38 tucked in it against my back. I thought of it as my little odds evener, and the closest thing I've ever had in my life to an insurance policy. I didn't tell Dougie about the gun. He was being so flippant and casual about it all when I knew it could turn serious. It was serious already, in fact, cos there was half a million quid involved and that is serious fucking money and people will do you some serious fucking damage to get it.

We drove out of Amsterdam into the country. It was another lovely, hot day. Bit too hot: I couldn't take my jacket off because the money was in there, and I had to keep the cardigan around me to hide the gun. The drive took the best part of an hour. The Bee Em was a fast motor but I didn't gun it because I didn't fancy being pulled by the Dutch Old Bill. I wasn't sure what their powers of 'stop and search' were over there, and I didn't fancy having to explain away 500 grand and the .38.

By the time we got there the car had lost some of its shine, what with all the dust, but in the sun Dougie's suit was bleedin' radioactive. We pulled up outside this café in a little village where we'd been told there would be someone waiting. They were outside at a table. Two Dutch geezers: one all blond and the other well-tanned. Both of them in summer suits and flip-flops. They looked a lot cooler than they acted, though.

They both seemed nervy. They weren't big, gangstery types, either of them, but they were keyed up. They looked charlied off their heads. My antennae were already twitching even before we got there, so now they were going ten to the dozen.

We sat for a minute. I just had a soft drink but Dougie ordered a beer and I had to sit there while he conversed with them in Dutch. Now, I *know* this cunt talks double-Dutch even when he speaks English, so now he's speaking double double-Dutch! What's that? Quadruple shit, in my book. And I had to sit there while he represented us. He kept flipping between talking Dutch and English, which I didn't like cos I got the feeling that all the serious stuff I wanted to hear was being spoken in Dutch.

The two geezers were being overly friendly and all smiley and it was just not working for me. Blondie kept looking at me and nodding and Mr Tan was listening to Dougie but not really listening. By this time, before we'd got there, I'd moved the .38 round to my side when Dougie had fallen asleep in the car. As we sat there I had to resist the temptation to feel for it, just to check. I knew it was there, of course, but you get that feeling anyway. Like when poker players keep checking their cards even though they know what they've got.

They got in their car, a blue two-door Mercedes sports, and we followed them. A few minutes away we pulled up to these high walls, went through big, black, open gates, which were electric gates but broken, and up this red-clay driveway which led to a country-style mansion house. Inside the perimeter walls it was set in these pretty grounds lined with conifer trees and music speakers out on the lawns, like some kind of health farm. The mansion was all painted pale yellow and had black, fancy wrought ironwork on the windows in the shape of flames. They looked nice, very decorative and all that, but really when it came down to it they were just bars. They looked like they were there to keep people from getting out. And it goes against my nature to willingly walk into a gaff that has bars on the windows. It all looked very picture-book, there in the blazing sun, all daffodil yellow, but I took just one look at this place and thought one thing: prison. It's just a pretty prison.

Then I saw what looked to me like a 'For Sale' board pegged

to the building. Everything then just went *zhoom!* – like every doubt I'd had and every bad thing that had happened went through me like a voltage jolt: Dougie nicking the money, getting stoned and pissed and acting like a junkie, Phil's warning, the two twitchy cunts in the car ahead, and now this tarted-up excuse for a prison whorehouse.

Sometimes you get a gut instinct, and in my experience it's never wrong. It's a real animal thing. Like it's a leftover from when we were all running round in furs trying to avoid being eaten by dinosaurs. Call it intuition, or whatever you like, but never ignore it.

I didn't ignore it. I took it all on board, but I still couldn't back out. There was still the possibility that it might go ahead as planned and I couldn't afford to jeopardise that. It weren't even my job. If we left now and then got a phone call saying the stuff had arrived, it would be too late. But now I was hyper-alert. Very, very few situations are, literally, a matter of life or death. I knew this one was and I was determined I wouldn't find myself dropping to the floor ten minutes later with a bullet in my chest thinking, Oh if only I'd known! I knew, mate. I fucking *knew*.

We followed them through the front doors. On the way in Blondie turned round and went to search me, trying to pat me down.

I said, 'What's your fucking game?'

'I'm just checking,' he said. 'Don't take any offence.'

'Fuck the offence! What are you on? We're your *guests*. You should be pleased to see us. Be nice!'

Blondie then looked at me as if to say, You fucker! He really, really wanted to have me there and then, but he was holding himself. That was when I realised he didn't know I had the money on me.

Dougie then went all daft on me, grinning at them like a retard, and started telling me to calm down. I said, 'Fuck it, I won't.' I felt things getting wonkier by the second.

Suddenly, Mr Tan cut Dougie off by saying to me, 'Where's the money?'

There was a second's pause before I answered, and in that time I knew things had moved up a gear. I said, 'The money's close by.' But fuck me if Dougie don't then go, '*He's* got it!' –

meaning me; meaning I've got it on me. Now, I knew that if they knew it was on me then we'd suddenly outlived our usefulness. We were then surplus to requirements. I quickly turned it round by saying what he meant was that I knew where it was, that I'd had it.

Then Blondie, who hadn't taken his eyes off me, chipped in: 'Is it in the car?'

'Don't worry about it,' I said. 'When we get the call, you get the money. No problem. Right?'

He looked really pissed off, but tried to switch his face back to happy, as if it was no big deal. Then he put his hands out. 'OK, OK. Come in and look around. There's the bar, you can have anything you want.'

They walked off into a big living room on the right. Dougie followed them and I left them to it and went for a wander around. Even at this stage it all seemed iffy enough for me to want to check out possible escape routes.

The ground floor was large and open and had a casino, a bar and, at the back, set a few steps down, a big indoor swimming pool. Downstairs in the basement was a nightclub. I could hear muffled music coming through the floor but I think it was just being relayed to the speakers outside. There couldn't have been anyone in the club cos it was the middle of the afternoon. In fact, there was only about thirty or forty people in the place and most of them were women. Most of them half naked and looking pretty strung out.

Upstairs, the first floor had only one door into it, and behind that a big, heavy firedoor with this guy sat beside it. I figured he had to be a guard. He didn't look like anything else. So people could go through the door and further upstairs, if they were allowed, but anyone upstairs couldn't just walk out.

I came back down and through a doorway to the right saw a fat geezer fucking this bird in a chair, sweating all over her. To my left I could see Dougie in the big living room with the two Dutch blokes. I went in and Dougie and Tan were talking in Dutch and Blondie was at the French windows behind them. He came over to me with a real shit-eating grin and again started saying I could have anything I wanted – drink, drugs or any of the girls.

'We are making movies upstairs. Go and watch or join in if you want. You like?'

I turned to where he was pointing and saw this wasted-looking Chinese bird flopped in a chair in just her knickers. I said, 'No, I'm all right, mate.'

He said how 'my friend' seemed to be enjoying himself, and I looked at Dougie and, even though he was blathering on to the other guy, Mr Tan wasn't listening, he was looking over at me. I walked back out thinking, This is just getting creepier by the minute.

I went over to the swimming pool down the bottom, and sat by the pool's edge was this young bird, real pretty she was with long blonde hair. She was wearing pink fluffy slippers, a see-through pink négligée and a bikini. She was crying her eyes out.

'What's the matter, darling?'

When she saw it was me (apparently, she'd seen me and Blondie arguing earlier) she just started spilling her guts. She was English too. Laura was her name. She said she was trapped here. Said she'd come here with her friend, months ago. Her mate had met this flash prick in Ibiza and he'd given her the full fairy story and said he'd marry her. Laura had come out here with her but he turned out to be a right bad cunt – slapped them both around, took their passports and put them into prostitution in the house. I asked if she meant the blonde geezer, and she said, 'Yeah.' She said no one ever talked back to him or answered him back, which is obviously why he got such a cob on when I told him to fuck off.

She'd been told her friend had left, but she knew that was crap because they didn't let anyone leave. All the girls started off wanting to leave, but then got so strung out on free gear that they couldn't be bothered. And they knew they wouldn't get the stuff free anywhere else. They were also making porn films and snuff movies upstairs, she said, and she thought her mate had been killed in one. She was proper terrified, this girl, and I genuinely felt sorry for her.

Then and there I just wanted out. The scene was so bad it made me want to shit. The whole thing just felt like an accident waiting to happen. She must have been able to see in my face that I didn't trust them either, and she asked if she could leave with me. I knew I might have my hands full myself and didn't want to make my problems any bigger. So I just said I'd see what I could do. As I walked away I decided that if the deal did go down as planned, I'd try and sneak her out anyway.

I went back into the big living room and Dougie was sat down with his Y-fronts round his ankles with the Chinese bird on her knees sucking his cock. He looked up at me and smiled and said, 'Dave? Don't worry.' I thought, I am *completely* on my own in this one. I noticed there was another guy in the room now, a big bodybuilder in a T-shirt – a real thick-necked, steroid monster. Then I saw something come out from behind the sofa, and it was only a bloody Rottweiler! I thought, Fuck me and bring on the clowns – what next? It padded round the room, and when it passed anyone, even the Dutch guys, it growled. Even the dog didn't like these guys.

It was really hot now. I still had my jacket on and was sweating my bollocks off. I loosened the knot a bit on the cardigan round my waist and checked on the position of the .38. Mr Tan left and out the window I caught sight of him going over our car. I knew that we were counting down to something not right. The guy came back in and Blondie asked me if he could count the money and if it was in the car.

I nodded at the other geezer and said, 'He should know; he's just had a fucking good look!'

I could feel sweat running down my face. The three Dutch guys kept looking at each other. Then they'd catch me looking at them and smile. I kept checking the gun. It was already in my head to that extent. I'd now accepted what was gonna go down. They meant to kill us both. The only thing stopping it was they weren't sure if we had the half mill on us. I felt like I could almost hear a ticking, like a clock on a bomb.

The dog was still prowling round and it curled its lips as it passed me. I'd already made sure I was stood by the door, near the corridor that led out to the entrance. I looked at my watch and saw that we'd now been here nearly two hours! I was double, hyper alert. It's funny, but your body seems to take over, like it's gathering itself together to save you.

The bodybuilder disappeared, taking the Chinese girl with him. Just as Dougie was doing up his pants, the mobile went off and everyone seemed to give a little jump at the same time. Dougie listened for a second and then said, 'Eh? You what?' The container was obviously empty. It had been a scam from the start. Dougie was too stupid even to disguise his reaction. I thought, You dozy, fucking *cunt* – you've just killed us. If I can tell what's being said, then so can the Dutch. I looked round at them and found them both looking right at me. I looked back at Dougie and his chest exploded out his back.

Everything went into slow-motion for a second. Even as I went for the .38 I clocked Dougie, his body flying slow but his guts going much quicker out the back of his jacket. Then a thousand noises blew up. Glass smashed as Dougie's body hit the French windows. The dog barked and leapt. I dived and tried to get the gun out. I felt like I was diving in a cloud of glass, blood and dog snot. I pulled out the .38 and in the middle of the arc, as I brought it round, I saw Mr Tan dead in line and shot one off. He was holding a vase above his head. The shot got him in the shoulder. I saw it bang in and puff out. I heard the boom of another shot – not mine – and the dog yelped. I came up and levelled the .38 out in front of me at Blondie. He already had a gun on me. I immediately saw it was a little Derringer. A tiny gun, but it carries big, fuck-off .45 bullets, like a Magnum, which is why Dougie was blown to fuck, *but* it only carries two rounds. And he'd used them. He had nothing left! I thought, Right Dave, hold your breath, don't pant, easy now . . .

He looked at me and he knew. The geezer knew he was fucked. I shot him right in the forehead. His head snapped real quick as if on elastic, and a massive ball of blood blew out behind. I thought – Wow! *Right* on the fucking button. Then I was suddenly aware of everyone in the building screaming. I didn't even look for Dougie. The French windows were red. I tightened the knot on the cardigan and went for the door. A crowd of women, including Laura, ran in a panic past the room. I didn't know if they'd seen it all happen. People were running in and out of rooms all over the place. I ran out, grabbed her hand and pulled her down the corridor. Someone else started shooting. They shot straight through the walls and the bullets came through at us. I could hear the wood splitting. I didn't want to go into the room and try to shoot him in case he got me, so I took a chance and ran down the corridor, pulling her with me. It was like running a gauntlet of bullets. I was thinking, This is just mental. Proper, proper mental!

In the hall it was fucking bedlam: people running everywhere and the girls all crying and screaming and doors banging. I told her to stay with me and we ran down the stairs into the basement. I looked at her, thinking she'd be in bits, but she wasn't. She wasn't crying or hysterical or anything, she'd slipped right into gear; calm and right on it. She looked really determined and I could see she knew this was her big chance to get out.

We came out in a corridor full of beer barrels and out into an underground car park. The ramp came back out the front of the building, by the main doors. They'd blocked in my Bee Em with the Merc so I jumped in it and drove it out the way. It had one of those yellow steering locks on, jamming the wheel round, so I could only drive it in an arc. It bumped up on to the lawn, and when I jumped out I saw Laura was in the car waiting, just staring at me like she was saying 'Hurry up!' People were running out the doors on to the grass. And from here I could see the French windows of the living room smashed open and the curtains blowing out.

I jumped in the car, revved it, and just as we were starting to pull away, the bodybuilder leapt out from nowhere and grabbed her. I couldn't speed off cos he looked like he'd rip her arm off. She started whacking him, but it was like a fly on an elephant. I pulled out the .38 and banged one off at him, but deliberately wide because I didn't want to hit her. He yelled, let go and pissed off sharpish as I floored it. We must have wheel-spun for thirty seconds before the tyres bit.

And then we were back out on the lane and speeding away, leaving behind one dead Dutch, one wounded one, one probably dead dog, one definitely dead Dougie, one bodybuilder with his pants full of crap, one knickerless Chinese bird and a yellow insane asylum full of freaked-out nutters. The kind of weekend break you don't get Judith Chalmers recommending on *Wish You Were Here*, put it that way.

I kept checking the mirror because I was half expecting the Merc to come zooming up behind us. Nothing showed, but I kept it as fast as I could on the twisty roads. I glanced round at this bird Laura and she was just sat still, all tensed up and staring ahead. She still looked focused on getting away. I thought she might have been in shock. She hadn't even noticed that one of her tits had popped out of her bikini top. Funny how men notice these little things in a woman. I didn't know whether to mention it or not – ain't that ridiculous? So she's sat there in a pink bikini and fluffy slippers, see-through négilgée and hair blowing in the wind, blasting through Holland in a red BMW with one tit out. And I'm thinking, Three days ago I was in the boozer with my mates. Now I'm in *The Great Escape* with Barbarella. Steve Mc-fucking-Queen, or what!

There was no-show behind us, so I eased off a bit but still kept us moving sharpish. I wanted to put as much distance as possible between us and that nuthouse. She still hadn't spoken. That suited me cos I just concentrated on getting us away.

I started shaking my arms and looking round myself to see if I'd been hurt or hit. Sometimes you don't know until after, when you're coming down. The pain can get lost in the surge of adrenalin. I felt like I was coming down from the biggest surge of the stuff I'd ever had in my life. And all the time I was thinking, Am I doing everything right? Don't screw it up now. Constantly thinking, Keep cool, Davey – you've got this far. I'd slowed the car but my brain was still doing 95 mph. But I was elated! I had this weird feeling of relief and this kind of . . . electric excitement at having been right in it, and survived it, and lived. And just knowing that gave me a hard-on. Actually, that ain't strictly true, cos I'd had a hard-on right through the gun battle and I still had it. Now that's something they never tell you in the films. Never saw John Wayne with a stiffy, did you? (Mind you, maybe that explains his walk.) But it's true, it does happen, believe me. Take it from one who knows. Must be some kind of primal thing. Beneath every boxer's groin-guard in a title fight, there's a boner. Either take my word for it or, if you feel up to it, ask Mike Tyson or Nigel Benn.

I started replaying it all now in my head, and when I did I realised how lucky I'd been. Much more than you know at the time in the middle of it all. Seeing someone shot just slips you into turbo on self-preservation. All your senses go on overdrive and soak things up. It sinks in and stays there.

Driving along now – still shitting because I still didn't know if they'd come after us – it all came out. And in funny little details: the colour of the vase that Mr Tan had picked up to throw (daft cunt); the puff of blood when I shot him; dirty Dougie with his cock in that bird's mouth (which is one of the ugliest sights it's been my misfortune to witness); his lungs flapping out his back in bits and hitting the windows; the dog snot; Blondie's head snapping sideways, and this little twitch his lip did just before I shot him; the sweat patches under the bodybuilder's armpits; and one other thing, which even shocked me when I remembered it: how, when I turned to go for the door and saw Laura and the others going past, I'd clocked her and thought, Nice legs. Now, ain't that just mental? Who would've thought you'd have the time, eh?

I'll tell you another thing I felt, and that was pride. I don't know if that sounds conceited – maybe it does, and I don't really care because I just felt so fucking chuffed with myself at the way it had all turned out. I think I had good reason to feel that way. You know what they say about 'when all around you are losing their heads'? Well, I didn't do that. If I hadn't done it right at the time they would have put a hole in me first. Fact. I felt like standing on the seat, driving with my feet, punching the air and shouting '*YES!*'

I knew I'd come out better than them because I'd stayed sober and on the ball. And because I wasn't stoned, pissed or too frightened to act. I didn't give anything away with my face like they all did. I kept my head, I had a gun and kept that too. Didn't fall under the spell of free fanny, free drugs, free beer and free everything else they offered. And when it came down to it, it all paid off. Thank fuck that time I did everything right, did what had to be done to get out of there alive. To stay alive, everything had to be done right. And I fucking did it. I was meant to die today. And I fucking didn't. Keeping my head is what saved me. It's not an easy lesson to learn, but if you do, you'll come out on top every time.

And to top it all, I'd managed to get this bird out as well. I looked over at her and she was nodding off beside me (tit still out, by the way. Nipple like a bullet). You might think that in the middle of all that shit back there, having to pull her along with me would have been a handicap, but it wasn't. It helped. In a weird way it made it easier because it gave me a mission. Someone to do it for. Sometimes that happens: you do things more determinedly for someone else cos you know they're relying on you, than you would normally do for yourself. And saving a damsel in distress, so to speak, was nearly as important as getting out myself.

I knew I was over here doing wrong and people had got blown away and someone I'd been with was now dead, but driving away now it felt like the real thing of the day was saving the girl. I know saving myself was a really big thing, obviously, but if I wanted to take any blame off myself for what had happened then bringing her out did that in one fell swoop. Justified me doing what I'd done. Even if saving her was more by accident than design. I'd fucking well still done it.

That's truly how I felt, real pleased that I'd got her out. I felt like it cleansed me of killing the geezer because it had been done for that. He was fully entitled to die anyway, for trying to kill me, but her asking me for help like she did . . . justified it all.

As we drove on, another element of the come-down hit me. That's when I started piling up the 'what ifs' in my mind. There seemed to be hundreds of them, and only one would have been enough. What if Blondie had felt the money when he tried to search me? What if we had put the cash in the car? What if someone had run in with a shotgun or AK-47? Or if I hadn't gone to see the Outcasts when they'd suggested carrying a piece? Or if one of them had come up behind and dropped me. Or the bodybuilder had come out to the car with a gun . . .

All these things I didn't really want to think about cos it was scary just thinking about them. It had been scary enough already. All of it. Every bit. But thinking about things made me realise how much of it had been out of my control. Fate seemed to play too big a part in it all for my liking.

And, one of the biggest 'what ifs' of all: if the blond geezer had gone for me first, and not Dougie. That still puzzled me. Surely he hadn't thought Dougie was a bigger threat than me? If he had gone for me first he would have painted the wall with me, no doubt about it, just as he had with Dougie's guts, cos I couldn't even remember seeing the gun come out. All I could think of was that it was because Dougie was much closer to him. But even so, the smart move would've been to pop me first.

Then something clicked into my head that suddenly seemed to make some sense of it. I thought about when you're playing pool and you've got one hanging over the pocket – you *know* you should leave it till later cos it's easy, but sometimes you just can't resist dropping it to hear that sound you know it's gonna make when it goes down. That might sound silly, but I think it was exactly the same feeling the blond geezer had. Out of the two of us, Dougie was the one over the pocket.

I looked at the dashboard clock and saw we'd been driving nearly an hour now. She was still asleep beside me. Unfortunately this convertible didn't have an electric roof and I didn't even fancy stopping to put it up. And I didn't want to wake her. So, now all I had to do was figure out how to get her tit back in before we hit the border.

We just drove and drove. I kept the .38 with me as long as I dared, then ditched it. I still had my passport, which made things easier, but I would have preferred it to be a moody so I couldn't be identified. I'd made sure I had my passport on me, though, in case everything went wonky and so I wouldn't have to go back to the hotel. Some stuff of mine and Dougie's would still be there in our room. I didn't know if Dougie had anything in his jacket that they could use to ID me. I was still shitting myself cos I didn't yet know how big an organisation they were and if they'd have people out after us at the borders or ferry or at the airport. Or if they might go to the police and try and paint themselves as victims of an attack or something. And I know what a murder hunt is all about. Once the Old Bill get on it, if you haven't covered your tracks they'll find you.

We spent one night in Holland, back with the Outcasts. They looked after us. Laura bedded down straight away (she'd still barely said a word) and I stayed up into the early hours telling them about what happened. When I saw their faces react as I told them about it all, it suddenly hit home even more than before what an amazing escape it had been. Phil was amazed I'd got out by only using three of the .38's six. He reminded me of how I'd asked him for spare rounds before. I said, 'Yeah, but I was joking, obviously.' Before I went to bed I gave Phil a hug and thanked him, and I really, really meant it. I tried to ring Jenny but got no answer, so I rang my mates

Rooster and Seymour and explained I had to be picked up at the docks.

Next day we drove into Belgium and spent a night there. I was frightened to be in the car now in case it had been ID'd. I left it at a car valeting place and was told it would be ready in a few hours. I just never went back. They could have it. I still had all the money on me so I bought a cheap Volkswagen camper van, hid Laura in the back in the cupboard under the sink, and drove on.

She was now dressed in some clothes of Phil's. I'd given her the big cardigan I had with me. It swamped her and made her look really tiny and frail. She had begun to say more as we travelled down, but not much. When I asked her what was the matter she said she didn't want to count her chickens. She wouldn't allow herself to believe it was really all over until we hit Dover. I knew it was that cos that's how I felt, but worse, because I knew when we got home that it still might not be over for me.

She hid in the van and I covered her with a blanket. On the ferry I called Jen. I could tell she was worried though she tried not to let it show. I didn't say too much cos I didn't want her worrying more. Just said it had gone wrong. We have a pact, me and Jen, that in a situation like this she only need ask me two questions: Are you hurt? (I said, 'No') and, Need I worry? (I said, 'No need to worry, babe'). And that was enough. I told her that I'd see her soon and that I loved her. Being so close to death makes you realise *exactly* what and who are important to you. And it's my policy to make sure those people know that. I can't begin to describe how good it was to hear her voice. She made me feel like a fucking winner.

Now that she knew not to worry I knew she'd be annoyed with me as well. She had reason to be, though. I'll tell you why. She knew I didn't like Dougie and what I thought of him, and that would piss her off cos I'd still got involved. When I can see what I think is going to happen, I can't help predicting it. I can't stop myself. Because if you don't and then it comes true, it's too late to say anything. And if you do, you end up turning into Mr I-Told-You-So! Then people just think, Oh shut up, you silly cunt! I only say what I think to people I value, so they trust me when I give advice. Though, in this case, I was guilty of 'do as I say, not as I do'.

The next call was to the guys we'd been on the job for. They knew it had all gone bad already, of course, because the container was empty, but they didn't know details. I told them that Dougie was dead and I'd had to pop somebody, and that they'd been making snuff movies there and I had this girl with me and that I'd got out. The geezer I was talking to freaked out and started telling me not to go to them, not to ring again, and that they'd be in touch.

'What shall I do with the money, then?' I said.

There was a long pause.

'What, you've still got the money?' He sounded surprised.

In that moment I thought, Fuck! I could have kept it. What with everything happening and the thousand things going on in my head, I hadn't even thought of saying that it had been on Dougie or nothing. His manner changed then, and he started saying how we should meet up as soon as I landed. I told him that I'd be in touch and hung up. Cheeky bastard.

I drove from Dover down to Folkestone where my really good mate Marcus lived. Laura stayed in the back all the way. We got to Marcus's and as soon as she tried to climb out the van she started to cry with relief. She really did start crying. Because her legs had gone dead from being curled up, Marcus carried her inside. Being a bodybuilder, a really huge geezer, he just scooped her up like a baby.

While she was asleep and waiting for her family to collect her, me and Marcus sat up and I told him what had happened. I was getting more used to telling it by now, but it was something you didn't need to elaborate at all. Just telling it was enough. Like when I told the Outcasts, seeing Marcus's reaction made me feel better and worse at the same time. I felt brilliant cos I was still here to tell it, but all those 'what ifs' started coming back to haunt me as well. But you can't dwell, can you? What if this and what if that. If your auntie was your uncle she'd smoke a pipe, as they say.

A couple more hours went by before her family came for her. When she woke up she borrowed some of Marcus's bird's clothes to change into. I was surprised by the way she had coped and kept it together. I looked at her and thought, Now ain't you got a good story to tell in a few years when you're picking the kids up from school.

I thought how lucky it was that those geezers had done it so amateur. I would've thought they'd done it lots of times. Maybe that was it, though. Maybe they had, and just got too clever and casual about killing these two English blokes. That'd explain that dozy blond prat only having a two-shot Derringer for the pair of us. Well, my heart bled for him.

Before Laura left I said it was best if we didn't know where each other was going in case we got caught. I didn't particularly want to know her address and I definitely didn't want her to know mine. As far as I knew there might be an Interpol bulletin out for us right now. But, I must admit, there were times afterwards when I wished I'd been able to keep in touch. I dare say this will do it.

The people waiting to take Laura away were from up north, I think. She left and I never saw her again.

I bypassed London and travelled up to Glasgow to stay with some mates. I still weren't sure what the outcome of it all would be. There might have been someone looking for us right then.

I called the blokes in London and they hadn't heard anything. They'd been having Dutch newspapers sent over, but there were no stories. Although the Dutch geezers weren't really in a position to go to the police and complain about anything, you just never know. They might have come up with some story.

I called Jen and she came up to see me. It was just so good to see her, I can hardly tell you. Brushes with death and disaster always give you a kick up the arse and give you back a little taste for life, don't they? And there's only one way to celebrate *that* . . .

18 Playing with Bulls

I met Danny Dyke through my mate Jonathan Evans. Danny was another public school boy with a perfect plum-in-the-mouth voice, a judge's son from a very rich family. He was a bit infatuated with the whole gangster scene, though, was Danny, but, unlike Jonathan who was happy enough to hang around the fringes of it, Danny wanted to be involved. It was all so different from his life. Well, you can imagine, can't you? From a twelve-grand-a-year private education to knocking around with us lot in pubs and nightclubs.

He was a really nice fella and people would've loved him for just being him; they would've liked him just as he was, but he wanted to be something he weren't. And like I explained to you right at the beginning, about that geezer Guy, don't do a 24-carat walk with 9-carat feet. There are certain worlds you just don't act in. Cos if you do you'll get sussed and the real ones will gobble you up whole.

Right at the beginning I got involved in a disagreement over Danny. He was pretending to be what he weren't and it rubbed some people up the wrong way and shit hit the fan. It was gonna lead to him either getting hurt or me stepping in and stopping it, which I did. I took on the row for him, won it, and then went back and had a few words with Danny. I could've not got involved, but Danny would have got a fucking good kicking. And that would've upset Jonathan too cos he was constantly, *constantly* worried about Danny and trying to get him to stop, telling him not to get sucked in by the excitement and the nightclubs and all that. But Danny was gone, mate. There was no telling him, unfortunately.

He was an osteopath by trade. He worked with the Welsh rugby team, stuff like that. When he was up in Wales he must've been bragging about the blokes he knew in London – this villain and that villain – and some people asked if he could get hold of any good puff (marijuana to you). So he said that he could.

Now he's never been a drug dealer in his life, and he's not really cut out for it, but he saw it as a way to get involved. These people told him how much they'd pay, he asked around in London how much the stuff would cost, and then did the figures. If one kilo of puff cost him, say, £1,400 and he sold it for £2,250, he's making £850 per kilo. He started off selling two kilos a week, then ten. He ended up shifting fifty fucking kilos a week!

That's an awful lot of money. He was getting the stuff cheap and selling it up in Wales for top dollar. But he weren't doing it for that; he didn't need the cash. He was just doing it for the buzz.

And the worst thing anyone can do is that first deal, because it makes it easier to do the next. I've seen it happen time and time again to people. Once they've done that first one their minds won't let them work eight hours a day, five days a week for a few hundred pounds when with one phone call they can make ten grand. And they can make ten phone calls a day. Please believe me, it's true, that selling drugs is more addictive than taking them.

So Danny got deeper and deeper in. He could see that the only way you get trusted in the gangster world is if you have a history and background in it that could be checked: old pals, associates, recommendations, that kind of thing. You can't buy that. And without that you ain't going nowhere. So he just lied. These geezers up in Wales that he was dealing with, he told them that all these names worked for him. I think he even said I worked for him. And he said that he had his own yacht and went out to Morocco to get the puff himself, y'know, that kinda crap. What he didn't realise was that he was signing his own death warrant.

After a few weeks of knowing him, these Welsh blokes saw right through him. They knew he was lying. Then when they knew he had no back-up, no muscle behind him, they thought,

Right! We can have him over here with no repercussions. So they asked him to get 200 kilos. Danny had never been late with a penny before, with the people he was dealing with in London. So when he asked for £280,000 worth he was given it. Then he shot up the motorway one morning to meet these Welsh geezers.

A couple of days went by and I got to hear about it. People started to get worried. Big Mark got hold of Danny's mobile phone bill and found out who he'd talked to on the day it happened. We found out the addresses and a few fellas piled in a car and went looking for him. We kicked in a few doors of people he'd told me he'd dealt with in the past, all drug dealers. None of them knew nothing or had seen him.

People were panicking now. The blokes in London thought he'd done a runner. Everyone else thought it might be something worse. No one knew where he was.

The next day his car was found burnt out in Brecon. So first they put him on Missing Persons, and then they made it a murder hunt and the police came in. They had thirty officers on it. You can imagine the little motivation speech they got from their chief after they knew it was a judge's son gone missing. A few Brownie points on offer there, you can bet. They tried to trace his movements by visiting the same people we had. And when the Old Bill questioned them about Danny, they started saying, 'Oh, yeah, Dave Courtney came round looking for him a few weeks ago.' You can imagine how that looked. The police put two and two together and came up with an iffy four.

So the police came and lifted me. They had videos from motorway cameras showing me driving up there. This was a bit of a bastard cos I knew I was fucking innocent of it, but all I had as a defence when they asked me if I done it was, 'No, I never.'

Anyway, these three cunts up in Wales, who were already known to the police as dealers, suddenly start pulling up outside their council houses in thirty-grand Shogun jeeps! One bought a new caravan, another one got a second new car. Now that little lot ain't come from an extra couple of quid rise in their giros. Clever cunts, obviously.

So it's pretty obvious who done it. The police have a rough idea what's happened so they nicked the three geezers and let me go. Now it's all falling into place. They had forensics crawling all over these guys' houses. Some spots of blood were found and they identified it as Danny's. The blokes just said that Danny had called to see them and they'd had a massive argument and a fight and he was bleeding. Then he drove off. So cos they explained it that way it was up to the police to prove otherwise. If they do them for murder and they get life, and then two years later Danny Dyke shows up . . .

Also, they didn't want it to go to court and risk them getting off cos you can't be tried twice for the same thing. As I well know. So because they couldn't produce a body, the case was dropped. You didn't need to be Albert fucking Einstein to work out the truth of it, but proving something's true is a different matter.

A while later, though, Danny's body did come to light. Then the full story came out. They found him in a scrapyard nearby, and when they searched it they found all this blood-soaked carpet, plaster and floorboards. They arrested the three blokes again, and one of their wives bubbled them.

She'd come home in the middle of it all and seen what they'd done. They were decorating the front room so the carpet was turned back and the walls were stripped down to plaster. One of them had come up behind Danny and smashed him to bits with a scaffolding pole right there. There was so much blood it went through the carpet on to the floorboards and into the dirt underneath. So the floorboards came up. And the bloodied bits of plaster were hammered down and dumped with the rest. The body was taken off by another bloke in a JCB so that none of the other three would know where it had gone. The JCB driver was the disposal man. In between their first arrest and the second one, this driver had mysteriously committed suicide.

All of them bar one got found guilty.

And that was that. A nice, smart young fella like Danny went out walking on thin ice and didn't come back. And he was an only child. Imagine what that did to his parents.

If you lie about being a boxer, you get knocked out. You pretend to be a lion tamer, you get your arm bit off. And, as the Yanks say, 'You play with the bull – you get the horns.'

Chisel that one in stone.

* * *

Around this time there was a proper meeting of old bulls. It was one of the things I've been most privileged to be part of.

Reg got in touch with me and said he'd like to arrange a meeting with some of his old rivals: Charlie Richardson and Frankie Fraser. In the old days the Krays and Charlie Richardson's firm had been enemies. Ronnie was sent down for shooting one of Charlie's boys, George Cornell, and Reg did Jack 'The Hat' McVitie. Frankie was part of the Richardsons. He got ten years in 1967 and was famous for something that supposedly involved one of their enemies' teeth, a pair of pliers and no anaesthetic. Frankie, in his own book, though, denied it ever happened. Charlie Richardson was given a 25-year stretch for something along similar lines. Boxing promoter, Alex Steen, was also to be at the meeting. Alex was another legendary figure, definitely one of the chaps and well respected in the boxing fraternity.

It was thirty years since they'd all seen each other. *Thirty* years. The Berlin Wall had been up and down in between!

On the day, we all drove down to see Reg in Maidstone nick in Kent. Reg's brother, Charlie, was also at the meeting. The screws allowed it to go on. They realised the importance of it. I think they considered it an honour just to witness it happening. In fact, one prison officer did say it was a privilege to be there. (On the day, at the table there was someone there who shouldn't have been. Gary Piper, who had chauffeured someone down, was a complete wanker. Hello, Gary.)

When we walked in, the chaps all hugged Reg. Then we sat down at one end of the visiting room that they'd set aside. They'd pushed all these tables together. Normally you can only have three visitors to a table, but the rules didn't apply on this day. It was like a boardroom with them all sat across from each other.

It was very emotional. I mean, at one time they'd been sworn enemies out to do each other, and now they were all here together. And seeing these men – who were older now but had once been the young lions of their day – just sat together talking . . . well, I'm never normally lost for words, but right then I was. And it just wasn't the right place for me to speak. Breathing almost seemed like an intrusion.

They swapped photos of old friends and reminisced about

the old days. There was something very, very nostalgic about it, just like it would be with any guys that had been in the same business; footballers, boxers, whatever. They admitted a few nasty things they'd done to each other, but ended up laughing about it. They even caught up on what had happened to a few that went missing in action.

'What about that albino geezer of yours?' one of them said.

'Oh, yeah. Him. *We* done him, didn't we, Frank?'

Someone said, 'Yeah, I thought you did.'

'Sorry 'bout that, Reg,' another one replied, like they'd just forgotten to return some garden shears they'd borrowed.

It was just funny little things like that, which probably sound odd to everyone else, but it was these men's pasts. They'd been right up there at the height of it all when it was still possible to live that life with some style. And they gave it glamour. That's just the truth. I think that's why the establishment, or the authorities, or whatever you want to call them, came down like a ton of bricks tipped off Everest. And the longer you're at this game, the shorter the odds get. You go from being a 100–1 outsider to the Old Bill's odds-on favourite.

I think they were all surprised at how well they got on. They realised that they could've been good friends instead of enemies. Think about what might have happened thirty years ago if they'd teamed up.

When they left, it was handshakes and hugs all round again. They'd talked about what they all hoped for the future but they knew they might not ever see each other again.

I gave Frankie Fraser a lift home in this black Mercedes 500SEL that I had. We ended up going the wrong way up the motorway so I spun it in the fast lane and dived through a gap in the central reservation where there was some traffic cones. We flattened a fair few and got back on the other side. Frankie was loving it.

'Oh, this is excellent!' he said. 'I ain't had a drive like this since that bank job in sixty-six!'

In fact, they all got together again not long after, but for a reason none of them would have wanted.

19 Two Funerals

My dad died on Tuesday, 14 March 1995. He'd been ill for some time, about six, seven years, suffering with angina. I remember first thinking that I was glad he was out of his pain now. And he was one of the very few people who are fortunate enough to die peacefully in their sleep. If you asked anybody how they'd want to go, that's how they'd choose, wouldn't they?

You get loads of weird feelings when someone dies. Guilt and regret and wishing you'd said things, and knowing it's too late afterwards to do anything now. So many things. And that odd feeling that you can't quite believe you'll never see them again. Especially when it comes to your parents. You always think they're gonna be there.

Over the last lot of years we hadn't seen each other as often as we should. That's another thing that can happen with family: you take each other for granted. I'd started seeing him more, though, over the last few years. You feel so many things, stupid things – am I visiting enough? Because in the last year he was very ill.

I think I embarrassed my family with what I was doing. On one occasion my mum said how it might be good for me down the pub with my mates when I was on the front page on the *Sun* and stuff like that, but it weren't nice for her at the bus stop having to answer questions about me. I didn't really realise that at the time. I'd thought by distancing myself, earlier, it would have made it easier. I'd always known I was very different from the world they were living in, and I hadn't wanted to force myself and my life on them.

Without meaning to, everything I seemed to do just went against the grain at home: prison, then the documentary, the court cases, the Kray twins thing, everything. It just weren't very nice for my family and they suffered for my choice of lifestyle.

They knew that a lot of what was printed and said about me was bollocks. No one knows the difference between the man and the myth more than your mum and dad. They just *know* you. But, at the same time, they didn't see me running around denying a lot of it either. So I couldn't really start moaning about that cos there was some truth in it. And in the end, your mum is Mum, ain't she? And your dad is still Dad. They can still tell you off.

I knew I'd broken his heart by how I'd turned out. That must have been hard for him to understand. Especially when everything he'd done for me had been right. Not exactly the model first son, was I? But I think cos I was his first boy that's why he found it difficult to give me as hard a whack as I deserved. Or maybe it was because he knew Mum was a harder hitter!

I remember when he'd had his heart operation, a triple by-pass, and they wouldn't let me see him in the hospital cos he was in one of those seclusion tents. I thought, Hang on, that's my dad and I want to see him. So I went downstairs and found the doctors' changing rooms. I put on a set of greens. The gown, the mask, the J-cloth on my head and the gloves. The works. When I walked back up all these nurses were saying, 'Morning, Doctor'! I just hoped that someone didn't grab me and pull me off to do some emergency brain surgery. But I guess everyone's got to start somewhere. Like Dr Frankenstein.

I went into the tent and tapped Dad and started talking to him in a whisper. He woke up and was trying to focus in on me but he saw me in these surgeon's greens and couldn't get his head round it. He must've thought he was still dreaming. Either that or, Christ! the NHS are getting hard-up these days. Then all the machines he was plugged into started bleeping! I think he overloaded them trying to compute the information. I thought I'd given him another bloody heart attack. All these nurses came in and started passing me respirators and stuff, like I knew what I was doing.

Anyway, the old man pulled through. Afterwards, when we'd talked about it, he said he'd thought a whole new career had opened up for me.

I said, 'What, as a doctor?'

'No,' he said, 'a silent assassin!'

Three days after my dad passed away, Ronnie Kray died. Ever since I'd first met Ronnie and Reggie Kray we'd become good friends and I'd often visited them inside. On the Friday I heard the news, like everyone else, that Ronnie had died of a heart attack in Broadmoor. He was in the twenty-seventh year of his time.

I got a call from Reg asking me if I'd go see him. I went down to Maidstone nick and he asked me if I'd arrange the security for Ron's funeral. I said I'd consider it an honour. The Krays weren't my guv'nors, but there was a feeling of mutual respect, and they were from the old school so I did look upon it as an honour to be the one who was asked. I knew it was gonna be a big affair, of course, but as I started the planning of it I realised just how huge. It turned out to be the biggest security operation of my life.

The funeral was planned for 29 March so we had over a week to prepare. That sounded like more than enough until the scale of it and all the possible problems started to hit home. And my old man's funeral was on the twenty-fifth, so there was all that in my head. It never rains . . . Reggie himself would be allowed out on day-release for the funeral, and that, in itself, meant that the security would have to be spot-on and run really tight. The eyes of this country and a lot more around the world would be on us that day. It was a proper big job to take on and a good one to do if it went well, but a bastard if it didn't.

There was loads of talk in the papers about what the day would be like. Already there was criticism from those who thought it'd be a chance for more Kray twin hero worship. There was talk of a hundred thousand people turning up. Some were calling for a police clamp-down to try and stop it altogether and prevent Ron being turned into a martyr. Police spokesmen started giving interviews to try and calm things down. And this was all before the day had even come.

I arranged a meeting with the Old Bill and at this meeting

were some of the most senior officers of the Met, superintendents and chiefs. In fact, it was all chiefs and no Indians.
I felt like fucking Custer! Quick, put the Jags in a circle – we'll
hold them off here! Funny one that, though, don't you think?
I mean, me and them sat around a table, with no lawyers
present. When they asked me anything it was all I could do not
to blurt out 'No comment!' just on instinct.

We discussed the route that would be taken. There were
certain roads we couldn't take the procession down because of
speed bumps; not a lot of dignity in two hundred people in
thirty limousines all playing trampolines. And cos the hearse
was going to be an old-fashioned horse-drawn one, there were
some roads that had a certain kind of tarmac that would make
their hooves slip. We'd have to get in touch with the council
to grit those.

And then there were the crowds expected, the security
needed and who would be where and doing what. I knew that
not every single person in the crowd would be pro-Kray; there
might be some nutters and troublemakers as well. It weren't till
one of the officers said something, though, that I realised what
that might lead to.

'I mean, what if someone decides to throw a tin of paint at
the hearse, for example?'

I thought, Fuck me, yeah. I could just picture it: a pot of
red paint smashing the glass and splattering everywhere. I
pointed out that cos of who was being buried the crowd would
probably contain a very small element of people who don't
have the most respect for the police.

'Look, don't take this the wrong way,' I said, 'but who
do you think these people would listen to most – a spotty
eighteen-year-old copper or a six-foot-four, bent-nosed geezer
with a lump in his jacket who looks like he eats babies on
toast?'

That little phrase 'lump in his jacket' sparked a bit of interest. We were already talking about the possibilities of some
sniper nutter taking pot-shots.

'*We* have men with firearms, Mr Courtney.'

I said, 'So have I. They just don't have certificates for them!'

I was told that any of my men spotted with a gun on the day
would be arrested like anyone else. I said that was fair enough,

but they weren't exactly gonna be brandishing them about. I also pointed out that when it came to deciding who and who not to let into the funeral parlour and the church and the cemetery, me and my lads would be a better bet. A normal policeman ain't gonna know that some geezer in front of him asking to be let in, who might look like just an ordinary fella and not all gangstery, might actually be the biggest face from Glasgow or Manchester, or wherever. And he ain't gonna look too kindly on some skinny constable barring his way.

What with the crowds expected, the difficulty of the route, the nature of the Krays, the TV and press scrutiny, and everything else that went along with it, I think the police had already sussed out what a fucking nightmare it could be. And that was confirmed in what one of them said to me, off the record (and I remember this word for word): 'We are more than happy to hand the reins for the day over to you, Mr Courtney, but if anything goes wrong the axe would fall squarely on you.' Which cheered me up no end, I can tell you.

No, actually, I did accept that. It was fair comment. In any situation, if there's a chance of you getting acclaim then there's also a risk of getting the blame. But I was determined that on this day, as much if not more than any other, everything was gonna run smoother than a Rolls-Royce in oil.

So, I got one hundred and fifty of the tastiest, biggest, baddest-looking, best-dressed naughty blokes that I knew. From all London and around the country. The old Filofax got a right pounding that day. I think I went through it from A to Z.

I looked at it this way: I didn't really need the best fighters there, although these blokes were some of the best, but the best *deterrents*. Because it was going to be so highly publicised I didn't want them to have to prove anything. I wanted prevention rather than cure. If some anti-Kray people did turn up I wanted them to be so intimidated that they wouldn't even want to see what these geezers were capable of. And just on looks alone these fellas were quality trouble-stoppers.

Among the many there was, in no particular order of naughtiness (deep breath), Marcus from Margate, Brooklyn John, Tucker, Big John and Jim from Birmingham, who brought a firm down to help me, Bernie and the Welsh boys,

Big Marc, Warwick, Andy, Tim, the Hastings firm, Southend
Chris, Coventry Stuart, Lance and Manny, Windows, Ian
Davies, some of my good friend Jamie's boys from Glasgow (I
ain't forgot the eight grand!), Adam, Ron and the boys from
the warehouse, Big Jamie, Bill, Bulldog Dean and Pete, the
boys from the Isle of Man, Mark Bates, doormen from the
Yacht Club, Legends, The Frog and Nightgown, Sunny Side
Up, the Hippodrome, Stringfellows, Browns, the Gas Club,
Camden Pally and the Ku Club, Rhino from *Gladiators* (he
was ready), Big Steve from SW1 and firm, Johnny Jacket, the
loan of some of Ian Waddley's top men, Terry Turbo, Steve
Raife, Locks and Boogie and the boys, Eddie and Dennis,
Frankie Baby, Seymour, some of Albert Chapman's firm and
some of Carlton's boys, Big Bird and Matthew and Spud,
Lenny McLean's son Jamie, Cecil, Don, Al Benson, Johnny
McGee, Rochester Les, Northern Billy, Big Joe from Gravesend, Billy Bonkers, Bill the Bomb (Canning Town), Bizmark,
Big Mel (Woolwich), H, Jimmy Andrews, Christian and Andy
(representatives from New Zealand), Big Bernie, Big Neil and
Hammer. Oh, and Ken the Dog. Is that enough colourful-
sounding characters for ya? Fuck me, I nearly had an asthma
attack reeling that list off!

In the week before, the preparations started. I'd contacted all
the boys I wanted and arranged for a big briefing session on
the day before. Then there was walkie-talkies, head mikes,
bulletproof vests and cars to be ordered. The undertakers
usually used grey Volvos so we had to track down thirty black
Daimlers. And then there was the wake to arrange, which was
done by the twins from The Guv'nors pub, and flowers to
order. The whole thing cost me the best part of ten grand but
I didn't begrudge any of it. It was going to be a day to
remember.

Then I had to visit the undertakers handling it all,
W. English & Son in Bethnal Green, to talk about flowers and
wreaths and floral tributes. Also there was the sorting out of
seating in the thirty limousines that would follow the hearse:
who would sit in which car and what position in the
procession. And the arrangements for letting people into the
funeral parlour, where Ronnie lay in an open casket for
mourners to come and pay their respects, and security for that

night and day. Everything really, bar getting God on the phone and sorting out the weather – 'Clear and bright would be nice, mate, if you can manage it. Cheers.'

I talked to Reg again and he said that he'd already rung the funeral parlour and they were expecting me. I walked into English & Son undertakers and introduced myself to a lady who worked there called Terry. She asked if I had anything proving I was Dave Courtney, which was quite right of her; better to be safe than sorry, as they say. Not being one for carrying a lot of official documents, I just reached in my pocket and pulled out my knuckleduster – solid gold with diamond-studded ridges and 'D.C.' engraved across it. I said it was my version of an American Express gold card. She looked up and laughed.

'Well, that'll do nicely,' she said.

'Yeah, never leave home without it.'

In the week before the funeral I drove around the route several times with Tucker and Terry Turbo. The route had been kept very hush-hush. I also took a friend of mine, Alastair, who had the knowledge to know where a sniper would position himself. There was about half a dozen rooftop locations that were prime spots.

During that week leading up to it people came to the funeral home to pay their respects to Ron. They were all carefully vetted by the chaps on guard there. I'd stationed lads in and around the place all week, day and night. And it's fucking hard to get someone who is willing to sleep over in a funeral home, especially when there's the deceased lying in state. I had to get rid of one of the people working for me in the parlour, a female member. Not that she'd done anything wrong to me, personally, but the other men didn't trust her judgement. Which was later proved to be right because she turned out to be a friend of the supergrass Bernard Mahoney, and in a book he wrote she moans about being sacked from the funeral. In that book, Mahoney grasses up everyone and says how I tried to put him out of his misery of being a grass, which I ain't denying.

Anyway, before the actual day I was in close contact with Reg. I had meetings with him and rang him up to let him know how things were going. I was able to ring Maidstone, and as long as it was during 'association' hours – that means the inmates are not locked in cells – then they would bring him to the phone. I've never known that before, where someone could ring a nick and ask to speak to a prisoner and they'd actually bring him to the phone! But cos of the scale of this thing all the normal rules were put on hold. When I rang Maidstone I did get tempted to reverse the charges.

A few days later, on the Saturday, it was my dad's day. He was buried in Honor Oak Cemetery. It was a well-turned-out service with family and close friends. It was a much smaller gathering than I knew Ron's would be, but it was a lot more hurtful for me. All those feelings that I'd had after his death, I'd been able to put them to the back of my mind during all the preparations for the other funeral. But on the day they all came back. In a way I felt like I hadn't even been able to give him enough time in death, in the same way I hadn't during his life. Afterwards I only asked for one thing of his, and that was his slippers. That might sound silly, but it was just something that made me think of him.

From that I had to immediately go back to the planning of the Ron's funeral. There was four days to go to the ceremony on Wednesday. The Tuesday night before the funeral I stayed over at the undertaker's with some of my boys. That was a strange one. Being in this darkened parlour with all these candles flickering around the casket. I didn't sleep much at all, actually.

About two in the morning I heard a noise outside, and when I looked out I saw these two blokes bent down looking at my car. What with it being so late at night (or early in the morning), mine was the only car in the street. It was a metallic black Jaguar XJS convertible V12. Every chrome part of it I'd had gold-plated. Every single part: the bumpers, the window trim, the wing mirrors, the door handles, the aerial, the badges, the windscreen wipers, the steering wheel, the dash dials, all the locks, even the radio switches. The leaping jaguar on the bonnet was gold-plated with two diamonds for eyes. I modelled it after the 'John Player Special' Formula One racing car colours. It was villainy on wheels. Flash but tasteful, that motor of mine was. Tastefully flash. It had been customised for me by Les, Joe and Gary from Rochester, all really good, long-term friends of mine who'll always be close to my heart.

This car, by the way, was the one that led to one of the funniest lines I remember hearing – and it was from one of the Old Bill. I was flying through central London one night at three in the morning with some of the boys, foot flat to the floor, top down, cigar in, music on, head stubble vibrating in the wind. A police car clocked us and pulled out. I didn't even see them, but it must've taken them a few miles just to catch up. I pulled over and the copper got out and strolled up to me. He was already smiling. He leant on the door and gave the car the once-over.

'Having a bit of trouble getting her off the ground, sir?'

Oh, yes! Nice one. That was a cracking little line, that was. I had to tip my hat to that little witticism, and I told him it was worth getting the six points just for that. Turns out I'd been doing 140 mph. Fuck me, I was shocked. The geezer I'd bought the Jag off said it did *one fifty*! Lying bastard.

Anyway, these cunts outside the funeral parlour giving it a good inspection obviously thought it looked fast enough, so I went out and chased them off up the road. Fancy, trying to rob a car outside a funeral home. In the times I'd had it parked outside English's, when I was visiting or staying over, I'd picked up loads and loads of parking tickets. I don't know about the 'rest' bit, but you couldn't even fucking park in peace! All those tickets, though, they did make a good bonfire.

Anyway, when I went out in the morning I found the Jag's windscreen in bits on the front seats along with a hammer. I was absolutely gutted cos it was the perfect mourning car to use at a funeral.

We did one more sweep of the route and I checked my boys were stationed on the rooftop spots with nothing more than binoculars (honest, officer). Trouble was, the police had had the same idea. So my lads were looking at them and they were looking back, everyone wondering who was who. Because of all our lot and all the police, there weren't no room for a bloody sniper. I rang one of the superintendents and he radioed the situation through to his lads. I think when the police knew I'd stationed my boys at the same place as theirs, they knew I was doing the job proper.

I'd been in English's all night so I went home early in the morning and got bathed and ready. Black three-piece suit and black shirt. Versace, black leather overcoat. Freshly shaved head.

I went back to English & Son. Vanloads of flowers started to turn up until the whole pavement in front of the building was lined with bouquets and floral tributes. As well as tributes from all the chaps, there were hundreds more from showbiz people, sports stars, actors, actresses, and rock stars. People from the music world like Roger Daltry from The Who and manager Bill Curbishly, Morrissey, Madness, UB40, East 17, Lulu, even Frank Sinatra. And ones from the boxers Nigel Benn, Charlie Magri and Henry Cooper, and boxing promoter Frank Warren; sports stars like Lester Piggott, Oliver Skeet, Jimmy White, George Best; David Bailey (who had taken the most famous photo of the twins in the sixties), Twiggy, Vivienne Westwood, Ray Winston, Michael Caine, Oliver Reed, Jamie Foreman, Patsy Kensit, Bill Murray; Steve McFadden, Mike Reid, Barbara Windsor and the *EastEnders* cast; Jim Davidson, Peter Stringfellow, crime writers Toby van Judge and Tony Thompson, Gary Bushell, the *Sun, News of the World*, BBC and ITV.

Among the many, many tributes from admirers and business associates far and wide were ones from America: a photo of Manhattan in a frame of flowers and signed 'From New York'; Wilf Pine, good friend of the Krays and their link with the American boys (he'd be there at the funeral; he's still got a 24-hour minder, a guy called Big John); John Gotti; Danny Simms sent big flowers, and so did the American serial killer the Black Widow; and Angela (I can't say any more than that). There were also tributes sent by the Isle Of Man Boys, one from the Irish contingent with no name, the three big bike gangs, all the main traveller families, and a big fuck-off white wreath with Chinese writing on.

Then there were flowers from all the British families: the Hunts, Hendersons, Mapps, Chevralls, Hawards, Frenches, Arifs, Brindles, Rileys, Smiths, the Halls from Battersea, the Webbs, Oliphants, Lambrianous, Taylors, O'Brians, Callaghans, Pintos, Bowers, and more.

Nearly everyone I've already mentioned at some point sent their own tribute, so I'll just list the others (bear with me); it was a proper, *proper* history book of villainy: Tommy Wisbey, Ronnie Biggs, Jimmy and Johnny Nash, Teddy Dennis, Roy Shaw, Lenny McLean, Paddy Monaghan, Buster, Bruce Reynolds, Ronnie Knight, Alex and Greg Steen, Kevin and Kenny Noye, McVicar, Charlie Richardson, Frankie Fraser, Joey Pyle, Mick Colby, Ronnie Easterbrook, Albert Chapman (of the Elbow Rooms, Birmingham), Freddie Foreman, John Colbert (close friend of Charlie Kray and me), Dave Simms and Tony (of Sophisticats) and Tony's dancer wife, Lee.

Fuck me, the scent from them all nearly turned me into a tree-hugging hippy on the spot. Talk about flower power!

And there was more (c'mon, I'm on a roll now): Charles Bronson (the prisoner, and a good, close friend of Ron's), Joey Martin (the longest-serving prisoner in British jails), Jay, Mickey Regan, Caesar the Geezer (a good friend of the twins, and every prisoner), a right South London face called Dave Thirston, a big name called Frankie Simms, Brendan McGirr, Dean and Julie, Kevin, Shaun, Perry, Roy, Dean and Chrissy the Greek and the whole of Premier, Laurie Scott, Joe and Gary and the boys from Dexters, Robbie and the boys from Propaganda, Matt and the boys from Welling, the ICF (Inner City Firm), Jimmy Andrews, Robbie and Johnny and the big scouse firm, Terry and Eileen (mates from the Wood), Beau, Bish, Gavin, Nath, Si and Conor (the Rainham posse), Rubber Ron and Keith Winn, Ian Studdard and James Cohen, Ralph Haeems and Sid Ray (Ron's solicitors during the original murder trial), all the top guard security firms, over a hundred doormen from every club, loads of football teams; One Nation, Dreamscape and Garage Nation (mine and Terry Turbo's rave companies), and – last, but not least – a big fuck-off 'Thank You' wreath from all the shareholders at Interflora!

And any bees lucky enough to be in the vicinity that day fed themselves so fucking big they had to catch buses back to the hive. I nearly took a couple of the fuckers on as minders.

Nearly all of those who sent flowers (at least those who were at liberty to do so) also attended as mourners.

Right across the length of the wall of English's was Reggie's tribute which said TO THE OTHER HALF OF ME, spelt out in white flowers.

The press turned up first, and took up strategic positions.

Hundreds of them, on scaffolding and boxes, stood on walls and up on roofs. Some of the cameras looked more like rifles and machine guns.

Because most of the people with me didn't want to be on camera, I had a dozen of the boys, hand-picked by me, stood in a line right across the front of the place, every single one impeccably dressed. All bang in a straight line as if they were at attention. Everyone did their utmost to look the part for Reg and Ron. All the security were black-suited up with dark sunglasses. Two ranks in front and more round the back. When the limos arrived I had one of my blokes opening the doors. Then there was about ten more inside the parlour, half a dozen with rifle sights placed on rooftops along the route, more by the church and up by the cemetery, and every single last one of the others placed strategically along the roads. It looked like, and was, a proper army. When I looked around at them, I thought, This little show of strength is gonna kick the whole world up the arse.

The crowds had been gathering outside. They were kept back by barriers, but they stood on everything and anything to get a better view.

Then certain mourners close to the twins started arriving to pay their respects to Ron and give him a kiss on the forehead before the casket was closed. And who should turn up but the woman I'd taken out from guarding the place the day before.

The hearse pulled up outside English's. Now that was something else: an old Victorian style horse-drawn carriage; all black and gold it was, and pulled by six black horses with black plume head-dresses. Both sides of it carried big flowered letters. One side said RON and the other THE COLONEL, his nickname. The roof was completely covered in flowers. Two of the tributes were boxing gloves made from red flowers. Brother Charlie had done an excellent job of arranging all the classy bits around the procession in a way that only Charlie could, cos the man oozes class and quality. And he worked very hard at helping me at the funeral.

Then Reg arrived at the parlour to pay his respects. He was brought in a Home Office car with two prison officers, a man and a woman. They were about the nicest screws you could get, respectful and quiet. They knew they were in for some flak for keeping Reg handcuffed the whole time, so they had nice screws, not nasty ones. But not uncuffing him was pretty naughty, when you think about it. They even kept him cuffed in church. They tried to lessen the impact of that by keeping the wardens low-key, which is something they must've learned from when the twins' mum died in 1983. For that funeral Reg and Ron had been handcuffed to the two tallest prison officers then serving. For no reason you could think of. And the twins ain't the tallest geezers themselves, so it just looked well over the top, ridiculous and really insensitive.

I don't give a fuck who you are or what you've done, when your mum dies you deserve as much respect as the next man.

As soon as he left the car the crowds started cheering and whistling. I'd knew he'd get a warm welcome, but it surprised me a bit (I didn't know then it was gonna grow even more). I met Reg at the door. He put his arm round me, kissed my forehead and thanked me for the arrangements for the day. I walked in with him. Inside he was met by everyone with handshakes and kisses. Then he went in to see his brother for the last time.

The route for the procession had been kept from everyone except the ones who had to know. It was gonna be this: the hearse leaves English & Son and goes along Bethnal Green Road, past Vallance Road where the twins grew up, and round the corner to St Matthew's Church nearby for the service; from there the procession goes off through Bow and then north to Chingford Mount Cemetery, which was about an eleven-mile journey. There would be thirty cars following the hearse, which wouldn't be going much more than walking pace, so God knows how long it would take. I estimated a couple of hours. And then, after the burial, back down to Andy and George's place, The Guv'nors, for the wake.

The casket was brought out. It was oak with gold handles and had a white crucifix on top. Then the funeral procession set off with the head undertaker, Paul Keys, leading the way. Behind him, holding the first horses, was Michael Santry, known as 'Johnny Jacket'. Half a dozen of my boys walked alongside the hearse, but because it was higher than we thought, they ended up shielding the coffin with just their heads. Then there was Reg's car, and behind that the one with me, Brendan, Terry, Dave, Steve, Tucker and Wolfie.

The slow drive to the church was the most harrowing part for me cos the streets were the narrowest and most densely packed. Bethnal Green was the twins' old manor so there was a mass of people there. Some of the older ones would've lived there when the twins ran the place, but the younger ones that were hanging off lamp-posts and railings to get a look, they wouldn't have even been born. Where the streets were narrow the police linked arms as a barrier, with their backs to the crowd. In front of them I stationed some of my men, who stood looking back into the crowds. I must admit that the police did an excellent job just keeping that amount of people on the pavement. It weren't that people were pushing deliberately, but more kept coming and the pure volume of people crushed everyone forward. The coppers stood fast, though, and a lot of them went home after that with their little arms hanging off. I take my hat off to them for that.

Along Bethnal Green Road we paused for a few seconds at the top of Vallance Road, and then moved on. Two streets down we all turned into St Matthew's Row. Now, St Matthew's is a church, not a cathedral, and the road it's on is fairly narrow, but there were thousands and thousands of people all crammed around the church and up the row. Just everywhere. I could see if it did go wrong here it would go wrong in a big way. And it could even go wrong because people who were fans of Ron and Reg's were almost hysterical, crying and pushing. This was the nervy bit, cos the hearse had difficulty getting through the mourners. It took them twenty minutes just to get the coffin off the hearse, through the crowds and into the church.

The church only took two hundred, but they squeezed in three. Everyone who was anyone was there. It was like a *Who's Who* of gangland Britain, past and present. I saw Reg in and then stood at the entrance with my lads. A few people got the hump that I didn't let them in, but once it had gone a hundred over capacity there's not a lot you can do. Everyone left outside listened to the service on a public address system.

Like I said, Reggie was kept handcuffed during the service. The police even had an armed officer hidden behind the funnels of the organ.

It had been a bright day since the morning, so God must

have got my little request about the weather (I'll pay you when I get there). By the time Ron's casket was carried out, the sun had got even stronger. Four of the pallbearers had been chosen because they represented different parts of London: Charlie Kray for East (obviously), Teddy Dennis for West, Freddie Foreman for South (he was out on parole for the Security Express job) and Johnny Nash for North. It was a kind of tribute to Ron that all the old manors, who hadn't always seen eye to eye, came together to carry him out.

When Reg came out of the church the crowds went mad again. I mean really mad. I was like somethng you used to see with The Beatles. People were crying and screaming out, 'We love you Reg!' and 'Let him go!' and loads of hands were reaching out to touch him or shake his hand. It was really strange. He couldn't have possibly got a better welcome from so many different kinds of people, from celebrities to road sweepers. Outside the church, I looked out and saw young and old, black and white, tramps and posh people; everyone wanted to see him or be near him. I thought, That kind of fame is power. But the trouble comes when you get infamous more than famous. Infamy is something you can't always use for yourself like fame, it's more out of control.

Frankie Fraser, who was travelling in a car with Paddy Monaghan, an ex-bareknuckle fighter, told me later that one of the crowd handed him a ten-quid note to autograph. He did it, and then turned to Paddy and said some of the chaps from the old days wouldn't have believed that – someone handing Frankie Fraser a tenner and him giving it back!

Right from the start I knew things would go like clockwork cos I'd planned it so strict. I'd gone over all the possibilities and sat down with others and bounced ideas around in case I'd missed something. The only uncertain thing was the crowd, really, but when I started to see how Reg was received I knew this would be OK. In fact, because they were so pro-Kray, especially in the East End, if anyone had done anything out of order I think the crowd would've ripped them to bits before any of my boys even got there.

The procession set off for the cemetery. Nothing had been seen like this since Winston Churchill's funeral, the old Victorian hearse pulled by the six black horses being led, on foot, by the head undertaker. Behind him, walking next to the coach and horses, another six top-hatted undertakers and, outside them, half a dozen policemen. Immediately behind was the car carrying Reg. I hadn't been told but I'd assumed the car had bulletproof glass, but I stationed six of my stockiest lads to walk alongside it. Outside them were another six police. Directly behind that was the car with me, Tucker, Wolfie and Dave, and behind us there was a line of thirty black Daimler limousines with family and friends. This line of cars was a quarter of a mile long itself. At the head of the hearse were police motorbikes with blue lights on and more along the length of the procession. It was a real, proper gangland burial. The pavements and road were full of people right up to both sides of the cars. All shopkeepers were out watching and office workers looking out from windows. I'd never seen anything like it, and don't suppose I will again. The only other person you could imagine it happening for is Reg himself.

I sat in the back of the limo thinking about the difference between this and my dad's funeral. At this one there were crowds cheering and taking photos, not what you'd expect at a burial, and at my dad's I just thought of the crying.

People walked alongside us for miles, some taking pictures, sometimes running from the back to get ahead and see Reg and the hearse. A police helicopter followed us all the way. The police actually cordoned off the A2 where we crossed it. That was how big it was. Normally they wouldn't do that for anything but a state funeral. Then we went through Bow, over the flyover and up through Hackney, towards Chingford. The crowds thinned out here and we picked up speed a bit from walking pace.

I knew there would be loads more people at the cemetery, but I wasn't prepared for what was waiting. On top of all the people already there I think all the others from outside the church had gone up there as well. Everything slowed down to a crawl up Old Church Road. People were lined five deep solid on either side. The whole place was completely covered with people. It was unbelievable. You could not see the grass in the cemetery because of the crowds. People were on the walls and even up trees with cameras and binoculars. But there was no noise like before. And that amount of people being silent is really strange. It was really eerie.

It had taken nearly two hours to get there. The horses looked shagged. All of them were drenched with sweat, and steaming. The purple and black saddle blankets they were wearing were stuck to their flanks. When Reg got out he stopped and patted them. Before he went to the open grave he stopped and laid some flowers at the graves of his mother and wife and kissed both headstones.

At the cemetery it was the same story as the church – everybody wanted to get close. Everyone wanted to be around the hole looking in. A few dirty looks got thrown my way when I had to stop a few and tell them they couldn't go any further. But everyone was really well behaved.

As soon as the burial service was over, Reg was taken out the back of the cemetery to a waiting car and driven to Maidstone with a police escort. These last few hours had been the first time he'd been out of prison since his mum's funeral twelve years ago. What a bastard that is, only seeing the light of day when one of your family dies.

We all left and went down to the wake at Lenny McLean's old pub, The Guv'nors in Stepney. It was now run by two other twins, funnily enough, Andrew and George. They laid on a beautiful spread, but so many people turned up – about five hundred – that they had to send out for more food and drink. Then me and all the fellas on security went on to another pub on our own. It was the first time that all the blokes on security duty had been back together in one place, so I took the chance to thank them for a job well done. Everything had gone sweet. I didn't realise then that things would turn sour.

The press coverage the next day was massive. I mean huge. Front pages and full-colour double-page spreads. Some just reported what had gone on and how amazing it was, and others, like some of the tabloids, did their usual hysterical bit: VILLAIN BURIED LIKE HERO, GONE AND BEST FORGOTTEN, crap like that. Which is pretty fucking hypocritical when you think about all the copies they've sold on the back of all the Kray twin stories over the years. But everyone wanted to have their say. And one of the two most famous villains in the country being buried, and being buried in such style, was bound to make the papers wank themselves cross-eyed over it.

There were loads of pictures of Reg, of course, and a lot of the boys in front of the funeral home cos that was just too good a photo to resist; all those black-suited wardrobes lined up on parade. Most of the photos of me were taken at that point. Apart from that, I kept a pretty low profile, which was unusual for me (generally I'd run towards a camera, not away from it), but I knew this weren't the time and place for that. I'd wanted to run a proper tight little ship that day and not let any ego distract me from that.

It didn't stop the papers from running articles on me, though. The crime desk reporters knew me well from all the past stories. It's an odd thing reading about yourself from someone else's point of view, especially when they were using phrases like 'Boss of London's toughest bouncers', 'Burly minder' and 'Kray twin henchman and heir'. I thought, Well, two out of three ain't bad! One of the reporters just went on and on about how we were all dressed. Nothing else but that. My leather overcoat (thanks for that, Joe) nearly gave him a heart attack. He said I looked like I'd stepped off the set of *Mad Max*! The prat meant it as an insult, but I just thought, Brilliant – I love that film.

The police chiefs sent me a really nice complimentary letter commending the handling of the security, which was another hypocritical thing cos from the second the funeral had ended, and I mean from that *second*, they decided to come down on me like a ton of bricks and either put me away or put me out of business.

I didn't realise till I got back in the country how bad it was.

Straight after the funeral I took forty of the boys away on holiday to Tenerife to wind down and celebrate things going well. Get some real sun as well, not that forty-watt stuff that passes for sunshine in Britain. A big mate of mine out in Tenerife looks after all the timeshares, so we got the accommodation for free and I paid for the flights.

It was a proper man's holiday it was: just the boys having a good time. And ain't Linekers, Bobby's Bar and all those places on the strip the best place to be when you're buzzing? Friends of mine, Tony and Sue, who are residents out there, made sure it was a very good holiday. We were a real floorshow for the other sunbathers – forty burnt, tattooed lumps playing football with crates of beer for goalposts and having a laugh. Yeah, spot the English.

So, I'm sat there on the beach with a hole dug in the sand full of water and a bottle of champagne in it, like you do, going redder than a baboon's arse and reading the *News of the World* like any good Brit abroad. I turns the page and sees this headline: GHOULS SNORTED COKE OFF RONNIE KRAY'S COFFIN! A mouthful of champagne made a quick exit down my nose. There was a photo of Ronnie laid out in the coffin, a photo of Reg (caption: 'Reggie: Planning action') and under that a picture of me (caption: 'Courtney: Security boss'). And next to that another, smaller headline: ANGRY REG CALLS FAMILY SUMMIT OVER OUTRAGE.

I thought, *What*? Fuck me, where's this come from? It went on to say that the blokes guarding Ron in the parlour had snorted coke off the coffin, played with a Ouija board and put a Sony Walkman on the body! I was thinking, Oh please, someone kick me in the nuts and wake me up. Reg was said to be 'seething with rage in Maidstone jail and has now summoned brother Charlie so they can discuss what action to take'. It got better: 'The first person they will want to interview is David Courtney.' The article was trying to make out that some kind of big gangland meeting was being organised, and I was gonna get shot!

Now don't you just hate it when that happens? That's the kind of thing that can completely fuck up a holiday. And I thought the worst thing I'd have to worry about would be sunburn and headbutting a few lairy sharks out at sea. I was sat there like an even more outraged version of Victor Meldrew, going, 'I don't fucking *believe* it!'

All the boys gathered round to have a gander. Then I got straight on the phone to Reg.

'Do I have to explain?' was the very first thing I said.

He went, 'No, no. Listen, Dave, I've been in prison for thirty years and you should see some of the rubbish they've wrote about me. Don't lose any sleep over it. I know what you did on the day and thanks for that.'

He said he hadn't even talked to the paper, even though they'd quoted him saying some things. He knows how the press works, but he didn't have the slightest idea where the story came from. It turned out later it had been the work of the woman I'd taken out of the funeral parlour the night before. I knew she had got the hump about it but didn't realise it was that bad. She'd got more hump than a camel farm.

But the good news from telephoning Reg called for only one thing: more champagne! And then following that, of course, a near-death experience. Well, no holiday's complete without one.

Next day we all went out to sea on Sue's boat to watch the whales mating. Being out in the middle of the ocean they probably thought they were safe from David Attenborough and his film crew, and then us lot turn up to watch them having a shag. Fancy that, forty flat-nosed fuckers staring at you giving your missus one. Talk about a passion killer. Didn't put them off, though. They must have been humpbacks.

While we were miles out a freak storm blew up from nowhere. One minute, nothing, and then the next, the sea and wind going *Arrgghh!! Die you bastards!!* Everyone was downstairs being sick. I could see the old captain panicking a bit, so I tried to keep the morale up by standing on deck, hanging on to a bit of rope and shouting out, 'Forward! Forward!' Then things got really bad. We all put on lifejackets. One of the fellas, Elliot, put on three. I asked him what the fuck he was doing. He said he was bigger than everyone else and he didn't reckon much to these flat lifejackets.

I said, 'Why don't you try *inflating* one of them, you silly fucker?'

I knew things had gone from bad to even fucking badder when I turned round and the bleedin' captain's *lashed* himself to the wheel with rope and he's screaming into the radio, 'MAYDAY! MAYDAY!' Now call me old-fashioned, but that's not what I want from the captain of a seafaring vessel. I felt a *Titanic* moment coming on.

The waves were like mountains. One minute they were there, fifty feet high with us bobbing on top, and then suddenly they'd disappear from under us leaving this massive empty drop. It was like that: wave rise – wave suck out underneath – boat drop into huge hole. Seriously, it was that bad. Proper, proper fucking scary. The sea don't respect some little geezers from London however big and hard they think they are. If the sea has got the hump, mate, it will just smash you to fucking pieces.

We finally got out of it somehow (I think we farted the boat clear) and limped back into port. Mark Bates kept asking whose idea this had been anyway. I definitely weren't gonna get credit for that – Batesy with the hump is a frightening sight.

They say that the only reason the Pope kisses the runway when he lands is cos he's terrified of flying. Well, we all did 'a Pope', big-time. We looked like the whitest bunch of Muslims you've ever seen, all praying to Mecca.

But, genuinely, everyone thought they might die that day.

I came back from holiday to find that half my doormen had been sacked. The fallout from the funeral had been immediate.

The public perception was that the Kray empire was alive and well. It gave the old Kray myth a big injection of adrenalin and made me look like not only a 'Kray henchman' but heir to the throne. First, I was never their henchman or a 'Kray gang member'. When they were in their heyday I was in a Silver Cross chewing a rusk! And, second, there was no throne to inherit. Things had changed since their time. London was different now. Everything had fragmented. Drugs had changed everything. A lot of the old allegiances and loyalties had gone with the drugs coming in big-time.

A lot of the romance had gone out of crime cos the crime of the moment was drugs. And there's not a lot of romance around drugs – a lot of wealth, but little romance. Less morals, less standards, less loyalty and less honour among the drug culture than there was among the more traditional forms of crime. Drugs changed everything. If someone can break into their mum's house and nick things to get their next fix, how can you expect them not to grass you up? And like a lot of junkies will do anything for a hit, a lot of dealers will do anything for their money. But with the huge sums of money that can be earned, you sometimes have to deal with people you normally wouldn't like to do business with.

Please don't think I'm getting on my high horse about this, saying I think it's wrong or bad, because I don't, not at all. I tried it, it didn't agree with me, and although I fell behind financially compared to some friends of mine, I'm just saying it wasn't right for me. But I do know people who do, and they're nice fellas.

I knew I was looked at as one of that kind of old-type villain, which I took as a compliment. Those were the men that had impressed me when I was younger, and I held them very close to my heart now I knew them. And if that's what I'd aspired to because I was around these people, then I thank them.

What standing I had in the crime world was because I got on with all the different factions in the country. Which was the same way I'd got on in the doorman world, by making friends not enemies. And, as with the doormen companies, London's different firms and families might not always have got on with each other, but they got on with me. And if some of them weren't talking because of some bother between them then I could step in and mediate. Sort of like a UN ambassador. With knuckledusters. It weren't gonna get me any Nobel Peace prize, though.

I'm only half-joking here, actually. I'm not meaning this to be big-headed cos it's just fact, but I knew, and the *police* knew (cos they'd admitted it to me), that because I was in a position to smooth things over I'd actually stopped loads of trouble happening. A lot of the coppers on the beat, and the ones immediately above them, secretly acknowledged that. I mean, they knew that if some war was brewing between two firms, those people wouldn't listen for one second to the Old Bill. And then they'd have to do something about it.

The weirdest thing happened when me and this other guy both went up for the door contracts at these seaside nightclubs. In the end he got it, which didn't bother me at all. Some you get, some you don't. Me and my boys went for a drink and ended up in the same club as the other geezer out celebrating with his mates. He ordered some champagne, and cos he was struggling to get the cork out he started having a go at it with his teeth. Not a clever one. The fucking cork fired out, straight down his throat, and he choked to death right there! And because when they took his body to the hospital it weren't apparent how he died (and they hadn't been told), they called the police. The Old Bill realised he was one of the geezers I'd been up against for the contract, and they thought I'd topped him. For *that*. Fucking hell! I thought, That takes the chocolate digestive, that does – being accused of shooting someone with a bottle of fizzy wine! In the end I got the contract anyway and, without him around, his company took a turn for the worse, so I took that over. On the back of that me and Terry ended up making our rave company, One Nation, even bigger.

So the frontline police weren't that against me. The order to go after me would have come down from high up. The police looked at all the security during the funeral as not only a show of strength by an army, but also an act of defiance. Like the IRA firing guns over a grave. The strength scared them and the defiance pissed them off. In their eyes, one villain who had been hero-worshipped had just been buried and they didn't want another one to come along.

That's how they looked at it. And me. The whole clubbing scene thing I was part of; the writing for the *Scene* magazine and co-running One Nation; the things I had done and not got nicked for; the things I'd done and got away with; and then saying 'Course I done it' on the court steps; the fact they'd tried to get people to grass me up and failed; the way I played them at their own game; the way I poked fun at them; the funeral, of course; me being on telly in stuff like *Minder* and *The Paradise Club* and, funnily enough, *The Bill* where I played a South London gangster and used all my villainy friends as extras (that went down well); making records with my sexy missus; me driving around in a Rolls-Royce and generally being a flash bastard; even the fact that I could make some of *them* laugh at the stuff I did. And . . . what else? Let me think. Oh yeah, me being devilishly handsome on top of it all. That didn't help. So just *everything*, really. All of it. The whole Dave Courtney Thing stuck in their throats like a sideways banana. And I was so upset by this I could hardly eat for ten minutes. I think they thought, Well we've been telling people for years that crime doesn't pay, and he's running around making it look like a career option! So they set out to lose me my work, get rid of my jobs, take away my driving licence, warn off club owners that used my men, and close down my pub.

Listen to this. I now know men who were in the force at this time – men who later went on to work for me as doormen – who told me exactly what the police's objectives were: shut him down, shut him up, raid his house, freeze him out, make him lose his doormen, stop this hero-worship thing and start some nasty rumours in the hope that if you throw enough shit, some will stick. Thank God I baby-oiled myself. I was told that they would not allow someone like myself to become a popular villain with the media.

They hit my pub, The Albion in Woolwich. I'd done The Albion out like a proper little theme pub; it was all gangstery: Tommy guns, violin cases and knuckledusters on the walls, signed pictures of all the big chaps in London, photos of Jimmy Cagney, Bogart and Edward G. Robinson, drawings by the prisoner Charles Bronson and loads of pictures and memorabilia from Ronnie Kray's funeral – like the hat I wore on the day, one of the horse's shoes that it had lost, the whole works. The best thing I had on the walls, though – listen to this – was a painting of the crucifixion done by Ronnie Kray in Broadmoor. He'd sent it to a good friend of his, the painter, Francis Bacon. After Bacon died, the painting belonged to a geezer that was friends to us both. He gave it to me cos he knew I'd appreciate it. I even had the letter that Ron had sent with it. It was valued at fifty grand and I had it hung on the wall of my pub. But places used by villains are always the safest, funnily enough. I mean, who's gonna cause trouble there? Even Evel Knievel wouldn't have risked that.

The Albion turned into a proper little tourist attraction and was always really busy. All the chaps used to meet there for a drink as well. One evening, some time later, me and a lot of the chaps were gathered in the pub for a photo-shoot. The dance artist Tricky had done an album of his music and sampled the voices of me, Tony Lambrianou, Frankie Fraser, Joey Pyle, Freddie Foreman, Roy Shaw, Tommy Wisbey and Jack Adams. No other press were there cos the record company didn't want any other photos leaking out. We all had a bit of a party afterwards as well, which was done by a mate, Gareth.

There was loads of big motors outside and some of them were parked illegally. This local beat copper was passing and came in the pub to get the cars moved. All he sees is the walls covered with guns, knuckledusters and gangster photos and half of London's naughtiest, past and present, sat there looking at him: Freddie Foreman, Joey Pyle, Tony Lambrianou, Frankie Fraser, yours truly and loads more. I think he thought he'd stumbled on to Base Camp One of Villains Incorporated!

The day after that two plain clothes police officers called at my house and told me that, although I wasn't down as a licensee, if I didn't take my financial commitment out of the pub they would close it down. Simple as that. I told them that I was doing fuck all wrong, I didn't even sell Rizlas in there, and there's nothing they could do about it.

'You know better than that,' one of them said. 'You know you don't have to do anything wrong to get nicked.'

I said, 'Oh, you're gonna "find" a kilo of charlie in there, are you?'

'Nothing as respectable as that,' he said. 'I'll nick you for a rape, something like that, put you on remand for a year and then see how many people go "Hail, Dave Courtney" then!'

I thought, Fuck me. It was then that I realised it wasn't me they were afraid of but my popularity. But what worried me most was what kind of copper would think a K of charlie was *respectable*!

They did make me remove my involvement. They were gonna go to the brewery and say, 'Oh, did you know one of the people involved in the place is a Kray-twin gang leader?' So that was another thing I had to hand over.

The surveillance on me, which had been there on and off for a while, now went apeshit. I knew they were bugging my house, my car and my phone. I didn't get a telephone bill for the next three years. Why's that then? Did BT overlook me, y'know, like they do? Or was it because the police had a word with them and told them not to cut me off, or even paid the bill for me (my favourite!), so they could carry on listening? That's a chapter title in itself: 'The Old Bill Paid My Phone Bill!' I even caught police going through my bins! I had a camera concealed above my front door so I could see who was knocking and we got two Old Bill on film, rummaging through my fucking rubbish. I sent a copy to the station with a note attached: 'Please improve the food in your canteen because I just find this – you scavenging for my old meat pies – a bit embarrassing. Thanks, Dave.'

But the best one was just before they stopped my involvement in my pub. This was a cheeky one. I found out the police had set up an observation point in an undertaker's across from The Albion. So I got all the regulars in, all good mates and people who've supported me: Dave Parks, Anita, Dave 2, Trevor, Scully, Kathy, Mickey and Peter Mapp, Chas, Kieran, Dave Thurston, Gary, Barry and Big Larry, Paddy, Anne, Michelle, Paul, Brian, Alan, Noel, David, Mel, Danny, Laurie, Phil, Ian and Corraine, Gary 2, Lou Anne, Kosheema, Les, Shena, Laura and Daniel, Steve, Sharon and Simon, Chas, Bizmark (who is in the business), Nicky and Gemma, Pit Mark and, of course, Jay. One of them brought a video and got it all on film. I walked across the road with a tray of crisps, peanuts and a couple of pints.

The best I could've hoped for, I thought, was that I dropped the stuff off and the coppers upstairs were told that Dave Courtney had left it for them. What actually happened was that as soon as I walked into the undertaker's a lady who worked there asked where I was going. I said the food and drink had been ordered by the police and I wanted to know who pays for it. She said 'Not us', picked up the phone and called them down! These two Old Bill on surveillance upstairs came down, saw me stood there smiling, and their jaws just hit the fucking floor.

I said, 'It must be really boring for you watching me drink and play pool all day, so come over for a couple of games yourself.'

Then I heard a massive cheer and whistling and turned to see that everyone from the pub was out on the pavement over the road. Oh, just how happy was I?! Proud of every one of them.

It was in the papers the next day. I made sure of that. The headline was: COP A LOAD OF UNDERCOVER POLICE! It said: 'Scotland Yard refused to comment on the alleged incident, saying information on secret observations is never made public'. I thought, It fucking will be when I send a copy of the video to *You've Been Framed*! And if that's their idea of 'secret', then keep up the good work.

But, like I said before, if they pick *you*, if they decide that you are the one and then they throw all their weight and resources and money and time into following you, listening to you and photographing you, into either nailing you or closing you down, then you are gonna get nailed or you are gonna get closed down. No two ways about it. They'll find something. Especially with these laws of 'knowingly concerned' and conspiracy.

'Knowingly concerned' was, as we amateurs in the legal profession put it, a real cunt. It made it illegal, actually against the law, to introduce one person to another. Which was basically my stock in trade. It said that if I, for example, introduced one party to another party and then both these parties went on to commit a crime then I was responsible because it would've never happened without me 'effecting the introduction', as a lawyer would say. Or, as I would say, 'Bollocks!' Talking about my nickname as the *Yellow Pages* of Crime, 'knowingly concerned' was like prosecuting the geezer who actually publishes the *Yellow Pages* because a plumber you phoned came round and cracked your U-bend! Or, another example: if the shit did hit the fan then the fan could be prosecuted, for just carrying on doing its own thing – spinning – when the turd hit it, and so 'effecting the turd's introduction' to a lot of shit-faced people.

That all might sound silly, I know, but it also might put across the depths of fucking silliness in the law they were trying to convict people with. One thing that weren't silly was this: anyone convicted of being 'knowingly concerned' would be given a sentence *greater* than the longest sentence handed down to whoever had done the crime. And that, my friends, is what's commonly known as the cherry on the cake. Or, in this case, porridge.

So, when I got back from Tenerife I found that the police had gone round to the club and pub owners that used my men and said I was a Kray twin gang member. They even sent videos of the funeral out to people! The owners knew that was all bollocks and tried to defend me. The coppers said, 'Look, we don't care what you think. You can be his friend and not have a licence for the club or you can sack his doormen and stay open.' I didn't want them to be in an awkward position, so I bailed out. I handed all those door contracts over to others. And from then on my doorman firm began to be chipped away at. The number of men working for me went from 500 to 200. But I still had their telephone numbers if I needed a hand.

If I'd been the boss of 500 cleaners I wouldn't have been a problem. But in the police's eyes I was in charge of this army of London. And the fact that my missus was black made that army become bigger and so much stronger. It was never meant as a threat, but just fell that way. The ironic thing is that they were slowly but surely ruining all that I wanted to *legitimately* do. Shutting me down meant that I had to sack my mates. It was awful.

So my public image went up, but the doorwork went downhill. And even though I couldn't do debt-collecting myself now cos I'd been in the papers and on telly too much, the actual offers of debt-collecting jobs came flooding in again. I just picked the best and most profitable ones.

And because the police were now watching me more than ever I couldn't even have as many friends around my house as I would've liked, or fence out all the jobs I could have. They really did clamp down on me. Things were said to me, off the record, that made me realise how bad things had got.

If you're the kind of person that's had no run-ins with the police then you probably still have that Dixon of Dock Green image of them. Modern policing just ain't like that. I don't think it ever was, to be honest. In the 'good old days' it was even easier to fit people up than today, in many ways, by them just verballing you up in a statement. So, it's easy to look in from the outside and say, 'Well, I just wouldn't stand for it' – in fact, I only usually stand for 'God Save The Queen' and injections in the buttocks – but it wasn't a case of 'standing' for anything. There's not an awful lot you can do about it. I did write to my MP, of course, and heard *fuck* all back!

The only thing I could do was give them no reason to do anything. From the day of Ronnie's funeral, from that day on the transformation started from infamy to the celebrity thing. It began to change from one to the other. That day propelled me. Or compelled me to propel myself, shall we say. And the more straight I got, the more publicity I got. TV and radio and magazine people came after me. The more TV and film work I did, the less I could actually be an active villain. Which, in effect, is what I'd been after all along. Now something had come along that could give me the lifestyle without me having to look over my shoulder.

Because I'd been a visible villain people knew I knew what I was talking about. So the chaps didn't mind me being up there and talking about stuff or even being a kind of spokesperson, cos they knew I'd done it and I was one of them. Also, because

TV and film people are used only to dealing in people who fake it, when they actually meet a 'real one' they absolutely cream themselves.

So the police got stronger about how much they wanted to shut me down and the media got stronger about how much they wanted to use me. Both of them worked. I went into magazines and telly. I thought, Give me half a chance and within a few years I might even be on *This Is Your Life*! 'And do you recognise this voice? . . . *You have the right to remain silent* . . . Yes! It's your very first arresting officer from all those years ago!'

Something else came back to haunt me more than any voice from the past and that was that little thing called 'knowingly concerned'. Before that, though, another incident happened that would have effects. This geezer turned up dead in a Range Rover parked near to my old flat, the one that I'd shared with 'Lone Wolf' Dave (Dave was living somewhere else now). I had known the dead guy's brother but had never met the guy himself. Still, they put me under investigation, and that would be used against me in the not-too-distant future.

20 The Criminally Minded Club: (Members Only)

After getting away with loads and getting off with loads of things in the past, ironically, I ended up looking at the longest prison sentence I'd ever faced for something I hadn't even done. Funny that. Fucking hilarious, mate. Not so funny at the time, though. I knew that if I was found guilty I wouldn't be coming out till the year 2010. Two thousand and ten! That sounded more like a space film than a prison sentence.

It started when me and a few pals – Keith Masters, Tode Rnic, Paul Hawksford, John Keefe and Mark Riggs – went out clubbing one Saturday night. We all ended up back at my house at about six on the Sunday morning, all still up buzzing and wide awake. They were due to go pick someone up from Heathrow who was coming back from holiday, and they asked if I wanted to go with them. I'd only met the geezer who was arriving a couple of times before, but it was a really nice sunny day and I had nothing else planned so I said I'd go along for the ride.

Down at Heathrow the incoming plane was late, as seems to be per fucking usual these days. They ask you get to check in two hours before the flight, don't they, and then there's still always a delay. Anyway, we waited around for ages and then I went off to the bog, and when I came out no one was there. I asked around and it turned out that the guy they were waiting for, Marc Curno, had come through and all six of them had gone off in the direction of the train station. Which surprised me. I thought we'd all be returning by car. I followed them down and caught up with them on the platform.

That's when all the customs jumped out and grabbed us.

You could say I was ever so slightly surprised; you could say that. Personally, I would say that I was abso-fucking-lutely gobsmacked. It wasn't till the copper said he was arresting us for the importation of narcotics that I knew the geezer we'd met had more on him than a few duty-frees. And a nice little Sunday drive had suddenly turned into this. You know that feeling when you wish you'd just gone straight to bed?

It turned out that when they'd searched Marc Curno when he came through customs they had found six kilos of cocaine on him but told him to carry on through so they could see who he met.

We were all taken to the cells at Heathrow and kept there for two days. Tode Rnic was exonerated and freed from the station.

I had introduced John to Paul and Paul had introduced Marc to John, so that then made me 'knowingly concerned' in the eyes of the law. Paul realised he had plane tickets in his house, had made phone calls to Bogotá and was on video, so he had to go 'guilty'; Marc was caught with the suitcase, so he had to go 'guilty'; John was caught with bits and pieces in his Filofax, so he had to go 'guilty'; but all I was guilty of was introducing these people to each other, and in my eyes that ain't a crime. From the second I got nicked I knew all I could be done for was introducing them, and I wasn't gonna deny that.

At one time you could say nothing, but things had changed. Now there was a law saying that if there's something you don't mention which you later use in your defence, then conclusions can be drawn from that. So much for the right to silence and innocent until proven guilty, then. What bollocks.

During questioning it was easy to go 'no comment' to questions about plans of the operation cos I knew fuck all about it, but I wasn't going to deny knowing the geezers cos I knew telephone bills would show it. There's not a lot you can do with that. They get you by the bollocks with the phone bills. (But I'd only talked to them on the phone like I do with hundreds of people I know.)

And although I broke my own rule by not going 'no comment' to everything, seeing as I was the only one going 'not guilty' here, I was gonna act not guilty. Under any other circumstances, always go 'no comment', *always*, no matter what the fucking police say. Unless you are, like I was, in the very rare and lucky circumstances where all the others have already gone 'guilty'. So that meant there was no danger of harming them. In fact, all my co-defendants made it easier for me by saying it was nothing to do with me. Still, I was charged.

As it happened, when I was being questioned I could hear Mark Riggs being interviewed next door and doing the same thing – going 'no comment' to everything. Now I knew that Mark was as innocent of this as me, but I also knew he was doing the 'no comment' bit for everyone else. So I told them that he was just along for the ride, just doing the driving actually. Mark was eventually released without being charged. The only one out of all of us.

The rest of us were transferred. I was taken to Twickenham and that's where I was charged. When I'd first been taken in and I'd given my name, the coppers had gone, 'Dave Courtney? Fuck me!' They couldn't believe it; Dave Courtney – 'The Heir to the Krays', as they saw me – banged up in their little nick. It was like a massive stroke of luck to them, to nick me for this, accidentally, when they'd been after me for so long. So me saying I had nothing to do with it went down like a gas leak at a bar mitzvah. They had me pegged as the Mr Big organiser of the whole thing.

That's one of the downsides to having a reputation: as well as getting the acclaim for things you were not involved in (which had happened in the past), you also get the blame for things that are nothing to do with you.

The Old Bill were on a high, though. They'd been waiting for this for years. A common-or-garden drugs bust had suddenly turned into what they saw as The End of Dave Courtney. The fact that I was innocent made me sleep a bit easier, but not much. I'd seen innocent men, especially those with previous, fitted up and jailed. Or just convicted because the jury were swayed by the reputation of the man. Sometimes they end up thinking like the police: he must be involved because look who he is!

I was charged with being 'knowingly concerned', which I've already told you about. So, the basis for my arrest and charge was basically this: because I am Dave Courtney, the police cannot believe that I did *not* have something to do with the crime. And because they had telephone records of me calling the others involved, to them that was enough. It don't mean a thing that I've called these blokes loads of times a year since I first met them, like you do with friends. There was no more evidence against me than that, but the general gist of it was, 'We think he is involved somewhere down the line'. And since 'knowingly concerned' had been brought in, that's all they needed.

In fact, ever since I'd first heard of the 'knowingly concerned' thing coming in it had really started me thinking about getting out of the game. I'm not saying this as a brag, more a statement of fact, but after so long in the business and because I always tried to get on with people first, I'd ended up knowing as many people as anyone else, and more than most. So people naturally came to me. And, after so long living the life, I couldn't turn around and refuse a request or favour. I couldn't suddenly go from being Mr In-the-know to Mr I-don't-know, could I?

I applied for bail at Uxbridge Crown Court before a magistrate. It was turned down. Twice. During my appearance for the first application, while I was being held I wrote a letter for Jennifer laying out some instructions of things I wanted her to do. I knew whatever happened over this I was gonna be off the streets for a while. And Jennifer being Jennifer, she knows the score, and whenever I've got banged up she has slipped straight into it: organising things for me and keeping in touch with people. She had the black book with all the names and numbers, and whoever holds the Filofax holds the power. So whenever I've been inside she ran things. Like I've said, I think women are naturally stronger, or can be over many things. Jennifer was all that, and if you find a strong woman, and a naughty one at that, and she is on your side, then that's a real asset. Jen could carry on running the show for me and be the perfect ambassador.

Anyway, I wrote this eight-page letter to her saying a few things and gave it to my solicitor to give to her. The cells are videoed, so they saw me do it, but that don't matter cos it falls into the confidentiality laws between a client and his lawyer. But the solicitor was a young fella, just a junior clerk or something that had to be there with me for legal reasons, and he didn't know the full score. So on his way out one of the police said he had to confiscate the letter and the geezer only went and gave it to him! Fuck me. I wanted Perry Mason as my brief and I got Mickey Mouse. The police ended up not being able to use it as evidence anyway because of the way they got their hands on it. How sad.

After being charged I was taken from court to Wormwood Scrubs. When I walked in the Scrubs I got a really great welcome. There was, at the time, a big black community in there and loads of them I knew through the club scene and because of Jenny. I knew half the inmates by first name. They started shouting hello, and that really touched me. That really meant a lot. It's bad enough walking through the gates, but it makes it easier when you get a reception like that. Other inmates came to visit me, and within twenty minutes I'd been given really nice clothes, fags, biscuits, extra pillows and gifts from them. And the guy in my cell, who I'd never even met before, gave me his prison job in the kitchen. A nice, soft job. He did that for me. I felt honoured. Just goes to show what I'd said was true: if you're good to people they'll be good back to you. And that was true even with people that had never met me, because they knew I was like that.

The screws had a different view. They couldn't stand to see me being treated like that so a pack of them came running downstairs and marched me off to solitary, high-security cells. I'd only been in the Scrubs for 45 fucking minutes! Their excuse was that they'd heard there was gonna be an armed escape attempt for me, a storming of the barricades by 500 doormen, or some such bollocks. Obviously, I didn't tell them about the laser-pen and loaded wristwatch that had been given to me by James Bond. They made me a Double-A category prisoner because of the risk I supposedly presented. Being made Double-A is a bastard. I knew I'd be carted off to the Double A-CAT at Belmarsh Unit.

They kept me in solitary in the Scrubs for two days while they got a cell ready at Belmarsh, put up net curtains for me, that kind of thing. Then I was transferred by armed guards in an armoured van to Belmarsh prison. My cunning plan to have a magnetic helicopter pick us up off the street and fly me to Cuba never came off, though. You just can't get the staff these days.

What happens when you're made a Double-A and sent to the unit is that you go into the normal induction system, double handcuffed, and then put in another bus and this bus drives into the Double-A Unit. The unit is something else. It's a little prison within the prison, a miniature replica. Like a cage within a cage. The A-CAT at Belmarsh is one of the world's most high security. When it was first built they dropped in a squad of the SAS to try and escape and test its security measures. They didn't even dent it; in fact, I think there's still three or four of them trapped in there. There's no way in the world anyone would get out of it. Houdini would've had a nervous breakdown.

It was built to house what they regarded as the forty most criminally minded people in Europe. Not the most murderous or the biggest serial killers, but the most criminally minded. The men who have the money, the manpower, the knowledge and wherewithal to get things done on a big scale. That's their view of you. Biggest backhanded compliment I've ever had, come to think of it.

The security measures were unbelievable. First I went through double steel doors (everything's fucking 'double' in the unit), then I had to strip off (even the screws had to do this), walk through into another room stark bollock naked, be searched, and then put on another set of clothes. All the time there are lights and cameras trained on you videoing every move. Being an old hand at the filming lark I gave them my best side. That's my backside, in case you're wondering.

Every new incoming gets the usual induction speech from the guv'nor. Bit like a red coat welcoming you to Butlin's. Without the laughs. I had this one down as a prat right from day one.

'Mr Courtney,' he said, 'I don't care who you are or who you think you are, how much money you have or how much outside help and influence you have . . .' – he paused for effect (I nearly yawned) – '. . . because this institute was designed to *break* you.'

'I'm ever so sorry to be the little hiccup in your theory,' I replied, 'but this place ain't gonna break me. In fact, it ain't even gonna *dent* me. I'll be going home.'

He went on to say how that was quite common cos inmates couldn't face the reality of their situation. I thought, We'll see, sunshine.

So I entered the unit as prisoner PW2426.

There were four units in a star shape. Ten single cells in each quarter. I was taken to my cell. The cells were all spare and identical: stainless steel sink, a lump of stainless steel as a mirror, a metal sheet jutting out from the wall as a table and another one as a seat. So that fucked up my plans for rearranging the furniture and turning it into my little Camelot. I was gonna ring that *Changing Rooms* programme, but didn't see the point. It had an ordinary window, but it only opened six inches out and there was tungsten iron mesh over it on the outside. So there was a kind of net curtains after all.

At the end of the corridor, by the last cell, there was a big, glass-walled room where all the screws sit monitoring you through cameras and listening devices. The phone was on the wall next to this room, and whenever you made a call you could see the guy inside listening in. If they hear one word they don't like or are suspicious of, anything they think is a coded message, then they cut the phone off. The line from the BT ads about 'it's good to talk' obviously didn't mean fuck all in Belmarsh.

Outside the cells there was a common area: ten chairs around five tables, a telly up on the wall, a tumble dryer and some books, two toilets and two showers, and a dining table. There was a little gym downstairs where you could spend thirty minutes a day (but it took you that long just to get there).

You never went out of there. You were segregated and never saw all the other prisoners.

So, I'm in the unit. The bad side is that just by being there it does your case no good at all. Very, very few people have walked out of the Double-A after being found not guilty. In fact, I don't know if any have at all. You could say it's the kiss of death to your chances of freedom. Just the massive amount of security that accompanies you to court immediately prejudices the jury.

The upside is that you're in with a much better class of criminal. I ain't painting myself as that, but that's where they sent me. I didn't exactly have a big say in the matter. The other guys in the Double-A with me at the time were, Tony White of Brinks Mat fame (the biggest single robbery ever done); Charlie

Kray, who was in on cocaine smuggling charges; Charles Bronson, rated as the most dangerous prisoner in the country; Ricardo Heinz, a big big-time yardie, and Chunky, another yardie; John Short; David Rose, who had escaped from Parkhurst; E.J., another yardie; Mickey Steel and a geezer called Jack; Ronnie Easterbrook, in for armed robbery and shooting a copper; some IRA boys; Ronnie Field and Bobby Gould, co-defendants of Charlie Kray; John Gilligan, a very big name in Ireland (and what I saw the authorities do to this man was disgusting); Mickey Boyle; Steve Seaton; Warren 'Attitude' Edwards; Big Kenny; Dingus McGee, another IRA bloke; a French/Algerian terrorist; an animal rights activist; a guy who threatened to poison the water system with anthrax unless he got a million quid; political prisoners from around the world that had been caught in this country; and my co-defendants John Keefe and Paul Hawksford. Paul was kept segregated, but I didn't know why at the time. Marc Curno was on an ordinary wing but one with such a bad reputation it was called Beirut.

Before we get on to my fate, I'll tell you something about these chaps cos they've all got interesting stories.

Tony White was allegedly on the Brinks Mat job in 1983 when £26 million in gold was robbed, the biggest there's ever been. Charlie Kray you know about. He was seventy years old, I think, and had been banged up in the Double-A on remand until his trial. I gave evidence for him at that. Charles Bronson you'll also probably know (there's a book in itself). Charles was rated as the most dangerous inmate in the country. He fucking looked it an' all. He's this big geezer with a shaved head but a really long fuzzy beard. He'd been sent down in 1983 for an armed robbery but kept kicking off inside and getting more years slapped on his term. And – get this – out of those 23 years he's done so far, over 20 of them have been in solitary confinement. That must be some kind of record. It ain't the only one: he's in the *Guinness Book of World Records* for doing the most sit-ups – 3,750. He's had only 69 days of freedom in his time out, and during that period he had three fights, and won them all. He writes poetry and draws, but everyone thinks he's completely mental. I reckon Charlie isn't mad at all. I think he's borderline genius. Some of the nicks he's been in haven't shared that view, though. He's been treated like a dog in some: fed under the door, chained up to go in the exercise yard and chained up to come back.

Me and Charles got off to a bit of a shaky start, actually. When I was brought in to Belmarsh they confiscated my stuff. I happened to have two Rolexes on me, one for me and one to sell. Word got back to Charlie about this – the screws deliberately put it about to shit stir – and he thought I was some kind of flash cunt. Who – *me*? Although the Double-A was a special prison inside a prison, there was still another unit within the Double-A! That's where Charles was kept. We couldn't talk, so after he'd heard of the two watches he sent me a little note about it. Anyway, we sorted it out, and eventually became good pals.

David Rose had escaped from Parkhurst and tried to nick a fucking aeroplane. That's not going about things half-hearted, is it? But I suppose if you're gonna try to get away you might as well get far away. Funny, cos David Rose looked so harmless you'd no more imagine him the type to do that than the Pope.

Mickey and Jack were in charged with the killing of Tony Tucker, Pat Tate and Craig Rolfe, who were found dead in a Range Rover in some deserted part of Essex a few months before. That was the one that when Jen heard about it, and heard the name 'Tucker', she thought it was my mate Ian Tucker and didn't know if I was one of the three.

Ronnie Easterbrook had done an armed robbery and got shot. He played dead until the Old Bill went for him, and then he shot one of them. When he was being taken to court with some of the IRA, he smuggled some plastic explosive into the van and tried to blow his way out. The roof just came down on them.

John Gilligan was a big-time name in Ireland who didn't give a fuck, a real Robin Hood. He weren't into the politics and religion of the scene over there. He was in the unit after the death of an Irish woman journalist. She'd door-stepped him at his place, they ended up having a row, and he threatened her. Not long after she was shot. There was no evidence against him other than the police suspicion. Another 'knowingly concerned' thing. He was nicked transporting money from England to Ireland which, even though he'd genuinely won it on the horses, he was banged up for. Then they hit him with the thing about the journalist. A real stitch-up job, I think.

Dingus McGee was another IRA one. He was kept down in the unit within the unit where Charlie Bronson was held. He did the old 'dirty protest' routine and smeared his cell with shit. Any time a screw opened his door they got a faceful as well.

The vegan, Save the Whale, Greenpeace animal activist had burnt down some lab where they tested on animals and killed three people in the process. And he had the balls to bang on at me for eating meat! I told him my favourite meat was swan (which only the Queen is allowed to eat, by the way – did you know that?). I said my mates went into parks, threw bread down for them and then cut off their heads with garden shears. That freaked him out for days. Whenever he went on about not eating meat I'd remind him that Hitler was a vegetarian, but it didn't stop him from cooking six million Jews. He was next door to the IRA guy that blew up Canary Wharf, so the Ban the Bomb symbols drawn on the Veggie's cell didn't exactly make them two the best of mates.

The poisoner geezer was some student of biochemistry who had tried to hold the water companies to ransom. He got caught and got twenty years for his trouble. One day he started telling me about the amount of bacteria in one square inch of pond life, or something daft (you can tell how riveted I was, can't you?). 'When you get it under a microscope you've never seen anything like it in your life,' he said. I told him I'd seen worse, and he asked me where.

'Inside a hippy's sleeping bag at Glastonbury.'

Warren Edwards. Now he was a living nightmare for the screws. From Cheshire, he was. A fitness fanatic and a real hardnut. He'd escaped from a nick and beaten up the screws. He'd been in Belstone prison with some other high-security prisoners and they'd ended up practically running the place. So the authorities decided to split up their little firm. It was when he was being ghosted to a dispersal prison that the break-out happened. He told me the story one day when we were out in the yard.

'When I came out and saw what we were being taken in I couldn't believe it, Dave. I was expecting some armoured sweat-box and this thing that pulled up was more like a fucking Sunshine coach!'

They drove on to London. I don't really know the ins and outs of what happened but it ended up with them jumping out of the coach at Holborn and the screws getting a good kicking. Someone nicked all the prison paperwork from the coach and it turned out a nice day after all! I nicknamed him 'Attitude'. Warren was the original NWA: Northerner With Attitude.

When he was caught, they banged him up in the Double-A. Because of the hiding the screws had got he knew he had a fucking good hiding due in return. That's one of the screws' perks of the job. I'd seen some guys in other nicks given ferocious revenge beatings. So he was wary about going in the showers or being in his cell. I tried to tell him that because of all the video cameras they wouldn't be able to get him, but he couldn't get his head round it.

Cos Belmarsh was so different from any other nick you'd been in, it did take time to grasp that; the fact that though the cameras helped them watch you, they also stopped them doing anything to you. The surveillance in there was incredible: 24 hours a day, every day, all year. Anything you did or said was taped. Every time you walked, stood, sat, shat, farted or wanked, it was caught on camera.

We'd be let out of our cells for an hour in the morning. Three times a week we could come out between four and eight. The food was a bit better, but you didn't get the benefit of it because it took over an hour to clear security. So by the time you got it it was freezing cold. I never thought the day would come when I looked forward to salad. If a banana set off from the kitchens green, it was well fucking ripe by the time it arrived. I bet half the stuff went past its sell-by date just getting to us.

I didn't have a visitor for months cos that's how long it takes them to vet people. When you submit a list of people you want to see they start investigating their background, their friends, their associates, and if they've got any previous, and if there's any terrorist connections. They even do all this with people you just want to telephone. It's a joke. Just really ridiculous. Three months to clear a phone call. I've known marriages not last that long. Anyway, I said I was a devout Catholic and put the Pope on my phone list. It was never cleared, so fuck knows what they found out about him! It took them two years to clear John Gilligan's brother for a visit. Fact. *Two years.*

They were really strict about what you could have in your cell as well. Only a certain number of books, a certain amount of paper and pens. Only a certain kind of trainers, and the laces couldn't be above a specified length. Even your radio could only be of certain dimensions! Just ever so over the top with the old security measures, I think you'd agree. I mean, I didn't even waste my breath asking if it was OK for me to be sent my lucky knuckleduster.

I tried to brighten the place up a bit and painted a picture rail round the top of the wall. Then I painted a picture in a frame as if it was hanging there. I was quite proud of that – the Mona Lisa with her tits out. Anyway, that got me straight in trouble. They put you on report for just writing your name on the wall. So you couldn't even mark down your days by chalking them off in traditional Hollywood prisoner style.

You could fill in a form and apply for books from an outside library. So I put down *The Great Escape*, *The Life of Houdini* and *Tunnel Diggers Monthly*. Didn't hear a dicky bird.

One of the screws asked me what sport I was into. I said pole-vaulting and long-distance running, but I'd prefer it if they took the barbed wire off the top of the wall in case I only just made it. He knocked back my request for a pole and a pair of trainers.

The exercise yard was this little bombproof pen with wire mesh over the lid to stop a helicopter air-lifting you out. So I had to ring the chaps on the outside and cancel that one, obviously. Well, the cost of hiring a chopper is fucking outrageous . . .

I applied for bail two more times to the magistrate, and both times I was knocked back. And I had said to me, actually had said to me by a police officer (and I quote), 'No muggy magistrate will dare give you bail now that we've put you on Double-A!' He went on to say that the police knew that I was innocent but if they could nick a year of my life by keeping me on remand then that would be better than nothing.

My bail was set at one million pounds. Four benefactors provided the money for me. My next appeal for bail went to a judge in chambers. A judge was more likely than a magistrate to grant bail. But the police also fucked that up for me by saying that I was a leading suspect in an ongoing murder investigation (meaning the guy found dead in the Range Rover a short while back). That remained unsolved, and looked like it would. They knew it was nothing to do with me, but they used it to fuck the bail appeal.

The judge said to me, 'No amount of money, Mr Courtney, will make me even consider for one second giving you bail.'

I replied, 'Thank you. And I hope you win the lottery!' Never let the cunts grind you down. Never.

So, I settled down to however long I was gonna be in the Belmarsh Hostelry for the Wayward.

Because everyone in there knew what trouble they were in and the number of years they were looking at, it weren't exactly the happiest bird I'd ever done. Everyone was looking at double figures and that don't really make for a humorous atmosphere. Cos if you looked on the black side and started talking about what our release dates would be if we got guiltys, we were all looking at well into the next century. Oh, how we laughed! My fucking sides hurt, I tell you.

Actually, I did have reason to be more optimistic than most. I thought so anyway, even if no one else did. I was convinced I'd beat this and get back home. And that weren't me just denying the truth, like the guv'nor had said; I knew when I got my day in court that that would be enough. And knowing that, I took it upon myself to become court jester for all the other chaps because I knew, and they knew in their heart of hearts, that there was a good chance they weren't gonna be going home. I wanted to cheer them up. They were all bang in it, caught on surveillance and all that.

Surveillance is a cunt. The thing is, if you choose anyone in the world, and I don't care who it is, Prince Charles or Mother Teresa, and you subject them to 24-hour surveillance – bug their car, bug their house, bug their phone, open their mail, follow them everywhere and video and photograph them – then you will eventually catch them doing something you can say is wrong. Charles with Camilla, for instance. *And* if that person happens to be a bit naughty anyway then they're definitely gonna be caught for something.

Listen, even if you have been to prison you can't imagine what the Double-A unit is like. You really have to be there. I'll try to give you some idea.

Everything we did was recorded so they could analyse it. So every hour of the day and night we were filmed: in the cell, in bed, on the bog, in the shower, watching telly, eating, sleeping, talking, walking, exercising, relaxing, reading, writing, having a shave, a shit, a shower and a shoeshine, and everything else in between, basically. Every *single* thing. It was like being in a human zoo. And then they gather all this information together on a computer and in a daily log book. That'll be where they recorded what you'd done on the bog, I guessed – the log book.

Yeah, they recorded everything. Who you speak to and for how long and what you both said; who you didn't speak to; who you seemed to avoid, if anyone; how many steps you usually took around the exercise yard; if you read one particular page in a magazine more than the others; and any deviations from all that pattern of things. They even recorded what you had for dinner and how you ate it so they could work out ... oh, I don't know – whether the most 'criminally minded' always ate their sausage first, or some such bollocks. And every letter you wrote went to a sorting and investigations room where they scanned it for hidden messages and code words. Like the code-breakers used to do during the war. Just in case every eleventh word on the fifth line, for instance, could be pieced together into a sentence. So in some letters I made sure that certain words were in the same place on each page, like 'tunnel', 'finished', 'tomorrow', 'fly', 'Brazil'. Pretty fucking uncrackable that one, eh?

The thing is, because they've already got this image of you in their heads as the most criminally minded, they just overestimate what you're capable of and go completely OTT. I think they seriously thought a 500-strong Dave Courtney Army was gonna roll up the streets in tanks and blast me out. Which was ridiculous. It had been years since I owned a tank.

Anyway, so the little system they had in the unit – all the security, all the pathetic rules and all the petty regulations – I played it for all it was worth, mate. It was like a challenge to keep myself and everyone else amused. I like to think of that as one of my fortés – rising to a challenge. With this regime

being run so tight, though, you only had to loosen a few nuts
to get the wheels wobbling. And did I fucking wobble them?
You *know* that! I made it my mission.

One of the screws was called Mrs Crabtree, and she took a
dislike to me right off the bat. So I did to her. Early on she did
say something to me that I'd been hoping she'd say cos I had
an answer ready and waiting. It was in the common room as
well, with all the chaps there, which made it even better.

'You seem to have taken an instant dislike to me, Courtney,'
she said. 'Why is that?'

'Well, it saves time,' I said.

Everyone fell about. Oh, it was funny. They hate it when
you stick it to them with a joke cos there's fuck all they can do
about it. Absolutely fuck all.

Here's another one I used (on the outside). You'll like this.
One time I was out with the boys at some posh restaurant and
we were being a bit loud as usual. This snotty old dear on the
next table made some remark about us to her old man,
deliberately loud so we could hear. I said something to her – I
forget what, but it weren't complimentary – and she was
horrified. She said, 'Really! I've never been so insulted in my
life!'

I said, 'Well, you should get out more!'

Bang! One nil. That got a big laugh. From us lot anyway.
And I think even her old man had a little smirk.

Another one of the screws looked just like Fred Flintstone,
and I don't just mean a passing resemblance; I mean this guy
was a spot-on, dead ringer lookalike. Big flat head, massive
stubbly jaw, barrel chest and six inch legs. I swear I could *not*
take my eyes off him. No one could.

One time he started lecturing me about something I'd done,
something against rules and regulations.

'Now you know there are certain do's and don'ts in here,'
he said, 'and that is a definite don't.'

'Oh, I am sorry,' I said, 'I thought it was one of the
Yabba-dabba-*dos*!'

I'm afraid that didn't even raise a titter with him. Went right
over his head. Which was a feat in itself, considering the size
of it.

Because you're banged up so much in the Double-A,

you learn to tell each screw just from the sound of their footsteps; some squeak, some shuffle, some march, some walk fast or slow, some have shoe tips. Fred Flintstone, for instance, was heavy-footed. Must've been the weight of that head, obviously. I could tell Mrs Crabtree's footsteps. She sounded like a Russian shot-putter carrying a fridge-freezer. She was a proper, *proper* horrific sight she was, like something bad left too long in front of the fire. In fact, she looked just like Zelda from *Space 1999*. She was spiteful and nasty with it, and it radiated from every pore of her. And that's not just me being cheeky either; every one of her colleagues said the same behind her back.

Anyway, one night I heard that familiar sound of her knuckles dragging daintily on the floor and I looked out the little cell window and saw she was doing the night-watch. The screw on night-watch would come round every fifteen or twenty minutes and look into your cell. When she was on watch she would open the window hatch really loud to wake you up, then switch the cell light on, have a look round and shut the hatch back – but not all the way. She always left a little gap so that next time she came round she could sneak up and catch you having a wank. (You do a lot of wanking in prison cos it's the only thing that's nice and free. You end up coming out with one big muscley arm.) When Mrs Crabtree came back for the second patrol, even though she was shutting all the gates quietly, trying to sneak in, I was ready and waiting for her. I picked something up off the table and I thought, Right! You want something to look at, then I'll give you something tonight. So, when she slid up to the hatch and peeked through, what she saw was this: me stood stark bollock naked on my bed, dick in hand, wanking away with a green apple balanced on my head. I just saw her eye widen with the shock and then heard her move away!

Now I know that because of the rules and regulations about reporting everything we do, she has to go back and write that down: '11.30 p.m. – Caught inmate Courtney (PW2426) masturbating with Granny Smith on head'. And because I knew they had to write down everything to be analysed, I decided to really give them something to write about. Silly things, like in the exercise yard I started bending down and pretending to pick something off the floor in exactly the same place every day. I knew it would be written up in the Big Book. And then one morning I came out of my cell and queued up for breakfast completely starkers except for a sock on my knob. The screws came up to me and asked me what I thought I was doing. 'Getting my breakfast. What does it look like!' And then I just stood there looking really outraged that they'd even asked me. So that one will have gone in the Big Book.

Another time I came out to collect my last meal of the day and the man in front of me was given a massive big plate with sandwiches, milk, apples and all that, so I said I'd have the same as him. They said I couldn't cos he was Muslim and he was on Ramadan. I said so was I. He argued that I weren't.

I said, 'Look, I remember when I got arrested they asked me my name and address but no one asked me what fucking religion I was. I could be a Moonie for all you know. But I am actually a Muslim. I want my Ramadan.'

So I caused a right big scene and they had to go get more food for me. And cos I was quoting rules and regulations at them and they can't fuck around with religion, they put me down as a fucking Muslim on Ramadan. Result! (Or so I thought.)

Anyway, on Ramadan I'm supposed to eat at two o'clock in the morning and five o'clock in the morning, and you're supposed to pray at these times as well. So they came round, banged on the cell door and woke me up! So I got up in the morning, still with the hump cos they kept waking me up all night, queued up to get my bacon sandwich and they went, 'No, sorry, you can't eat. You're on Ramadan.' I told them that I'd been on Ramadan yesterday. They told me that Ramadan lasted for 28 days! So I was on fucking Ramadan wasn't I, for the next fucking month! I lost a stone and a half. They wouldn't let me have any chocolate or cups of tea. When Jen came to visit me and everyone else was having a cuppa I had to sit there with a mouth like Gandhi's flip-flop. I weren't even allowed to kiss her cos it was a Ramadan rule. Because I'd thrown the rule book down their neck they went by the rules and Ramadaned me right off! So I turned into the skinniest fucking Muslim you've ever seen.

Another thing they had to do was read and analyse every

single bit of literature you had sent to you in case there was one word scribbled in each piece that built up to a message. So I started sending off for anything and everything. I was getting holiday brochures from every travel agent going, Argos catalogues, clothing catalogues, furniture catalogues, insurance plans, bibles, Buddhist self-help books, leaflets on how to join the Samaritans, book club offers, and junk mail for just about anything you could think of. And the screws assigned to 'sort and search' had to go through every single bit of paper addressed to 'Dave Courtney, The Unit, Belmarsh'. Which meant them scanning every page of the fucking bible for code words! *Yes!*

And on top of the stuff I ordered myself from the back of magazines, I also started to get even more stuff sent to me by people. Wolfie, Brendan, Tucker, 'Lone Wolf' Dave and others all sent stuff in to me. I got books like *The Singer Sewing Machine Self-Repair Manual, London's Sewage System Through The Ages, Sheep Farming – An Illustrated History*, stuff like that; all of them big, thick, boring as fuck books about absolutely anything. And every one had to be searched page by page. *A Beginners Guide to Traction Engines*, that was a good one. There was loads. Some of them were so dull I immediately forgot what they were called. I had a mate who was a printer, and he made up a book cover with the title *How to Escape from Belmarsh Prison – Dave*. He wrapped that around a book and sent it to me.

One thing that was sent to me and that I did actually get some solace from was, funnily enough, a bible. Now I know you're looking for the sign – 'Caution! Joke Approaching!' – but I'm serious. It was sent to me by the father of Jonathan Evans (Posh John). I'd always got on really well with Jonathan's old man, and his mum; really, really lovely people. They sent me this beautiful, antique, gold-embossed bible. I read it right through. Twice. And whether you're religious or not you can find lessons in there to learn.

Back to the funny stuff – I got sent a banana. No, really. Not wrapped up either, just a banana with the address written on the skin and a stamp stuck on it. The screw had to deliver it to my cell because it was sent by registered post. All mail is property of the Sovereign until it arrives, did you know that?

So it's a brave man who tampers with the mail cos who'd want to go down in history as the bloke who interfered with the Queen? The screw said he was gonna confiscate the banana (maybe they thought I would leave the skin on the stairs as a booby-trap), which I knew meant he would throw it away. Because it was registered, though, I insisted he put it in my property for me to pick up when I left.

'And,' I said, 'don't eat the fucker and just leave the skin!'

Another thing I got sent was a massive cardboard beer bottle. It was from a shop window display and was about three feet high. It arrived at Belmarsh with my name on and loads of goodwill messages written on the back. That was mental. And, listen to this: I got sent a hacksaw! But every bit of it was wrapped really tightly with paper so it just looked exactly like what it was. There was a label tied to it with my name and the prison address and some message like, 'See you in a week's time!' Then a trowel arrived the week after with another message: 'Just in case the hacksaw blade snaps – try digging a tunnel!'

Then I went one step further and came up with the most cunning escape plot in the history of British prisons: I attempted – listen carefully now – to *post* myself home. Clever, or what?

On that morning, the locks went on the cell doors and I walked out completely naked. Well, not completely naked: I had a stamp on my forehead and my address written on my chest in marker pen. Then, casual as anything, I laid down across the OUT tray for that day's mail. Everyone was just stood around laughing their bollocks off. A few of the screws weren't amused, like Mrs Crabtree and this other one who was a real by-the-book jobsworth character. Like Mr Mackay out of *Porridge*. He ran up and asked me what I thought I was doing.

'What does it look like? Dave Courtney, PW2426, sending myself home, sir!'

He just went spare. 'What is the matter with you, Courtney?! What the fuck is the matter with you!'

Lying across this desk, bollock naked, I looked up at him and said, 'Oh no, *don't* tell me I haven't put enough fucking postage on!'

Charlie Kray was there, laughing with all the others.

Afterwards, when he did a book about his experiences (*Me And My Brothers*), he wrote about that incident.

It started to become a big thing when my mail arrived. Everyone looked forward to it, even the screws. If you think about it, though, the screws have a pretty boring job. Especially in a nick like the Double-A where the security stops anything out of the ordinary from happening. Prison officers are imprisoned as well, in a way. Yeah, they can go home at the end of the day, but years and years of their working lives are spent banged up in a prison! That's where a lot of the bitterness and spite comes from. I said that to one screw; I said that even after I'd gone home he would still be in here. That didn't go down too well.

I said that to the Mr Mackay character, who was a real nasty little bastard. Because of all the mail arriving for me and the fact that I wound them all up, this cunt really had it in for me. He made it his mission to really go out of his way to try and piss me off. A lot of the other officers were OK, to be honest. I told them that if they went out to any club in London I'd make sure their name was on the guest list. A lot of them took me up on that, and when they arrived at the club there'd be some mate of mine waiting for them, giving them champagne and a couple of Es. They had a fucking good time, mate, let me tell you.

This nasty cunt wasn't like that, though. And over the course of a year, or whatever, you can talk to a screw and learn about him. Even though they don't think they're giving much away, they do. I learnt that this geezer had a new 3 series BMW. He was bragging about it one day so it weren't exactly a secret. So I got one of my visitors to find it in the car park and take the number down. Then a contact of mine on the force traced the address from the number plate. That address was sent to me bit by bit, word by word in different letters. I memorised it and ate the paper it was written on. Now that might sound a bit like *Mission Impossible*, eating bits of paper with information on, but every day in the Double-A your cell is searched when you're out on exercise. All your rubbish is turned out and photocopied and all your letters go through the Home Office special police to be checked. So I memorised this screw's address and waited.

He was such a cocky, horrible piece of work that I knew he had to say something to me; he just couldn't help himself. Sure enough, a few days later he made some comment to me. And he always did it in front of the other screws and inmates as well, trying to humiliate you as much as possible. I leant towards him so that only he could hear, and whispered his own home address in his ear.

'So now I know where you live,' I said.

He went absolutely apeshit, but because no one else was in hearing distance even the other screws had to admit they didn't know what I'd said. They all thought he was a prat anyway. He started spluttering and shouting, saying that I'd threatened him. And because we are supposed to be 'the most criminally minded', and this is drilled into the screws from day one, he genuinely believed he was in danger. They're told how we might pretend to be nice and befriend them to find out where they live so we can take their kids hostage, stuff like that. So this geezer went barmy.

I just acted the innocent. 'How could I possibly know where you fucking live!? I ain't exactly got a front door key to this place!'

That really did his head in, and he deserved it.

Because of all the cameras they can't get to you in the usual way, like giving you a good kicking, so they do it psychologically. For instance, there was a rota next to the telephone where you'd put your name down to make a call. If the screws wanted to be clever they'd always open your cell last so every day you'd be bottom of the list. And in the little amount of time you're allowed out of the cell you'd never get your turn on the phone. And then they'd make you last at night as well.

They could use the system against you. They could pick and choose who to strip-search, and whose cell to search and mess up. I'd get back from the exercise yard sometimes and there'd be paw prints all over the bed where they'd let the sniffer dog go mad inside. And every twenty days they made us switch cells in case we were trying to dig a bleedin' tunnel, or doing something daft like stitching bedsheets together to make a hot air balloon and do a Richard Branson out the fucking window!

One day I was out in the yard playing volleyball with some of the chaps. This diamond bracelet, which I'd been allowed to keep, broke off and one of the diamonds fell out. We all got down and started looking for it but our time was up before we found it. They made us go back inside. Anyway, I look out of my cell window and I see the screws down on their hands and knees! The bastards were only on the floor looking for the diamond. And I'm sure it weren't for my benefit.

When it came to them listening in to telephone conversations and prison visits I threw in the odd curve-ball there as well. In the middle of a normal conversation I'd suddenly say, '. . . and remember, the eagle flies at dawn!' or '. . . and don't forget what I said before: five bananas in a bunch, unless I wink twice'. Really daft, spy-talk kind of stuff, but I knew they'd end up replaying it over and over looking for clues. (In fact, years later I did actually run into one of the screws who was in the Double-A at that time and he said that I wouldn't believe how much trouble and extra work I caused them. To which I would say, 'Oh dear, how sad, never mind.')

One of the blokes in there was John Short. John was a proper man's man, pushed the weights and all that. He's a nice geezer, but a real hardnut. The prison had just brought in something called a listener. This was a screw who came on all nice and friendly (Mr Barraclough in *Porridge*, this one would be), and inmates could call him into the cell and tell him about bullying or any problems they might have. The listener has to swear confidentiality.

So, one day, I called the listener into my cell and told him that one of the other prisoners was making sexual advances to me. I said I told the guy to fuck off but he took it the wrong way and I was afraid it was gonna lead to trouble. I said I didn't know what to do. The listener sat there taking it all in and then asked me who it was. I said it was John Short.

Now John Short is the most un-gay geezer you've ever met in your life: this dirty great big six-foot-six, flat-nosed hardnut. Not that you couldn't look like that and still be gay, but John just *wasn't*, in the slightest, y'know what I mean.

Anyway, there was this long pause as the screw tried to get his head around it.

'Err . . . John *Short*?!' he said. 'Are you sure you're not . . . y'know, reading it all wrong?'

I said I was sure and this listener left and went upstairs with the information, like he had to.

I told John and his co-defendant Tony White about all this and we were just laughing about it. Next thing, though, the bloody guv'nor comes down to see me. He had to take the complaint seriously cos he's got to cover his back, so to speak, but I could see he was well pissed off. He knew as well as anyone what John was like.

He said, 'Listen to me, Courtney, if this thing goes any further it involves an awful lot of time and paperwork. It has got to be recorded in the books and, if it isn't true, will involve a lot of people and a lot of wasted time. I understand that this must be a joke on your part but don't, for one *second*, stand there and tell me that *John Short* is trying to fuck you!!'

That was really funny. I didn't try and take it any further because just getting the guv'nor to come down and make that little speech was enough.

All the time I was inside I was still writing for this clubbing magazine called the *Scene*. The magazine was run by my good pal and partner Terry Turbo. Me and Terry were partners in a club called One Nation. We met on the club scene and became really good friends (we'd been nicked together and got 'not guiltys' together). We decided to get together and combine the two things we were good at, me doing security, and Terry doing rave and club promotions. Together we figured we'd make a good team. The Butch Cassidy and Sundance of the rave scene! Terry had been into clubbing since the year dot and had learnt the business from the bottom up. He became one of the best club promoters in the whole country. Terry was into clubs and kick boxing. I'd tried that once with him and ended up hurting so much the morning after that I just went out and bought myself a bigger knuckleduster to make me feel better!

I'd always written a page for the *Scene* and I carried on doing it from the unit. The title changed, though, from 'Dodgy Dave's Funny Page' to 'Not So Dodgy Dave – Live From Inside!' It was still fucking funny, though!

My missus, Jen, was not only good on the outside keeping in touch with everyone for me and helping keep things together, but she was the best any man inside could have wanted. She was so understanding that she arranged for me to judge a Readers' Wives competition run by the magazine! Get that! So, every single day I was getting between ten and twenty letters from women who had entered the competition. Sexy letters with photographs. The Double-A had all this filthy correspondence coming in the like of which they'd never seen before.

I was sending out letters to people: friends, female admirers, nutcases, readers' wives, celebrities, the Pope, and hundreds of other prisoners. I'd write out to people on anything I could find. Not just bits of paper but on fag packets, cornflake boxes, the little cardboard bit inside bog rolls, sweet wrappers – absolutely anything I could get a stamp and address on. So when they emptied the OUT tray, with all my stuff in, it looked like I'd just tipped my litter bin into it.

Tucker sent me a Laughing Tape. A tape of really mad laughter, like the Laughing Policeman at the funfair, funnily enough, which went on for a solid half hour. I played it non-stop through the night. Everyone else was shouting out 'Shut it off!', but it was so infectious that you just couldn't help but laugh with it. Then some of my mates sent in tapes they'd made. They might be out in a club or something and they'd pass the tape recorder round loads of people to say hello. All these tapes were checked and analysed before they gave them to me. The screws played them backwards and at all different speeds to see if there were any hidden messages like, 'The hang-glider's nearly ready, we're just waiting for a strong wind!' or 'Put on the nun's outfit and slip out incognito!' I even got sent a tape by a woman, who shall remain nameless (she knows who she is!), of her having a really long and really loud wank! This particular tape took the longest to be cleared by the screws who listened to it, though. Funny that.

Because of all this mail of mine coming in and going out, and the fact that it all had to be checked, they took on an extra member of staff to sort it. Then they changed the rules and said we were only allowed to spend a certain amount of money on stamps.

I finally started to get people cleared to visit me. On visiting days I was taken, handcuffed, by two guards to the visiting room. Then I'd strip off, be searched, put on new clothes out of a box and go through into the room. Just so I could talk to someone behind a bit of glass, on a telephone, with a screw sitting beside me and a camera up top looking down on us. Then I'd leave and be stripped again, X-rayed, and have someone look in my mouth and up my bum – even though we'd been talking through glass! It's a joke, a fucking joke.

It was difficult making up a list of people because I didn't like to put them through the intense scrutiny you were subjected to when you visited the Double-A. It took over an hour just to get in past all the security measures, and that was before they even got to see me. What a palaver. I was visited by Jennifer, Harry Haward, Dave ('Lone Wolf'), little Jenny Brown, Terry Turbo, Jay, Tucker, Nicky, Posh John, Ian Brown, Lenny Lucas, Dean and Pete, Mum and Tracey and the kids.

The most visits you could have was three one-hours each week. Jennifer didn't miss one. And kept things afloat on the outside. She had the black book and the phone. If anyone rang for me Jennifer took the call and no one went away not pleased. More than that, though, she kept me brave. She had a hundred per cent faith in me.

After three months of visits the glass came down and you could talk across a table. Everything else was still there and the table was so wide that you could only just touch fingertips.

I'm really glad I went through it, strange as that may sound, cos it taught me an awful lot. There's always something good you can draw from bad things. Some people don't recognise that and they just get lost in suffering. As I've said before, it really puts things in perspective when you go in prison: who's important in your life – your missus, your kids, your mates. And when you're not on the outside then the only people who are there for you are the people who genuinely love you. Sometimes even friends stop writing. The longer you're in, the more that happens. Then you really do need the people who stick by you. They mean an awful, awful lot. And when you get out you remember that – who's who and what's what. I needed that, a little kick up the arse.

And I was in such illustrious company inside that I just soaked it up again, like a sponge. Anyone can enjoy the good times, that's easy, but you also have to be able not to just take the bad with the good but learn from it as well.

And, on top of all that, I got to meet an old childhood hero of mine. I mean, not everyone can say they've met Fred Flintstone.

Christmas inside is a funny time. That's a big reminder of all that you're missing. Home life, wife and kids. Not to mention decent grub. Or at least food that wasn't stone cold. They did send in a turkey, but I told them to stuff it.

I sent a message to the guv'nor asking if Santa had been cleared for a visit, but I didn't even get the courtesy of a reply. Honestly, manners cost nothing, do they?

Christmas Day itself just showed up how ridiculous the whole Double-A security thing was. One of Charlie Kray's co-defendants, Ronnie Field, had a heart attack. We were all sat in the common area when he just keeled over. It took the ambulance and orderlies over an hour to get into him. Listen, the man was dying and we could hear the ambulance outside, but they made them go through the whole fucking security rigmarole before they let them in, searching them and X-raying all their equipment. Eventually they got in and got him out to hospital. More by luck than anything else, Ronnie survived. But they still had him handcuffed to a screw at his bedside.

Merry fucking Christmas.

I knew that for me the new year would bring the biggest thing I'd faced yet: my trial. And if it went badly I knew I was looking at not seeing Jenny and my kids and my mates for a long time. The kids would be all grown up by the time I got out.

So while everyone else was making new year's resolutions to give up smoking and all that bollocks, mine was to play the most important card on the Monopoly board, that one you always kept tucked up your sleeve: 'Get Out Of Jail Free'.

21 The Clap Theory

I'd been on remand in Belmarsh for eleven months before my case came to court.

Pleading guilty to a charge immediately knocks a third off the sentence you'd get if you insisted on it going to court and then still got guilty. So they ended up with an eight each instead of a twelve. And working out what they would've got if they'd gone to court enabled me to figure out what they would hand down to me.

Because I was up on 'knowingly concerned' and was also marked out as the supposed 'ringleader', then I'd get more than a twelve. Probably fifteen years. But because the others had already gone 'guilty' and been sentenced it meant that they couldn't be mentioned in my trial and be used against me.

Paul Hawksford, one of the guys along on the drive to Heathrow, ended up doing a deal with the police to try and get a lesser sentence. They wired him up and he taped his conversations with his cellmate in the Scrubs. He did a lot of his bird in solitary after that cos he couldn't mix with the prison community for his own safety. And they only knocked him a year off and gave him seven years. So fuck all good it did him, and a lot more damage. His excuse for doing what he did was that they'd threatened to arrest and nick his wife if he didn't do it. Now, in my eyes that ain't an explanation for doing that. If that had been said to me then my missus would've had to get used to prison food and I would've had to get used to writing letters. It's not that I think more of my mates than I do of Jennifer, it's just that grassing is an unacceptable thing to do and she would understand that. She wouldn't like it, but she would understand that cos she's got the knack of being able to put herself in other people's shoes. And if the boot was on the other foot, as they say, she knows I'd do the same. And not only would I expect my missus to leave me if I did that, but that's exactly what happened with him. His own wife divorced him for it. Paul Hawksford never grassed me up or did me any harm personally whatsoever, but by his actions and what he had done I had to disassociate myself from him because it was thought of so badly.

Just before the trial was due to start the guv'nor called me up to see him. He did like his little speeches, and I knew I was in line for another one. It was his chance to gloat. He started going on about how I seemed to have taken it all as a bit of a joke. I think he was peeved that his speech to me when I'd first come here hadn't turned out to be true. I hadn't let the place 'break' me, as he said it would. In fact, I'd just given the impression of having a fucking good time!

Thinking that I was gonna get guilty and would soon be back down in my cell, he said, 'May I be the first to come and visit you after the trial?'

'Course you can,' I said, 'but I don't know if you'll be welcome down at the pub in Woolwich. We'll be having a celebration drink at The Westminster Arms.'

'I think you'll find you will be back down on the unit. I meant I'd like to visit you in your cell.'

'You can fucking *live* in it, mate,' I said, 'because I will not be there!'

I was being really cocky, but I was determined not to let him get away with having the last word. Or to walk away all downhearted like he wanted me to be.

I made a big sign from a piece of cardboard and hung it outside my cell door: TO LET! PETS AND DHSS WELCOME.

The trial was held in Belmarsh Court next to the prison. Transporting me there was a circus in itself. I was handcuffed to two screws, then uncuffed, stripped, searched, put through a metal detector and given a new set of clothes. Then I was handcuffed back to the screws and, with a ten-man guard around me, taken through all the gates and cameras to a waiting armoured van. During the ten-foot walk to the van I was accompanied by another two screws with a guard dog each. That's because the time it takes you to walk from the prison door to the van is the one and only time you are actually, technically, 'outside', the only time you're not surrounded by walls and cameras. And they thought you might make a run for it. While dragging the two prison officers handcuffed to you along beside you, obviously. Piece of piss, really.

So then they put me in the van with the armed guards all sat around me. The van then drove about forty feet and stopped outside the courthouse door. *Forty feet.* I didn't even have time to unpack my sandwiches. We had to wait inside until the two screws with the dogs ran across to catch us up! Not until they arrived was I allowed to get out and cross the few feet from the van to the court. And you think British Rail are bad.

So I got out and the two Alsatians are there looking at me like, 'Fuck me, what was that about?' Then me and my little fan club went down two floors and into the underground tunnel which leads to the dock. Still handcuffed to the two screws, we went through the tunnel and another five gates with cameras all the way.

Then I was put in a holding cell. This cell was all solid, stainless steel. Every bit of it. It looked like it was cast from one big lump of metal. Nothing was attached to anything else, it was all moulded. As if the shape of the chair and the bed and the toilet had been punched in from the outside. And I'd asked for the presidential penthouse suite as well! I'd a good mind to complain.

It was in here that I had my meetings with my defence council, David Martin-Sperrie QC.

I could've dressed down for the trial and worn a tweed jacket with elbow patches and jumbo cords, something daft like that, to try and make me look like a picture of innocence. But I thought, Fuck it. I ain't exactly been a shrinking violet during my life and it's too late to start now. So I wore my flashiest clothes. Much to David Martin-Sperrie's horror. First time he clapped eyes on me he went, 'Oh, Dave . . . can we not tone it down a little?' I agreed to take off the gold-plated, diamond-studded knuckleduster I had around my neck on a big chain, remove the Versace sunglasses and not use the gun-shaped cigar lighter. Can't say fairer than that. I'd already let my hair grow out from stubble to make me look 'less intimidating', in my brief's words. So now I just looked like someone with a dodgy haircut.

My old mate Terry Turbo came up to be a character witness, but when my brief saw him he said, 'He needs a character witness himself; he'd get two years for looking like that in court, witness or not!' Thanks anyway, Tel. One of the guys who'd already had to go 'guilty' to it, John Keefe, was waiting downstairs for three days, willing to come up and say I was never involved. It was explained to him that by doing so it might affect his appeal, but he came and did it anyway and I thank him for that. In the end I didn't call him up. I didn't think I'd need it and I didn't want to risk him getting into more trouble.

From the holding cell I was taken back up two flights into the court. I came up into the dock, straight out of the ground like Thunderbird fucking Two. The dock was closed in with bulletproof glass. An armed guard sat each side of me and a high-ranking officer at the end of the dock. Looking out over the court I could see my defence and the prosecuting councils' desks to the right of me, the judge to the left, and dead ahead the jury. The public gallery was above the jury so they couldn't see each other.

Now, by law, everybody is presumed innocent until proven guilty, right? Everyone knows that. And things that have no bearing on the case but that might prejudice the jury against you are not allowed to be mentioned. Like previous convictions or cases not proven or even others under investigation. Also, if a case is high profile and reported in the papers and on TV then the jurors are not supposed to see those things. And all those measures prove that the law acknowledges that it would be unfair to the person on trial.

Well, imagine you were one of the jurors that opening day of my trial, and see what you think of this . . .

First you are escorted from your house or hotel room by an armed guard. The same guard that you have been told will be living with you and sleeping in your house until the trial is over. Then when you get to court you see Armed Response police posted outside, the road is cordoned off to limit access, and you might, if it's flying low enough, notice the police helicopter hovering above. When you get in the courtroom you find that you have to sit behind bullet-proof glass as your guard stands by, along with all the other eleven guards assigned to your fellow jurors. You look to the right and see an armed officer behind the judge, more armed officers stationed at the back of the court and, if you visit the lav and overhear two people from the public gallery talking, you'd learn that there were armed guards up there too. If you look out across the court you'd see the defendant, in this case me, also behind glass with an armed guard either side of him. You may also have learned, if some of the reporting has leaked out to you, that the courthouse is bomb-searched every day and the manhole covers in the street outside are removed and the drains also checked for bombs. You might also learn, if you haven't guessed already from the whole three ring circus, that it all costs something like twenty grand a day to provide.

Now you answer me this: *has all that you've seen prejudiced you in any way towards me?*

I know that everyone likes to think they're fair-minded and smart enough to just look at the evidence, but I think you'll find, in your heart of hearts, that the answer to my question is OF COURSE IT HAS FUCKING PREJUDICED YOU!

Sorry, I didn't mean to shout ... but when you're on the other side of all this, like I was, and looking down the barrel of fifteen fucking years in prison I think you'd also have reason to be ever so slightly miffed.

The whole set-up is like the world's biggest example of the old phrase 'No smoke without fire'. And I know you remember me going on about how my nan used these old sayings and I learnt that they were often true, but living your own life by them and deciding someone else's life on them are two different things. And once something has been planted in someone's mind it's difficult to get it back out. I mean, if I'd stood up and said, 'Never judge a book by its cover', for example, that wouldn't have magically evened things up, would it? So, if you had been a juror, not only did the police want you to think 'No smoke without fire', but they actually provided the fucking fire and fanned the flames! And if (like the old song says) smoke gets in your eyes, then how can you see clearly?

And with that, I rest my case. Sorry to get all human rights and preachy-sounding about it, but it just ain't right, is it?

My way around all that crap was to get the jurors to like me. Not by conning them or tricking them or trying to put one over on them to make me think I'm something I'm not, but just by getting them to see me as a person and not some 'most criminally minded' monster. That was my way of trying to even things up. Because everything the jury saw was like a big arrow pointing at me saying, 'Look at the baddie! Look at the baddie!'

I'll tell you something now: when I came up from underground and first came out into the dock and I saw the whole 24-carat, no-expense-spared, bulletproofed, bomb-searched, 'do-or-die', armed-to-the back-teeth, right royal song and dance of it all, even I thought I was fucking guilty! So Christ knows what the jury were thinking.

Fuck me, I thought, maybe I should've worn the tweed jacket after all.

I wish I'd been able to sell tickets for my trial, or even get the hotdog van concession for outside, cos it was packed to the rafters every single day. The public gallery was so crammed they had to operate a 'one out, one in' system. There must have been close to a hundred and fifty people there.

It was heartening to look up and see everybody, though. A proper *This Is Your Life* collection of people for me. Give yourself a Brownie point for everyone you recognise from my life: Jennifer, Brendan, Lone Wolf Dave, Marcus, Tucker, Amon, Santos, Birmingham John and Jim, Les Moore and his brothers Gary and Joe, Posh John, Warwick, Danny Dolittle, Ian Davis, Mark Bates, Mickey, Carl, Boss man Mick from Aquarium, Tony and Junior, Daves 1 and 2, Terry, Adam, Johnny, Wish, the two Steves, Dean and Julie and Peter, Big Mark, the two Rickys, Bob Tanner and his brothers, Jimmy-boy from Leeds, scouse Brian, Jimmy Andrews, Johnny and Robbie, Christian, Peter and Keith Watson, Ian Edmondson, Jenny Brown, Candy, Tracey and the Astral girls, Sheena, Flanagan and husband Derek, Steve McFadden, John Colbet, both Jamies, Steve Raith, Lenny McLean, Freddie Foreman, Joey Pyle and Joey Pyle Jnr, Wilf Pine, Jay, Rod, Northern Billy, Big Marky, John Saint, Denis Firmen, Eddie and Derek, Aquarium Lou, Alfie, Paddy and Mel, Dave Simms, Tony and his wife, Lee, Mum, my brother Patrick and sister Susan, Drew and Jenson, and my boy Beau. In fact, Beau was the first face I saw when I came out into the dock. It made me feel good, and a bit bad at the same time. I didn't like to think this would be the last time I might see him or any of my kids: Levi, Chelsea, Drew and Jenson. There were loads more as well who came during the trial, and I do apologise if I've neglected to mention you. Your presence was greatly appreciated.

Who else have I missed? My old mate Tinky Winky, now a big star (he was in disguise), John Lennon, Elvis, Buddy Holly, Madonna, Batman . . . oh shut up! Let me dream.

The prosecution put their case first. The arresting officer was the first to give evidence, followed by other police and then the forensics bloke and a list of things supposedly connecting me to the crime. Which was fuck all, actually. Like I say, the basis for it all was this idea that I must be involved just because of who I am and cos I was there on the day.

Because of the nature of what they were charging me with it was a pretty hard thing *not* to prove, if you get what I mean. First of all they've got me on the back foot by presuming me to be guilty and then saying, 'Go on then! Show us you're not.' It was more like character assassination than anything else, led by the police. But you start talking about conspiracy theories and people's eyes just glaze over. Having said that, I'm sure that I did see one of the prosecution team on a grassy knoll . . .

Halfway through, some mates of mine – Warwick, Andy Finlater, Mick Warrel, Chops and Yorkie – burst into the courthouse. They were all wearing T-shirts saying DAVE COURTNEY IS INNOCENT! WRONG PLACE, WRONG TIME! The prosecution objected and the trial was stopped. They requested a mistrial on the grounds that it may prejudice the jury! *Get that!* Half a dozen fucking T-shirts against what I had to fight against.

The judge overruled it.

The prosecution evidence was pretty boring stuff. I started to make these signs that I'd bring in every day and hold up to the jury, saying things like, HELLO – HOW ARE YOU? or BAD JUMPER! if one of them was wearing a nasty pullover. Or YAWN! – that one got a big laugh. And cos I was behind glass and they were behind glass, we couldn't hear each other and no one could hear them laughing. You'd just see them falling about. It looked like a film with the sound turned down.

Because one of the problems when you know you're gonna be in court for a couple of weeks is how to look at the jury. They're all studying you closely so do you not look at them, do you smile and risk looking like a cocky cunt, or do you try and look sad and innocent? Even though I was innocent, trying to look it was something I didn't think I could pull off with a mug like mine. So I went for the upfront cheeky-chappie route and started making the signs. That got me a ticking off and a threat of being made in contempt of court. Like I had nothing else worse to worry about.

Some of the table-dancing girls from Stringfellows came along to show their support. A couple of them lifted up their tops, took their supports off, and pressed their tits against the glass. That caused a bit of a stir. And you know what table dancers are like; some of them girls have got world-class knockers. I noticed the prosecution didn't object too fucking strongly to that little display. Seemed to go down well with the fellas in the jury as well.

Then the day came when it was my turn in the witness box. I wasn't nervous at all, just eager to get up and have my say. By that time I could walk in there, wink at the jury and get smiles back.

The first thing said to me was, 'You are, are you not, David John Courtney?'

I said, 'I am, your honour. But right now I wish I fucking wasn't!' That got a big laugh and set the tone. Start as you mean to go on, that's my policy.

I've said it before, but I'll say it again, laughter is such a good weapon. It really is. And in a situation like this you ain't got much else. Let's dig out one of my nan's old sayings here, shall we? Let's see: 'Laugh, and the world laughs with you; cry, and you cry alone'. *Bang on!* Thanks, Nan. Too fucking true. I might have been getting some of the jury with me, but the prosecution were putting up a good show of resisting. There's just no pleasing some people, is there?

I made an opening statement to the court, addressed to the jury cos they were the most important people in there. Me and David Martin-Sperrie decided there was no point in me trying to present myself as a choirboy. If I was honest about what I was then they would know I was telling the truth about other things. Maybe some other lawyers and law books would say, 'Don't even think about it'. Well, I did think about it. And that's why I did it.

'You all know me,' I said, 'and I'm worse than you think . . . but I treat you with enough respect to know you can look at me and know what I am. I've done most of the things you might have heard of – debt collecting, beating people up, even burying people – and been pretty fucking naughty in my time. But I've never dealt drugs.

'And because I'm good at what I do, the people who don't like that don't like me, and they've just roped me into this. I've been visited in my cell and told that they don't think I'll get done for this, but if they can steal a year off me on remand then they will do that. And, you never know, maybe if things go a certain way on the day and they make me sound bad enough to you, I might even get a guilty.

'But I'm not having that; I'm just not fucking having it. So I'm telling you how it is. I've been dragged into this, but I'm innocent. Thank you.'

That's exactly what I said right from the word 'go'.

'And,' I added, 'if going "no comment" during the police interviews has led to me being here and got me in trouble just because I didn't want to get my co-defendants in bother, then I accept that. And I will do the fucking bird.'

That got a big cheer from the public gallery.

The prosecutor weren't too impressed. Every time I protested my innocence he got his wig in a right little uproar.

'I put it to you, Mr Courtney, that you are an out-and-out liar!'

'And *I* put it back to you,' I said, 'that it don't fucking matter what you put to me – that don't make it true! You are the prosecution and it's your job to do that to anyone standing in the dock. If I was the Pope stood here you'd put exactly the same thing to me.'

One thing I knew was that the jury didn't know what kind of sentence I was looking at. The police know that most jurors don't realise what the implications are of being charged with 'knowingly concerned'. They try and trick the jury into thinking it's nothing. It was a fairly new charge and it sounded quite innocent, really. It don't sound like 'manslaughter' or 'murder', but it can carry the same sentence. The first the jury would know about it was if they found me guilty and then the judge went 'Fifteen years!' Then they'd be thinking, Fuck me, I never knew! But by then it's too late. So I decided to make it known to them.

They never ask you to make a little speech. It ain't like that. It's not like in the films. You might try to get a point in during questioning and the prosecutor will cut you off and say, '*Thank* you, Mr Courtney! – A simple "yes" or "no" will do!' But if the judge starts speaking to you then you can answer him and make a point. The judge is king in his court. He can put the prosecutor in contempt if he likes.

So what I did was this: instead of prettifying my language like a lot of people do in front of authority, I just talked in my normal way, the way I always talk, with quite a fair few 'fucks', 'fuckings', 'cunts' and 'bastards'. Soon enough the judge interrupted and asked if my 'rather colourful language could not be moderated somewhat'.

I said, 'I'm sorry, your honour, but I'm fighting for my life here today and you are all using words and legal terms that I don't even understand. And if I can't say what I mean in my words, and I get it wrong, then I get *fifteen* years! Now I don't know if the jury know that and if I'm wrong about it then someone jump up and tell me . . .'

None of the prosecution team broke a leg getting up to deny that one, so that sent a proper little ripple through the jurors. Like I said before, I weren't tricking anyone or saying anything that wasn't true, I was just trying to even up the odds that they'd deliberately stacked against me.

Then, when I'd established it was OK for me to talk as I did, I said, 'Right, now what these cunts are aiming to do . . .'

Every evening I'd go back to the unit, through the whole palaver of the tunnel and the guard dogs and the armoured van. It never got any quicker. I've had holidays that didn't last as long as that trip. The screws kept taking my TO LET sign off my cell door and I kept putting up another one. I mean, what were they gonna do? Arrest me?

I kept the other chaps informed about the current state of play. It was better than fucking *Coronation Street* for them. It's funny, but even in the middle of it all, and even though I was fighting against such a big thing that could completely fuck my life up, you still get moments when you see it as if from the outside looking in. You see it for what it is. Like you're floating above watching a play. *(Enter stage left) – Courtney takes the stand . . .*

The others involved in this, the ones that had already gone 'guilty', had been sentenced weeks ago so the prosecutor weren't allowed to mention them as much as he would've liked. He skirted around it pretty skilfully, though. He kept asking me these very carefully worded questions about them. I kept refusing to answer; I said I'd only speak on my own behalf and no one else's. He wanted to know who had planned it all and which ones were lower down the ladder, so to speak. I just said I'd only answer for myself. He carried on, though, and the judge (who was the same geezer who'd presided over the trial of the others) finally got pissed off and interrupted.

'All prosecuting council wants to know, Mr Courtney, is who was the horse and who held the whip.'

'Well, you sentenced them, your honour,' I said. 'You know what you gave each person, so if he wants to know that much, you fucking tell him!'

The prosecutor was a snide little bastard. He thought that cross-questioning me would be an easy touch. He asked me why he had to worm things out of me, and why wouldn't I give him anything!

'You are paid £500 a day to worm, mate, so worm away cos I'm giving you fuck all. In fact, I wouldn't even give you a cold.'

He didn't have to worm that answer out of me, but he didn't seem to like it.

Then the old question of my reputation reared its ugly head. There was no point in me trying to present myself as Little Bo Peep, and I could only damage their picture of me as the Big Bad Wolf by being open and funny. I mean, the Big Bad Wolf was a sly and deadly serious little fucker, wasn't he?

'You are well known for using a knuckleduster,' the prosecutor said. 'Do you always take one to "work"?'

'Yeah. Would you come to work without your wig?'

'So you think of yourself as being a bit of a hardman?'

'Oh, yes,' I said, 'very much so!'

He eventually abandoned that little line of questioning as a bit of a non-starter. Another thing he kept doing, which was downright snide, was he kept banging on about the 'street value' of the coke found on Marc Curno. I thought, Give it a rest. Street value this, street value that. And all the time trying to associate me with it. 'Drugs with a street value of six *million* pounds!' he said at one point. I saw all this street value crap sinking into the jury and decided to prick that little bubble.

I interrupted him. 'I'm sorry, but could you tell me exactly *which* street in London values it at six million, cos I would fucking love to know!' That caused another silent, shoulder-shaking session among the jury.

The question of being 'knowingly concerned' was what the whole thing spun on. The prosecutor spelt out what it meant in great detail to the jury. Then he turned to me.

'*You* knew these men. *You* introduced them to each other. *You* helped facilitate this crime!' Well, I fucking jumped right on that one, mate. I spoke directly to him. 'OK. If, for the sake of argument, I introduced you that lady there –' (I pointed to the woman custom officer that had arrested me) '– and you got off with her, and then afterwards found that she'd given you the clap, would that be my fault?'

Oh, listen – the whole fucking court just fell about. I'm telling you. It was unbelievable. The judge started calling for order and tried to calm things down. The prosecutor quickly tried to move on to something else, but I wouldn't let it go. I kept insisting that he answer the question (what a turn-up for the books; who was 'worming' now?) until the judge finally stepped in and said he should answer. The prosecutor looked really sheepish and admitted that, no, it wouldn't be my fault. Oh *yes*! I thought, Take *that*, you clever cunt! He'd been sticking it to me ever since I took the stand. I had one more thing to say, though.

'I'd just like to apologise to the officer, your honour, for using her in that example. I bet she's of impeccable character.' I turned to her and winked. 'Sorry, darlin'!'

I don't think everyone could quite believe some of the things that were going on in court. David Martin-Sperrie came down to see me in the holding cell afterwards and he said to me, deadly seriously, 'Dave . . . you are slowly and surely carving your way into the history books of British crime.'

I nearly came on the spot. I thought, Wow! Then I asked him, equally seriously, if he wouldn't mind saying that line back to me, but really, really slowly this time. He asked me why.

'Cos it sounded so good,' I said, 'that I want to have my hand on my cock when I hear it again!'

After over two weeks on trial and two days of me being in the witness box, the jury finally went out to decide. It took them three days. So for all that time I was sat down below in this cell no more than the size of a broom cupboard. A sterile tin box with a plank-bench and me plonked on it in my best suit. Trying not to get it creased.

I'd felt sure of the outcome for most of the way, but those three days waiting for the verdict was the worst bit of bird I've ever done. It just went on and on. I really felt like I was in the fucking twilight zone. I daren't start making plans in my head for when I got out in case I didn't. And just thinking about getting sent down for fifteen could fuck your head up. I thought, Am I gonna get a shag tonight, for the first time in a year, or am I gonna be wanking for the next fifteen?

The door opened eventually and I got called upstairs. I got all set for the big moment, but it turned out they just wanted to ask me a few more questions to clear up a few points! Fuck me. So I went back down and spent a few hours trying to keep the suit half decent.

They called me up again. Here we go, I thought, get ready either for 'lift off' or 'splash down'. Fuck me again if it wasn't the same thing! A few more questions. Laugh? I nearly shat a pony.

Third time lucky, it was. The third call-up was for real. There was a full turn-out in court, as usual. It was really quiet, though, this time. You could've heard a fly's prick drop.

The little ceremony the court goes through before the judge asks the foreman to deliver the verdict is like some kind of slow torture.

'Not guilty.'

Everyone went kind of . . . noisy. Ever so slightly mental,

actually. Everybody in the gallery jumped up together like they were the Olympic Synchronised Leaping-Out-Of-Chairs team. Fucking gold medallists every single one of them. I grabbed the two screws next to me and gave each one a big kiss. And just how happy would you have to be to do *that*?!

I was taken back downstairs, and that's when they hit me with it: I had to go back to the unit to collect my things.

I said, 'You must be fucking joking! I'm not wasting another second in there let alone another hour just getting back in! They kept insisting that I had to. Rules and bleedin' regulations again. Just to pick up my gear. 'Look! Keep the magic markers, keep the smelly trainers, keep the dot-to-dot books: I don't care and I'm not going back. Listen to me, what did the man say upstairs? Just repeat to me what he said.'

One of the screws said, 'Not guilty,' and I told him I was awfully glad for him that he weren't hard of hearing and I wasn't going anywhere but out the front door like any other man would. I caused such a stink about it that they gave in. And too right. I shouldn't have even had to fight for that.

On the court steps was everyone from the gallery and all the ones that couldn't fit in. Must have been nearly two hundred people. Jenny gave me a big hug, so did Beau and Jenson and Drew. And I nearly got battered to death with back slaps.

I heard a noise and looked across at the car park and started laughing. Tucker had come to court on this go-ped he'd just bought (go-peds are like a skateboard with a handle and motor – silly little things). He was buzzing round with all the car park attendants chasing him and shouting that it wasn't allowed. It was like something out of *Tom and Jerry*. He was just bombing around, laughing and waving at me.

Everyone piled into the Westminster Arms for a drink and then went on to 'my' pub, the Albion, to carry on celebrating. We all started reliving the best bits of the trial. I half expected Jimmy Hill to pop up with slow-motion action replays.

At the end of the night me and Jen booked into a five-star hotel in Hyde Park, the Lanesborough. And after three of the worst days of my life, when I'd been left stewing in that cell waiting, I now had three of the best. That's how long me and Jen spent holed up in the room. We just talked and talked. Well, not *just* talked, obviously. Every inch of the bed and floor was put to good fucking use. Literally. We kept room service busy and the neighbours awake.

After I came out of hiding with Jenny, Mick Colby and the boys arranged a big party for me at his mansion with the swimming pool. The house was decorated with 'Not Guilty' posters and the party was such a blinding success that Mick's been finding an excuse to have one every month since!

I was already a bit of a name among the 'silks', as the barristers are known, because they'd had some of their best work from me. But that little routine I'd used with the prosecutor and 'knowingly concerned' went down as a bit of a classic, if you don't mind me saying so myself. I heard that it became known as 'The Clap Theory' and was later used by barristers in other cases. I think their wording of it might have been a bit different from mine, though.

My barrister David Martin-Sperrie was the absolute bollocks. And so were his two assistants, David and Michelle Haeems. And I'd like to take this opportunity to thank you for your hard work.

I toyed with the idea of keeping a low profile (for about ten seconds), then I thought, Fuck it! and promptly had 4,000 big posters made with this photo of me taken in a witness box, sticking up two fingers. Above and below the picture it said DODGY DAVE SAYS – NOT GUILTY!! I had most of those plastered up around London and the rest we advertised for sale in Terry's club magazine the *Scene*. Like I said, all the while I'd been inside I'd carried on writing for it under the heading, 'Not So Dodgy Dave, Live From Inside!' Now I was back out and writing again as 'Dodgy Dave's Funny Page'.

You know what the funniest thing was, though? Despite what he'd said about wanting to see me after the trial, the guv'nor of the Double-A unit never did make it down to the pub after the verdict. Laugh? *Stop* it. I made a fucking half-hour tape of myself!

I was back in court a few months later. Not for me this time. Charlie Kray's case had come to trial. He'd been on remand in Belmarsh with me. Me and a couple of others were called as character witnesses, which might seem like a bit of an own goal at first glance, but the idea was to call up some faces that really would have known, so we could point out that Charlie wasn't what they were saying he was.

And he weren't. He had two very naughty brothers and was tarred with the same brush. And when they got banged up he had all that and what was left behind to deal with. He was charged with plotting to supply cocaine.

Taking the stand again after being there only a few months back was a weird one. I gave it my best shot. Charlie was seventy now and looking at a ten to fifteen.

'Sorry to burst your bubble,' I said, first looking at Charlie and then back to the barrister, 'but Charlie couldn't deal cards let alone drugs. Charlie has never done anything, not when he was younger and not now he's a seventy-year-old man. And I've known him for years.'

The defence council questioned me on the cocaine allegation and whether Charlie could have been involved.

I said, 'The only coke Charlie ever had was in his Bacardi.'

Then I talked a bit about his brothers and how I knew them, and by knowing them knew that Charlie wasn't involved in anything.

'When I organised Ronnie's funeral I liaised with the chief of police, Sir Paul Condom.'

'I think it is Con*don*, Mr Courtney,' the wig said. At least that got the jury laughing.

Not much else to laugh about a few weeks later, though. Charlie got a guilty and twelve years. *Twelve* years at seventy. That was a scary one just to think about. (I wish you all the best, Charlie, and I will always consider us good friends.) I thought, There but for the grace of God and good judgement . . .

22 Understand This

Debt collecting, fraud, forgery, protection, pimping, handling stolen goods, cheating customs & excise, bank robbing – in fact, the whole villain lifestyle thing; when the risks of all these are getting hurt, maimed, banged up, going on the run, or even being killed, why do the people who do it, do it?

Because the end justifies the means. The money justifies the risk. And the money gets you what you want. Which is a lifestyle you wouldn't get any other way except through bank robbing, cheating customs & excise, debt collecting, blah-blah-blah.

Understand this: it's not that you're addicted to being a villain but that you're addicted to the lifestyle. And the only way you can fund that lifestyle, I'm afraid, is villainy. Plus, the higher bracket of people you get in with, the more money you need. So it is a bit like the everyday rat race in that respect. It has that in common.

I remember when I was younger and other blokes would be talking about going out on Friday *and* Saturday night, and I'd be thinking, I've got enough money for one night, but where can I get the money for both? Or they wouldn't just go on holiday, they'd go and buy a villa there. You get into a different bracket, so you get into a different racket. That's why I understand addiction very, very well. Whatever kind it is: drugs, sex, gambling, whatever. It's just using something to help you get where you wanna go.

You're not a perpetual villain, which is what people put it down to; they say, 'You just can't stop thieving' (for example), but that ain't it at all. What you can't stop is having a fucking good time, and for most people that comes with the kind of money you ain't gonna get flipping burgers in McDonald's. Now, doing a takings snatch on the van that picks up at McDonald's, that's different.

And once you've got into it and earned anything from a couple of hundred grand in five minutes through doing a bank to five hundred quid in the same time for collecting a debt, you are not, abso-fucking-lutely *not*, gonna go on an assembly line checking wheel nuts at a tractor factory. Yeah, there's all the risks, but then again there's all the things it ain't: getting up at 7.30 to commute to work for nine to work all day till five, five days a week, 48 weeks a year, till the age of 65. Up to forty-nine years of grind and taking shit from the boss and paying shit-loads to the taxman until you finally retire (if you don't die first) with a piss-poor pension. Then you've got maybe another twenty years, if you're lucky, which you can't really enjoy anyway cos you've not enough money, before your kids bung you in a home and forget you're there.

Don't get me wrong, I am not, believe it or not, for one minute knocking you if you do that. In fact, I think you're a bit of a fucking hero, to be honest. Because I could not do it. I could no sooner do that than you could do what I did. Each to his own, as they say. But think about this: more ordinary workers do the lottery than anyone else. That's their dream of escape. I had mine.

Personally, I wouldn't bet on a horse that was fourteen million to one. That's how I look at it. I'd give better odds on myself, though. I had my own way of making my numbers come up. Sometimes they did, sometimes they didn't (and I didn't have to rely on the drop of bingo balls). But as you will now have gathered, I had a *fucking* good time along the way.

I was fortunate enough to have some kind of natural talent for what I did and to realise, early on, that I had to learn from others who had already been there and done the crime (and usually the time).

They say everyone's got a book in them trying to get out. Well, I had to try to keep mine in. Until the right time. I could hardly have written about that side of my life while I was doing it, could I? Well, I could've, but then how many of you would've come to Wormwood Scrubs for the book signing?

Oh, *shut* up!

23 Banged Up, Buried or Mills & Boon

I had another mate called Brendan who was a good mate of mine. You couldn't help but like him. He was always happy, always had a big smiley grin on his face. He was sort of like a mini version of me, really: shaved head, lots of jewellery, always up for a laugh. He even started smoking a cigar. We'd go out clubbing together and you always knew you were in for a good time. He was one of those people who just naturally looked on the bright side, always buzzing. People tend to warm to you if you're like that cos so many people aren't. A lot of people get down easily. With good reason sometimes. You only have to watch the news too often to realise that. And because of how he was, girls loved him. He had loads of girlfriends and they all adored the geezer. He was the best company to have on a night out. He was just into being naughty, was Brendan, like I'd been at his age. But he was a genuinely nice lad. That's the reality. If you'd met him you'd have thought, *What* a nice bloke.

Being in the game he was in, of course, people he dealt with often owed him money. Like this one guy who owed him a fair bit. Now this geezer who's in debt, he got done for something and he was gonna get sent down. Not for too long, mind, so Brendan says, 'OK, see me when you get out.' As a friendly gesture, a kind of thanks, I suppose, the guy gives Brendan a gram of coke. Thank you very much, don't mind if I do, I imagine he said.

Back at his flat later, Brendan laid out the powder in two big lines, rolled a tenner into a snorting tube and sucked one line straight up. But what had been given to him was a concoction of coke, heroin and some other crap – battery acid, for all I know. As soon as it hit something moist, Brendan's nasal membrane and brain, for example, the concoction re-liquidised. It went back to its natural form, and that's something that definitely don't belong in the human body. He died sitting in his chair alone with his computer game in his hand.

Because of the kind of lad he was, you really noticed him not being around any more. I know we're all supposed to be equal and special in our own ways, and all that bollocks, but some people do leave a bigger space behind than others when they leave a room. He was only 28 and yet there were nearly two hundred people at his funeral. That's a lot for a young man. A good proportion of them were girls, as well. I think that would've pleased Brendan.

That's just one of the ways you can go. Because there's only three reasons makes a man get out of this particular lifestyle: getting nicked, getting killed or walking off into the sunset with a lady. Those are the only things that happened if you hung around in my life long enough.

Tony Smith was an old mate of mine from way back. He was one of the kids who was with me on the waste ground when I threw the slate into that kid's head. A few years ago Tony was shot in the face in the VIP lounge of the Emporium nightclub.

A friend of mine called Vannie got shot dead on his doorstep not too long ago. Vannie and me had both used each other in our professional capacities over the years.

Billy Gale, a big name in the Inner City Firm, flipped his Range Rover over the central reservation and got killed. He had a massive funeral. Some shooting broke out during the wake at a pub in the East End.

Tony Tucker, Pat Tate and Craig Rolfe all got shot dead in a Range Rover in Essex in 1995. That became really big news. (This was the one, remember, that Jenny heard about and thought 'Tucker' might be the Ian Tucker I knew.) The police pulled me in about that one as well. Since organising Ronnie Kray's funeral a dog only had to crap on the pavement and the Old Bill pulled me in.

Francis was a doorman and a big friend of mine. I was stood right next to him when he was shot. It was a few years ago when we'd just come out of the Frog & Nightgown pub in the Old Kent Road. We were walking on the pavement when I just heard this bang and Francis fell down. All I saw was the back of this guy as he jumped into a car and it drove off. Francis was in a really bad way. I'd never seen so much blood. He actually died, technically, in the ambulance, but they revived him. Cos he seemed to be on the mend I sent him a card in the hospital saying, 'Well done. I knew it would take more than one to finish you off, you big fucker!' Next day there were complications with blood clots, and he died.

The police even tried to rope me in as something to do with it. I mean, fucking hell, Francis was a good mate of mine! But that's how desperate the police were to have me. At Francis's funeral the lead car carried a wreath I'd had made for him as a tribute from me and all the doormen: a four-foot-sqaure dinner jacket and shirt made from black and white flowers.

The ex-Foreign Legion geezer I told you about, Kevin, the human fighting machine, he took the third option: the old Mills & Boon route. After forming his own security company, Strikeforce, he met a lady and fell in love and got out of the game while he was ahead.

A lot of guys who avoid a bullet or getting bird, or survive getting both, do the old gangster bit of going to live in Spain. They get the villa in Marbella but then realise they ain't got one mate there, don't speak Spanish and miss an awful lot of the things about England that everyone moans about. A lot of these blokes – fugitives, or ones who've retired – are lonely out there. So they start flying all their mates out. I mean, there's a lot nicer places than Marbella but they go there cos it's close enough to get your mates out to see you.

That was always the dream when you started out: make it big and buy a fancy gaff abroad or out in the country. Then when you get that you see it ain't all it's cracked up to be, and you miss the thrills. Even the ones who move out to Kent or Surrey, after a couple of years it wears a bit thin and they think, Is this it? No one's popping in and out the house all the time like they used to; the phone ain't ringing off the hook like it did before; all the fellas are back up in London and you might have a million in the bank, a really nice car and a really nice house, but so fucking what? After living the life you've had for the last twenty or thirty years, sitting watching the mustard and cress grow is a real cunt. You try going from that to *that*.

The gangster thing bewitches people, but it isn't really anything like what they think. But they see it like they dream it, see what they want to believe; they think there's Dave Courtney out in the big Roller, in the nightclubs and all that. They think that's all you are. They don't see me banged up 23 hours a day in Belmarsh, seeing my family through bulletproof glass a few hours a week. They just see all the glittery bits and get sucked in by it. I know how they get sucked in cos I did! I remember it. Some people just remember the outcome of something, but I don't forget *why* it happened.

I ain't moaning, by the way. I chose the life and stayed in it because I fucking *wanted* to, mate, no two ways about it. There will always, always be men who want to do this. As each decade goes past the only thing that changes is the popularity of certain crimes. Like anything else they go in and out of fashion. Once it was armed robberies, then frauds and stings, then drugs (it's always drugs now). The other big thing now is importing booze and fags cos the sentences aren't like those for drugs, but the profits are. The desire was to choose the crime with the least penalty if you were caught, but the greatest rewards if you weren't.

Some crimes are seen as being more acceptable than others, and the further back you go the more morals there were. As each decade comes and goes the morals erode. That's why they called me the Last Remaining Villain cos I was old-school; I caught the tail end of it.

I became more of a monarch, for want of a better word, than an active member. I get asked for advice. They don't come to me no more if someone gets killed cos I'm out of the frame. I haven't got doormen working for me either – the police saw to that. It's more to do with respect now because of what I've been about for a very, very long time. People don't say bad things about me but they do it for the right reason – not out of fear (although, if I decided to stamp my size nines then a lot of people would listen) but because, with me being me, I always just tried to get on with everyone. Right from being a kid, I just genuinely liked being around people, having loads of mates and making them laugh. That was always the biggest kick for me, having a giggle and getting everyone else to join in. It's just human nature that people warm to you if you're like that rather than growling and throwing your weight about. Amazing, really, how much just seemed to grow from that. And when certain opportunities came along I didn't shirk away from the responsibility. I saw it as a challenge.

Because I have an awful lot of sparkly friends it means that you can be guilty by association. The police will never believe I've stopped because of some of the company I keep. They forget that I know as many so-called 'straight' people. I know butchers and bakers, but that don't mean I'm in the bacon sarnie business. But the Old Bill can't believe I've cracked it, that I've done that life and got out. They won't have it that they've had their chance and fucked it and I'm getting on with the other stuff: acting, singing, making records, boxing promoting, writing books and for magazines, with Jenny beside me shining in her own way, singing and dancing. You'd think they'd be glad about that, wouldn't you – me making a go of it? One less for them to worry about. Maybe they think my acting and writing career is a bigger crime than any of the others! Cheeky monkeys. Or maybe they just miss the laughs in court whenever I took the witness stand.

My boys Beau and Jenson (I consider Jenson – and Drew – mine cos I've raised them, with Jenny, from babies) – I don't want them to follow me in what I done, and like any dad I want to help them do whatever work it is they choose. Beau has just gone sixteen now and I know being the son of Dave Courtney can be a fucking big weight to carry on his shoulders but he's handling it very well and I'm so proud of him. And it ain't only people in the street that sometimes look at him differently. Do you know what the police did to him? This happened really recently.

Him and his mates were out pissed and they started mucking around with a plastic toy gun. One of them ran into a garage shop and said, 'Give me all your Mars bars!' Daft stuff like that. Obviously a joke. Beau ran into a vet's with the toy and said, 'You killed my cat!' Bloody silly, I know, but no more than that. The people in the vet's were laughing about it. But someone in the street saw him and called the police. They took him down the station to give him a telling off, but when they heard the name 'Courtney' and realised who he was, they nicked him! Two hours later they got the top bloke out of bed and then charged Beau with firearms offences! Fuck me. They got on the ball with that one a lot fucking quicker than they did on the Stephen Lawrence case. What sense does that make?

I moved recently to a house in Plumstead. A big place that used to be a school. I've called it 'Camelot' (remember me saying that at school the only thing that grabbed me in history was tales of King Arthur?), and I've done it out like a castle. All wood and gold inside, suits of armour and swords as decoration, a sword in the stone in the garden and lances down the walls outside; even a massive round table in the dining room that me and my 'knights' can sit round. A recent visit to Monte Carlo just blew me away. I absolutely fell in love with the place; it's just pure class. Even the road sweepers look like guardsmen on parade. Monte Carlo rekindled all my images of Camelot and inspired me even more to style my house that way.

My old mate Dave ('Lone Wolf') is a dab hand at the old building lark and he took a bit of time off from his new acting career and called around to help. Those two snakes of his are long dead, thank fuck, so at least he couldn't sling those over the back of the Harley and bring 'em round. He built a proper little castle at the foot of the garden for the kids to play in. It ended up being nearly as big as the house. I'm thinking of moving in.

When I first moved in my next door neighbour saw me arrive and came running round and knocked on the door. I opened it and she took one look at me – shaved head, gold rings, fat cigar – and she said, '*Please* tell me you're one of the builders!'

Well, what could I say to that but, 'No, darlin'. I'm gonna be living here.'

She's a lovely lady, as it happens, Reima. Bit spiritual, she is. Said she could feel my aura. (No, I'm not even gonna rise to that one! Too easy.)

The house is the absolute bollocks. You'll have to see it, and maybe you will in *Hello* magazine or *Through the Keyhole*! I can just see Loyd Grossman wandering around: 'And here we have pictures of Reggie Kray and a gold knuckleduster next to the soap dish: now who could *possibly* live here?'

Only the other day I was sat in my living room talking about how I ain't had a phone bill in three years (I told you why that was) and minutes later, literally minutes, the phone went. It was BT calling me about this unpaid bill! Don't tell me that was a coincidence.

The only deals they hear me making now is with TV companies. I seemed to find another way of getting out of the scene other than the three I've mentioned. By turning all the notoriety and infamy into fame. After Ronnie's funeral things really went big-time with the media (although my profession at the time was affected badly and very noticeably). Magazines came knocking and I ended up being interviewed by the *Independent* and the *Mail*, and having a five-page spread in the *Times*. Granada TV took me up to Manchester to do a show there. Me and Jen were on the *Vanessa* show. The BBC's *Inside Story* series made a documentary called 'Gangster's Molls' and interviewed my Jenny; Rennie Wisbey, wife of Tommy, one of the Great Train Robbers, and her daughter Marilyn, who is Frankie Fraser's girlfriend; Wendy Lambrianou, wife of Tony; Jo-Jo Laine, who went out with one of the Knightsbridge safe deposit robbers; Georgie Ellis, the daughter of Ruth Ellis; and the missus of another Great Train Robber, Charlie Wilson. It was a good angle for the programme to take because it's not often that the woman's view is put across. They're usually overlooked, and you know my view about how important a good woman is to the man. And Jennifer just *shined*, mate. She was so supportive and classy with it. I was so proud I can't tell you. And they even used an old clip of me from the *Bermondsey Boy* documentary, evicting some squatters. A rare clip of me in action. With a fringe!

I also got a knock on the door from that friendly neighbourhood vigilante Roger Cook. He'd seen all the press after the funeral and decided to do a *Cook Report* programme on me. He got a lot more than he bargained for.

The mistake I'd seen a lot of people make when Roger Cook came knocking was to turn their face away from the camera and leg it up the street, with Fat Rog huffing and puffing behind trying not to have a heart attack. Now if that don't make you look like the dodgiest, most guilty fucker in the world I don't know what does.

So, one day I answered the door and find Cook wedged there with a cameraman and two bodybuilders for back-up. They were shoving the camera right in my face trying to get me to react by swatting it away in the usual manner.

'Mr Courtney!' he went. 'Roger Cook here! I'd like to question you about your past! Do you deny . . .' and he went on and on about this, that and the other. And I'm stood there in my dressing gown with a bowl of cornflakes going soggy on the kitchen table!

I told him to calm down before he did himself an injury, and said if he gave me five minutes to get dressed I'd answer anything he wanted. That took the wind out of his sails.

'You mean you will answer *any* questions?' he said.

'Listen, mate, I'll even tell you what Santa brought me for fucking Christmas! But at least let me put my pants on. We don't want to scare the horses.'

They waited around outside like a group of lemons while I went back in and put on my smartest clobber, my best jewellery, tweaked a few nostril hairs and took the shine off my head. I'm ready now, Mr De Mille! I rang a mate of mine, Colin G, who has a big yacht moored up in London, and sorted that out for a venue. I thought, I'm not gonna let that fat cunt Cook get me on the back foot like he always tries to.

We drove down there, and when we arrived there was Tucker and Northern Billy, Mark, Ian, Dean and Pete waiting to meet me. I'd called them before, from the house. I told Roger Cook to get on the boat and wait for me. Then me and the boys went up to these two lumps that had come along with the camera crew.

'Did you or did you not come along today to give me a clump if you thought I was getting out of line?' I said. They looked at each other and then back at me, Tucker and the boys. They wouldn't even answer cos they were shitting themselves so much. I told them to stay on the dock and not move while we did the interview.

Roger Cook and a lady called Sylvia interviewed me. They said they'd got on to me after Ronnie's funeral because some of the blokes they were already investigating turned up that day to do security. Then when they found out they were working for me and I'd organised the funeral they said that came under 'organised crime'! (Like anyone does any crime without 'organising' it to some degree.) And what we're talking about here isn't even a crime – it's what most people call organising a fucking funeral.

So we sat on this yacht for two whole hours with them throwing questions at me. They let me talk on and on, thinking I'd talk myself into trouble. Which a lot of people do: give them enough rope and they'll hang themselves for you. But I just justified what I'd done. Which weren't me lying or anything because, right from the start, I'd decided only to do things that I could justify.

'But you attacked five Chinese waiters with a sword, Mr Courtney!' he said. 'Are you telling me that is the behaviour of a normal person?'

I said, 'What I'm telling you is that if you were surrounded by half a dozen geezers with knives and kebab skewers trying to turn you into the dish of the day, what would you do? I think it's normal to defend yourself. Don't you?'

There's nothing he could say to that. He couldn't catch me out cos if you're telling the truth then there's nothing to catch you out on! They kept taking a break and having a little conference between themselves. I thought, bring 'em on Rog! Bring on those questions and I'll bat them all right back over the net. With a little topspin for good measure. He came out with the old chestnut of me admitting I done it on the court steps.

'Course I done it. I did it and said I did it. He said he was gonna shoot me so I shot him.'

I could see him thinking to himself, 'You cunt!' I put a proper little hole below the waterline in his battleship.

He's been doing his programme for more than ten years and people have got proper sentences because of him; eight, ten and twelve stretches. But now they're all coming back out, the first ones, I'll bet Roger Cook's now thinking, Hang on – I was a bit naughty back there doing all that for no other reason than a TV programme.

And not just once. He did it nearly every Thursday night for ten years. Well, now, a few of those 'Thursdays' are coming out and some of them ain't the kind of geezers to take it lying down. Which is why he's spent so many thousands on iron gates and surveillance around his house. Think *forward*, you silly bastard!

Years ago we were told not to tell tales. That's the culture we all grew up in. Especially those a bit on the naughty side. It was inbred. Now things have changed. We are turning into a nation of grasses. And they make it entertainment. If, fifteen years ago, you'd said there's gonna be a prime-time TV show with appeals from the police to shop someone, everyone would've said, 'Rubbish! What're you talking about?' Trying to explain how horrible grassing is to someone not in the crime world is difficult. In that world, that's like saying in the future there will be a programme for paedophiles. The old-school gangsters would've never believed it could happen.

When I was in a studio filming some programme or other I met this really nice geezer called Piers Hernu. He was the editor of this new magazine that was just being launched called *Front*. Piers asked me if I'd write for them, and I ended up with my own monthly column! They call me 'His Royal Dodginess'. It's fucking wicked.

One of my best ones, though, happened when I got a call to be part of that record I mentioned before. Three top dance artists from different countries – Britain, America and Japan – were chosen to do an album each featuring known villains in each country. The top British guy in that field is Tricky. He's had number one albums and the lot. He's really respected. Tricky's LP is gonna be called *Products of the Environment*.

So me and some of the chaps – Roy Shaw, Freddie Foreman, Joey Pyle, Tony Lambrianou, Frankie Fraser, Jack Adams, Tommy Wisbey and Tony Guest – all went into a studio. Tricky recorded us speaking some lines to put to his music. The track with me opens with me saying, *My name is Dave Courtney and my position in the London crime world is I have five hundred, six foot, flat-nosed geezers ... only choose the weapon you're prepared to do the bird for ... knuckledusters? I swear by 'em!* That kind of thing. Guaranteed to get bumped off the Radio 4 playlist.

Freddie Foreman I met when I was debt collecting in Spain.

We struck up an instant friendship. He was the one who shot the Mad Axeman. At the height of it all he was the very top of the tree, was Freddie. The genuine, real McCoy. And although he was an excellent organiser he went on jobs himself. The Express job and the Dairy Milk jobs and all that. He was actually out there. Freddie's book *Respect* is another massive book full of excellent advice. He got extradited from Spain after he was drugged. They got him on the plane but it took ten geezers to get him off after he came round. He's a geunine leader of men and men don't mind taking orders from blokes like Freddie.

Tony Lambrianou I've already mentioned. He was one of the Krays and another one of the old-style chaps – very much his own man. His book was a bestseller and a very enlightening book about that period of time. His brother, Chris, is a proper one as well.

Frankie Fraser you already know, of course. Top man. I can't say any more that hasn't already been said. And another fantastic book.

Joey Pyle, another 24-carat geezer: Big Joey. I've told you how he was one of them that impressed me when they came into the gym when I was a lad. He was one of South London's best, and is now a successful boxing promoter with his son, also called Joey. Young Joey used to be a good boxer himself and is now a fucking excellent promoter. Me and Joey junior recently opened a gym with our own stable of fighters and went into partnership. Our gym is opposite another good one called Squats run by Big Ricky. Big Ricky did bodyguarding with me for people like Madonna. He was also on one of the funniest debt-collecting jobs I ever did when I had to repossess this massive, bright pink car that had been customised to look like Penelope Pit-stop's car from *Wacky Races*. We got it back but it was fucking embarrassing driving it away, let me tell you. We looked like two gay lumps going cruising!

Me and Joey put on our first boxing show at the Royal Kensington Gardens Hotel. That was a real big success. All the tables were taken by people from the fight, film, TV and publishing worlds. Ernie Shavers, the heavyweight that fought all the greats like Ali, Fraser and Norton, he was there presenting prizes.

Jack Adams was a driver for some of the firms during the height of it all. He didn't do jobs himself, but being the trusted driver he got to know an awful lot from the things he saw in the back of the car and the places he had to go. A man with many secrets. He's long since gone very straight and is now a successful businessman.

Tommy Wisbey, of course, one of the Great Train Robbers. What more can you say about a legend like that? It was an honour to meet him.

Roy Shaw had been another boxing idol of mine. I knew both Roy and Lenny McLean well, so sometimes it was a bit of a difficult one being between them. What a pity they didn't team up. But like Lenny, Roy was a hard one as well. A real man's man. In his heyday he was the hardest fighter I've ever seen. And he was a legend in whatever field he went into. When he was in prison his antics and bravery were legendary; when he boxed his fights were legendary; and when he did armed robberies, the same. He put a pool table on his back and broke down a wall during a prison riot. On a bank job he picked up a wounded geezer with one hand and shot back with the other. That's proper film stuff. Roy is a gentleman to ladies, well dressed, all that; but at party time he'll jump up and sing karaoke with everyone else. He's a one hundred per center

He'd have man-to-man chats with me and give me the benefit of his experience.

'I don't need to go around firm-handed any more, just me and Alfie,' he said once. 'Cos when you get to a certain level, because of your merits, you get an inner confidence that shows.'

He's been out there and fought the biggest men, done fifteen years, had shoot-outs, the lot. His business head is well respected too. He's made a lot through property and land. He recently published his own autobiography, which is an excellent book and went to No. 1. The launch party at Epping Forest Country Club was a big success. All the chaps were there.

I once gave Roy a bulletproof vest for his birthday. He said it was just what he wanted, 'cos they used to just bounce off, but now I'm a bit older'.

Talking of which, I turned forty recently. Yeah, I know, I

don't look a day over 39! Life's supposed to begin at forty, they say (and my new one certainly is), so I decided to push the boat out a bit. Me and some of the chaps had all chipped in to get a big house where we could hold events like this. We thought, why should we burn holes in our own homes' carpets?

My birthday bash really turned out to be one to remember, though. You only hit forty once, so I invited everyone I knew. Right from old school friends like Colin Robinson and Rob Hanson. There was a five-piece band and singer performing in the main room, Nigel Benn DJing for the dancefloor in the big marquee we put up in the garden, roulette tables where guests could have a flutter, and a massive buffet with salmon, lobster and caviar, and two bars giving out drink and bottles of champagne. The guest list was pretty starry too: Babs Windsor, Steve McFadden, Jamie Foreman and Carol Harrison, Ray Winston (all good friends of mine), boxers Charlie Magri and American heavyweight Ernie Shavers, Julius Francis (British heavyweight champ), snooker player Jimmy White, Oliver Skeet, Roger Daltry, Mark Morrison, Fun Loving Criminals, Goldie, Tricky, Shane Ritchie, Chris Quentin, Peter Stringfellow and Peter and Emma Page, Gary Bushell, Mark Bosman and the Naughty Boys, Mark Goldberg from Crystal Palace, Warrior from *Gladiators*, Piers Hernu, Sally O'Sullivan and Andy Sutcliffe from *Front* magazine, Danielle Montana (DJ) and MC Creed, MC Shorts, footballers, Page Three girls, and Tracey and the girls from Astrals. Among all the great presents I got was a black Harley Davidson by Dave Legeno ('Lone Wolf') and a painting given me by Dean Cuddy ('Bulldog' to me), his missus Julie, Jamie, Mandy and Peter. Jamie's dad Jim had painted a portrait of me sat on a throne, holding a cigar and with a big knuckleduster behind me. This picture is the absolute bollocks, mate. It really knocked me out.

Which is exactly what I did to these two geezers that gatecrashed the party, would you believe. They walked in behind Babs Windsor and everyone thought they were with her. Turns out they weren't. I went over and asked who'd invited them. 'What's it to you?' one of them said. Fucking cheek. So I gave them both the old swift one-two, they were carried out, and we partied on as before.

Imagine gatecrashing that gaff. That's about as unlucky as

the geezer who had to pay Hitler's gas bill. Either that or they had more spunk than Monica Lewinsky's dress.

Apart from all my mates you've already heard of, also having a good old knees-up were: Kevin, Alistaire, Outcast Phil, Gypsy John and his boys, Blackpool Garth, Birmingham Ray and boys, Big Mel, Andy B, Boxer, Sister Beckford, the Blue Orchid boys, Steve Gordon, Wally Angus & Co., the Deja Vu boys, Aquarium Michael and his men, Thailand Phil, Israel, Jazz, Kaz, Faz and his brothers and Pard (more new neighbours), 8 Ball Pete and Angela (who flew in from America), Tony Montana, Toby von Judge, Keith, Tall Alan and Karen, Jeremy 'Terracotta', Lambros, boxer Lester, Herbie, Tracey the bongo player, Tony MacMahon, Tony Thompson (who wrote about me in *Gangland Britain*), Lee Brown (who does it for me with the South London Press), David Bond (who's helped with his chosen words), Suzanne, Pike, Steve from Bedford, Steve Gordon, Stevie Street, Steve Holdsworth, Paddy, Big Noel, Birmingham Keith, Gary Baron, Steve Raith, Lee McKenzie, Albert Chapman, Jeff Goodall, Charlie Rickson, Roy Hall, Jason Steel, Chris Head, Ken the Dog, Ian Woolen, Paul Ravinelli, David Mullany, Fiona Boothroyd, Matt, Julie, Sidney, the Woolwich Car boys, Clive and the Hanover boys, Brendan's mum Sheila, Marcus & Karen, Paul & Elisa, Glen & Don, Billie & Gillie, Bradley & Hazel, Martin & Jitt, Bev & Ricky, Danny & Ted, Nicky & Gemma, Uncle Jack, Aunt Trish and Auntie Mertle. Fuck me, now I'm running out of space and breath!

Great Train Robber Bruce Reynolds and his son Nick were also there. Nick is a sculptor, and has just done a cast of my head! That's a fucking strange one – looking at a lifesize replica of yourself. It's gonna be in an exhibition of Nick's called 'Cons to Icons' along with ones he's done of Freddie Foreman, Frankie Fraser and all the other chaps.

This Tricky LP thing just got better and better. Steven Spielberg was due to choose one track from all of them to shoot a video for. And guess what? You better fucking believe it! This was one thing I didn't mind the old Courtney card getting marked for. So I really will be ready soon for the new Cecil B. de Mille of Hollywood.

Then the guys who made *Lock, Stock and Two Smoking*

Barrels used me to put some of my stories in the film. Top film it is, too.

Carlton TV interviewed me for *Britain's Most Wanted*. No, not cos I'm one of them, silly, but cos they wanted my views on the scene today and stuff about hitmen. Y'know, the usual family viewing kind of thing. It must've gone down well, though, cos Carlton got back in touch to do a documentary about me and my Beau.

Then Jonathan Block, the manager of the American band the Fun Loving Criminals, gave me a call. They wanted me to appear on stage with them at this gig they were doing at the Forum in London. On the night their singer, Huey, said to the crowd, 'I'd now like to introduce you to the original fun loving criminal, Dave Courtney!'

I walked out on stage and went up to the mike. 'You might have heard about some of the things I've done. But I've just got one thing to say: "No Comment"!'

Afterwards I took Huey and the boys out to the table-dancing club in Soho called Astrals. And a good time was had by all.

Nearly as good a time as when I was being taught scuba diving recently by my pal Gary the diver. We were underwater in a swimming pool doing the old air-tank breathing bit and he was showing me how to let air out to make yourself rise to the surface. I showed him the Courtney way when I took the knuckleduster out of the back pocket in my shorts, dropped it on the floor of the pool and rose up to the surface. That caused a few fucking bubbles to come out, I can tell ya.

One of the best things happened just the other day. Me and Terry Turbo went to the annual dance music awards at the Kilburn National, and fuck me if we didn't win 'Best Large Promotions of the Year' award for One Nation! And that really meant something to us. Happy? I nearly exploded on the fucking spot, mate. What a buzz that is – getting up on stage to accept something like that. I milked the applause, like you do, then just said, 'Ohhh, *stop* it!' It was a wicked night.

I've seen mates of mine get killed, I've seen them succeed. Several of them are now millionaires or just big successes in their own right: Larry, Les and Mick Sprat, Roy Shaw,

Brendan, Big John and Jim, Timmy and Heidie and Lou from Aquarium, Mad Jack, Ian Tucker, Mick Colby and loads more too numerous to mention. But they've all been at the sharp end in their time and paid their dues.

In my time I've been lucky enough to do a few special things I ain't mentioned yet: boxing with Nigel Benn (I went easy on him!), horse riding with Oliver Skeet, motorbike riding with Eddie Kidd and an American bike-trick specialist called Gene Wilson; I was even taught to fly helicopters by my mate Warwick. The horse riding weren't such a success, though. Me, Jen, Tucker and Debbie went down to this farm with Oliver (me in full cowboy gear – hat, gun, spurs). I ended up jumping Oliver's quarter-of-a-million-pound Olympic horse over a fence and it ended up dumping me on my arse. I was sat there in a puddle of horse piss, half paralysed. I think I'll stick to my Harley in future.

Things have just gone mental. I can't believe it myself sometimes, all this stuff that's happening: TV, films, books, magazines, records. And to think I was *that* close to suicide. Oh *stop* it! I'm loving it. And who wouldn't? It's what I always wanted: the lifestyle without all the looking-over-the-shoulder business. You see, before, in the profession I'd chosen, if I did something really really well I couldn't tell anyone about it! Cos I'd have got nicked. No matter how blindingly I did a bit of work there was only so many people I could tell. So I went for getting known for the *overall* gangstery thing, rather than one big job. You tell me if it's worked.

I don't think the Old Bill will believe I've knocked it on the head until I'm lowered into a hole in the ground. Even then they'll probably have a bug planted in the fucking coffin.

But screw them. Let's end on a high note with Jennifer giving birth to our daughter, Courtney de Courtney (or Lulley-girl, as we call her). What a little beauty she is. Just like her dad: blue eyes, pot belly and no hair!

Epilogue – Sleep When You're Dead

I dream, but they're really short, my dreams. They have to be because I don't sleep for long. Don't like to. We ain't here long enough on this earth. I've learnt that – we are just not here long enough. Life's too short for long sleeps. Even eight hours a day is one third of your life, over *23 years* out of your seventy. Get your head round that.

I can't stand the thought of it, so I usually try to get by on four or five hours. Margaret Thatcher always said she did the same. Mind you, if there was ever a person lacking in beauty sleep, she was it. But then she'd probably say the same about me, if we ever talked, ex-villain to ex-villain.

They say you're 'dead to the world', don't they?, when you're spark out. That's too close to the truth. When you're asleep you might as well be dead. And there's gonna be plenty of time to be dead when you're dead, mate. You *know* that. Sleeping just interferes with me having a bloody good time. And I certainly ain't banking on reincarnation. You get once round the track, in my book. Anyway, you might come back as something really sad, like a worm, or a slug. Or someone who drives a Volvo.

Considering I've done so much, there's not much I regret. I only regret not doing more, to be honest. But there's still time to change that. When people say they have trouble sleeping, they mean they can't sleep and they want to. My trouble with sleeping is I don't want to. I've still got too much to do.

Because when one ride ends, there's always another one waiting to begin.

And I know that too . . .

Index